RESEARCH IN MARITIME HISTORY
NO. 12

A COMMUNITY ENTERPRISE: THE HISTORY OF THE PORT OF FREMANTLE, 1897 TO 1997

Malcolm Tull

International Maritime Economic History Association

St. John's, Newfoundland
1997

ISSN -1188-3928
ISBN -0-9681288-2-3

Research in Maritime History is available free of charge to members of the International Maritime Economic History Association. The price to others is US$15 per copy.

Back issues of *Research in Maritime History* are available:

No. 1 (1991)	David M. Williams and Andrew P. White (comps.), *A Select Bibliography of British and Irish University Theses about Maritime History, 1792-1990*
No. 2 (1992)	Lewis R. Fischer (ed.), *From Wheel House to Counting House: Essays in Maritime Business History in Honour of Professor Peter Neville Davies*
No. 3 (1992)	Lewis R. Fischer and Walter Minchinton (eds.), *People of the Northern Seas*
No. 4 (1993)	Simon Ville (ed.), *Shipbuilding in the United Kingdom in the Nineteenth Century: A Regional Approach*
No. 5 (1993)	Peter N. Davies (ed.), *The Diary of John Holt*
No. 6 (1994)	Simon P. Ville and David M. Williams (eds.), *Management, Finance and Industrial Reslations in Maritime Industries: Essays in International Maritime and Business History*
No. 7 (1994)	Lewis R. Fischer (ed.), *The Market for Seamen in the Age of Sail*
No. 8 (1995)	Gordon Read and Michael Stammers (comps.), *Guide to the Records of Merseyside Maritime Museum*
No. 9 (1995)	Frank Broeze (ed.), *Maritime History at the Crossroads: A Critical Review of Recent Historiography*
No. 10 (1996)	Nancy Redmayne Ross (ed.), *The Diary of a Maritimer, 1816-1901: The Life and Times of Joseph Salter*
No. 11 (1997)	Faye Margaret Kert, *Prize and Prejudice: Privateering and Naval Prize in Atlantic Canada in the War of 1812*

Research in Maritime History would like to thank Memorial University of Newfoundland for its generous financial assistance in support of this volume.

A Community Enterprise:
The History of the Port of Fremantle, 1897 to 1997

Table of Contents

List of Tables

List of Photos

Acknowledgements

I would like to thank the numerous people who have contributed to this book. I am especially indebted to Professor Frank Broeze, Professor Keith Norris and Ms. Kerry Sanderson, the Chief Executive Officer of the Fremantle Port Authority, who commented on drafts of every chapter. I would also like to thank Mr. Peter Ridgway and Mr. Bill Latter for commenting on the drafts of Chapters 3 and 6 respectively. I am, of course, responsible for any errors or omissions that remain.

I would like to acknowledge the assistance given by the staff of the Fremantle Port Authority, especially Ms. Helen Hicks, Public Affairs Coordinator, Ms. Ainslie de Vos, Public Affairs Manager and Ms. Sunita Thillainath, the Librarian. I would also like to thank the numerous people, too many to list in full, who answered my questions about the history of the port. My thanks also go to Dr. Paul Weaver for compiling the index.

This book draws on the following previously published work: "The Development of the Port of Fremantle, Australia's Western Gateway," *The Great Circle*, vol. 7 (1985); "Blood on the Cargo: Cargo-Handling and Working Conditions on the Waterfront at Fremantle, 1900-1930," *Labour History*, No. 52 (May 1987; and "The Financial Performance of the Fremantle Harbour Trust, 1903 to 1939," *Australian Economic History Review*, vol. XXVIII (1988). I would like to thank the editors of the respective journals for permission to use the material.

Last, but not least, I would like to thank my wife and children for their understanding that has helped make this book possible.

Abbreviations

ASIA	- Australian Stevedoring Industry Authority
ASIB	- Australian Stevedoring Industry Board
ASOF	- Australian Steamship Owners' Federation
FHT	- Fremantle Harbour Trust
FPA	- Fremantle Port Authority
L.A.	- Legislative Assembly
L.C.	- Legislative Council
MUA	- Maritime Union of Australia
P&O	- Peninsular and Oriental Steamship Navigation Company
P.D.	- Parliamentary Debates
WIRA	- Waterfront Reform Authority
WWF	- Waterside Workers' Federation

Conversions

IMPERIAL TO METRIC
1 foot = 30.5 centimetres
1 yard = 0.91 metre
1 statute mile = 1.61 kilometres
1 nautical mile = 1.85 kilometres
1 bushel = 0.0364 cubic metres
1 gallon = 4.55 litres
1 acre = 0.405 hectares
1 ton = 1.02 tonnes

MONETARY
One penny (1d) = 0.83 cents
One shilling (1/-) = 10 cents
One pound (1£) = 2 dollars

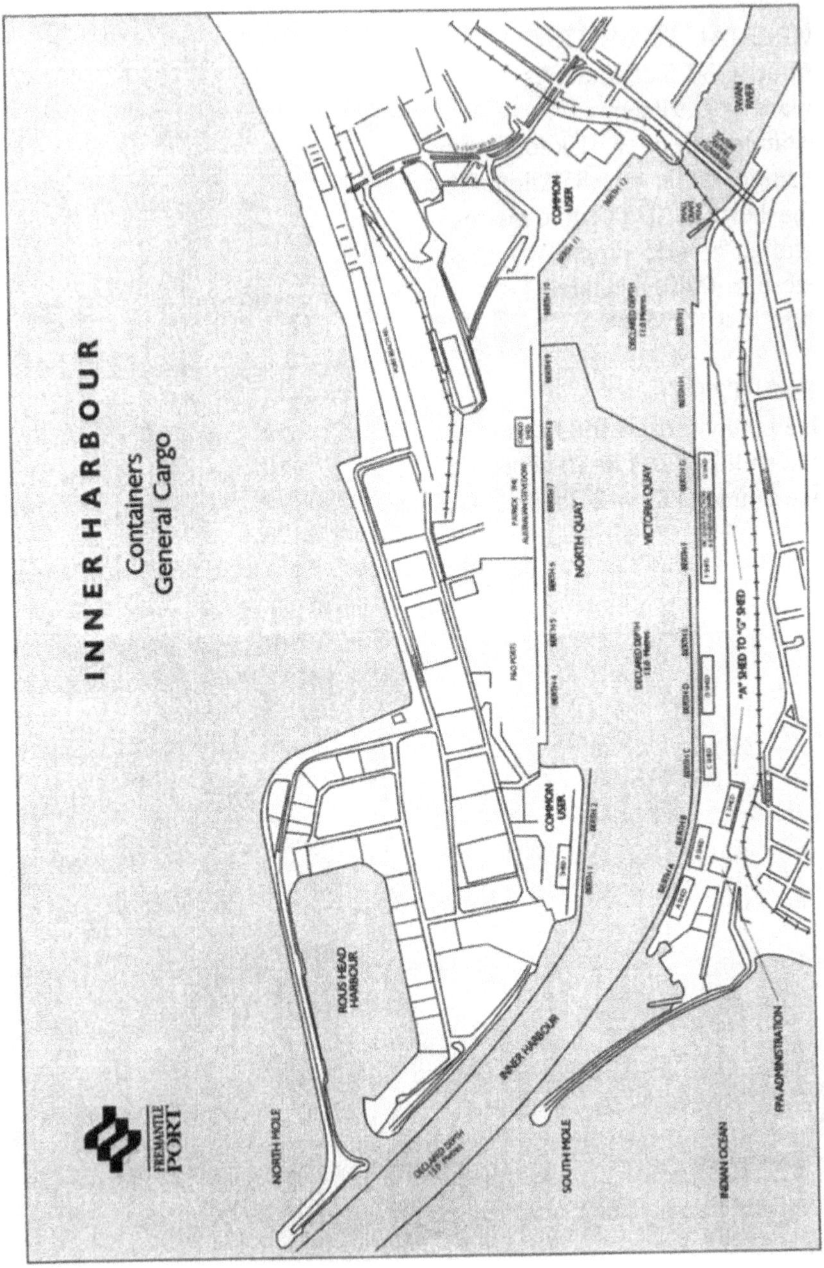

Photo 1: Map of the Inner Harbour

Source: Courtesy of the FPA.

Introduction

Ports are vital links in the international transport system and, for an island nation such as Australia, assume a special importance as gateways to the rest of the world. The basic function of a port is to provide a link between land and sea transport and to furnish means by which transfers of freight and passengers between the two systems can be made efficiently. A port is

> the place of contact between land and maritime space, and it provides services to both hinterland and maritime organisation. It is, therefore, a knot where ocean and inland transport lines meet and intertwine.[1]

But a port is not merely a "knot" where land and sea transport intertwines: it can also be a centre of population and of political, economic and social activity. During the nineteenth century Asian ports such as Bombay, Singapore and Shanghai formed the hearts of cities which constituted the meeting places of European and indigenous cultures. Such ports facilitated western economic penetration into the less developed nations of the world. The Australian capital city ports that were established between 1788 and 1837 similarly provided the British Empire with gateways into the vast Australian continent. Australian ports, of course, never became cosmopolitan meeting places to the same degree as the Asian ports because the Aboriginal population was relatively small and, until after the Second World War, trade and shipping was mostly with Britain.

The Port of Fremantle, which is located on the edge of the Indian Ocean, was developed to provide a gateway to the western part of the continent. The port has been a vital link in every phase of Western Australia's development: from the difficult early years of the colony, through the convict era, gold rushes, wars and depression it has remained a vital point of entry and exit for people and goods; its shipping and trade a barometer of the state's prosperity. Yet in its early years Fremantle was far from an ideal location for a port because a rock bar blocked the mouth of the Swan River and ships had to use a few exposed wooden jetties. The

[1]G. Weigend, "Some Elements in the Study of Port Geography," *Geographical Review*, XLVIII (1958), 185.

provision of an adequate harbour had to wait until 1897 when the rock bar was finally removed and ships were provided with a safe harbour in the lower reaches of the Swan River. One hundred years later Fremantle had developed into a modern port with deep-water berths, bulk handling equipment and container facilities. The centenary of the opening of the Inner Harbour was celebrated on 4th May 1997 when the patrol boat HMS *Geraldton* re-enacted the arrival of the *Sultan*, the first ocean-going vessel to enter the Inner Harbour. A port open day and an official luncheon hosted by the Fremantle Port Authority were also part of the festivities.

One of Britain's leading port historians, Gordon Jackson, has observed that "ports are living organisms" and must adapt to changing circumstances if they are to continue to prosper and grow.[2] Since the nineteenth century the world's ports have been forced to adjust to major changes in trade, shipping and cargo-handling technology. In the nineteenth century the ports had to adapt to the development of iron ships, the replacement of sail by steam as a source of propulsion and the requirements of large mail steamers; in the first half of the twentieth century, the ports were required to provide bulk handling systems for liquid and dry cargoes; and, since the Second World War, the development of huge bulk carriers and technological innovations such as containerisation, have revolutionised the international transport system. The handling of general cargo has been transformed from a manual activity, requiring a large labour force, to a capital intensive one. Unlike conventional general cargo operations, which required berths with covered storage for stacking and sorting of the cargo, containers themselves provided physical protection for the cargoes, and made existing wharf sheds largely obsolete. Containers require open facilities with extensive space for stacking and storage -- space which was lacking in many capital city ports. Thus many ports were forced to develop new facilities with access to adequate deep water and land areas. Sometimes the existing facilities, which were no longer required for commercial port operations, fell into decay and this eventually led to moves to redevelop the old waterfront areas. A well known example is found in the Port of London, where the old docks, stretching from Stepney to Woolwich, were made redundant by new facilities downstream at Tilbury and outside the Thames estuary at Felixstowe. The London Docklands Development

---

[2]D. Williams, "History of Ports and Harbours - Adaptations to Change. Conference Summary," in P. Holm and J. Edwards (eds.), *North Sea Ports and Harbours - Adaptations to Change* (Esbjerg, 1991), 226.

Corporation redeveloped the area for commercial industrial, residential and recreational use.[3]

As long ago as the 1870s, an official at the British Board of Trade, no doubt to the dismay of those who entertain romantic notions of life at sea, declared that "a ship is an instrument for making money."[4] In order to "make money" a modern vessel - whether a bulk carrier or container ship - needs to spend as little time as possible idle in port and as much time as possible at sea carrying cargo. If ports fail to provide up-to-date facilities and reliable services they perish as commercial ports.

All these changes and pressures have been reflected in varying degrees in the history of the Port of Fremantle. In the 1950s new deep water port facilities were developed at Cockburn Sound some twenty kilometres south of Fremantle. The new facilities attracted trade away from the Inner Harbour and by the 1970s parts of the Inner Harbour and, to some extent, the City of Fremantle, had acquired a "decaying" image. A long line of obsolete wharf cranes straddled the wharves, idle and unsaleable; some of the wooden wharves on Victoria Quay were crumbling; and most of the cargo sheds echoed only with the memory of bustling stevedoring activity. In 1983, Alan Bond, one of Western Australia's most colourful and controversial entrepreneurs, succeeded in ending the New York Yacht Club's 132-year winning streak in the America's Cup Races and brought the Cup home to Fremantle. The rejuvenation of the city was speeded up in preparation for the defence of the America's Cup in the summer of 1986-87 and some port facilities were adapted for alternative uses including leisure activities and a boat museum. But the relative decline of activity in the Inner Harbour could not be reversed by temporary success in yacht racing and in the 1980s the port was saddled with excess capacity and crippling financial problems. In addition, Fremantle as all Australian ports, suffered from industrial militancy and restrictive practices of various kinds. A new management perspective and new policies were required to guide the port through the painful restructuring required to improve efficiency and restore its financial position. In particular, microeconomic reform and commerciali-

---

[3]C.J. Evans, "New Ports for Old," in C.R. Ford (ed.), *Ports into the Next Century* (London, 1991), 225.

[4]T.H. Farrer, evidence before the *Royal Commission to Inquire into the Alleged Unseaworthiness of British Registered Ships*, 1874 (C.1027), XXXIV, Q.11,489. Cited by Williams, "History of Ports," 230.

sation led to massive changes to established work practices and procedures.

Port cities such as Fremantle traditionally enjoy a cosmopolitan atmosphere: they are open to the world and are places in which "races, cultures, and ideas as well as goods from a variety of places jostle, mix, and enrich each other and the life of the city."[5] In his autobiography Xavier Herbert recalled his youth in Fremantle:

> Besides the big ships, steam and sail, were the little ones, the tugs, yawls, schooners, ketches, the tight little pilot pinnace that could battle any sea, the dredges eternally groaning and grumbling as they bucketed up the river mud, the diver's tender with the man in the helmet coming up in a cloud of silver bubbles or going down. There were the things ashore that served the ships, steam cranes and electric gantries, coal grabs and whip [sic] winches, spare parts of ships like propellers, anchors, chains through the links of which a boy could crawl, and the stuff that went into the ships or came out of them, sandalwood, karri, jarrah, mother-o'-pearl, wool, wheat, hides, multicolored mineral ores, and curry, coffee, sulphur, crated automobiles and railway locomotives... The town itself was no less colorful than its waterfront, peopled as it largely was by seafrarers and globetrotters that the ships of half a century had left behind. The packed shops and restaurants, the wine bars, pubs, hash-houses, wash-houses, whore-houses, doss-houses, were run by people of all breeds...Everyday was a market day in that town of ships' chandlers and providors and sailormen and globetrotters ashore. The narrow streets seemed always to be thronged, always uproarious with voices, the clatter of horses' hoofs and the roll of iron wheels, the honking and grinding of the clumsy motor vehicles of the day, the clanging and groaning of the old fashioned trolley cars.[6]

---

[5]R. Murphey, "On the Evolution of the Port City," in F. Broeze (ed.) *Brides of the Sea. Port Cities of Asia from the 16th-20th Centuries* (Kensington, NSW, 1989), 225.

[6]Xavier Herbert, *Disturbing Element* (Melbourne, 1963), 95-97.

By the 1990s technological change and microeconomic reform had transformed the port: less than four hundred skilled workers handled cargo and shipping but they did so more quietly, more efficiently and more profitably than before. Yet compared to the port of Herbert's youth, it had become a ghost port and many Fremantle residents feared the implications of the changes for the economy and culture of the port city.

Despite its importance and colourful past, there is, as yet, no detailed history of the port or, for that matter, Fremantle itself. The main study of the city and port of Fremantle is still J.K. Ewers' *Western Gateway*, a popular history first published in 1948; Robert Reece and Robert Pascoe published a pictorial history of the port city in 1983.[7] Patsy Brown's book, *The Merchant Princes of Fremantle*, published in 1996 relates the struggle for a modern harbour but dealt only with the period 1870-1900.[8] The objective of this book is to help rectify this deficiency by charting the history of the Port of Fremantle between 1897 and 1997.

Broadly speaking, the development of the port will be analysed from the perspective of maritime history.[9] Maritime history is not a narrow, antiquarian discipline, but embraces "all aspects of man's relationship with the sea."[10] In view of their importance in the port's history, a great deal of attention is given to economic issues but in order to understand the port's development it is also necessary to consider a variety of issues in social and political history. Maritime history is essentially multi-disciplinary in scope.

It has been observed that studies of ports and port cities tend to fall into two extremes. On the one hand, there are works dealing with port activities such as shipping and trade; and on the other hand, there are

---

[7]See J.K. Ewers, *The Western Gateway* (2nd ed., Perth, 1971); and R. Reece and R. Pascoe, *A Place of Consequence. A Pictorial History of Fremantle* (Fremantle, 1983).

[8]P. Brown, *The Merchant Princes of Fremantle. The Rise and Decline of a Colonial Elite 1870-1900* (Nedlands, WA, 1996).

[9]For a general discussion see F. Broeze (ed.), *Maritime History at the Crossroads: A Critical Review of Recent Historiography* (St. John's NF, 1995); and R. Davis, "Maritime History: Progress and Problems," in S. Marriner (ed.), *Business and Businessmen. Studies in Business, Economic and Accounting History* (Liverpool, 1978), 169-197.

[10]D.M. Williams, "The Progress of Maritime History," *Journal of Transport History*, Third Series, XIV, No. 2 (September 1993), 29.

works dealing with the city as a whole but neglecting maritime activity.[11] This book is primarily a detailed study of the Port of Fremantle and makes no claims to provide a comprehensive history of the port city although it should serve as a useful stepping stone for such a work.

The book adopts a thematic rather than a chronological approach to the port's history. Chapter 1 deals with the establishment and early development of the port and discusses C.Y. O'Connor's visionary scheme for the development of the Inner Harbour. Chapter 2 charts the evolution of formal port administration and control at Fremantle and the establishment of the Fremantle Harbour Trust (FHT) in 1903. The next two chapters discuss the growth and changing composition of port activity as measured by cargo flows and passenger flows (chapter 3) and ship movements (chapter 4). Port trade mirrored developments in the state as a whole so chapter 3 charts the growth of the Western Australian economy between the 1890s and the 1990s. In chapter 3 it will be shown that Western Australia remained a basically primary producing state, with a small manufacturing sector, although in the 1950s there were attempts to expand manufacturing activity. It will be seen that the result was that Fremantle's export trade was dominated by grain, wool, timber and other primary exports, and the import trade by oil and manufactured goods originating from both overseas and interstate. Fremantle, aided by its geographical location and favourable transport connections, remained the state's premier port from the 1890s to the 1990s.

The implications of trade for the port varied not only according to its volume and pattern but also according to the nature of the ships in which the cargo was carried. Thus in chapter 4 considerable attention is given to changes in the types, sizes and technology of ships calling at Fremantle. In chapter 4 it will be shown that one of the most striking changes was the tendency towards increased vessel size: between 1919-1920 and 1995-1996, the average vessel calling grew from about 5200 to 19,000 gross registered tons. But by the 1990s the port had to cope with vessels as large as 130,000 tons which required costly deep-water channels and berths.

Chapter 5 examines the physical evolution of the port in response to these changes in trade, passenger and ship flows. The port authority's endeavours to make Fremantle a "first class port" led, among other things,

---

[11]P. Reeves, F. Broeze and K. McPherson, "Studying the Asian Port City," in Broeze (ed.), *Brides*, 29.

to the progressive deepening of the harbour, an abortive attempt to provide a dry-dock, the provision of bulk grain handling facilities, the development of the Outer Harbour, and the introduction of containerisation. The port's basic physical lay-out remained unchanged until the mid-1950s when the Outer Harbour was developed in response to a state-sponsored programme of industrialisation; such physical longevity was a testimony to the soundness of C.Y. O'Connor's work.

Chapter 6 deals with the key area of cargo-handling practices, working conditions and industrial relations on the waterfront at Fremantle. A wide range of people derived employment opportunities from the operation of the port but probably the most important single group of workers was the wharf labourers who undertook the physical handling of cargo. As late as the 1940s, their task remained a basically manual one, requiring considerable physical strength; moreover, it was often undertaken in arduous and hazardous conditions. The wharf labourers were employed on a casual basis, a system of employment associated the world over with low and irregular earnings, poor working conditions, industrial unrest and restrictive work practices. In the 1950s forklift trucks and pallets were introduced on Fremantle's wharves and paved the way for the more revolutionary container handling technique. These technological changes led to massive reductions in port employment: the number of waterside workers fell from about 1800 in the mid-1950s to about 370 in the early 1990s. The introduction of permanent employment in 1967 did not lead to the hoped for improvement in industrial relations and in the late 1980s a radical programme of microeconomic reform was introduced to reduce disputes and improve work practices.

A major turning point in the port's history occurred in 1903 when the Fremantle Harbour Trust (renamed the Fremantle Port Authority in 1964) became the central administrative authority for the port. In chapter 7 we discuss the administrative structure of the port and use a number of yardsticks of administrative efficiency in order to assess the performance of the port and its administrators between 1903 and the 1990s. In view of the impact of the port's financial capabilities on the port's response to change, it is necessary to examine charging practices, sources of capital funds and the profitability of port operations. The port authority's finances and, in particular, its tariff policy were shaped by a variety of pressures including revenue requirements, political bargaining, state development policies, as well as historical inertia. Over the years the port authority developed into a rather inward looking organisation; it shared with other port authorities a tendency to over-staffing and over-investment. Not until the 1990s did Australian port authorities become targets for microeconomic reform and all aspects of their operations including their objectives, functions, accountability, competitiveness and management and work practices, receive close scrutiny.[12] As a result, the Fremantle Port Authority underwent a radical transformation into a commercialised, customer focussed organisation designed to meet the needs of the port and its users well into the next century.

Although the port authority is the major public organisation responsible for the development and operation of the port and hence occupies a central place in this book, other organisations and actors, both public and private, are involved in the working of the port. These include overseas and interstate shipowners, shipping agents, consignees, stevedoring companies, tug operators, ship repairers, waterfront businesses, waterfront unions, the Fremantle Council, police, railway, customs, immigration and other state and federal public servants. The profusion of organisations and actors, and the interconnections between them, creates a complex network of relationships extending throughout Western Australia and, indeed, Australia as a whole. In a very real sense the port is "a community enterprise."[13] The multiplicity of decision-makers affecting and affected by port activities gives ports a unique complexity. It is this complexity, in particular, that ensures ports are more than "passive" links in the international transport chain and are worthy of serious attention by historians.

Lewis Fischer and Helge Nordvik have stressed the need for maritime historians not to limit themselves to regional or national boundaries but to adopt a more international perspective in their work.[14] This book discusses general themes and issues in port history and may offer some insights to historians seeking to understand the evolution of ports throughout the world in the twentieth century.

---

[12]See Industry Commission, *Port Authority Services and Activities* (Canberra, 1993).

[13]M.L. Fair, *Port Administration in the United States* (Cambridge, MD, 1954), 4.

[14]L.R. Fischer and H.W. Nordvik, "The Context of Maritime History: The New *International Journal of Maritime History*," *International Journal of Maritime History*, I, No. 1 (June 1989), viii.

Chapter 1
The Birth of A Modern Port

On 1 June 1829 the *Parmelia* and the *Sulphur*, under the command of Captain James Stirling, anchored off the wind-swept Western Australian coast. They had come to found a new British colony on the banks of the Swan River. One of Captain Stirling's first tasks was to choose a site for the capital of the colony. He later wrote:

> On our arrival here with the expedition the imperfect knowledge which I had of the country was of course soon extended and it was found in consequence that a Town at the mouth of the Estuary would be requisite for landing goods and as a Port Town, while another sufficiently high on the River to afford easy communication between the Agriculturalists on the Upper Swan and the Commercial Interest at the Port would tend much to the speedy occupation of that useful District. In selecting a site for this purpose, the present position of Perth seemed to be so decidedly preferable in building materials, streams of water and facility of communication that I was induced on these grounds to establish the Town there.[1]

The capital was named "Perth" after the parliamentary seat of Sir George Murray, The Secretary of State for Colonies, and the port town "Fremantle," after Captain Charles H. Fremantle, who had taken possession of this part of the continent in the name of His Majesty King George IV on 2 May 1829.

Although it appeared natural to Stirling to site the colony's port at the mouth of the Swan River, it was far from an ideal location because a rock bar blocked the mouth of the river, preventing the entry of ocean

---

[1]Stirling to R.W. Hay, Permanent Under-Secretary for the Colonies, 7 January 1832, cited in M. Uren, *Land Looking West* (London, 1948), 99.

going vessels.[2] Ships had to anchor in the exposed Gage Roads and lighter their cargoes ashore. It was then transferred to river craft and ferried up-river or carried by horse and cart over a rough road to Perth. This multiple handling led to delays and, of course, increased the cost of transport. In 1832 the Commissariat Officer, John Lewis, estimated that provisions could be handled up to six times before they reached their destination and that the cost of bringing two tons of flour from Fremantle to Perth, a distance of thirteen miles, "cost as much as the freight from England."[3] Another unfortunate consequence of the separation of port and capital was that in the early years of the colony "ships" captains, who did not venture upriver to see the improvements at Perth, carried back to England tales of a colony on the brink of collapse.[4]

The first port facility at Fremantle was a small jetty built near Arthur's Head in 1832. By 1875 there were three lighterage jetties, one in the river in five feet of water and two south of Arthur Head in eight and twelve feet of water.[5] A tunnel, which survives to this day, was cut through the limestone of Arthur's Head to provide access to High Street. In order to cater for the increasing size of ships one of the latter jetties, known as the Long Jetty, was extended into twenty feet of water in 1893. This was, at best, only a makeshift arrangement, because the jetty was unusable in heavy weather. A south-westerly gale did so much damage to one ship that the Captain declared:

> It is certainly the worst place I or anyone else ever saw. No place to send a ship of this size ... I would not come

---

[2]For accounts of the choice of the site for the capital and port see G. Bolton, "Perth: A Foundling City," in P. Statham (ed.), *The Origins of Australia's Capital Cities* (Cambridge, 1989), 141-155; F.K. Crowley, *Westralian Suburb: The History of South Perth, Western Australia* (Perth, 1962), ch. 3; and J. Bird, *Seaport Gateways of Australia* (London, 1968), 19-21.

[3]T. Fletcher, "Stevedoring Efficiency at Fremantle, 1829-1903. The Problems Experienced by a Waterfront Industry in a Developing Port," *The Great Circle*, XVII (1995), 24.

[4]P. Statham, "Patterns and Perspectives," in Statham (ed.), *Origins*, 10.

[5]F.W. Tydeman, *Report on Port of Fremantle* (3 vols., Perth, 1949), II, 53. Henceforth referred to as the *Tydeman Report*.

> to this port again and be obliged to discharge at this wharf, if they made me a present of the vessel.[6]

Bad weather also interrupted cargo-handling and delays for this and other reasons caused ships to spend a long time in port. In 1869 it reputedly took six months to unload the cargo of the *Lady Louisa*.[7] The barque *Catalina*, which arrived in March 1886 with 600 tons of cargo, took five weeks to unload even though she was equipped with steam winches to help unload her cargo into lighters.[8] Poor port facilities at Fremantle and the north-west outports contributed to:

> a high incidence of shipping casualties, higher freight rates and insurance rates, slower turnround potential, and consequently an absence of larger vessels on the coast. The lack of facilities was also to delay for a time, but not prevent, the introduction of steam on the various routes to Fremantle.[9]

Not surprisingly, shipowners considered Fremantle "a port to avoid" and demanded high freight rates in order to compensate for the risk of calling.[10] The vital overseas mail steamers refused to call at Fremantle: instead they called at Albany, over 400 kilometres to the south, because it offered a safe deep-water harbour.[11] It hardly needs to be said that

---

[6]J.S. Battye Library of West Australian History, Deposit 2602, A/1-3, Captain D.B. Shaw to Messrs. Simpson and Shaw, New York, 8 November 1892. Also cited in J.K. Ewers, *The Western Gateway* (2nd ed., Perth, 1971), appendix 16.

[7]P. Brown, "Western Australian Merchants and Political Agitation: The Struggle for Fremantle Harbour in the Late 19th Century," *The Great Circle*, XII (1990), 75. For a more detailed treatment, see the same author's *The Merchant Princes of Fremantle. The Rise and Decline of a Colonial Elite 1870-1900* (Nedlands, WA, 1996).

[8]*West Australian*, 13 July 1903.

[9]G. Henderson, "From Sail to Steam: Shipping in Western Australia 1870-1890" (Unpublished MA thesis, University of Western Australia, 1977), 23.

[10]M . Tauman, *The Chief. C.Y. O'Connor* (Nedlands, WA, 1978), 56.

[11]F.K. Crowley, *Australia's Western Third* (Melbourne, 1970), 24.

compared to Albany and some other Australian ports such as Sydney (Port Jackson), Fremantle was originally a very poor location for a port.

Port Jackson, for example, was an almost perfect choice for the site of the first settlement, as it offered sheltered mooring for ships, deep water close to the shore and access to the interior, water supplies and building materials.[12] Thus, as was normal in new colonies, port and city were combined in one location. Yet the passage of time can significantly alter the viability of locations: what was once an ideal location can become an inferior one; a poor location may become more favourable. So it was at Sydney and Fremantle. In Port Jackson the nature of the terrain limited the availability of land physically suitable for port development. The presence of deep water close to the shore became, paradoxically perhaps, a further constraint on port expansion. The steep foreshores and limited flat land at the waters edge meant that expensive rock blasting and/or reclamation was required in order to create sufficient space for terminal facilities. Even if reclamation was undertaken it was restricted by the need to retain an adequate area of water for the safe manoeuvring of ships. By the end of the Second World War Port Jackson was "precociously supplied with deep water, yet now hemmed in on all sides not only by a great city but also by its beautiful and unyielding sandstone."[13] By contrast, at Fremantle, as we shall see, political action, helped overcome the port's locational disadvantages.

The Development of the Inner Harbour

Fremantle's merchant class depended upon the port for their livelihoods and were dismayed by the state of the port and the competition from Albany. They began to agitate for improved facilities but it was to be many years before their efforts were rewarded.[14] From the 1830s onwards various public and private proposals were made to make Fremantle into a safe and efficient harbour.[15] In 1839, for example, J.S. Roe, the Surveyor General, submitted a design for a harbour constructed under the

---

[12]Bird, *Seaport Gateways*, 27.

[13]*Ibid.*, 67.

[14]See Brown, "Western Australian Merchants," 73-89.

[15]For a summary, see *Tydeman Report*, 50-52.

shelter of a breakwater off Arthur's Head. The first proposal for a harbour in the river was made by W. Phelps, Assistant Surveyor, in 1856. This involved dredging a 300 feet wide channel up-river and reclaiming land on both sides of the channel. Some experts on harbour construction even suggested abandoning Fremantle and building a new port at Cockburn Sound. In 1870, W.T. Doyne, an engineer, recommended against the development of Fremantle because of "the numerous natural difficulties to be contended with, and the consequent great cost and uncertainty of works undertaken for such a purpose."[16] It appears that he reached this conclusion after studying timber transport in Western Australia.

Timber was cut east of Fremantle in the Darling Ranges and drawn by horse and cart to "the muddy dyke called the 'Canning River'." It was then ferried downstream to Fremantle by river boats. In rough weather these boats could not go out to Gage Roads so the timber had to be transferred to more seaworthy craft. Doyne argued that this multiple handling could be avoided by sending the timber by rail to Cockburn Sound. In 1872 timber companies built a railway from Jarrahdale to Rockingham; the timber trade flourished until the opening of the Inner Harbour in the 1890s. But it was over seventy years before any major port facilities were located at Cockburn Sound.

In 1877 an eminent British engineer, Sir John Coode, without visiting Western Australia, submitted two schemes for a harbour outside the mouth of the Swan River. He was opposed to a harbour in the river because of marine surveys made by Captain Archdeacon, Admiralty Surveyor in 1873. These suggested that there was large scale sand movement along the coast. The tidal movements at Fremantle were too small to flush out the river mouth so that any river port would quickly silt up unless continuously dredged - an expensive operation. So the consensus amongst Coode and other engineers was that the port should not be developed in the Swan River. Coode eventually visited Fremantle in 1886 but remained convinced that sand movement would cripple a river port. The following year he submitted a revised scheme for a viaduct extending from Arthur Head providing 2,500 feet of wharfage with water depths of between twenty-two and twenty-nine feet at low tide.

---

[16]Great Britain, Public Record Office (PRO) Colonial Office (CO) 18165, W.T. Doyne, "Report Upon Proposed Harbour Works at Fremantle, and Improvements in the Navigation of the Swan River," 28 February 1870.

Coode's schemes, like those of Doyne and others, never reached fruition. There was one simple reason for this: the cost of most of the proposals was beyond the economic resources of the fledgling colony. For example, Coode's 1887 proposal was estimated to cost £495,000, more than three times the amount the government proposed to spend.[17] Money for developmental works was limited until the granting of responsible government in 1890. Before then, governments of Western Australia were not free to borrow money on their own account, without reference to the British Government.[18] But, above all else, it was the gold rushes of the 1890s that provided both the means and the incentive for investment in harbour and other transport facilities.

Gold transformed the economies of the eastern colonies in the 1850s; it produced a similar transformation in Western Australia in the 1890s. The population of Western Australia grew from about 48,500 in 1890 to 180,000 in 1900; a fourfold increase within a decade. Government revenue rose from £1.2m in 1894-1895 to £3.08 million in 1899-1900. External trade leapt from £1.55 million in 1890 to £12.81 million in 1900.[19] The tonnage of shipping calling at Fremantle rose from 44,000 tons in 1888 to 66,000 tons in 1891; by 1900 shipping tonnage had passed the million mark. This massive expansion of port activity overtaxed the capacity of the port's facilities, echoing the experience of the ports of Sydney and Melbourne, forty years or so earlier.[20] There was an urgent need for investment in harbours, railways, water supplies and other infrastructure required to service the needs of a growing economy.

---

[17]Ewers, *Western Gateway*, 93.

[18]F.K. Crowley and B.K. de Garis, *A Short History of Western Australia* (2nd ed., Melbourne, 1970), 46.

[19]Data are from R.T. Appleyard, "Western Australia: Economic and Demographic Growth, 1850-1914," in T. Stannage (ed.), *A New History of Western Australia* (Nedlands, WA, 1981), 219, 222 and appendix 6.3, 236.

[20]For a discussion of the transport crisis of the 1850s, see N.G. Butlin, *Investment in Australian Economic Development 1860-1900* (Cambridge, 1962), 299-305.

Photo 2: Charles Yelverton O'Connor (1843-1902), the engineer responsible for the design of Fremantle's Inner Harbour.

Source: See photo 1.

Photo 3: Harbour construction, c. 1897.

Source: Courtesy of B. Farrington.

Western Australia's first premier, John Forrest, "a man of forthright rectitude, robust commonsense, and homely hardheadedness,"[21] embarked on an extensive programme of public works. During the decade in which he was premier the public debt increased from £1.4 million to £12.2 million.[22] In 1891, in what proved a particularly astute move, Forrest appointed C.Y. O'Connor as engineer-in-chief.

O'Connor, who was born and trained in Ireland, had acquired extensive experience of public works projects in New Zealand, and provided the professional skills necessary to translate Forrest's plans into reality. He was an outstanding example of "the general practitioners" of the engineering profession, men who could turn their hands to a wide range of projects, including in his case railways, a water pipeline and harbour works.[23] The gold rushes led to large increases in the demand for engineers and skilled tradesmen, especially in the mining industry. In 1890 there were only about 477 engineers in Australia and most of these

---

[21]F.K. Crowley, "Sir John Forrest, The Statesman," in L. Hunt (ed.), *Westralian Portraits* (Nedlands, WA, 1979), 84.

[22]*Ibid.*, 86.

[23]In this respect, colonial engineers appear to have differed from British engineers, who became increasingly specialised. See R.A. Buchanan, "Institutional Proliferation in the British Engineering Profession, 1847-1914," *Economic History Review*, XXXVIII (1985), 42-60.

were located in the eastern states; Australia had only 157 engineers per million of population, compared to 354 per million of population in Britain.[24] O'Connor faced serious shortages of personnel but he gradually built up a skilled workforce which he used on other public works projects. R.T. Appleyard has said that "in this trilogy of circumstances - discovery of gold, responsible government and political leadership - lies the key to understanding the nature of economic change in the decade prior to federation."[25] Doubtless, Appleyard would also acknowledge the contribution of dedicated engineers and public servants such as C.Y. O'Connor.

John Forrest's government was primarily representative of the Swan River area and was determined to attract the mail steamers to Fremantle in order to ensure that Fremantle became the colony's premier port. From the 1840s onwards the quest for adequate steam communications and mail services with Britain had generated considerable rivalries between the Australian colonies. The first comprehensive mail contract providing a weekly service from England to Albany, Adelaide, Melbourne and Sydney was not, in fact, developed until 1888.[26] However, as early as 1852 mail steamers had began calling at Albany, over 400 kilometres to the South of Fremantle. Mail for Fremantle and Perth was off-loaded and sent by small coastal steamers to Fremantle. Fremantle and Perth interests agitated for the mail steamers to call at Fremantle but they refused to do so until a secure harbour was available.[27] The opening of the Great Southern Railway connecting Perth and Albany in 1889 further enhanced the attractions of Albany over Fremantle. Alarmed that the railway would entrench Albany's position, the government decided that O'Connor's first task would be to provide a safe harbour at Fremantle.

After detailed investigation, O'Connor rejected the notion that sand drift would prevent the opening up of the river and recommended the construction of a commercial port inside the river. The scheme involved the construction of two moles to protect the entrance to the river estuary,

---

[24]M.R. Rice and B.E. Lloyd, *Professional Engineers in Australia. Population Analysis* (Brighton East, VIC, 1990), 17-24.

[25]Appleyard, "Western Australia," 219.

[26]See J. Bach, *A Maritime History of Australia* (Melbourne, 1976), chs. V and VII.

[27]Tauman, *The Chief*, 34; Brown, "Western Australian Merchants," 73-89.

the blasting and dredging of a channel through the rockbar to a depth of thirty feet, dredging of the river channel to thirty feet, reclamation of land for quay and warehouse space, and the levelling of Arthur's Head for railway sidings and the provision of a graving dock and slip. The total cost of the scheme was estimated at £800,000 although a first stage to meet initial requirements could be completed for £560,000.[28]

Photo 4: Fremantle Harbour from Arthur Head, c. 1904.

Source: Battye Library 24966P.

H.W. Venn, the Director of Public works, and a member of cabinet, was impressed by O'Connor's plan but Sir John Forrest initially favoured an earlier plan of Coode's for a harbour at Owen's Anchorage, just over three kilometres south of Fremantle. However, he suffered an embarrassing setback when the Legislative Assembly rejected his motion in favour of Owen's Anchorage. A Joint Select Committee of both houses was formed to inquire into the question of harbour works at Fremantle. The Committee included Venn, W. Marmion, Minister for Lands and member for Fremantle, C. Harper, A. Richardson, S. Pearse, W. Moore, E. Hooley, T. Burges, G. Leake, and M. Grant. Of these, Marmion, Pearse, Moore and Hooley, directly represented Fremantle commercial interests.[29] O'Connor's professional and diplomatic responses to persistent questioning impressed the Committee and it concluded:

---

[28]For a detailed discussion of the harbour works, see Western Australian *Yearbook*, 1902-1904; and J.S.H. Le Page, *Building a State* (Perth, 1986), 182-199.

[29]Brown, "Western Australian Merchants," 81.

> That the evidence given and the opinions expressed to this committee by the engineers and nautical authorities consulted point strongly to the superior advantages of opening the mouth of the Swan River over any other project, and this committee is therefore of the opinion that the scheme as recommended by the Engineer-in-Chief and shown on drawing P.W.D. 1468 be adopted.[30]

Forrest agreed to abandon his plan for Owen's Anchorage and the Legislative Assembly gave approval for O'Connor's plan in March 1892.

On 16 November 1892, Lady Robinson, the wife of the Governor, officially started the largest engineering project in the history of the young colony by tipping the first load of stone into the water at Rous Head. By mid-1894 the North mole was long enough to provide sufficient protection for work to begin on the south mole. The rock bar across the entrance was destroyed by explosives and the rubble removed by dredgers. The dredger *Fremantle* was able to pass through the bar on September 13, 1895 and the dredging of the Inner Harbour started in January 1896.

By 4 May 1897 enough of the rockbar had been cleared to allow the first ocean going vessel, the Blue Funnel Line's *Sultan* of 2,063 tons to enter the new harbour. The Premier Sir John Forrest and his wife were aboard, the latter reputedly with her hands on the wheel. The *Sultan* was designed for the Singapore-Western Australia run and continued in service until 1908 by which time she had made eighty-eight round trips.[31] The first mail steamer to enter was the Norddeutscher Lloyd's *Gera* of 5,005 tons on the 10 August 1898. But the celebrations were dampened by the fact that the Peninsular and Oriental Steam Navigation Company (P & O) and the Orient Line, the holders of the government mail contracts, refused to switch to Fremantle from Albany until their representative, Captain T.S. Angus, had had a chance to inspect the new harbour. Also, the inter-colonial shipping companies, especially the Adelaide Steamship Company and McIlwraith McEachern, had a vested interest in delaying the move because they would lose the lucrative business of shuttling passengers and

---

[30]Western Australia, Parliament, Minutes, Votes and Proceedings, Session 2 , vol. II (1891-1892), Select Committee to Consider Harbour Works at Fremantle, 808.

[31]Nestorian Association, *Newsletter*, No. 5 (May 1997).

mail between Albany and Fremantle.[32] Sydney and Melbourne interests were also not keen on a switch to Fremantle because the extra distance could add up to twelve hours to the scheduled voyage times.

Photo 5: The SS *Sultan*, the first ocean-going vessel to enter the Inner Harbour, 4 May 1897.

Source: See photo 1.

In 1899 P & O's Captain Angus visited Fremantle and expressed concern that steamers might be unable to leave Victoria Quay in rough weather. Forrest authorised construction of a special mail boat jetty on the north quay despite O'Connor's claim that it was unnecessary. In fact, the jetty was never used by mail boats and was eventually demolished in 1915.[33] As further inducement to the mail steamers, the government agreed to provide tugs free of charge until the Inner Harbour was

---

[32]Brown, "Western Australian Merchants," 87.

[33]Fremantle Port Authority (FPA), 31/03, FHT to Premier, 16 May 1903; FPA 18/14/2, FHT to Under Secretary for Lands, 30 July 1914; FPA 92/16, "Fremantle Harbour Works. Progress Report for Year 1915."

completed, much to the chagrin of local tug owners.[34] Furthermore, a concessionary rate of £30, introduced in 1892 to cover all dues paid by mail steamers at Albany, was extended to Fremantle for the life of the current mail contract.[35] These concessions suggest that the government was determined to attract the steamers to Fremantle, regardless of cost, and that the British shipping companies were not slow to exploit their bargaining power.

In August 1900 Captain Angus reported that the harbour was safe for mail steamers; Albany's days as the colony's mail station were effectively over. The first British mail steamer to enter was the Orient-Pacific Line's *Ormuz* which arrived from the eastern states on 13 August 1900; the first British steamer outward bound from London to enter was the Peninsular and Oriental Company's *Himalaya* on 13 September 1900.[36] O'Connor's scheme and the government's concessions had finally succeeded in establishing Fremantle as the colony's leading port.

Construction work on the harbour was largely finished by 1903, by which time 6,840 feet of breakwaters (the north and south moles) had been built, 1,503,099 cubic yards of rock had been drilled and blasted, 9,637,501 cubic yards of sand had been dredged and 8,805 feet of wharves and jetties had been constructed. Although a major subject of discussion in parliament and the press from 1900 onwards, work on a dock did not commence until 1908. Opening up the river, however, cost almost £1.5 million, testifying to the advantages of a port such as Albany, which was endowed with a natural deepwater harbour. Thus Fremantle's history demonstrates how man's political will and engineering capability can succeed in creating a viable port even when geographical conditions are not immediately favourable.

It is a tribute to O'Connor's foresight that the basic structure of the Inner Harbour remains unchanged to this day. Fremantle's wharves were of the marginal type (constructed along the shoreline) rather than the finger piers (built at right angles to the shore) found in most other

---

[34]Western Australia, Parliament, *Debates* (WAPD), XIV (1901), 1183.

[35]FPA 153/03, Agents of P&O to Sir J. Forrest, 23 December 1903. The FHT had attempted to increase the dues but the shipping companies claimed that there was an unwritten agreement they would not be increased during the life of the current mail contract. Sir John Forrest confirmed that this was the case.

[36]FPA 20/27/1, E.S. Barker to FHT, 9 February 1927.

Australian ports. The latter had only a narrow opening providing access to the shore; they provided a maximum number of berths for a given length of foreshore and were adequate for cargoes and vehicles using ports in the early years of the twentieth century. But as trade and motor traffic increased, the narrow approach ways became bottlenecks and traffic was often forced to queue in order to get access to the wharves. This problem eventually led to the adoption of marginal wharves. It says much for O'Connor's foresight that, in the 1890s, he chose this type of wharf for Fremantle. Melbourne and Sydney, for example, did adopt this type of wharfage until 1917 and 1929 respectively. The breakwaters at Port Kembla (1901), Adelaide (1909) and Newcastle (1909) were modelled on O'Connor's design for the north and south moles.[37] O'Connor was responsible for other major projects including railway lines and the building of the Coolgardie pipe-line carrying water to the goldfields. His secretary, a young man called Frank Stevens, who later became Secretary of the Fremantle Harbour Trust, undoubtedly echoed the sentiments of his colleagues when he described him as "a man of brilliant genius and remarkable foresight."[38] But the pressure of work, the constant public criticism, and the need to justify his actions to numerous committees of inquiry, took its toll. On the morning of Monday 10 March 1902 O'Connor rode his horse into the surf at Fremantle and shot himself. A note left on his desk declared that

> the position has become impossible...Anxious important work to do and three commissions of enquiry to attend to... The Coolgardie scheme is all right and I could finish it if I got a chance and protection from misrepresentation but theres no hope for that now...[39]

In 1910 Pierro Porcelli carved a statute of O'Connor which is located outside the Fremantle Port Authority and, to this day, it serves as a reminder of a brilliant career cut tragically short.

---

[37]See Institution of Engineers, *Construction of Fremantle Harbour 1892-1901* (Perth, 1989).

[38]Tauman, *The Chief*, 245.

[39]*Ibid.*, 229-230.

The Fremantle Blockage

While the harbour works were still underway, the port had to cope with the trade boom caused by the gold rushes of the 1890s. The increased volumes of trade and shipping exposed serious inadequacies in port administration. During the nineteenth century the control of the port was split between four government departments: Harbour Masters, Customs, Railways and Public Works.[40]

The first Harbour Master, Commander M.J. Currie, was appointed by Captain Stirling whilst enroute to the colony on the *Parmelia*. The first port regulations for Fremantle were introduced in 1852 and gave the Harbour Master authority to control the berthing of vessels, pilotage and other navigation services. All construction work in the port was undertaken by the Public Works Department. Each department tended to pursue its own agenda and this led to confusion and inefficiency. For example, Customs officers checked the goods as they were unloaded, impeding stevedoring operations, rather than waiting for merchants to withdraw them from customs before calculating duty.[41] The jetties were connected to the railway system in 1891 and the following year, after complaints by merchants, control of the wharves was given to the Railways Department. But to the dismay of merchants, cargo-handling operations continued to take second place to the needs of the railways.

In January 1896, when inflows of migrants and goods were particularly heavy, Fremantle merchants began to complain about the "great Fremantle blockage."[42] A meeting of merchants and shipping agents claimed, for example, that the railway system was completely disorganised. Railway trucks were loaded indiscriminately, with "potatoes and onions at the bottom, with machinery on top; boxes of butter were exposed to the hot sun so that their contents melted and spread over the wharves."[43] The resultant public outcry eventually led to the dismissal of

---

[40]J.S. Battye Library, Deposit RN90, "Fremantle Harbour: Notes on Departments, etc., Responsible for Activities in the Port of Fremantle Prior to 1902."

[41]This paragraph draws on Fletcher, "Stevedoring Efficiency," 28-30.

[42]Brown, "Western Australian Merchants," 83.

[43]W.B. Kimberley, *History of West Australia: A Narrative of Her Leading Men* (Melbourne, 1897), 333.

H.W. Venn, the Minister of Railways and Public Works. Captain Laurie, a leading stevedore, complained that the Harbour Master could berth a vessel where he liked but that the Railway Department might refuse to take cargo away from the vessel.[44] The Railway Department adhered to a strict schedule: trucks were placed alongside a vessel at 8 o'clock in the morning and removed at 12 o'clock, regardless of the needs of shipping. It was necessary to travel to Perth in order to appeal to the Head of Department. The Public Works Department appeared to be unaware of the specialised needs of port operators: for example, it designed some sheds with a gap of 166 feet between them and the wharf edge, unnecessarily increasing trucking and handling costs. Even minor improvements were made only after long delays. The Railway and Works Departments' administration was characterised by "want of system, want of proper appliances, and...conflict of interests."[45] Merchants complained that due to the slow rates of discharging at Fremantle freight rates between Europe and Fremantle were twenty-five percent higher than those between Europe and the eastern states.[46] In 1899 it was claimed that London brokers were threatening to revert to the old practice of lightering goods ashore, rather than tie up at Fremantle's wharves.[47] In 1897 Fremantle had witnessed the opening of a modern harbour but the Fremantle blockage threatened to choke it off at birth. Clearly, there was a pressing need for a more unified system of port administration and control.

---

[44]WAPD, XXI (1902), 1534-1536. The following comments about government departments are also from this source.

[45]Hon. J.J. Higham, MLA for Fremantle, in *ibid.*, 1113.

[46]FPA 31/03, W. Sandover (in England) to Perth Chamber of Commerce, 27 November 1902.

[47]WAPD, XIV (1899), 1140.

Photo 6: SS *Manchester Merchant* at Victoria Quay, Fremantle, c. 1907.

Source: Battye Library 9627P.

Photo 7: State Shipping Service vessel *Kabbarli*, c. 1966.

Source: See photo 1.

Chapter 2
The Establishment of the Fremantle Harbour Trust

The beginning of modern harbour management and control can be traced back to Britain in 1857 when the Mersey Docks and Harbour Board was formed. Subsequently, similar forms of organisation developed throughout the British Empire.[1] Melbourne acquired a harbour trust as early as 1876. The creation of the Fremantle Harbour Trust (FHT) in 1903 marks the establishment of formal port administration at Fremantle. The Fremantle Harbour Trust Act was largely based on *The Sydney Harbour Trust Act* of 1901 and a New Zealand Act of 1878.[2] Throughout Australia, a large variety of port authorities have evolved with varying powers and systems of control, reflecting the impact of a multitude of factors, including geography, the nature of the hinterland, the type and volumes of cargoes, and national and state politics. By the 1960s there were about ninety major ports in Australia administered by thirty-five different sorts of authorities: "a system that grew up topsy-turvey from the days of pioneer settlement and sailing ships communications, developed during the days of State separatism and regional pride and jealousy and was never consolidated when the fragments became the Commonwealth."[3] The FHT is, however, of special interest because it acquired the power to engage in cargo handling operations, a profitable task usually left to private enterprise.

---

[1]See F. Broeze, P. Reeves, K. McPherson, "Imperial Ports and the Modern World Economy: The Case of the Indian Ocean," *The Journal of Transport History*, VII (1986), 1-20.

[2]For a general discussion of Australian port administration, see J. Bach, *A Maritime History of Australia* (Melbourne, 1976), chs. XII and XVIII; and M.T. Tull, "The Development of Port Administration at Sydney 1901 to 1936," *The Great Circle*, IV (1982), 92-104.

[3]*Australian Financial Review*, 18 June 1963.

The Formation of the Fremantle Harbour Trust

The departure of the Premier, John Forrest, for federal politics in 1901 led to a short period of political instability that delayed attempts to reform port administration. However, in July 1902 Walter James' Government assumed office and the following month the Colonial Secretary, the Hon. W. Kingsmill, introduced a bill in Parliament designed to establish a harbour trust at Fremantle. After considerable debate over the details of the bill, it was passed on the 11 December. From 1 January 1903 *The Fremantle Harbour Trust Act* vested exclusive control and administration of the harbour in a body corporate, the Fremantle Harbour Trust, with common seal, power to hold land and perpetual succession.[4] Although some modifications have been made to cope with changing circumstances, the Fremantle Harbour Trust, renamed the Fremantle Port Authority in 1964, continues to guide the destiny of the port to this day. Such longevity suggests that the 1903 Act must have incorporated sound principles of port administration. It is helpful to consider the provisions of the *Fremantle Harbour Trust Act* under the following three headings: area of jurisdiction; administrative structure; and statutory powers and responsibilities.

Area of Jurisdiction

The FHT was given jurisdiction over the Inner Harbour from the seaward ends of the moles up to the Railway Bridge - an area of about 152 acres (sixty-two hectares) of land and 250 acres (101 hectares) of water. The land area, on both banks of the river, provided ample space for berths, wharf sheds, railway lines and other port facilities. The Trust was also given control over an Outer Harbour, bounded by a line extending from a point about seven miles north of Fremantle; then in a south-westerly direction to Bathurst Point on Rottnest Island; thence along the eastern shore of the island and Garden Island to John Point on the mainland. This Outer Harbour covers a vast area of 114,000 acres (46,200 hectares) of water. No land in the Outer Harbour was vested in the FHT but in 1911 the Commonwealth decided to establish a naval base at Cockburn Sound and acquired a strip of land along the coast six miles long by one and a quarter miles deep. Plans for the naval base were abandoned in 1918 and

---

[4] *Fremantle Harbour Trust Act*, 1902 (No. 17).

the land remained largely undeveloped.[5] Thus in the 1950s when the state government attempted to attract industry to Western Australia, through a quirk of fate there was ample land in the Outer Harbour for port facilities and waterfront industry - an attraction not readily available in cramped metropolitan ports in the eastern states.

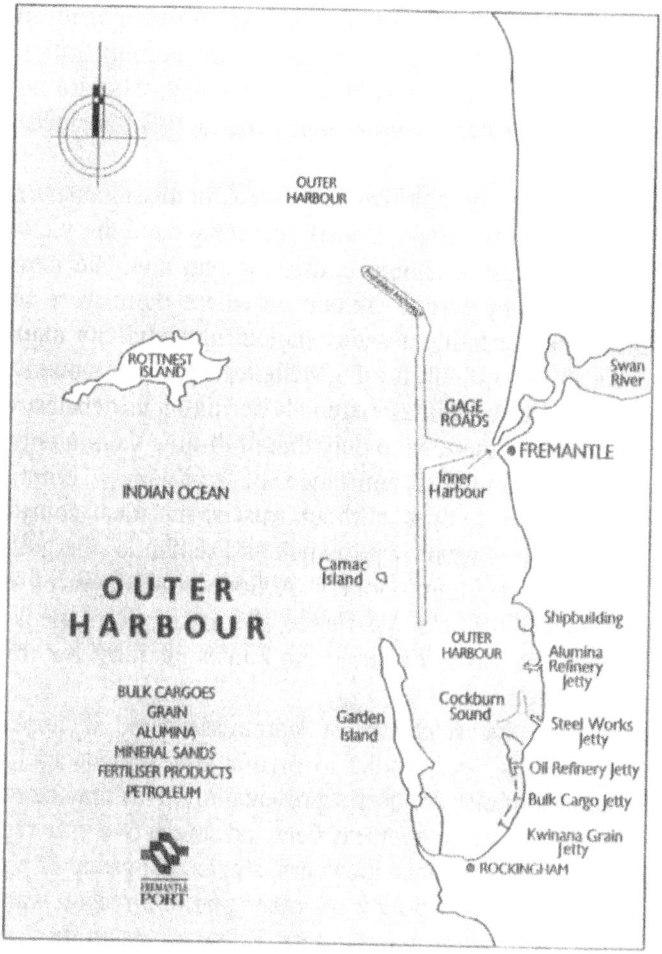

Photo 8: Map of the Outer Harbour.

Source: See photo 1.

[5]M. Berson, *Cockburn. The Making of a Community* (Cockburn, WA, 1978), ch. 13.

Administrative Structure

The control of the FHT was vested in five part-time Commissioners appointed by the Governor in Council. Their appointment was for a three year term, and they were eligible for reappointment at the end of that period. The Commissioners were paid two guineas per meeting subject to an annual limit of £150; the Chairman got four guineas per meeting with an annual maximum of £300. The day-to-day administration of the harbour trust was placed in the hands of a secretary, who did not have a seat on the Board. Ministerial responsibility for the FHT resided with the Colonial Secretary.

The decision to appoint five part-time Commissioners was arrived at only after long debate. The Colonial Secretary cited the view that the ideal harbour commission should consist of one man; he expressed a desire to avoid the situation at Melbourne where there were seventeen Commissioners, representing a wide range of port and city interests. As a consequence, it was difficult for the Melbourne Commissioners to reach a consensus, long and sometimes extremely acrimonious debates resulting. By contrast, at Sydney there were only three full-time Commissioners and "for the purposes and in the circumstances of the Sydney Commissioners the constitution of the Sydney harbour trust is the ideal constitution."[6] Nevertheless, for a less wealthy port such as Fremantle, the government favoured five part-time commissioners. A General Manager of the FHT, looking back on a life-time's experience of running ports, declared that the best arrangement was a "dictator who knows his job," but this option has not been pursued.[7]

Regarding the selection of commissioners, it appears that Australian authorities have tended to favour government appointments rather than the idea of elective user representation. This may be due to the fact that Australia lacked an overseas fleet and so elective user representation would have given foreign shipowners, a principal group of port users, an undue influence on port policy. Another possible reason was the fact that Australian ports were mainly state financed; Australia lacked the

---

[6]Western Australia, Parliament, *Debates* (WAPD), XXI (1902), 867.

[7]Interview by the author with Mr. Frank Tydeman, General Manager of the FHT between 1950-1965, 17 February 1983. The typescript is in the Battye Library.

private harbour companies which were common in Britain.[8] Nevertheless, West Australian governments usually consulted the principal interest groups such as merchants, shipowners and even, on occasion, waterside unions, before making an appointment.

The port's administrators, from Commissioners downwards, had a tradition of long, often lifetime, service to the FHT. Commissioner Bateman served for thirty-six years (eleven years as Chairman), Commissioner Carter for seventeen years (all as Chairman) and Commissioners McMahon, Taylor and Wilson for nineteen years each. Mr. McCartney, who became Manager in 1929, served the Trust in various capacities for forty-seven years; Mr. Stevens, the first Secretary, served for over one-quarter of a century. In subsequent chapters we will see how the port developed under the guidance of these men. Meanwhile, we turn to examine the evolution of the powers and responsibilities of the port authority.

Statutory Powers and Responsibilities

The powers and duties of the Commissioners were summarised in Section 24 of the Act:

> The commissioners shall have the exclusive control of the harbour, and shall be charged with the maintenance and preservation of all property vested in them under this Act.[9]

In addition, the Commissioners were to provide and control the pilotage service and maintain the lights, buoys and signal systems of the port.

Although the FHT Act vested sole control of the harbour in the hands of the Commissioners there were significant limitations on their autonomy, especially in financial matters. All revenue had to be paid to an FHT account controlled by Treasury, and was chargeable in each year with interest, sinking fund, and all costs of operating the port. Any balance remaining was paid to Consolidated Revenue. All expenditure,

---

[8]See, for example, H.J. Dyos and D.H. Aldcroft, *British Transport. An Economic Survey from the Seventeenth Century to the Twentieth* (Leicester, 1971), chs. 7 and 8.

[9]*Fremantle Harbour Trust Act*, 1902 (No. 17).

other than purely maintenance work funded from the Trust's own revenue, had to be approved by the government: the Trust complained that it could not even promote a man from fireman to engine-driver of a steam launch, "without bringing into operation the whole paraphernalia of the process of approval by His Excellency the Governor in Executive Council, and publication in the *Government Gazette*."[10] Furthermore, although the Trust was responsible for the maintenance of the port all works of construction and extension were still to be carried out by the Public Works Department. Section 25 of the Act provided for this as follows:

> The completion and extension within the harbour of all harbour works shall be deemed Government work within the meaning of the Public Works Act, 1902, and may be undertaken by the Minister for Works on the recommendation and under the advice of the Commissioners.[11]

Thus, as far as capital works were concerned, the Commissioners were merely an advisory body, with the government having final say.

Initially, there was some disagreement over the value of the capital works to be vested in the Trust. For example, the Public Works Department wanted to charge the Trust £71,157 for the cost of the original sea jetty.[12] Following the opening of the Inner Harbour this was useful only as a public promenade, and the Trust argued that it was unreasonable to charge it for a structure which was now earning no revenue. The jetty eventually became unsafe and was demolished in 1921. The Commissioners stressed to the government that they were "striving by all their power to cheapen the port and to provide efficient and rapid services," but that heavy capitalisation could only result in high port charges.[13] In 1905 the Trust complained that despite its continuous efforts, no schedule of property had been produced by the government: "the Government have simply preserved a stoical silence, which seems as

---

[10]FHT, *Report for Half-Year Ending 31 December 1903*, 5.

[11]Fremantle Harbour Trust Act, 1902 (No. 17).

[12]*The Mail*, 17 April 1905.

[13]FPA 15/03/3, FHT to Hon. Mr. Taylor, 5 December 1903.

impenetrable as it is incredible."[14] However, the following year it was finally agreed that the Trust assets be valued at £1,390,783.[15]

The 1902 Act made no provision for the creation of reserves for the renewal of assets and in February 1905 the FHT requested the establishment of a Renewals Fund. The Treasury argued that a Renewals Fund could lead to loss of government control over port finances and that its creation would require an alteration to the existing Act.[16] But the government eventually recognised that the 1902 Act was something of a "half-and half" measure and in 1906 introduced an amending bill into parliament.[17]

Captain Laurie, the first chairman of the FHT, and a member of the Legislative Council, argued that "the time has arrived when full power should be given to the Harbour Trust."[18] Initially, the bill proposed to give the Trust powers to borrow money on its own account and undertake harbour works, including the construction of a dock. However, opponents claimed that the government planned to invite "Parliament to lay aside its authority," and that an item of such importance as a dock should remain under parliamentary control.[19] Opposition was also expressed to increasing the Commissioners' term of office from three to five years. These controversial proposals were eventually dropped, but the Amending Act

---

[14]FHT, *Report for Half-Year Ending 30 June 1905*, 5.

[15]These were made up of the following:

Land	£ 40,154
Entrance moles	325,188
Inner harbour and channel	663,521
Wharves and jetties	226,112
Sheds and buildings	61,855
Slipway	21,644
Miscellaneous	52,309
Total	£1,390,783

[16]FPA 32/05, FHT to Under Secretary, Colonial Secretary's Department, 1 February 1905; FPA 40/06, Under Treasurer to Colonial Treasurer, December 1906.

[17]WAPD, XXI (1902), 1101.

[18]*Ibid.*, XXIX (1906), 1528.

[19]*The Sunday Times*, 12 September 1906.

granted the Trust power to construct harbour works subject to a limit of £2000 on any one undertaking, thereby providing a legal basis for maintenance expenditure.[20] The Act also provided for a Renewals and Replacement Fund to provide for the replacement of assets. But appropriations to this fund were limited to £2000 per annum, a sum which, incredibly, remained unchanged until the late 1960s. Thus the Trust was prevented from building up substantial internal reserves; this move appears to have been designed to ensure maximum government access to port profits. The Amending Act did allow the Trust to levy a Harbour Improvement Rate not exceeding one shilling per ton on all goods discharged or shipped from the port (Section 43). This provision was based on arrangements at Wellington, New Zealand, where a similar rate was introduced specifically to pay for the construction of a graving dock.[21] However, once again control was retained in government hands because Section 55 of the Amending Act gave the Governor power to revise dues if port revenue was considered excessive or insufficient to meet the needs of the Commissioners. The Amending Act generally clarified the Trust's financial arrangements and stated that interest of 3.5 percent was to be paid on loan funds, together with a sinking fund for redemption purposes at the rate of one percent of the capital debt.

The Amending Act provided the Trust with the power to employ labour and handle cargo (Section 31), a unique move which contrasts markedly with the severe restrictions placed on the Trust in the financial sphere. We will consider the reasons for this important provision below. Other general provisions of the bill dealt with the estimation of cargo tonnages, licensing and regulation of boatmen, porters, carriers and cab-drivers on the wharves, and limitations to the liability of the Commissioners for loss or damage in certain cases.

The Acquisition of Cargo-Handling Powers

During the nineteenth century, as we saw in chapter 1, the Railway Department was responsible for handling cargo to and from ships. But in 1902, when new wharf sheds were erected on Victoria Quay, the Railway Department arranged for shipping companies to handle cargoes through the sheds, apparently in order to save putting in their own labour. The

---

[20]*Fremantle Harbour Trust Amendment Act* 1906 (No. 35).

[21]FPA 78/06/2, FHT to Hon. Premier, 24 April 1906.

shipping companies received 1s 3d per ton for performing this service, a sum which was not always adequate to cover the costs involved. In addition, they collected wharfage on all general cargo for which they received 2.5 percent commission. The FHT continued this practice but reduced the commission to 1.5 percent in May 1903. In November of that year the steamship companies decided that this commission was not sufficiently remunerative and discontinued the collection of wharfage charges. The Trust undertook the collection of charges itself and estimated that this led to a halving of collection costs. However, the change precipitated considerable controversy over responsibility for cargo. The shipping companies argued that in the past they had collected charges as agents for the FHT and while they would continue to handle cargo from ships for a fee they would take no responsibility for losses or damage. The Trust responded that it was acting only as a wharfinger, that is, as a body in charge of a wharf. It collected a charge to cover the cost of wharf facilities but left the question of who was to do the handling to be settled between the shipowners and the owners of the goods. But neither shipowners, stevedores (contractors in general for loading and discharging cargo) nor consignees would accept responsibility.[22]

In an attempt to find a solution, in June 1903 the government asked for advice from W. Leslie, at that time resident engineer for the Harbour Trust. Leslie declared:

> that the present system of permitting the stevedores to own and use plant on the public wharves for handling cargo is to be condemned, as tending to build up private monopolies at the public expense.[23]

However, this upset his superiors, the FHT Commissioners who declared that it was their policy to:

---

[22]FPA 147/03, "Report of Conference between Trust, Shipping Association and Fremantle Chamber of Commerce," 28 October 1903; FPA 127/03, "Notes for Interview with Hon. Premier and Ministers," 25 June 1903; FPA 34/04/1, "Cost of Collection by Trust's Officers as Compared with the Old System of Commission to Shipping Companies," undated; FHT, *Report for Half-Year Ending 31 December 1903*, 3-4.

[23]Western Australia, Parliament, *Votes and Proceedings*, II (1903-1904), 5-13, W. Leslie, "Report as to the Best Method of Providing Appliances and Accommodation for Dealing with Cargo and Vessels at Fremantle."

> hold aloof from the work of handling cargo on the wharves...it being their contention that the Harbour Trust Act did not place upon them the onus of this work.[24]

In 1904 a conference of commercial and shipping interests formally requested the Trust to take over cargo-handling on the wharves. The Fremantle Chamber of Commerce even went so far as to say they were willing to pay higher rates to get the protection they desired.[25] Frank Stevens, Secretary of the FHT, wrote to William Ferguson, his counterpart on the Wellington Harbour Board, requesting details of arrangements at that port. Stevens, a New Zealander, was a journalist in Wellington earlier in his career and knew Ferguson. The Wellington Harbour Board handled all cargo on the wharves; Stevens was impressed by the "perfect unanimity" at Wellington compared with the turmoil in Australian ports.[26] This evidence appears to have swayed the FHT Commissioners because, after obtaining permission from the government, the Trust commenced cargo-handling operations on 1 May 1904. Given that the Chairman of the FHT, Captain Laurie, also ran the port's main stevedoring business, the decision was surprising to say the least.

The 1906 Amendment Act provided a legal basis for the FHT's new role:

> The commissioners may provide servants and labourers for loading and unloading goods on the wharves vested in the commissioners, and for working cranes, weighing machines or other machines and conveniences erected or provided by the commissioners for such purpose.[27]

The FHT introduced the custom of fixing the point at which the ship's responsibility ended and its began, at the moment when a man from the ship unhooked goods from the ship's gear. A similar custom was adopted in other Australian ports but with private stevedores assuming responsibil-

---

[24]FHT, *Report for Half-Year Ending 30 June 1904*, 3.

[25]*Ibid.*, 4.

[26]*Ibid.*

[27]*FHT Amendment Act 1906* (No. 35).

ity for the goods on shore. It is unclear why private interests at Fremantle were unwilling to do this; presumably if the Trust had not intervened they would have had to reach an agreement. No Australian port followed Fremantle's example, although there was some agitation for Melbourne to do so on the grounds that Fremantle's system was "the most advanced in Australia."[28] In 1907, the President of the Sydney Harbour Trust, Mr. Hickson, declared that he was strongly in favour of private enterprise doing cargo-handling.[29] One can only surmise that Fremantle's system may have followed from the appointment of a New Zealander, Stevens, as the first Secretary of the FHT. It was natural for Stevens to look for guidance from his home country, where the state was already involved in cargo-handling. A hint about Stevens personal views on this matter can be gauged from a talk he gave on the radio station 6WF in April 1925. He stated that "Fremantle is the only port in Australia where vested interests have not been permitted to get their clutches on to this great national asset."[30] Port authority control of cargo-handling led to a greater share of profits from the port accruing to the community, rather than to private interests. Between 1904-1905 and 1938-1939 the Trust earned an average surplus of £13,000 per annum from cargo-handling which represented about eighteen percent of total net profits.[31] On at least four occasions prior to the Second World War, the FHT would have made an overall loss without these profits from cargo-handling; they were a valuable financial life-line.

The Trust received praise for its "smooth and satisfactory" working of cargo.[32] It was claimed that tighter control over handling operations led to lower levels of cargo pilferage, but the Trust eventually needed to request additional policing powers.[33] The Trust quickly became the main employer of wharf labourers, with whom they appear to have enjoyed good relations. Wharf labourers were employed on a casual basis

---

[28]FPA 18/03, cutting from *The Age* (Melbourne), 24 November 1904.

[29]*Ibid.*, cutting from *Sydney Daily Telegraph*, 2 December 1907.

[30]*Ibid.*, 56/25, typescript of talk broadcast on 6WF, 30 April 1925.

[31]Calculated from data in FHT, *Annual Reports*.

[32]*West Australian*, 13 September 1904 and 9 January 1907.

[33]*Ibid.*, 27 July 1912.

and preferred working for the FHT because it "has always something in hand."[34] We will examine cargo-handling practices and the organisation of the wharf labourers in chapter 7.

The honeymoon with port users lasted until about 1910. The FHT refused to accept responsibility for losses or damage to cargo handled at night owing to the difficulty of obtaining accurate tallies after dark. A dispute arose when it refused to compensate a consignee for damage to his goods and the inter-state shipowners offered to take over cargo-handling. However, the Trust was unwilling to relinquish its cargo-handling profits and eventually agreed to accept responsibility for cargo handled at night for an extra charge of 3d per ton. The Trust recognised that night handling, although slower and less profitable than day time working, was beneficial, as it speeded up turn round and reduced the pressure for further port expansion.[35]

On the whole, merchants appear to have been satisfied with the Trust's work. In 1916 the Perth Chamber of Commerce declared that merchants prefer Trust control which "under no circumstances should be abandoned."[36] But two years later Mr. Griffiths, MLA for York, introduced an unsuccessful motion calling for the FHT to withdraw from the handling of goods.[37] However, little more was heard about this matter until the 1920s when the Overseas Shipping Representatives Association (OSRA) formally expressed dissatisfaction with the system of dual control at Fremantle. Stevens asked for concrete statements of complaint as so far he had received only "nebulous nibbling and grumbling."[38] However, local companies claimed they were reluctant to make individual complaints for

---

[34]*Ibid.*, 9 January 1907; and FPA 18/03, cutting from *The Age* (Melbourne), 24 November 1904.

[35]FHT, *Annual Report*, 1910-1911, 7-8; and FPA 86/11/2, Accountant to Secretary, 24 May 1911.

[36]FPA 102/24/1, Perth Chamber of Commerce to FHT, 24 October 1916.

[37]WAPD, LIX (1918), 1207.

[38]FPA 105/26/4, OSRA to FHT, 19 June 1925; and Circular No. CIV, 2 June 1925.

fear of reprisals.[39] It appears that OSRA recognised that dissatisfaction was not wholly due to matters over which the Trust had control; its push for privatisation appears to have been more a matter of principle than a result of deep-seated dissatisfaction with the Trust's performance. Certainly, powers once gained are not readily relinquished, and the Trust retained them until the beginning of the 1990s.

The Reorganisation and Operation of the Pilotage Service

When it was established in 1903, the FHT found that pilots based on Rottnest Island, located about twelve miles off the coast, were guiding ships to the Inner Harbour where they handed them over to shore-based pilots: a cumbersome and costly system. Reorganisation of the pilotage service was clearly necessary. Before discussing the FHT's reforms, it is useful to briefly examine the development of pilotage services in the nineteenth century.

Prior to the nineteenth century pilotage tended to be a private arrangement between the shipowner and a local mariner practising the calling of a pilot. The shipowner might hire the services of a pilot where he thought local knowledge of tide action, shoals and currents was necessary to safeguard his ship.[40] At Sydney, as late as 1813, pilotage was determined by bargaining between the pilot and ship's captains. Pilots were known to refuse all inducements to go out on stormy nights.[41] As ship size increased and the extent of harbour facilities grew, pilotage tended to come under government control "not so much for the protection of the ships ... as for the protection of commercial ports that had cost large sums of money to construct, and for the protection of other shipping using such ports."[42] At Fremantle a government pilot was available from 1835 onwards.[43]

---

[39]FPA 105/26/4, Australasian Steamship Owners' Federation to FHT, 24 June 1925.

[40]This discussion draws on a legal opinion of N. Keenan, K.C., cited in WAPD, LXXX (1928), 2327-2328.

[41]H. Shore, *From the Quay* (Sydney, 1981), 114.

[42]WAPD, LXXX (1928), 2327-2328.

[43]Bach, *Maritime History*, 38.

In 1848 it had been found necessary to establish a pilotage station on Rottnest Island because of difficulties in communications between Rottnest and the mainland, the poor quality of the Rottnest Light and the lack of pilot boats capable of taking pilots out from Fremantle in headwinds and calms.[44] During the nineteenth century communication with Rottnest was by boat, fire, flag and, after 1879 heliograph.[45] These rather primitive communications contributed to the wreck of the *City of York* in 1899 when the lightkeeper gave a non-standard signal which lured the ship too close to the dangerous shore. The FHT later claimed that "almost every wreck which has taken place on and around Rottnest Island is directly attributable to the fact that the pilots were to be looked for there."[46] The Premier, John Forrest, promised improved communications, and in March 1900 opened a telephone link with the mainland. Later the same year a second lighthouse was brought into operation at Bathurst Point, supplementing the main one which had been operating since 1851. Finally, in 1903 the FHT took delivery of a modern steam boat, the *Lady Forrest*, which had been built in England at a cost of £6,800.[47] Thus by the early years of the twentieth century the Rottnest pilotage station was obsolete and in August 1904 the Trust transferred all pilotage services to Fremantle. A look-out and signal station remained on Rottnest; once a vessel was sighted the news was telephoned to the mainland and a pilot boat despatched. The reorganisation was estimated to save about £2,000 per annum.[48]

Despite "a great outcry from persons who considered themselves as special authorities on the subject,"[49] the new system worked well. When the Orient-Pacific Line's *Orizaba* was wrecked on the five fathom bank

---

[44]FPA 40/03/1, Captain Irvine, Chief Harbour Master, to FHT, 19 March 1903.

[45]See J. Moynihan, "Twelve Miles West of Fremantle," Australian Post Office, (June/July 1970), 2-4; and Moynihan, "Linking Rottnest and Fremantle," *Telecom News* (June 1982), 12-13. The following discussion of Rottnest communications draws on Moynihan's articles.

[46]FHT, *Report for Six Months Ending 30 June 1903*, 9.

[47]FPA 91/20, Minutes, 21 July 1922.

[48]FHT, *Report for Half-Year Ending 31 December 1905*, 15.

[49]*Ibid.*

some thirty-six miles outside Fremantle on 16 February 1905, visibility was very poor owing to coastal bushfires. The master declared that a pilot station on Rottnest would have made no difference as those in the lookout station could not have seen his ship or heard the siren.[50] Although the accident occurred outside the port limits, the FHT decided to instal a fog signal on Rottnest to help prevent future accidents. This commenced operation on 1 June 1906 and exploded a charge every seven minutes during foggy weather. However, because of atmospheric variations its effectiveness varied. For example, on one occasion it was heard by fishing boats off Mandurah some forty miles south of Rottnest, but not heard by ships' much closer to the Island.[51]

Generally, the Trust's pilots provided a safe and reliable service. The arrival of the pilot boat was a welcome sight for sailors longing for an end to a weary sea voyage. In June 1908, Captain Cleary greeted the near-starving crew of the *Denbigh Castle*, who arrived in Fremantle after spending eight and a half months at sea:

> it is doubtful if he ever saw such a flotsam of humanity before, with our unshaven, weatherbeaten faces, sunken cheeks and eyes, our clothes, patched or tattered; even our "home-made" boots of tarred canvas nailed to wooden soles.[52]

However, one pilot, Captain Tait was eventually retired, owing to accusations that he was navigating ships while under the influence of alcohol, though there is no record of him damaging any ships.[53]

The first serious accident in the Inner Harbour occurred in 1916, nineteen years after it was first opened to shipping; in that time over thirty

---

[50]FHT, *Report for Half-Year Ending 30 June 1905*, 14.

[51]FHT 68/12, FHT to Fremantle Branch Manager of Orient-Pacific Line of Mail Steamers, 3 April 1912.

[52]A.A. Bestic, *Kicking Canvas* (London, 1957), 101.

[53]J.S. Battye Library, Harbour and Lights Department Deposit, AN 16/3, Acc. 1056, XXXIX, FHT to Harbour Master, 31 July 1903; Harbour Master to FHT, 12 October 1905.

million tons of shipping had entered the harbour without mishap. On 8 March 1916 the troopship S.S. *Ulysses* ran aground just south of the entrance channel. A Court of Marine Inquiry found the pilot, Captain Williamson, guilty of careless navigation and he was promptly dismissed. However, he appealed against the Court's finding on the grounds that the charts were inaccurate and the government appointed a Royal Commission to inquire into the matter. It confirmed that the pilot was guilty of an error of judgement.[54]

The S.S. *Ulysses* was owned by the leading British shipping company, Alfred Holt and Co., and formed part of its Blue Funnel service between Britain and Australia. Alfred Holt and Co. informed the FHT that because of the accident they would limit the drafts of their ships using Fremantle to twenty-seven feet, "until circumstances enable us to repose greater confidence in the port."[55] The Trust considered this accident, "the most serious thing that has happened in connection with Fremantle Harbour in all its history."[56] It responded by sending an explanation of the accident, and proposed harbour deepening, to Lloyd's of London. Clearly, such events represented a severe body blow to the port's prestige.

Another accident occurred on 24 February 1924 when the Peninsular and Oriental Company's S.S. *Benalla* ran aground outside the north mole. The pilot, Captain Morris, was blamed but subsequent evidence suggested that the helmsman put the helm to starboard instead of port as ordered by the pilot.[57] Any doubts about Fremantle's ability to handle large ships were reduced later the same month when ships' of the Special Service Squadron of the British Navy called at Fremantle. The *Hood* of 45,000 tons drawing thirty-three feet of water and the *Repulse* of 26,500 tons drawing thirty feet of water were handled without difficulty.[58] The Commander of the Squadron, Admiral Sir F.L. Field, praised the

---

[54]FPA 113/16/2/1, FHT to Messrs. Alfred Holt and Co., Liverpool, 28 June 1917.

[55]*Ibid.*, 113/16/5, Messrs. Alfred Holt & Co. to FHT, 21 September 1916.

[56]*Ibid.*, FHT to Hon. Colonial Secretary, 12 May 1916.

[57]*Ibid.*, 94/24/1-2, files entitled "Grounding of SS *Benalla*."

[58]FHT, *Annual Report*, 1923-1924, 11.

ability of Captains Clack and Rivers who piloted the *Hood* and *Repulse* respectively.[59]

Ironically, the abilities of the Trust's pilots, especially Captain Rivers, were later questioned in parliament during debate on the *Harbour and Jetties Act* 1928. This Act was designed to ensure that shipowners paid for the repair of port facilities damaged by their ships, except when pilot negligence was proved. Previously, shipowners had successfully avoided liability on the grounds that they were not responsible for accidents occurring while their ships were under the command of compulsory pilots. This applied even if the accident was clearly due to a defect in the ship or to the negligence of the ship's crew. With the growing size of ships, the potential for extensive damage to port facilities was increasing and the FHT was anxious to reduce the costly repair bills. For example between 1926 and 1928 there were four minor mishaps involving ships crashing into wharves, which cost the FHT a total of £3,139 in repairs.[60]

The Commonwealth *Navigation Act* provided that shipowners should pay for damage except where pilot error was proved. However, the relevant section of the Act had not been proclaimed owing to opposition from the states to the transfer of pilotage services to the Commonwealth.[61]

The Harbour and Jetties Act met with considerable opposition, mainly on the grounds that shipowners could not be held responsible for any damage done, for whatever reason, while their ships were under the command of the Trust's pilots. The Trust privately acknowledged that this "was a phase of the matter which is hard perhaps for the layman to understand, but it is of course quite reasonable and practical in shipping and port management."[62] During the course of the debate, the safety records of the Trust's pilots received some criticism. The Hon. A. Lovekin, accused the FHT of appointing "cheap" pilots, "in that the

---

[59]WAPD, LXXX (1928), 2341.

[60]*Ibid.*, 2071.

[61]Bach, *Maritime History*, 312-314.

[62]FPA 102/29/1, FHT to Secretary, Dept. of Navigation, Sydney, 3 July 1929.

salaries are not sufficiently high to attract the best men."[63] In three out of the four accidents between 1926 and 1928 Captain Rivers was the pilot; the other accident occurred with a ship piloted by Captain Clack. On all four occasions the pilots were exonerated. But in the five years to 1928 Captain Rivers had averaged one accident for every ninety-five ships handled, compared to an average of one accident for every 332 handled for three of the Trust's other long serving pilots.[64] Rivers' run of bad luck eventually affected his health and nerves and he resigned in 1928. There was no evidence, however, that Fremantle's safety record was worse than that of eastern states' ports.

The FHT strongly defended its pilots against claims that they were not competent seamen and "could not handle a rowing dingy."[65] It claimed that Fremantle's appointment procedures were amongst the strictest in Australia.[66] Only men with the highest navigation qualifications and who had an exemption certificate from pilotage at Fremantle were accepted. They were appointed on six months probation and had to undergo annual medical and visual tests. When the State Arbitration Court made the first award for pilots in 1935 they were granted a maximum of £700 per annum plus quarters or an allowance of £65 per annum in lieu of quarters.[67] The award conditions did not exceed those already given by the Trust, with the exception that pilots were allowed two days off per week whereas previously they could be called when required. Thus the accusation that the Trust appointed "cheap" pilots was unfounded. The FHT argued that the men who counted - the ship's captains - had never complained about their pilots. The Trust's arguments were effective and the Act was eventually passed without amendment.

---

[63]WAPD, LXXX (1928), 2314.

[64]*Ibid.*, 2329.

[65]FPA 102/29/1-2, "General Notes for the Minister," undated.

[66]WAPD, LXXX (1928), 2332.

[67]FPA 109/35/1, Minutes, 24 December 1935. See also *West Australian*, 18 December 1935.

Further Development of the FHTs Powers and Functions

The Trust's powers were further extended by an Amendment Act of 1911.[68] The Amendment Act had three major provisions. First, it provided the Commissioners with the power to remove goods left on the wharves or in the harbour area. The Commissioners had requested this because the previous season a quantity of wheat had been left in the wharf sheds and it had become infested with weevils. The weevils became so bad that they were being blown across the wharves and the Trust was forced to clean up the mess.[69] The Amendment Act enabled the Trust to recoup the costs of the clean-up from the owner of the goods. Second, the Amendment Act gave the Commissioners the right to charge extra for night handling of cargo. They requested this in order to cover the extra claims likely to arise because of the difficulty of obtaining accurate cargo tallies at night. Finally, the Act gave the Commissioners power to appoint special constables who, within the limits of the harbour, could exercise the powers of police officers. This power was necessary to combat pilfering of the cargo. There was a saying that wharf labourers wages were "twenty quid a week and half the cargo,"[70] though pilfering does not appear to have been a major problem at Fremantle.[71]

An unsuccessful attempt to extend the powers of the FHT was made by Scaddon's Labor Government in 1912. The Scaddon Government established a large number of state enterprises, from brickyards to butchers' shops, and saw state intervention as the only means for "the salvation of the masses against their exploiters."[72] However, the conservative controlled Legislative Council "blocked" many of the government's

---

[68]*Fremantle Harbour Trust Amendment Act*, 1911 (No. 25).

[69]WAPD, (1910-1911), 3278-3279.

[70]W. Lowenstein and T. Hills, *Under the Hook: Melbourne Waterside Workers Remember Working Lives and Class War 1900-1980* (Prahran, VIC, 1982), 16.

[71]M.T. Tull, "The Development of the Port of Fremantle, Australia's Western Gateway, 1903-39" (Unpublished PhD thesis, Murdoch University, 1985), 197-198.

[72]J. R. Robertson, "The Foundations of State Socialism in Western Australia 1911-1916," *Historical Studies: Australia and New Zealand*, X (1962), 324, cited by D. Black, "Party Politics in Turmoil," in C.T. Stannage (ed.), *A New History of Western Australia* (Nedlands, WA, 1981), 383.

bills, including the proposed amendment to the Fremantle Harbour Trust Act.

The 1912 bill proposed to give the FHT power to undertake stevedoring (cargo-handling on board ship) at the request of the ship-owner, to enable reserves to be created out of the revenue of the port, to remove the Trust's liability for damage or loss to cargo handled at night, and to extend the powers of the FHT police beyond the Trust's property boundary. The clauses relating to stevedoring and cargo liability were the ones which encountered most opposition.

The Trust was already doing stevedoring on vessels of the State Steamship Service and this Bill was intended to provide a legal basis for this (the State Shipping Service had been formed by the Scaddon Government earlier in 1912 to provide shipping services to outlying areas of the state). The Bill also proposed to give the Trust the power to do general stevedoring, a move that private stevedores resisted strongly. They feared that shipowners would prefer to deal with the port authority and much of their business would be lost.[73] One employer feared that "if the men have a grievance it will be the easiest way out of the difficulty for the Trust to give the lumpers exactly what they want in the matter of wages or hours of working, because they have the power to make regulations and charge the shipping companies just exactly what they like."[74] Ironically, the Fremantle Lumpers' (wharf labourers) Union also opposed the new power: they feared that if the FHT acquired a monopoly their members would not get work if they ran foul of the Trust's foremen.[75] It is possible that the Bill was designed to counteract attempts by commercial interests to regain control of all cargo-handling in the port. Shipowners claimed that if cargo-handling reverted to them, rates would fall by 3d per ton.[76] In the Legislative Council the Bill was condemned as "one more advance, and a very large one, on the road to State

---

[73]WAPD., XLIII (1912), 1844.

[74]*Ibid.*, XLIV (1912), 3070.

[75]*Ibid.*, 1845.

[76]*West Australian*, 17 August and 29 October 1912.

socialism."[77] The Council passed an amendment restricting the Trust's stevedoring to state-owned vessels.

As regards the proposed clause removing liability for damage to cargo handled at night, this was opposed on the grounds that the Trust was trying to wriggle out of its responsibility as wharfinger. It was claimed that the Trust paid out claims averaging £109 per annum, which was well below the level paid by private stevedores.[78] Clearly, local importers and merchants rather than shipowners would have suffered most from the proposed change and the Legislative Council struck the clause out of the Bill. The government rejected the Council's amendments so the Bill was eventually lost. Other measures of the Labor Government met less determined opposition; not surprisingly, the degree of opposition appears to have depended upon the relative threat to established private interests.[79]

In 1927 the Trust considered asking again for the power to do stevedoring. A Commissioner, Mr. Taylor, himself a lumper, said that the lumpers' opposition to the 1912 Bill was led "by the argument of interested parties" and they now realised they would get better terms from the Trust than from private employers.[80] But the matter lapsed as not all Commissioners were in favour of such a move.

In 1913 the government requested the FHT to take over administration of the State Shipping Service (SSS), on the grounds that the existing administration was far from satisfactory. The State Shipping Service, as we saw earlier, had been formed to provide shipping services to outlying areas of the state. Mr. Allnutt, then Chairman of the FHT, opposed the move on three grounds. First, that the Secretary and staff were fully occupied with the affairs of the Trust; second, that the Trust would not have full control of the SSS; finally, that it would be preferable to engage a separate shipping man for the job.[81] In part, opposition appears to have been based on the fear that such an arrangement would give the SSS advantages over other shipping lines. However, Allnutt was

---

[77]WAPD, XLIV (1912), 3354.

[78]*Ibid.*, XLIII (1912), 1848.

[79]Black, "Party Politics in Turmoil," 383-384.

[80]FPA 125/12/2, Minutes, 15 July 1927.

[81]*Ibid.*, 141/13, Minutes, 19 August 1913.

outvoted and the Commissioners agreed to give the scheme a six-month trial. Allnutt resigned in protest.[82] So from 1 September 1913 Stevens became Acting Manager of the SSS for which he received an additional £350 per annum. The arrangement was continued after the six month trial period. In 1917 Mr. Nicholas, a Commissioner, argued that the administration of the Trust was suffering but the Commissioners rejected his motion for separation of the two institutions.[83] The Liberal Government, elected in 1916, appears to have been unwilling to make any changes which would increase administrative costs.[84] Stevens had stressed that the existing arrangement was the cheapest and, not surprisingly in view of his extra emoluments, he was happy for it to continue.[85] He argued:

> that the line between the two concerns has been honestly drawn and is being rigorously maintained...In my opinion the Harbour Trust is largely the gainer by the amalgamation as the first-hand information we now have of the actual running and working of ships trading to Fremantle has immensely assisted the Trust's staff in carrying out the Trust's work, and this the outside shipping companies have recognised as is largely evidenced by the complete cessation of aggravating criticisms and the continuous striving for doubtful points of advantage which went on previously.[86]

However, not all of the Commissioners shared Stevens' enthusiasm, and in 1919 the government finally established a separate management structure for the SSS. Mr. Glyde, the Trust's accountant was appointed manager and Mr. Hetherington, a chief clerk with the Trust, was

---

[82]*West Australian*, 27 August 1913.

[83]FPA 97/17/1, Minutes, 2 and 6 February, 11 April and 27 July 1917.

[84]FPA 97/17/1, Colonial Secretary to FHT, 22 June and 8 August 1917.

[85]*Ibid.*, Stevens, Acting Manager of SSS, to Colonial Secretary, 23 August 1916.

[86]*Ibid.*, 681 Pt. 1/1/1 (New Series), "Administration of State Steamship Service," undated.

appointed Treasurer.[87] The SSS was renamed the Western Australian State Shipping Service in 1965 and survived for another thirty years despite a number of setbacks and persistent losses. Regrettably, no one has as yet written a comprehensive history of its activities.[88]

A minor amendment to the Fremantle Harbour Trust Act, the last before the Second World War, was made in 1913.[89] This allowed the FHT to provide a bond to the Customs Department as security against payment of duty on cargoes in its possession. This was a machinery clause only and passed without opposition.

Conclusion

Following the establishment of a sound framework for port management in 1903 West Australians could boast that Fremantle was now "a model of what a modern harbour should be."[90] Several features of Fremantle's administrative structure stand out. First, although the act of formation failed to specify explicit financial objectives, it appears that the government was not prepared to grant the port authority large discretionary powers in the area of finance. The governments desire to preserve revenue led to political interference in the running of the port and, as we shall see, port users complained that the port was being used as a "tax collecting machine." Second, the FHT was given the power to undertake cargo-handling making it, at that time, unique amongst Australian ports. The implication of this for cargo-handling practices, labour relations and port revenues will be explored in subsequent chapters. Finally, the FHT was given control over a vast Outer Harbour, providing an alternative area for port development. Although the Outer Harbour remained commercially dormant until the 1950s, its exerted a substantial influence over port planning and development from the 1920s onwards. The passage of time eventually exposed inadequacies in the administrative framework

---

[87]FHT, *Annual Report*, 1919-1920, 17.

[88]For a brief history, see A.M. Stephens, *The Stateships Story 1912-1977* (Perth, 1977).

[89]*Fremantle Harbour Trust Amendment Act*, 1913 (No. 4).

[90]*Evening Mail*, 29 October 1906.

and, as we shall see in chapter 7, port management underwent a major transformation in the 1990s.

Chapter 3
The Development of Trade at the Port of Fremantle

The Port of Fremantle has been a vital link in almost every phase of Western Australia's development; its shipping and trade a barometer of the state's prosperity. The import trade of the port began in 1829 with the unloading of the colonists, their personal effects and stores from the *Parmelia*. In 1832 wool exports began with a tiny shipment of three tons; other exports to develop during the nineteenth century included fisheries products, sandalwood, timber, gold and, at the turn of the century, grain. In 1903-1904 Fremantle's import and export trade totalled 692,000 tons and was carried in about 800 ships totalling 1.4 million net registered tons (nrt). By 1995-1996 trade had grown to 20.2 million tonnes and was carried in 1,758 ships totalling 33.5 million gross registered tons (grt). Therefore, over almost a century, trade had increased by about 2800 percent in tonnage terms, the number of ships calling had risen by 120 percent, and the tonnage of shipping had increased by about 2300 percent.[1] During this period Fremantle remained Western Australia's leading passenger port, although the rapid growth of air travel after the Second World War caused passenger movements to plummet. These summary statistics suggest that Fremantle experienced major changes in cargo and passenger flows and ship movements during the first century of the port's operation.

The objective of this chapter is to identify and explain the major changes in cargo and passenger flows between the 1890s and the 1990s; ship movements will be considered in the next chapter. In order to explain trade and passenger flows we examine a variety of factors, including economic ones such as the growth of population, incomes and industry and the state of overseas trade, while political factors such as government tariff and trading policies, and industrial militancy cannot be neglected. It will be argued that to a large degree Fremantle's fortunes as a port were not determined by local decisions of port operators and users, but by wider forces emanating from the state, national and even international

[1]The comparison of nrt and grt overstates the actual increase but grt data is not available until 1919-1920.

spheres. But before we can consider these factors it is necessary to briefly discuss the measurement of port activity.

There are a number of possible measures of port activity including the tonnage of cargo handled; the value of cargo handled; the capacity of ships using a port; and the number of ships calling. All measures have limitations: tons weight favours bulk cargo ports; using value data gives rise to the problem of finding an adequate price deflator; net registered tonnage, the best measure of cargo carrying capacity, varies with vessel type; and number of ships favours small cargo ports.[2] No single measure is adequate, especially for ports such as Fremantle, which cater for a wide variety of cargoes and ships types. From an economic point of view the value of trade is probably most important, as it affects the willingness to invest in port facilities. But as the port authority had the task of relating physical flows of cargo to physical cargo-handling capacity it tended to be more concerned with cargo tonnages. For the predominant part of this chapter discussion of trade will be in terms of tonnages simply because value detail is often lacking at the port level.

Cargoes can be subdivided into bulk and non-bulk or general cargoes. Although there is no hard-and-fast distinction between the two types, bulk cargo is usually of a homogeneous character, has a low value per ton and moves in large quantities; general cargoes are more heterogeneous and before the advent of containerisation consisted of individual parcels and packages all needing to be individually sorted and handled. Cargoes of a homogeneous character, such as coal and wheat, presented fewer obstacles to the development of mechanised handling than did general cargoes. As we shall see in Chapter 6, the handling of general cargoes remained a basically labour intensive activity as late as the 1940s.

The Course of Trade Fluctuations, 1903-1904 to 1995-1996

Figure 3.1 illustrates the growth of total trade at Fremantle between 1903-1904 and 1995-1996, measured in tonnes. For about nine decades, total port trade grew at an average of 4.6 percent per annum. As a result of this growth rate, by 1995-1996 Fremantle's trade had increased twenty nine-fold to 20.3 million tonnes. Figure 3.1 shows that there were significant fluctuations in trade flows, with peaks occurring just before the outbreak

---

[2]P.J. Rimmer, "The Problem of Comparing and Classifying Seaports," *Professional Geographer*, XVIII (1966), 3-91.

of the First World War, in the late 1920s, during the Second World War, at the beginning and middle of the 1950s, in the mid-1970s and in the early 1990s. Peaks and troughs in exports and imports did not always coincide: for example, imports recovered more rapidly from the 1930s depression than did exports; the latter passed their 1930-1931 peak of 1.2 million tonnes only in 1950-1951, reflecting the severe impact of the depression on Western Australia's primary sector.

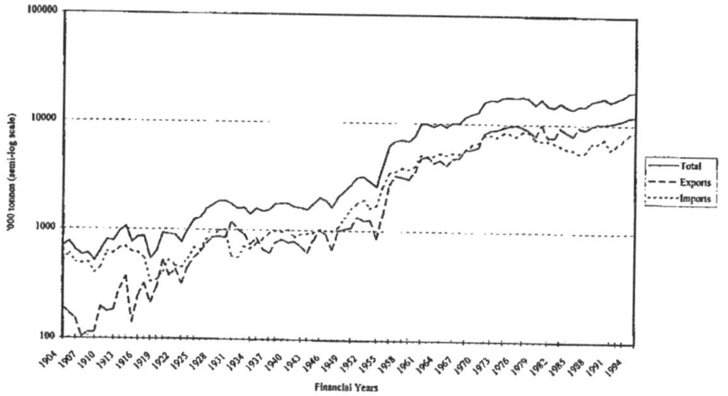

Figure 3.1: The growth of trade at the Port of Fremantle, 1903-1904 to 1994-1996.

Source: Appendix A.

Table 3.1 provides a preliminary snapshot of economic progress in Western Australia in relation to the rest of Australia between 1901 and 1991. The table reveals large relative increases in the area under crop, wool, wheat and gold production. In general, indicators of primary industry show substantial relative progress while indicators of industrialisation, such as factory employment, show relatively modest increases. As we will see below, even in the 1990s, Western Australia remained a primary producing state, a fact of immense significance for the progress of the port.

Before discussing the circumstances surrounding the major trade fluctuations, it is necessary to distinguish between foreign and domestic trade. Table 3.2, which shows the relative importance of foreign and domestic traffic, measured in tonnes, reveals that Fremantle was predominantly an "overseas" port. The main reason for this is the fact that port trade is dominated by exports of primary commodities. The opening of the Trans-Australia Railway in 1917, the decline in imports of bunker coal from Newcastle, and the increased competition from road and air transport after the Second World War also helped reduce the relative importance of domestic trade. By the 1990s eighty percent of port trade was accounted for by overseas imports and exports. Clearly, any discussion of trade must give due attention to the state of the economy, so we now turn to consider the economic circumstances surrounding major trade fluctuations between the 1890s and 1995. In order to facilitate discussion we consider the course of trade fluctuations in two periods, from the 1890s to 1939 and from 1940 to 1995.

Table 3.1
Western Australia in Relation to the Rest of Australia in 1901 and 1991

Indicator	1901 Level	Percentage of Australian total	1991 Level	Percentage of Australian total
Population	213,382	5.5	1,662,777	9.6
Area under crop ('000 hectares)	537	2.6	17,382	30.8
Wool production ('000 tonnes	199	3.4	222	26.3
Wheat production ('000 tonnes)	35	2.5	5,449	36.1
Gold production ($m)	15.9	53.7	2,900	70
No. of factories	586	5.1	2,561	8.4
No. of factory employees	11,828	6.0	67,000	6.7
Exports ($m)	18.1	20.6	14,039.5	25.5
Imports ($m)	14.4	17.7	3548.2	7.0

Source: Western Australia, *Statistical Registers* and *Yearbooks*.

Table 3.2
The Structure of Trade at Fremantle, 1910-1990
(percentages based on cargo tonnes)

Period	Foreign	Domestic
1910	45.7	54.3
1920	51.0	49.0
1930	77.7	22.3
1940	65.2	34.8
1950	75.0	25.0
1960	72.9	27.1
1970	61.8	38.2
1980	73.4	26.6
1990	80.0	20.0

Note: Averages of three financial years centred on the years shown.

Source: FHT and FPA, *Annual Reports*.

The Course of Trade Fluctuations from the 1890s to 1939

Graeme Snooks has used the leading sector concept as an aid to understanding Western Australia's economic growth during the nineteenth and early twentieth centuries. A leading sector is a sector which "initiates a process of change of substantial magnitude in an economy."[3] It expands in response to autonomous factors (factors external to the economy) such as new inventions, new discoveries of natural resources and changes in overseas demand. According to Snooks, at various times the goldmining, agricultural, and pastoral industries have acted as leading sectors in Western Australia.

---

[3]G.D. Snooks, *Depression and Recovery in Western Australia 1928/29-1938/39* (Nedlands, WA, 1974), 1.

During the 1890s gold mining was a leading sector, dominating the rest of the economy. Between 1896 and 1900 Western Australia produced an average of £3.98 million of gold per annum or just over one-third of Australia's total production. Over the same period exports averaged £31 per head of population, and imports £37 per head of population compared to £19 and £17 respectively for the nation as a whole. In chapter 1 we saw that the gold rushes created record levels of port trade and helped expose the inadequacy of existing port facilities. Gold production and gold exports peaked in 1903, when gold accounted for a massive eighty-three percent of the value of the state's exports. Subsequently, it declined in importance although as late as 1913 it still accounted for forty-seven percent of the value of exports and remained the major export earner. As the gold industry waxed and waned, so did the fortunes of the state and its major port. The decline in port trade in the first decade of this century, revealed in figure 3.1, clearly testifies to gold's importance. A period of readjustment followed for state and port alike. Fortunately, agriculture emerged as a new leading sector, boosting trade values and raising trade tonnages to record levels by 1914.

Estimates of Western Australia's gross domestic product (GDP) are available for 1913-1914 and 1938-1939.[4] The data show that real GDP (1938-1939 prices) grew faster in Western Australia than in Australia as a whole, but so did population, with the result that real GDP per capita actually fell by an average of 0.03 percent per annum. However, Australian real GDP per head grew by only 0.03 percent per annum, so that given the inevitable inaccuracies in the data, Western Australia's performance was probably the same as the national experience. Thus these years saw a general stagnation in per capita income growth. However, Ian McLean and Jonathan Pincus have suggested that the per capita GDP data failed to reflect increases in the standard of living due to unmeasured gains in areas such as life expectancy, leisure and housing quality.[5] Nevertheless, the over-riding impression remains one of, at best, extremely modest progress in living standards.

It might be expected that fluctuations in per capita incomes would be reflected in port trade, although clearly per capita incomes were not the

---

[4]G.D. Snooks, "Development in Adversity 1913 to 1946," in C.T. Stannage (ed.), *A New History of Western Australia* (Nedlands, WA, 1981), table 7.1, 238.

[5]I.W. McLean and J. Pincus, "Did Australian Living Standards Stagnate between 1890 and 1940?" *Journal of Economic History*, XLIII (1983), 193-202.

only factor affecting cargo volumes at Fremantle. Over the period 1913-1914 to 1938-1939 Fremantle's trade grew by about four percent per annum in tonnage terms, or about two and a half times faster than real GDP and population. However, there is no mechanical rule for translating growth in population and incomes into growth in port trade, at least as measured in tonnage, so that the 1:2.5 ratio of population and incomes to trade may not hold for different time periods. In order to cast further light on the factors affecting Fremantle's trade we need to examine the progress of the state's economy.

According to Sean Glynn, "in the first thirty years of this century, when the Australian wheat industry as a whole grew rapidly, Western Australia surpassed all other States in its rate of agricultural expansion, rising from an insignificant position as a net wheat importer to become one of the main wheat producing and exporting States."[6] Between 1900 and 1930 the area under wheat grew from about 74,000 acres to about four million acres; the value of wheat exports expanded from virtually zero to £6 million. This growth was aided by government intervention, including the provision of cheap land, the development of an extensive railway system and the provision of credit to farmers.[7] In view of the importance of the wheat industry for the state and the port, it is worth considering its growth in more detail.

The history of the wheat industry prior to the Second World War falls into four distinct phases, the first three of which were identified by S. Glynn.[8] First, there was an initial expansionary phase between 1903 and 1914, that was ended by drought and the outbreak of the First World War. Due to the shortage of shipping wheat piled up on Australian wharves awaiting shipment. The industry entered a second and contractionary phase that lasted until 1919. During this period unprecedented levels of government assistance were given to farmers: "a vast holding operation for the wheat industry until conditions improved."[9] The disruption caused by the war led to falls in real GDP throughout Australia;

---

[6]S. Glynn, *Government Policy and Agricultural Development* (Nedlands, WA, 1975), 2.

[7]*Ibid.*, ch. 1.

[8]*Ibid.*, 5-6.

[9]*Ibid.*, 6.

in Western Australia per capita GDP peaked at £140.9 (1938-1939 prices) in 1912-1913, a level not exceeded until after the Second World War.[10] Third, the wheat industry underwent a phase of rapid growth during the 1920s, which saw the extension of cultivation eastwards into marginal land areas. This expansion continued even though economic conditions became less favourable: wheat prices fell steadily from the mid-1920s onwards, and as the boundary of cultivation was pushed eastwards farmers faced higher production and marketing costs. The industry's expansion contributed to a boom in economic activity: between 1923-1924 and 1927-1928 real GDP per head increased by 2.62 percent per annum, compared to a decline of 0.02 percent per annum in Australia as a whole over the same period.[11] According to G. Snooks, however, the state's heavy emphasis on rural expansion and on boosting population with the aid of assisted migration, led to an unbalanced pattern of development, with disastrous consequences in the 1930s. The fourth phase in the history of the industry commenced in 1930-1931 when wheat prices slumped to only 2s 3d per bushel or about one-half of the level in the previous year. The ill-conceived campaign to revive rural incomes by growing more wheat had "turned a grave situation into complete disaster."[12] The 1930-1931 harvest was thirty-seven percent larger than that of the previous year but the gross return to farmers fell by thirty-one percent.[13] The collapse of wheat prices led to a period of drastic reconstruction, but recovery was slow: the 1930-1931 peak output was not reached again until the 1950s.

The fortunes of the industry were well reflected in the trade of Fremantle. The first recorded wheat shipment from Western Australia occurred on 23 August 1904 when the steamship *Essex* left Fremantle with 262 tons of locally grown wheat. The first wheat exports of any magnitude occurred in 1908-1909 when 14,774 tons was shipped from Fremantle. From these humble beginnings wheat exports grew to become a mainstay of the port's trade. In 1929-1930 a record 846,000 tons of wheat was shipped from Fremantle; thereafter wheat exports declined steadily

---

[10]G.D. Snooks, "The Arithmetic of Regional Growth: Western Australia 1912/13 to 1957/8," *Australian Economic History Review*, XIX (1979), 65.

[11]*Ibid.*, 67.

[12]Snooks, *Depression and Recovery*, 37.

[13]*Ibid.*

to about 348,000 tons in 1938-1939. But the 1930s depression had at least one far-reaching outcome for the port: the pressure to reduce costs led to the introduction of bulk handling of grain. Not surprisingly, the introduction of mechanisation in the midst of a depression proved controversial; we will discuss this important episode in the port's history in Chapter 5.

The depression led to a decline in economic activity throughout Australia but economic activity began to pick up in 1931-1932 in Western Australia, a year before the nation as a whole. This was mainly due to the re-emergence of goldmining as a leading sector, but also to the expansion of the dairying industries, and a general weakening of contractionary forces.[14] Goldmining began to expand in 1929 due to the introduction of more efficient production methods in the late 1920s and was further stimulated by an increase in the price of gold after 1930. By the late 1930s Western Australia was providing about three-quarters of Australia's gold production. In 1938-1939 gold accounted for forty-six percent of Western Australia's total exports of £23 million. According to G. Snooks, the goldmining revival provided Western Australia with a "breathing space," allowing time "to reconstruct an economy which had become badly out of touch with both national and international market forces."[15] However, Western Australia remained a basically primary producing state, exporting agricultural and mineral products and with only a small manufacturing sector.

A major reason for the slow progress of manufacturing industry in Western Australia was the removal of customs barriers between the states following Federation in 1901. Manufacturers in the more densely populated states enjoyed greater relative access to economies of scale and were able to make large inroads into the Western Australian market. Manufacturing industry in Western Australia was limited to the processing of primary produce before export and the production of goods where distance offered a measure of natural protection. Resentment about the effect of federation on local industry was a major factor behind the vote for secession in 1933.[16]

---

[14]Western Australia, *Year Book*, 1902-1904, 123.

[15]G.D. Snooks, "Development in Adversity 1913 to 1946," in Stannage (ed.), *New History*, 241-244.

[16]J. Hutton, *Manufacturing Industry and Western Australian Development* (Nedlands, WA, 1966), ch. 1 and 85-86.

Given the heavy reliance on imported manufactures, Western Australia tended to have high levels of imports per head of population. During the 1890s, when the gold rushes were underway, imports averaged £37 per head, about double the Australian average. By 1913 imports had declined to £31 per head but were still about double the Australian average. According to Graeme Henderson, in the nineteenth century many of these imports came from Britain via the eastern states and Singapore as direct overseas shipping services to this small, isolated colony, were naturally limited.[17] In 1900 overseas imports totalled £3,798,000 of which £511,000 or thirteen percent came via the eastern states. The practice of importing overseas goods via the eastern states continued in the twentieth century, although it steadily declined in importance. In 1912-1913 eight percent of overseas imports came via the eastern states, while in 1938-1939 the figure was ten percent.

As the twentieth century progressed, an increased proportion of Western Australia's imports, measured in value terms, were accounted for by interstate imports. In 1913 overseas imports totalled £5,898,000 or sixty percent of total imports; by 1938-1939 overseas imports were only £5,997,000 or thirty-three percent of total imports. J. Hutton attributes this change to a number of developments which include the gradual integration of the State's economy within the Australian national market; the development since 1902 of the Commonwealth system of tariffs against cheaper overseas imports; the growing sophistication and range of Eastern States' manufacturing output; improvements in communications between eastern and western Australia; and the shortage of adequate overseas supplies during and following the two world wars.[18]

As the state's principal seaport, Fremantle naturally reflected these changes in her own trade patterns. In 1907-1908 overseas imports totalled £3.2 million or fifty-five percent of the total value of imports; by 1938-1939 Fremantle's overseas imports totalled £5.0 million or thirty percent of the value of total imports.

As the United Kingdom was Australia's major overseas trading partner, it was the main loser from these changes. Data on the geographical origins and destinations of trade is not available at the port level in this period but the Western Australian data provides a good guide to

---

[17]G. Henderson, "From Sail to Steam: Shipping in Western Australia 1870-1890" (Unpublished MA thesis, University of Western Australia, 1977), 66-67.

[18]Hutton, *Manufacturing Industry*, 68.

trends at Fremantle. Between 1909-1910 and 1938-1939, the United Kingdom's share of Western Australia's exports fell from fifty-nine percent to forty-two percent, while her share of imports dropped from fifty-eight percent to thirty-nine percent. The slump in the United Kingdom's share of imports was, as we have seen, due partly to increased competition from eastern states producers sheltered by Australia's tariff wall. But the United Kingdom was also facing competition from other overseas suppliers, principally the U.S.A. and Japan. However, in 1932 the federal government signed the Ottawa Agreement giving preference to imports from Britain. In 1936 the infamous trade-diversion policy aimed at diverting trade away from the U.S.A. and Japan towards Britain was introduced. These, and other protectionist measures, helped halve the level of American imports at Fremantle.[19] Most imports from Japan entered Australia via eastern states ports: in the late 1930s only about two per cent of Fremantle's trade was with Japan.

Despite these protectionist measures, the United Kingdom's and British Empire's share of Fremantle's trade continued to fall. A major cause on the import side was the growth of trade with the Dutch East Indies, which during the 1930s emerged as a major supplier of oil to Australia. By 1938-1939 imports from the Dutch East Indies reached 255,000 tons or ninety-eight percent of Fremantle's total tonnage of imports from the Far East. This trade was primarily due to the growing use of petrol in motor vehicles: by 1932 there was one motor car to every twelve Australians, giving Australia fourth position in world car ownership, after the USA, New Zealand and Canada. Australia was the world's fifth largest importer of petrol; in per capita terms she imported thirty-two gallons per head, more than any other nation.[20] Oil was increasingly used in industry and also, as we will see shortly, by ships as a bunker fuel.

In summary, Western Australia experienced slow rates of per capita growth and structural change between 1913-1914 and 1938-1939. Primary exports, particularly wheat, grew strongly in the 1920s but suffered severe setbacks during the 1930s depression. Industrialisation proceeded even more slowly in Western Australia than in the eastern states. The proportion of Western Australia's imports from the eastern

---

[19]See K. Burley, *British Shipping and Australia 1920-1939* (Cambridge, 1968), ch. 3, for a detailed discussion of overseas trade and commercial policy.

[20]Australia, *Royal Commission on Mineral Oils and Petrol and Other Products of Mineral Oils* (Canberra, 1935), 23.

states gradually increased at the expense of traditional overseas suppliers such as the United Kingdom. All these changes were reflected in Fremantle's trade and help explain why the period was one of modest growth for the port.

The Course of Trade Fluctuations from 1940-1996

In many respects, the Second World War marked a significant turning point in Australia's history.[21] It led to a loosening of ties with Great Britain and the beginning of the reorientation of Australia's global connections towards the Pacific Rim, stronger support for industrialisation behind a tariff wall and a return to a programme of large scale immigration.[22] The arrival of American forces under the command of General Douglas MacArthur in 1942 marked the development of a military alliance with the United States. The presence of American forces helped preserve Australia from attack and the economy benefited from wartime demands and American technological know-how. As G. Bolton has observed:

> The American contribution to Australia's future development was not confined to the introduction of coca-cola and the provision of profits for the nightclubs, bars, taxi-drivers, and other service industries which sprang up in Australian cities to cater for warriors on leave. Of more lasting importance was the development of bulldozers, four-wheeled drive vehicles, "ducks," and light aircraft,

[21]There is an extensive literature on post-war economic history and economic policy. See, for example, R. Maddock and I. McLean (eds.), *The Australian Economy in the Long Run* (New York, 1986); B. Dyster and D. Meridith, *Australia in the International Economy* (Cambridge, 1990); C. White, *Mastering Risk. Environment, Markets and Politics in Australian Economic History* (Oxford, 1992); E.A. Boehm, *20th Century Economic Development in Australia* (3rd ed., Melbourne, 1993); G. Whitwell, *The Treasury Line* (Sydney, 1986).

[22]B. Pinkstone, *Global Connections. A History of Exports and the Australian Economy* (Canberra, 1992), ch. 5.

all of which would greatly facilitate the development of Australia's outback after the war.[23]

In the 1940s the Australian waterfront was a major beneficiary of American technology: they introduced forklift trucks to the wharves which speeded up cargo handling, an issue we return to in the next chapter.

Unlike the First World War when the Australian economy stagnated, this time there was a boom and industrialisation accelerated. Unfortunately, this boom was concentrated in the eastern states of Australia and the Western Australian economy stagnated: between 1938-1939 and 1947-1948 real GDP per capita increased by only 0.11 percent per annum, compared to 2.8 percent per annum in Australia as a whole.[24] The hostilities and shortages of manpower reduced output in Western Australia's agricultural industries.

As a result, port trade stagnated during the war. By 1942-1943, exports from Fremantle had fallen to 631,000 tonnes or eighty percent of their level in 1938-1939. Over the same period total port trade fell twelve percent to 1.6 million tonnes. However, Fremantle became an important submarine base during the war and visits by British, American and other warships led to record sales of coal and oil for ships' bunkers. At their peak in 1942-1943, they totalled about 222,000 tonnes or over seventy-five percent above their pre-war level.

After the war Australia shared in the world economic boom which lasted until the early 1970s. The economy experienced strong growth in population, production and living standards. Between 1948-1949 and 1975-1976, real GDP per capita in Western Australia grew at 2.8 percent per annum.[25] However, even in this "golden age" of economic progress, growth was not uninterrupted.[26] The major objectives of the Menzies and successive Liberal Country Party coalition governments (1949-1972) in the 1950s and early 1960s were preventing pressure on domestic resources

---

[23]G. Bolton, "1939-51," in F. Crowley (ed.), A *New History of Australia* (Melbourne, 1974), 469.

[24]G.D. Snooks, "Development in Adversity 1913 to 1946," in Stannage (ed.), *New History*.

[25]R.N. Ghosh, "Economic Development and Population Growth in Western Australia since 1945," in *ibid*.

[26]J. Perkins, *Macro-economic Policy in Australia* (Melbourne, 1971), 7.

from causing inflation and leading to an excessive level of imports, and achieving the maximum expansion of exports. In their criticisms of government economic policies, economists have rarely considered the effects on Australia's ports: for example, a reduction in tariffs can cause a surge in imports, creating serious bottlenecks in the ports. Therefore it is essential to consider Fremantle in the context of the national economy in order to clarify the effects of the state of the economy on the port's trade and on the conditions under which port services are supplied and consumed.

The immediate post-war years saw the economy undergoing adjustment to peacetime conditions, and although there were shortages of goods and services, there was high employment and fairly rapid economic growth. In 1948-1949 the government expanded the immigration programme which helped alleviate labour shortages in the economy. At the same time, overseas suppliers were recovering from wartime difficulties and were able to meet export orders in full, leading to a rise in imports. In June 1950 the Korean War broke out and the fear that it might spread led to a rapid rise in world demand for basic materials. Wool was in particularly high demand for military purposes and its price soared. In 1950-1951 Australia's overseas exports grew sixty percent in value, even though they fell six percent in volume. The record export earnings were used to finance increased overseas imports. But pent-up local demand, once released was not easy to check, and the country was flooded with all kinds of finished goods, raw materials and equipment, all of which was in short supply in post-war Australia. Many of the imports represented orders which had been placed long before, mainly with British manufacturers: the United Kingdom provided forty-four percent of the value of imports in 1951-1952. The flood of imports plus a fall of wool prices from their peak Korean War levels led to an adverse trade balance in 1951-52. This would have been worse but for the imposition of severe import controls in March 1952.

At their peak in 1951-1952, overseas imports reached $2,106 million or 14.4 million tons. Fortunately, domestic export tonnages were down that year, although the effect was undoubtedly two-way as the movement of exports was hindered by the imports. While the majority of the imports flowed through eastern states ports such as Sydney and Melbourne, about ten per cent entered via Fremantle. In that year imports at Fremantle reached a record of almost two million tonnes. The import boom led to serious congestion and long turnround times at Fremantle and most other capital city ports.

At Fremantle ships were forced to anchor in Gage Roads waiting for berths, a practice which quickly became known as the "Rottnest queue."[27] The FHT was frustrated by contradictory ministerial directions: on the one hand, it was urged to speed up turnround; on the other hand, it was told to continue to allow cargo to remain in sheds and on wharves so as not to "increase the cost of housing (that is, warehousing) to the community."[28] But in August 1950, the FHT was allowed to follow eastern states' ports and introduce increased penalty rates on cargo left on the wharves beyond a free storage period of three days. This was designed to ensure more rapid clearance of cargoes from the wharves. An indication of the pressure on the port is provided by the fact that between 1949-1950 and 1951-1952 revenue from storage charges increased by eighty-five percent to a record £48,600.

In May 1952, due to the delays and the high cost of chartering extra vessels to cope with the peak cargoes, UK shipowners imposed a surcharge of twenty-five percent on UK/Australia freight rates for general cargo. The surcharge was removed on 1 September but freight rates were increased by ten percent to cover higher operating costs. Therefore, the boom provides a good example of the way ports are enmeshed in the general economic situation. In this case, there was a line of causation running from the government's management of the economy to trade, to port congestion, to freight rates, and ultimately to the price paid by the Australian consumer for imported goods. Similarly, high transport costs reduced the competitiveness of Australian exports in overseas markets.

The congestion drew public attention to the state of the ports and the federal government commissioned an inquiry into the causes of the problem. The inquiry found that Australian ports were unable to cope with the level and nature of post-war cargoes: they were suffering from a lack of investment during the inter-war years and over-intensive use during the Second World War.[29] The British Board of Trade commented:

---

[27] *West Australian*, 6 April 1949.

[28] FPA 87/509/2, notes of a meeting between FHT and deputation from OSRA and ASOF, 11 November 1949.

[29] H. Basten, *Report on the Turn-round of Ships in Australian Ports* (Canberra, 1952).

> It was established that much delay was caused by slow forwarding of documents from the UK, failure of consignees to remove their cargoes quickly from wharf sheds, inadequate warehouse space and some lack of co-ordination by land transport organisations.[30]

The import controls introduced in 1952, coupled with other measures taken to check the boom, led to a short recession in 1952-1953. Fremantle's imports fell by about twenty percent which more than counteracted a rise of one percent in export tonnages. The storage charges fell by about seventy-seven percent to £11,000. Improvements in the balance of payments allowed the government to increase import quotas by ten percent in April 1953 and again in July 1953 by the same amount. There was a time lag of about six months between the granting of export licenses and the arrival of the goods, so port traffic did not increase immediately. In 1953-1954 imports into Fremantle rose by about six percent but the following year they grew by fifty-two percent as the relaxation of controls took effect. Another deterioration in the balance of payments led to the reimposition of import controls in 1955 but the impact on Fremantle's imports was more than counteracted by the opening of the Outer Harbour at Kwinana, south of Fremantle.

The state Liberal-Country Party government reached an agreement with Anglo-Iranian Petroleum (later known as BP) to establish an oil refinery at Kwinana. The background to this will be considered in a later chapter; for the moment we note only that it began operations on the 1 February 1955. This led to large increases in imports of crude oil and exports of refined petroleum products. In 1955-1956, the first full year of the refinery's operations, total port trade jumped by fifty-three percent; about sixty percent of this was handled in the Outer Harbour. The opening of the Outer Harbour represented a major turning point in the port's history: port activity, measured in tonnage terms, began to gradually shift from the Inner to the Outer Harbour.

Table 3.3 illustrates the breakdown of port trade, measured in tonnes, between the Inner and Outer Harbours in 1970 and 1990. In the two decades to 1990, the Outer Harbour increased its share of imports from seventy-nine percent to eighty-seven percent and its share of exports

---

[30]Great Britain, Board of Trade, *Overseas Economic Surveys: Australia* (London, 1954).

from fifty-six percent to eighty-six percent. After 1978-1979 bulk grain exports were relocated to the Outer Harbour and this further decreased tonnages handled in the Inner Harbour. The Outer Harbour was developed to handle bulk cargoes and the Inner Harbour increasingly concentrated on the more valuable non-bulk or general cargoes. Thus if value data were available it would present a different picture of the relative importance of the Inner and Outer Harbours.

Table 3.3
Breakdown of Port Trade Between the Inner and Outer Harbours, 1970 and 1990

Imports	1970		1990	
	'000 tonnes	Percent	'000 tonnes	Percent
Inner Harbour	1,401	21.0	902	13.4
Outer Harbour	5,268	79.0	5,823	86.6
Total	6,669	100.0	6,725	100.0

Exports	1970		1990	
	'000 tonnes	Percent	'000 tonnes	Percent
Inner Harbour	2,551	43.6	1,364	13.6
Outer Harbour	3,304	56.4	8,667	86.4
Total	5,855	100.0	10,031	100.0

Note: Three-year averages centred on the years shown.

Source: FHT and FPA, *Annual Reports*.

Until the late 1960s, the burden of federal government policy fell upon imports, but exchange rate variations had a great impact on the competitiveness of exports. The level of exports depended on the performance of primary industries, including the state of harvests and the level of world commodity prices. In view of the frequency with which serious droughts occurred between 1958 and 1968, this decade has been described as one of Australia's most intensive period of drought.[31] Climatic conditions varied across the country but in 1957-1958 a drought led to widespread failure of the wheat crop: Fremantle's wheat exports were more than halved and Sydney's fell to a mere trickle of 1000 tons. Australia was forced to import wheat from overseas; this was only the third time since 1900 that this situation had arisen. By contrast, in 1959-1960, a good season for primary produce, wheat exports increased by 202,000 ton or sixty-three percent at Fremantle. In 1970-1971, a record 1.7 million tons of grain, over half the state's total, was shipped from Fremantle. These fluctuations meant that demand for port facilities varied widely from one year to the next; in addition, the seasonal component in primary exports led to varying intensity of port use depending on the time of the year.

In 1960 the federal government lifted the export embargo on iron ore it had introduced in 1938 and this led to rapid development of the known reserves, especially in the Pilbara region of northwestern Australia.[32] The Western Australian state government enthusiastically assisted this expansion by providing large amounts of infrastructure. From a value of less than $1 million in 1965 iron ore exports grew to become Australia's major mineral export, accounting for $325 million or twenty-eight percent of the total value of mineral exports by 1970.[33] The development of the north-west iron ore industry and other mineral industries helped transform Western Australia from a "cinderella state" to a "state of excitement."[34] Western Australians began to enjoy a greater share of Australian income and purchasing power: total household income per head was traditionally the second lowest in the country, after Tasmania, but in the late 1960s it briefly surged above the national average. Frank Harman has suggested that residents of Western Australia continued to receive relatively low levels of income per head because the

[31]*Australian Yearbook*, No. 54 (Canberra, 1968), ch. 22.

[32]See A. Kerr, *Australia's North-West* (2nd ed., Nedlands, WA, 1975).

[33]J. Ward, "Australian Mineral Exports-Pattern in the 1960s and Possible Future Trends," *Australian Mineral Industry Quarterly Review*, XXIII (1971), 127.

[34]See G.C. Bolton, "From Cinderella to Charles Court: The Making of a State of Excitement," in E.J. Harman and B.W. Head (eds.), *State, Capital and Resources in the North and West of Australia* (Nedlands, WA, 1982), 27-41.

majority of the dividends, rents and interest generated by the mining industry did not accrue to Western Australians.[35]

This expansion altered the geographical pattern of trade through Australia's ports. By the mid-1960s Japan was the main customer for Australia's mineral exports, and had replaced the United Kingdom as Australia's major trading partner. Since the late 1950s, the prospect of British entry into the European Economic Community had increased Australian interest in trading with Asia but, for a variety of reasons, until the 1970s, Australia had only limited success in gaining access to other Asian markets.[36] By the 1970s, however, the progress of Asian industrialisation was creating a prosperous middle class and expanding markets for raw materials and food products in such countries as Indonesia, Malaysia, Singapore, South Korea and Taiwan. By 1992-1993 fifty-eight percent of Australia's exports were going to East and South-east Asia and thirty-eight percent of imports were coming from this region.[37] The United Kingdom received less than four per cent of exports and supplied only six percent of imports.

By the late 1960s the world's major economies were experiencing inflationary problems and declining productivity. The Organisation of Petroleum Exporting Countries increased the price of crude oil in the 1970s and these "oil shocks" helped plunge the world economy into an era of inflation and uncertainty. The combination of high rates of inflation, low rates of economic growth and high unemployment was termed "stagflation." As a trading nation, Australia was not immune from these problems and because of its reliance on primary exports and inadequacies in government policy experienced a prolonged period of "stagflation." By 1974 the post war boom was well and truly over.

Reflecting the economic climate, port trade in 1972-1973 fell for the first time since 1966-1967. The Whitlam Labor government (1972-1975), as part of measures to combat inflation, reduced tariffs by twenty-five percent in July 1973. As a consequence, the following year, all of Australia's capital city ports experienced an upsurge in imports. In 1973-

---

[35]F.J. Harman, "Resource Development and Personal Income Levels," in *ibid*, 359-376.

[36]See S. Tweedie, *Trading Partners. Australia and Asia 1790-1993* (Sydney, 1994), 1-11.

[37]*Ibid.*, 233.

1974, the value of total imports into Australia jumped twenty-seven percent and total imports into Fremantle increased by about 77,000 tonnes to 8.3 million tonnes. However, a better indication of the effect of the tariff cut is given by looking at general cargo imports at Fremantle, which increased by about 200,000 tonnes.

Another factor affecting the general cargo trade at this time was the introduction of containerisation. This topic will be considered in more detail in the next chapter and brief details only will be given here. Although not all cargo was considered suitable for containerisation, in 1969-1970, the first full year of container operations, 0.9 million tons of cargo was moved in containers. This was all handled in the Inner Harbour. Initially interstate container ships accounted for over one-half of the trade so the withdrawal of interstate container services in 1975 was a severe blow to the port. Container traffic fell by forty percent between 1974-1975 and 1976-1977 but the trade subsequently recovered and in 1984-1985 the port past the milestone of 100,000 TEU's (twenty foot equivalent units) of containers. In 1995-1996 containerised cargo reached 1.2 million tonnes and accounted for over seventy-five percent of Inner Harbour cargoes.

The Fraser Liberal National Party government (1975-1983) attempted to control inflation by cutting government expenditure and reducing the rate of growth of the money supply. There was a short-lived resources boom in 1979 but this quickly collapsed and inflation continued to be a problem. The Hawke Labor government (1983-1991) introduced significant changes including the adoption of a consensus approach to policy-making, the establishment of a prices and incomes policy (the Accord), the floating of the Australian dollar, deregulation of the financial sector and microeconomic reform.[38] Inflation was slowly brought under control and the economy began to recover. The Stock Market Crash of October 1987, while traumatic for financial markets, left cargo tonnages unaffected.

During the period 1981-1982 to 1991-1992, Western Australia, the Northern Territory and Queensland grew more rapidly than the south-eastern states. Western Australia was the fastest growing state between 1981-1982 and 1991-1992, increasing real GDP by fifty-three percent

---

[38]For an overview see Indecs, *State of Play 8* (St. Leonards, NSW, 1995).

compared to twenty-six percent for Australia as a whole.[39] This achievement has been attributed to three main factors. First, population increased by twenty-four percent between 1981-1982 and 1991-1992, compared to fifteen percent in Australia as a whole and this stimulated economic growth. Second, the further expansion of its export-orientated agricultural and mining industries boosted economic performance. The mining industry, which supplies the majority of exports, increased output five-fold during the decade ending in 1991-1992 and included a diverse range of products, including bauxite and natural gas as well as iron ore. By 1991-1992 Western Australia had overtaken New South Wales and Queensland to become Australia's largest exporter, supplying over one quarter of total exports. Finally, Western Australia, compared to the eastern states, had relatively few traditional labour intensive manufacturing industries. Since the 1970s the latter have been in decline because of moves towards lower tariffs. Australia has shifted from being an economy largely isolated from external competition by protective tariffs, to one exposed to the chill of global competition. With fewer affected industries, Western Australia's manufacturing output was able to grow by twenty percent between 1981-1982 and 1991-1992, compared to the national average of only three percent. Elaborately transformed manufactures accounted for about six percent of Western Australia's total exports in 1994-1995.

This expansion led to Western Australians enjoying a greater share of Australian income and purchasing power. Western Australia and Queensland increased their share of national GDP by a total of two percentage points and both obtained the reputations of being "states on the move."

In the early 1990s tight monetary policy pursued by the Keating Labor government (1991-1996) caused a slowing of growth and a fall in imports. The Inner Harbour, with its emphasis on imports of consumer goods, reflected the fluctuations of the Australian economy more directly than the Outer Harbour and imports into the Inner Harbour fell by sixty-one percent to 663,000 tonnes. However, the mining sector cushioned the West Australian economy from the worst effects of the recession. Total port trade reached a new record of 20.2 million tonnes in 1995-1996.

---

[39]Australia, Bureau of Industry Economics, *State Economic Performance 1981-82 to 1991-92* (Canberra, 1994).

In summary, the long boom of the post-war period came to an abrupt end in the early 1970s and an era of slower growth followed. However, in the 1980s Western Australia grew more rapidly than the eastern states due to faster population growth, the expansion of the agricultural and mining industries and significant progress in manufacturing industry. All of the booms and recessions, to a greater or lesser degree, affected the Port of Fremantle, and led to periods of feast and famine in port activity.

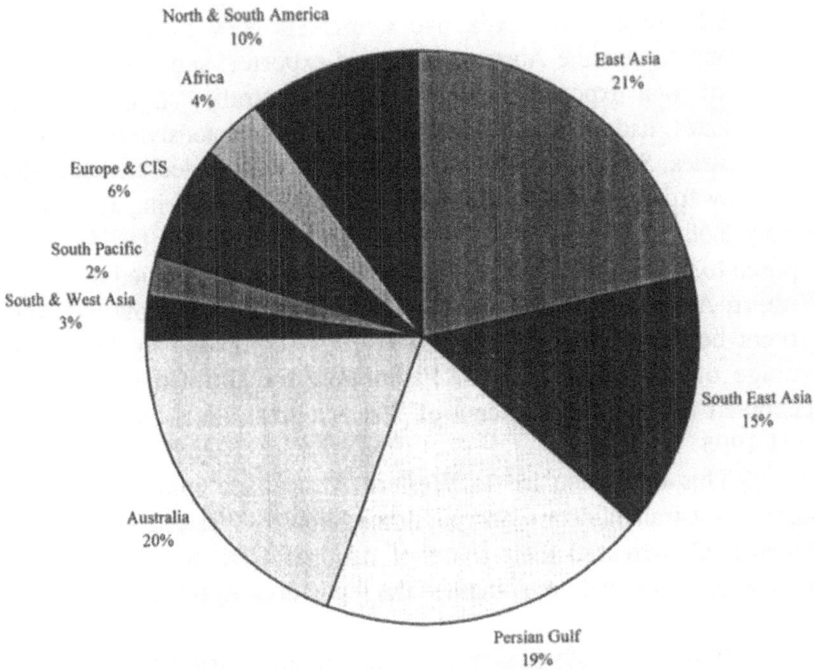

Figure 3.2: Principal Areas of Trade, Fremantle 1995-1996.

Source: FPA, *Annual Report* 1995-1996.

The bulk cargoes handled in the Outer Harbour were responsible for the major variations in the tonnages of cargo handled at Fremantle. For example, between 1978-1979 and 1982-1983, general cargo varied only by 88,000 tonnes from a minimum of 1.9 million tonnes but Outer Harbour tonnages varied by 2.3 million tonnes from a minimum of 12.2 million tonnes. Following the opening of the Outer Harbour in the mid-1950s activity in the Inner Harbour began to decline as bulk cargo handling operations were gradually relocated to the Outer Harbour. The fate of the Inner Harbour was increasingly tied to the flows of general cargoes and the growth of the container trade. Since the 1980s increased manufacturing exports have boosted the value of exports from the Inner Harbour and helped counteract the loss of bulk cargo to the Outer Harbour. However, because of the major exemptions given to Outer Harbour cargoes, the Inner Harbour cargoes made a greater contribution to port revenue than the cargoes discharged in the Outer Harbour. This, as we shall see, had serious implications for the long term financial viability of the port.

Figure 3.2 illustrates the breakdown of Fremantle's trade in 1995-1996. In that year trade with East and South-east Asia accounted for thirty-six percent of Fremantle's total trade, trade with the Middle East accounted for nineteen percent of total trade and trade with the UK and Europe only six percent of total trade. This was a far cry from the situation in 1938-1939 when twenty-five percent of the port's total trade was with the UK and Europe.

Fremantle's Hinterland

The hinterland or area of production and consumption served by Fremantle was clearly the major determinant of its growth. The hinterland of a port is difficult to delineate precisely: it will wax or wane as the port develops or declines and as production and land transport alters; equally, as the hinterland develops or declines so will the port. This two-way relationship is dependent on a wide variety of factors, including geographical location, proximity to population and industry, and port efficiency.

Australia's capital city ports (Sydney, Melbourne, Adelaide, Brisbane and Fremantle), have traditionally enjoyed a natural monopoly over much of their states and did not generally compete for cargo. Indeed, Keith Trace has argued that this fundamental lack of competition caused Australian ports to be tardy in adopting more efficient methods.[40] The European situation, with close geographical clusters of ports struggling for a share of trade, provides a striking contrast with Australia. For example, the Port of Hamburg, which in 1926 handled about 21.9 million tons of seaborne trade, was engaged in a commercial battle with other North Sea

[40]K. Trace, "Australian Overseas Shipping, 1900-60" (Unpublished PhD thesis, University of Melbourne, 1965), 279.

ports for the sea-borne, river-borne and rail-borne traffic of central Europe:

> Compared with the distances the ships have to cover on the highroads of the oceans, those between the various North Sea ports are of no account whatever. International trade has caused the development of economic areas independent of political boundaries...the close proximity to Hamburg of the other large seaports, however, has also given rise to a struggle for the possession of the industrial hinterland.[41]

Hamburg "spared no efforts and no money" in attempts to capture trade. By contrast, at that time Fremantle handled a mere six percent of Hamburg's tonnages, served a sparsely populated, relatively un-developed region, and was over 1347 nautical miles from Adelaide, the nearest Australian port of any size. In short, Fremantle was firmly on the periphery of world trade and shipping activity.

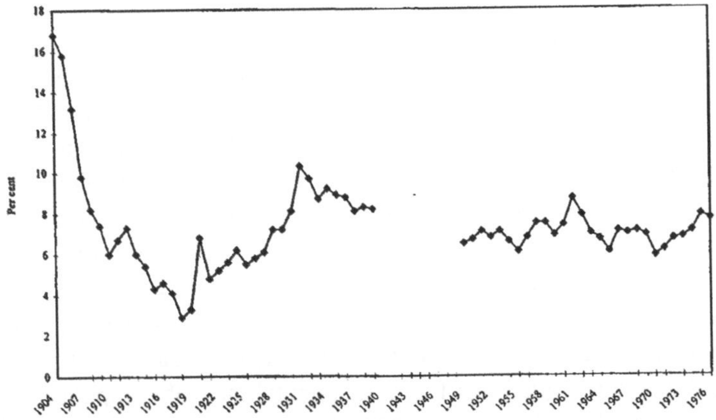

Figure 3.3: Fremantle's Share of the Value of Total Australian Trade, 1903-1904 to 1975-1976. Data not available between 1939-1940 and 1947-1948.

Source: Commonwealth Bureau of Census and Statistics, *Transport and Communication Bulletins*.

[41]L. Wendemuth and W. Bottcher, *The Port of Hamburg* (Hamburg, 1927), 1-2.

Fremantle's share of the total value of Australian trade is shown in figure 3.3. It plummeted from 16.8 percent in 1903-1904 to 6.0 percent in 1909-1910. A slow recovery began in the 1920s with a peak share of 10.3 percent of Australian trade in 1930-1931; thereafter Fremantle's trade share declined slowly to eight percent in 1938-1939. After the Second World War Fremantle's share of Australian trade averaged about 7.0 percent although the mineral boom of the 1960s led to a peak of 8.7 percent in 1960-1961. In 1990-1991 Fremantle accounted for 7.9 percent of the value of Australian trade. The port's trade share measured on a tonnage basis exhibits a similar pattern. In the early 1950s Fremantle accounted for about ten percent of the total tonnage of Australian trade, its share peaked at about seventeen percent in the early 1960s and then declined. By 1990-1991 Fremantle accounted for only 4.3 percent of the total tonnage of Australian trade.[42] Thus, regardless of whether or not trade is measured in values or tonnes, in the twentieth century Fremantle declined in importance as a national port. However, Fremantle's trade share at the beginning of the century was a result of the gold boom era and thus exceptional; subsequently, trade reverted to levels more appropriate to the state's population size and level of economic development.

After the opening of the Inner Harbour in 1897, Fremantle became Western Australia's major port but it has never possessed a monopoly of the state's trade. Since the nineteenth century it has shared trade with the adjacent ports of Geraldton, Bunbury, Busselton, Albany and Esperance; while Derby, Broome, Wyndham and a number of other tiny ports served the northern parts of the state. The latter ports were developed to serve small, isolated hinterlands. A lack of adequate land transport and the great length of the coastline made localised port facilities a necessity.[43] As population, primary production, and transport facilities expanded, the hinterlands of some ports began to overlap.

In 1938-1939 Fremantle's accounted for about seventy-two percent of Western Australia's overseas trade in tonnage terms and eighty-

---

[42]Data for values and tonnage in 1990-1991 are from Australia, Industry Commission, *Port Authority Services and Activities, Draft Report* (Canberra, 1993), table B3. Data for tonnages in other years are from CBCS, *Transport and Communications Bulletins*.

[43]Henderson, "From Sail to Steam," 19-23.

eight percent in value terms.[44] As table 3.4 illustrates, in 1989-1990 Fremantle's shares were about eighteen percent and fifty-nine percent respectively. This loss of market share is due to the fact that the State's mineral exports are largely channelled through northern ports such as Port Hedland, Dampier and Port Walcott. Port Hedland, for example, had a meteoric rise to the status of Australia's major port when trade is measured on a tonnage basis. By the late 1970s it was handling about forty million tonnes of cargo per annum, about forty times the level of the mid-1960s. The Port of Dampier was initially a privately owned port developed by Hammersley Iron Ltd to handle iron ore and salt exports and by the late 1970s it was handling almost as much cargo as Port Hedland. Similarly, Port Walcott was developed to export iron ore mined by Cliffs Robe River Iron Ore Associates.

Table 3.4
Shares of Western Australian Ports in Total Overseas Trade, 1989-1990

Port	Gross weight '000 tonnes	Percent of total	Value $ million	Percent of total
Fremantle & Kwinana	23,346	17.8	7,239	58.8
Albany	780	0.6	141	1.1
Broome	1,337	1.0	90	0.7
Bunbury	4,936	3.8	1,186	9.6
Dampier	45,344	34.5	1,827	14.8
Geraldton	2,234	1.7	556	4.5
Port Hedland	27,635	21.0	688	5.6
Port Walcott	19,153	14.6	288	2.3
Other	6,712	5.1	305	2.5
Total	131,477	100.0	12,320	100.0

Note: Where percentages do not add exactly to 100 this is due to rounding.

Source: Western Australia, *Yearbook*.

[44] F.W. Tydeman, *Report on Port of Fremantle* (3 vols., Perth, 1949), II, 40; and Western Australia, *Statistical Registers*.

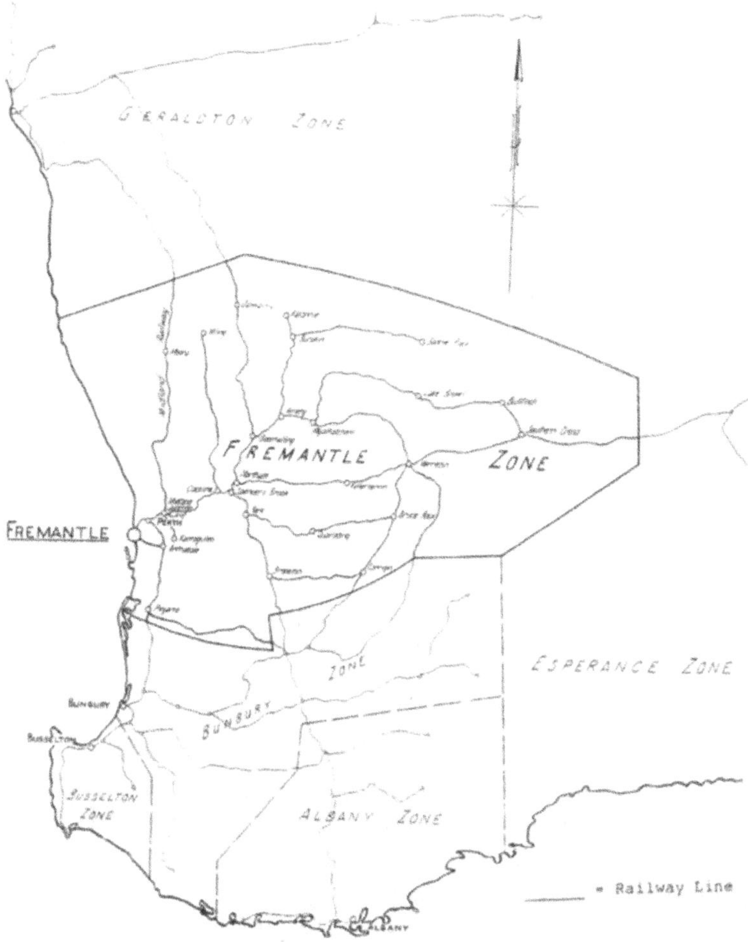

Figure 3.4: The Hinterland of the Port of Fremantle.

Source: F.W. Tydeman, *Report on Port of Fremantle* (3 vols., Perth, 1949), III, appendix 10.

As a rough approximation, Fremantle's hinterland can be defined by reference to major avenues of communication, particularly railways, and the grain collecting area of the port. The approximate hinterland of Fremantle for bulk cargoes is illustrated in Figure 3.4. In the case of general cargoes Fremantle's hinterland effectively covered the whole state. In a later chapter we will see that proposals to create a landbridge between Western Australia and the eastern states raises the possibility of extending Fremantle's hinterland for some commodities to the whole of Australia.

Fremantle's hinterland, as shown in figure 3.4, covers 95,800 square kilometres or only four percent of the state's area. However, it includes the centres of population and industry: in 1911 the metropolitan area contained 116,000 people or about forty-one percent of the state total; by 1933 the metropolitan region contained 230,000 people or fifty-two percent of the state total; by 1990 it contained 1.1 million or seventy percent of the state total. Thus the major port was developed in close proximity to the metropolitan area, although Western Australia differed from most other states in that the port (Fremantle) and administrative centre (Perth) were physically distinct, at least initially. From the mid-1890s onwards rapid suburbanisation began to link the two towns.[45]

Figure 3.4 also shows that Fremantle benefited from a radial pattern of railway communications; this was also generally true of road communications. The contrast with Albany, penalised by a non-radial pattern of railway development, is striking. When the Great Southern Railway was opened in 1889 Albany, with its fine natural harbour, began to threaten Fremantle's trade. This was a factor which prompted the government, which primarily represented Fremantle and Perth interests, to open up the Inner Harbour. Toby Manford has shown that the government ensured that subsequent railway development and railway tariffs favoured Fremantle at the expense of the outports.[46] Apart from Fremantle, Bunbury was the only port to enjoy a radial system of railways. But Bunbury specialised in bulk cargoes and offered no serious competition to Fremantle for general cargoes.

Albany was particularly severely affected by this "centralist" policy and after the First World War was "a dying port."[47] Following the implementation of the Navigation Act in 1921, which reserved the coastal trade for Australian vessels, less overseas steamers called at Albany. Previously mail steamers had often topped-up with parcels of interstate cargo which was off-loaded at Albany and railed to Fremantle. Yet another blow occurred the following year when control of wool marketing

---

[45]C.T. Stannage, *The People of Perth* (Perth, 1979), 240-251.

[46]See T. Manford, "A History of Rail Transport Policy in Western Australia, 1870-1911" (Unpublished PhD thesis, University of Western Australia, 1976).

[47]F.W. Tydeman, *Report on Albany Harbour* (Perth, 1948), 54-56.

passed to Fremantle buying and broking firms and an increasing proportion of the wool crop was railed to Fremantle for shipment. This was a victory for the FHT which had been attempting to centralise wool exports at Fremantle since 1913.[48] Given these factors, and the loss of the bunkering trade (to be discussed shortly), it is not surprising that Albany's cargo traffic fell from about 77,000 tons per annum before the First World War to 59,000 tons in the mid-1930s, a drop of twenty-three percent; over the same period Fremantle's trade almost doubled.[49]

Western Australia was not the only state to develop a transport network focussing on the major port. Aware that there was a close connection between railways and the fortunes of ports, city interests used their influence in parliament to ensure that as far as possible railway tariffs favoured the capital city ports.[50] In New South Wales, "Sydney interests" ensured that the bulk of that state's freight was funnelled through the metropolitan area.[51] But as production and consumption activities increased the growing volumes of freight put great strains on the transport network, particularly as only about thirteen percent of Sydney's trade (measured in tons) was carried by rail.[52] The combined pressures of port and city land use on a finite amount of road space led, at times, to severe congestion.[53] Fortunately land use pressures were less serious in a smaller and less industrialised state such as Western Australia. Moreover, even in the 1940s, half of Fremantle's trade consisted of bulk cargoes that

---

[48]C. Fyfe, *The Bale Fillers. Western Australian Wool 1826-1916* (Nedlands, WA, 1983), 277-279.

[49]Tydeman, *Albany Harbour*, appendix 8. The comparisons are based on the five-year periods ending in 1913-1914 and beginning in 1934-1935.

[50]See P.J. Rimmer, "Politicians, Public Servants and Petitioners: Aspects of Transport in Australia 1851-1901," in J.M. Powell and M. Williams (eds.), *Australian Space, Australian Time* (Melbourne, 1975), 182-225.

[51]G. Wotherspoon, "The Sydney Interest and the Rail 1860-1900," in M. Kelly (ed.), *Nineteenth-Century Sydney* (Sydney, 1978), 12-23.

[52]C.R. Bickford, "The Development of the Port of Sydney," *Journal of the Institution of Engineers* (Australia), XXIX (1957), 121.

[53]See A. Roberts, "Planning Sydney's Transport 1875-1900," in Kelly (ed.), *Nineteenth-Century Sydney*, 24-36.

were carried by rail to and from the port, reducing pressure on the road system.[54]

The changes in the pattern of consumption and production in Fremantle's hinterland caused alterations in the commodity composition of port trade. Table 3.5 illustrates the composition of Fremantle's trade between 1909-1910 and 1994-1995, measured in tons. Table 3.5 shows that Fremantle's import trade has been long dominated by petroleum products, but following the opening of the oil refinery at Kwinana the emphasis shifted from refined products to crude petroleum imports. In 1994-1995 petroleum accounted for sixty-five percent of imports. Another mainstay of the import trade are fertilisers (crude and manufactured) which supply the trace elements vital to the success of the wheat industry. The development of the aluminium industry has also led to regular imports of caustic soda. On the export side, the growth in the relative importance of commodities such as alumina and refined petroleum testifies to the growth of the state's mining and manufacturing industries. Nevertheless, agricultural exports such as grain, wool and timber still accounted for about one third of exports in 1994-1995.

Timber has been exported from Western Australia since the nineteenth century. The state's tough Jarrah and Karri timber was in demand both within and outside Australia for telegraph poles, railway sleepers, paving blocks and other construction purposes. In the mid-1970s excavations in a London street revealed Western Australian paving blocks: they were still in excellent condition despite being at least a century old.[55] Exports of timber took off in the 1870s and by 1909-1910 they were worth £972,000 or about twelve percent of total exports. The trade was shared between Fremantle and southwest ports such as Rockingham, Bunbury and Hamelin Bay. In 1909-1910 exports from Fremantle totalled 35,000 tonnes, or eighteen percent of the port's total exports, but they subsequently declined and did not approach this level again until after the Second World War. In the mid-1990s exports averaged 30,000 tonnes or less than one per cent of total exports.

---

[54]Tydeman, *Fremantle*, 44-45.

[55]J. Willinge, *Full Steam Ahead. Bunbury Port Authority 1909-1995* (Bunbury, WA, 1996), 25.

Table 3.5
The Commodity Composition of Port Trade

	1909-1910		1938-1939		1994-1995	
Imports	'000 tonnes	Percent	'000 tonnes	Percent	'000 tonnes	Percent
Agricultural produce	43	9.5	16	1.7	79	0.9
Coal and coke	100	22.2	71	7.4	33	0.4
Timber	16	3.5	14	1.5	22	0.3
Metal manufactures	53	11.8	71	7.4	35	0.4
Fertilisers	38	8.4	194	20.2	468	5.5
Petroleum	6	1.3	291	30.3	5,557	65.4
Residual	195	43.3	307		2,301	27.1
Total imports	451	100.0	961	100.0	8,495	100.0
Exports						
Alumina					2,667	22.5
Wool and skins	5	2.6	45	5.4	172	1.4
Timber	35	18.0	20	2.4	30	0.3
Grains	45	23.2	355	42.7	3,936	33.3
Refined petroleum (inc bunkers)			126	15.2	2,529	21.4
Flour	1	0.5	88	10.6		
Livestock	0.2	0.1	0.7	0.1	195	1.6
Residual	107.8	55.6	196.3	23.6	2,305	19.5
Total exports	194	100.0	831	100.0	11,834	100.0

Note: Only limited commodity detail is available on a continuous basis. Where percentages do not add to 100 this is due to rounding.

Source: FHT and FPA, *Annual Reports*.

It is apparent that the port's major items of trade by weight have always been relatively homogeneous cargoes such as grain and oil. As the twentieth century progressed, increasing proportions of these cargoes were handled in bulk. Coal and phosphates (for fertilisers) were the first cargoes to be handled in bulk but the major turning point came in the early 1930s when bulk handling of grain was introduced. Previously, at peak times wheat flows had reached three times their average level and "all available berths are occupied, congestion occurs and vessels, for want of accommodation, are kept waiting in the roads outside before they can enter the harbour."[56] But the development of bulk handling and the establishment of silos at rail-heads and the port, led to wheat flows becoming more uniform over the year. Other cargoes, such as wool, dairy produce and vegetables, exhibited marked seasonal variations, but only wheat had a significant impact in tonnage terms. Thus, from the 1930s onwards, the port's trade, measured in tons, became less seasonal in nature.

By 1994-1995 about eighty-six percent of the port's trade was handled in bulk. The dominance of bulk cargoes reflects the port's reliance on imports of cargoes such as oil and the fact that the export trade is basically comprised of primary products. Throughout Australia, general cargoes have traditionally been more important in the import than export trade. As we will see in the next chapter, this created problems for shipowners as each type of cargo had different requirements for shipping capacity, causing many ships to either arrive or leave only partly loaded.

It could be argued that table 3.5 would give a different picture of trade composition if value data were available at the port level. A variety of primary exports such as wool, sandalwood, livestock and fisheries products are more significant in value than in tonnage terms. In the nineteenth century wool rapidly became the most valuable export and although in the 1890s it was, as we have seen, replaced by gold as a leading sector, it has remained a valuable export. But the lack of value data at the port level means that its economic importance is not reflected in trade statistics for the Port of Fremantle. For example, in 1909-1910 wool exports from Western Australia amounted to £967,000 or twelve percent of the total value of the state's exports, but wool exports from Fremantle, which handled the lion's share of the wool trade, totalled only 5,000 tonnes, a mere five percent of the port's export tonnages.

Similarly, after the Second World War the development of the rock lobster and prawn fisheries turned fishing into a valuable export

---

[56]Alexander Gibb and Partners, *Report on the Fremantle Harbour* (Perth, 1929), 5.

industry. In 1979-1980 total fisheries exports were valued at $101 million but exports of fish products from Fremantle totalled 7,250 tons or less than 0.1 percent of total exports, although not all exports of fish products left via Fremantle. The fishing industry is considered in more detail in the next chapter.

Another export that has always been more important in value than tonnage terms is sandalwood. It is shipped to various Asian countries where it is turned it into a powder for use as incense or carved into boxes and ornaments.[57] Shipments began in the mid-1840s and most went via Fremantle, although significant amounts were also shipped from Bunbury and, after the 1870s, from Rockingham. In the early 1880s sandalwood was overshadowed by gold but it became known as the "the Gold-diggers best-friend," because unsuccessful prospectors often fell back on sandalwood as a source of income. In the boom years for sandalwood between 1896 and 1911, the annual quantities exported averaged between 8000-9000 tons of which about seventy percent were shipped from Fremantle. By the 1890s the indiscriminate cutting of sandalwood had led to the virtual disappearance of the trees in some areas but it was not until the 1920s that effective conservation measures were introduced. The trade is still continuing to this day, although it is now confined to dry and semi-arid regions of the state and in the 1970s exports averaged only 1200 tonnes per annum.

Shipments of livestock have long been a part of the port's trade. The trade began with the shipment of livestock from the northwest of the state for processing in Fremantle. This trade was supplemented in the late 1960s by a rise in overseas exports of livestock, mainly to the Gulf States, West Asia and North Africa. The number of livestock exported rose from 200,000 in 1966-1967 to almost four million in 1994-1995. The major emphasis is on live sheep exports, which in 1994-1995 accounted for ninety-nine percent of the trade. In the early 1990s Fremantle accounted for about seventy percent of the Australian live sheep export market. Although relatively insignificant in tonnage terms, this trade was worth $129 million in 1994-1995. It has attracted some criticism over the years regarding the care of the animals and the smells emanating from the sheep carriers. However, improvements in carrying and feeding operations have led to high survival rates for the livestock and specialised vessels now

---

[57]This paragraph draws on P. Statham, "The Australian Sandalwood Industry" (Unpublished paper given at the Sandalwood conference, East-West Centre, Honolulu, April 1990).

service the trade. Due to community pressure, in the mid-1990s the FPA began considering moving part of the live sheep trade to the Outer Harbour. This represented yet another threat to the viability of the Inner Harbour.

Fremantle's Bunkering Trade

After the opening of the Inner Harbour in 1897, Fremantle became the first and last port of call on the Australian coast for many overseas vessels. Thus the port was able to develop a valuable business supplying ships' bunkers and stores. In 1912-1913 Western Australia (principally Fremantle), supplied bunkers and stores worth £163,000 or eleven percent of the Australian total. By 1938-1939 Western Australia (principally Fremantle) supplied one-quarter of the £2,106,000 worth of bunkers and stores shipped on overseas vessels at Australian ports.[58]

The main item supplied was bunker fuel which accounted for about two-thirds of the total. According to Kevin Burley, fuel was the largest single running cost on the Australian coast between the First and Second World Wars, although it declined in importance due to a fall in the price of bunker coal, the adoption of oil as an alternative fuel and innovations in marine technology.[59]

Expenditure on bunker fuel in Australia was influenced by a number of factors outside the direct control of the port authorities, including the volumes of cargo available, the level of freight rates and the prices of bunkers at alternative ports such as Durban and Colombo. In 1907 Captain Irvine, the Chief Harbour Master, claimed that the Port of Natal (Durban) had captured three-quarters of Albany's bunkering trade, by charging 15s 6d per ton of coal, compared to 27s at Albany. Irvine estimated that every ton of coal sold at Albany and Fremantle meant 3s spent on labour; also, ships would outlay funds on items such as stores and port dues. He concluded that "nothing tends to popularise a port so much with shipping, as to know that coal at a reasonable price can be

---

[58]Statistics from Commonwealth *Yearbooks*. Value detail for each port is not available.

[59]Burley, *British Shipping*, 320.

obtained expeditiously."[60] Ships coming to Australia in ballast for cargoes such as wheat and timber naturally tended to bunker in cheaper overseas ports as far as possible. Also, when shipowners faced the possibility of leaving Australia with ballast space they tended to take on sufficient coal in the eastern states to carry them onto Durban or Colombo.[61] The latter port, for example, enjoyed a very extensive bunkering trade: in the mid-1920s it handled 825,000 tons of bunker fuel per annum, about seven times the level at Fremantle.[62]

Shipowners calling in Western Australia for bunkers could choose between Fremantle, Albany and Bunbury. Owing to its dominance of overseas trade, Fremantle naturally claimed the lion's share of the bunkering trade as well. Although Albany offered a natural land-locked harbour and adequate facilities for bunkering, many shipping companies preferred "to make use of Fremantle as a bunkering port on account of its geographical position and the advantages which it offers in many other directions, such as engine repairs, and the procuring of stores."[63] Moreover, in 1927 the International Load Line Convention amended Albany's winter (April to October) marks so ships could load 200 tons of cargo or bunkers less than at Fremantle where summer marks applied all the year round.[64] This move was due to the greater danger of encountering bad weather as far south as Albany. In 1924 it was reported that the *Queen Maud* picked up 100 tons of coal at Albany but spent four days and 140 tons of coal battling her way round Cape Leeuwin. The ship was forced to call into Fremantle to top up with coal.[65] Clearly, incidents such as these reinforced Fremantle's attractiveness as a bunkering port. However, at the same time dues at Albany were lower: in 1924 a steamer

---

[60]FPA 3/07/2, Irvine to Under-Secretary, "Proposal to Charge Wharfage on Bunker Coal," 2 March 1908.

[61]*Ibid.*, 107/23/1, memo, re: "Western Australian Bunkering Trade," issued by an unnamed coaling company, July 1924.

[62]Data for Colombo 1924-1926 are from K. Dharmasena, *The Port of Colombo 1860-1939* (Colombo, 1980), 67.

[63]FPA 107/23/1, memo re: "Western Australian Bunkering Trade."

[64]Tydeman, *Albany Harbour*, 56.

[65]FPA 107/23/2, FHT to Hon. Mr. Drew, 17 July 1924.

of 4000-5000 tons calling for 500 tons of coal, staying twelve hours in port, paid £25 at Albany compared to £47 at Fremantle.[66] It was claimed that some ships wanting bunkers alone preferred to take Newcastle (New South Wales) coal on at Albany and by-pass Fremantle. However, the FHT argued that "the charges at Fremantle and Albany have, in plain fact, little or nothing to do with the choice of port by shipowners, who have much greater aspects of each instance to consider than a few pounds difference in port dues."[67] Probably the only result of lowering charges at Fremantle would have been a loss of revenue to the FHT.

Bunbury also made efforts to get some of the bunkering trade although the Secretary of the Bunbury Harbour Trust offered to consult with the FHT over rate charges so that "the schedules would be kept uniform so far as practicable and competition would be avoided."[68] Bunbury's bunkering trade was basically confined to shipping that was loading there. It reached 46,592 tons in 1922 but declined thereafter; by the end of the Second World War it was virtually non-existent.[69]

Although local Collie coal was used in ships' bunkers as early as 1899, the bulk of Fremantle's supplies of coal were imported from the eastern states. Unfortunately, although the FHT kept statistics on coal imports it did not keep records of imported coal used for bunkering purposes in any one year until 1923. However, between 1907-1908 and 1912-1913 a total of 409,000 tons of imported coal was loaded into hulks at Fremantle for bunkering purposes; over the same period 136,000 tons of Collie coal was used for bunkering purposes.[70] Thus Collie coal accounted for about one-quarter of the bunkering trade.

As early as 1908, local coal interests were pressing for improved handling facilities at Fremantle in order to boost the use of Collie coal for bunkering purposes and also to facilitate the development of an export

---

[66]*Ibid.*, Johnson and Lynn Ltd. to FHT, 19 March 1924.

[67]*Ibid.*, FHT to J.B. Sleeman, MLA, 28 July 1924.

[68]*Ibid.*, 30/19, W.J. Cope, Secretary Bunbury Harbour Trust, to F. Stevens, Secretary of FHT, 12 April 1919.

[69]Statistics are from Tydeman, *Report on Bunbury Harbour*.

[70]Australia, *Report of the Royal Commission on the Collie Coal Industry* (Perth, 1916), appendices XXV and XXIX.

trade.[71] One difficulty was that Collie coal had a lower calorific value than Newcastle coal and users of coal for shipping purposes agreed that it took 25 percent more Collie coal to travel a given distance than if Newcastle coal was used.[72] Thus the State Steamships, for example, were reluctant to use the local coal as they had restricted bunkering space and its use would have encroached on space usually used for cargo. During the Newcastle coal strike of 1910 many overseas ships were forced to call at Fremantle and take a record 47,000 tons of Collie coal. But according to the 1916 Royal Commission into the Collie coal industry, such "was the greed of the coal owners that instead of supplying the best possible material with a view to the future stability of the industry, any rubbish which was sufficiently black to have the slightest resemblance to coal was dumped at Fremantle and Bunbury." Thus a golden opportunity was lost. Another problem with Collie coal was a supposedly increased danger of spontaneous combustion on long voyages.

Although the Peninsular and Oriental Steamship Navigation company (P&O) started taking Collie coal in 1901 the main users appear to have been German lines. Thus the outbreak of the First World War led to a setback for the local industry: Collie coal bunkered fell from 54,000 tons in 1914 to 26,000 tons in 1915. Despite the fact that freight and handling costs on imported coal were higher than on local coal - the freight rate from the eastern states was about 10s per ton in 1916 - the imported coal retained the major share of the bunkering trade. For example, between 1923-1924 and 1938-1939 a total of 193,000 tons of Collie coal and 393,000 tons of imported coal was loaded into ship's bunkers at Fremantle; therefore, imported coal accounted for about two-thirds of total bunkers. Collie coal was never popular with shipowners, some refusing to take any of it.[73]

---

[71]FPA 48/08/2, "Notes by F. Viles for Information of the Hon. J.D. Connolly, Colonial Secretary, on the Present Coaling Arrangements of Fremantle, and His Suggestions for Improved Facilities," 20 June 1908.

[72]*Report of the Royal Commission on the Collie Coal Industry*, xxxi. The rest of the paragraph also draws on this source.

[73]Australia, Tariff Board, *Report and Recommendations on Bunker Coal - Imposition of Duty or Payment of Bounty* (Canberra, 1932), 5, published in Commonwealth, *Parliamentary Papers*, CXI (1932-1934), 437-448. The following paragraph also draws on this source.

Figure 3.5, which illustrates the tonnage of coal and oil bunkers between 1923-1924 and 1994-1995, shows that from the mid-1920s onwards oil rapidly replaced coal as a bunkering fuel. By the end of the twenties over seventy-five percent of bunkers were oil; by the eve of the Second World War coal bunkers had declined to a trickle. The last bunkering coal was sold in 1968.

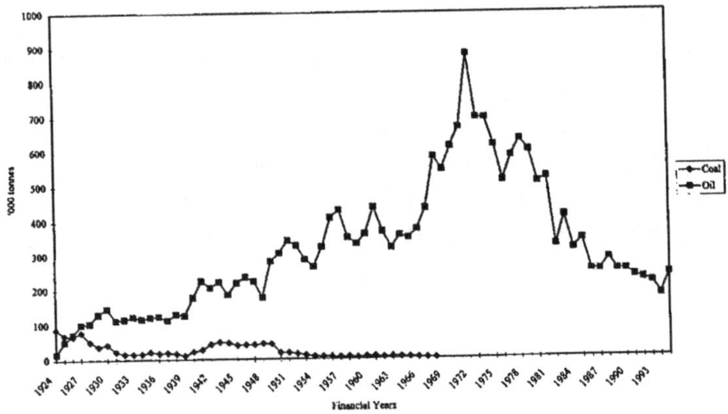

Figure 3.5: Coal and Oil Bunkers at Fremantle, 1923-1924 to 1994-1995.

Source: FHT and FPA, *Annual Reports*.

The switch to oil was probably encouraged by the high price of Australian coal. According to the Tariff Board, between 1913 and 1921 New South Wales coal prices were roughly in line with those of overseas coal centres, but between 1922 and 1928 the price of overseas coal tended to fall while New South Wales coal increased slightly in price. This was attributed to the high profits reaped by the coal owners and the relatively high wages paid to Australian miners. By the early 1930s the price of New South Wales coal had fallen to a more competitive price of 19s per ton at Newcastle. However, after shipment to Fremantle its price was often considered prohibitive by the shipowners. Even Collie coal cost 29s per ton at Fremantle. Moreover, shipowners often preferred to carry non-Australian bunkers as an insurance against strikes in Australian bunkering ports. Oil, on the other hand, was proving to be an economical bunkering fuel, offering quicker loading and freeing more space for cargo. By the early 1930s about forty percent of shipping tonnage visiting Australia was non-coal burning. In 1932 the Tariff Board recommended against any protection for the local coal bunkering industry on the grounds that it would merely speed up the switch to oil and further reduce the demand for Australian coal.

The switch from coal to oil had major implications for Fremantle. At a basic physical level it led to the gradual disappearance of the old sailing ships used as coal hulks. In the late 1920s there were ten in use at Fremantle; by the mid-1930s only three remained. But, more importantly, it led to the decline of interstate coal imports, a mainstay of the coastal trade. Coal continued to be imported for the Western Australian Government Railways but between 1909-1910 and 1938-1939 coal dropped from forty percent to nineteen percent of the total tonnage of interstate imports. Over the same period interstate trade, measured in tonnage terms, fell from about forty-six percent to twenty-four percent of total port trade. Oil was imported from the Dutch East Indies and the USA leading to growing traffic with these regions. By 1922 the FHT and port authorities at Melbourne and Sydney had allowed the Anglo Iranian Oil Company to develop oil-bunkering facilities.[74] These facilities posed new physical, financial and environmental problems for port authorities and will be discussed in more detail in a later chapter. The centralisation of oil facilities at Fremantle sealed the fate of Albany and Bunbury as bunkering ports and ensured that Fremantle would continue as one of Australia's leading bunkering and provisioning ports for overseas vessels.

During the Second World War, as we mentioned earlier, visits by warships and submarines led to substantial increases in bunkers. Sales of bunker fuels continued to expand after the war, reaching an all time record of 933,400 tonnes in 1971-1972. The closure of the Suez Canal in 1956 and between 1967-1975, and the development of new container services, boosted sales. Since then they have dramatically declined for two major reasons: first, the reopening of the Suez Canal; second, the reorientation of trade away from Europe towards Asia and the resultant loss of many passenger and cargo services. Since the 1980s an increased number of visits by Japanese fishing boats has helped improve bunker sales. By the early 1990s bunker sales had stabilised at around 220,000 tonnes per annum.

This discussion of bunkering has illustrated the inter-relationship between trade and shipping; to a large degree, it is impossible to discuss one without considering the other. In the next chapter we will discuss

---

[74]Burley, *British Shipping*, 95.

shipping technology and ship flows in more detail, bearing in mind the importance of the inter-relationship.

Passenger Traffic at Fremantle

Although passenger traffic is only a minor component of port activity, it needs to be considered because it generated demands for shipping and port services.[75] Moreover, for a small, isolated, state such as Western Australia, population flows through its ports provided an important index of prosperity. Due to its geographical position, Fremantle was the first and last port of call for many passenger ships and for thousands of migrants provided the first glimpse of their new homeland.

As Western Australia's leading port, Fremantle naturally accounted for the bulk of the state's passenger traffic. At the turn of the century Fremantle handled ninety-three percent of passenger movements, Albany four percent and Broome, the only other port with significant passenger traffic, about two percent. For many years Albany remained the only port of call for some ships travelling via the Cape of Good Hope, including P&O Branch Line steamers, while Broome attracted Asian labour for the pearling industry. Given Fremantle's dominance of passenger traffic figure 3.6, which illustrates passenger movements (arrivals plus departures) in Western Australia as a whole between 1901 and 1939, gives a good approximation of the trend of passenger movements at Fremantle. After reaching record levels in the gold rushes of the 1890s passenger traffic began to decline in the early years of the twentieth century. Passenger movements are, of course, a two-way affair, but with the exception of 1907 arrivals always exceeded departures. The net outflow in 1907 was due to the departure of many miners and goldfield residents as gold production declined. However, a revival of immigration, mostly assisted, led to a jump in arrivals before the First World War.[76] Passenger movements rose to record levels during the First World War, but this was due to troop movements; throughout the 1920s they averaged

---

[75]For a useful survey of the demands of the passenger trade for shipping see F. Broeze, "Our Home is Girt by Sea, The Passenger Trade to Australia and New Zealand 1788-1914," in K. Friedland, (ed.), *Maritime Aspects of Migration* (Cologne, 1989), 441-465.

[76]See F.K. Crowley, "The British Contribution To The Australian Population: 1860-1919," *University Studies in Western Australian History*, II (1954), 55-88.

only 33,000 per annum, or about one-half of the prewar level. The depression caused a further drop in passenger movements and they remained relatively depressed as late as 1939. Although the slump in passenger traffic was largely due to the decline in the state's economic performance, interstate passenger traffic was also reduced by competition from other modes of transport.

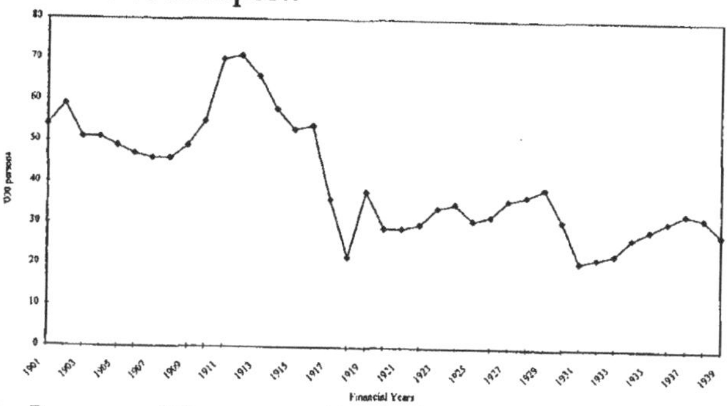

Figure 3.6: Passenger Movements (Arrivals Plus Departures) by Sea, Western Australia, 1900-1901 to 1938-1939.

Source: Western Australia, *Statistical Registers*.

After the opening of the Trans-Australia Railway in 1917 interstate passengers had a viable alternative to the long sea voyage around the coast (despite breaks of gauge, the journey by rail between Perth and Melbourne took only four days compared to seven to eight days by sea). Between 1936 and 1938, the railway was carrying a two-way traffic averaging about 10,000 persons per annum, or about twenty-three percent of total passenger movements into and out of Western Australia. But it was the aeroplane rather than the railway that was eventually to cause the demise of interstate passenger shipping, although this did not occur until after the Second World War.[77] Between 1936 and 1938 aeroplanes accounted for about 2000 passenger movements per annum or only four percent of the Western Australian total. Thus, by the eve of the Second World War, railway and air transport already accounted for over one-quarter passenger movements: the end of an era of leisurely sea travel was in sight.

Temporary visitors such as tourists, as well as migrants, generate passenger movements. From the port's point of view, migrants pass more or less directly through the terminals and require less elaborate provision

[77]J. Bach, *A Maritime History of Australia* (Melbourne, 1976), chs. XIV and XV.

than tourists, who might demand tourist guides, banking and other facilities. However, data on transit passengers at Fremantle is not available until 1957-1958 and details of temporary arrivals and departures are available at the national level only from 1924.[78] Between 1926 and 1930 temporary arrivals averaged about 125,000 per annum or twenty-seven percent of total arrivals; over the same period temporary departures averaged 126,000 per annum or thirty-seven percent of total departures. The depression of the 1930s led to a sharp reduction in tourist traffic and as late as 1937-1939 temporary arrivals and departures averaged only 29,000 and 31,000 per annum respectively. Doubtless, Fremantle reflected these national trends.

After the Second World War the Labor government, motivated in part by the old notion of "populate or perish," embarked on an ambitious immigration programme. Although the White Australia Policy remained in force, the government widened the net to include migrants from other parts of Europe, not just Britain. Large numbers of displaced persons were offered a new life in Australia.

The revival of immigration led to a boom in passenger shipping. Between 1945 and 1977 when the last migrant ship arrived, 169 vessels made over 2000 trips to Australia and carried a total of about three million people.[79] However, the introduction of jet travel in the 1960s severely affected passenger shipping. Between 1956-1957 and 1969-1970 the number of passengers carried into and out of Australia by air increased from 126,615 to 1,018,788 or by 705 percent. In the latter year eighty-five percent of arriving and departing passengers travelled by air and only fifteen percent by ship.[80] But about half of the Australians leaving on long overseas trips still travelled by ship and almost half of assisted migrants still arrived by ship.[81] However, in 1977 the federal government switched all official migrant traffic to air travel, ending the era of the emigrant ships.

---

[78]Burley, *British Shipping*, 148-151.

[79]K.M. Stodden, "The Post-War Migrant Ships," *BIMPR Bulletin*, No. 16 (March 1996), 24.

[80]Commonwealth, Bureau of Census and Statistics, *Overseas Arrival and Departures, Year Ending June 1970* (Canberra, 1970).

[81]Department of National Development, *Atlas of Australian Resources: Ports and Shipping* (2nd ed., Canberra, 1971), 17.

Figure 3.7 shows the trend of passenger movements at Fremantle after the Second World War. The passenger trade reached its peak in the 1960s and then began to decline due to the competition from air transport. Interstate passenger traffic was even more severely affected by competition from air and land transport: between 1951-1952 and 1959-1960 domestic passenger movements declined from 14.1 percent to 6.6 percent of total passenger movements at Fremantle. The State Shipping Service provided limited passenger services to the north west of the state until March 1973. After 1977 when the last liner carrying immigrants, the Greek owned *Australis*, arrived in Australia, passenger movements rapidly declined. By 1981 the *Centaur*, operating between Fremantle and Southeast Asia, was the only regular passenger ship calling at the port. The only other passenger ships calling were cruise ships but their visits were irregular and widely spaced. In 1983-1984 passenger movements plummeted to 2521 persons, the lowest level this century. The following year visits by six different passenger vessels, calling a total of nineteen times, increased passenger movements to 10,113 persons. The *Turkmenia* made thirteen trips between Fremantle and South East Asia and the liners *Queen Elizabeth 2*, *Canberra*, *Oriana*, *Coral Princess* and the *Mikhail Lermontov* (lost off New Zealand in 1986) provided a brief reminder of the time when passenger operations were a colourful part of port activity.

Given that first impressions of a country are very important for both migrants and tourists it is surprising that the port authority provided no special facilities for handling passengers: the usual practice was to clear part of a transit shed and use this for baggage and customs clearance. Fremantle was the first port of call for most migrant ships, so customs officers checked the passports and landing permits of all passengers even those in transit to the eastern states. They also administered the Immigration Act and prior to the abolition of the "White Australia Policy" (it died out in the late 1960s and was officially abolished in 1973) acted as "frontline troops in the battle to maintain racial purity."[82]

The experience of 1180 Polish migrants, who arrived in Fremantle on the American Army transport *General W.C. Langfitt* on 14 February 1950 was not untypical: their luggage was simply dumped on the wharf and they had to scramble to retrieve their meagre possessions. Many years later one of these migrants recalled her reaction on arriving at Fremantle:

---

[82]D. Day, *Contraband and Controversy. The Customs History of Australia from 1901* (Canberra, 1996), 255.

> After leaving beautiful green Mombassa we arrived in Fremantle where there were little tin barracks and lots of concrete. There was nothing there. I didn't want to get out and said, "I'm going back to Africa." I started crying. My Mother said that maybe it is not so bad and that, anyway, we couldn't go back. She was more philosophical about it than I was. As soon as I got off the ship a lady from the YWCA asked me, "How do you like Australia?" What could I say! We were given a pie, an orange, a piece of fruit cake and an apple by the YWCA.[83]

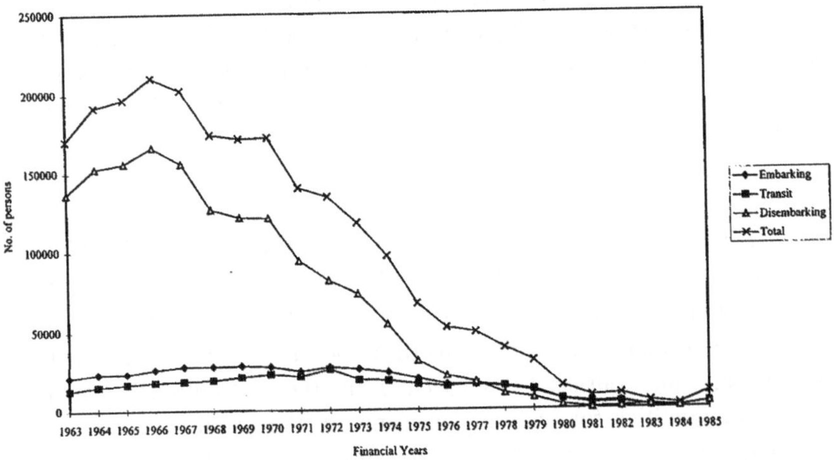

Figure 3.7: Passenger Traffic at Fremantle, 1962-1963 to 1984-1985.

Source: FPA, *Annual Reports*.

The primitive passenger handling arrangements continued until 1960 when a passenger terminal was finally opened. However, the terminal was built to cater for the needs of visitors arriving for the Commonwealth Games in 1962, rather than migrants. Ironically, it was opened just as air traffic was beginning to seriously reduce the number of overseas travellers arriving by ship. The terminal was grossly under utilised and by the 1970s the port authority was offering its use for dances

---

[83]M. Allbrook and H. Cattalini, *The General Langfitt Story* (Canberra, 1995), 109.

and other social functions. It has also been used to receive visiting British and American sailors and for the America's Cup Races in 1986-1987.

Conclusions

Thus far we have seen that Fremantle's growth between the 1890s and 1990s was largely dictated by factors outside its control: the port appears to have been a passive element, merely responding to periods of feast and famine in trade and shipping. The periods of feast and famine in port use were induced by a large variety of factors, including the level of primary production, world prices, shifts in economic structure and government policy.

After the gold boom peaked in 1903, Western Australia entered a period of slower growth. The economy remained heavily orientated to primary production as manufacturing industry, handicapped by competition form eastern states producers after federation, grew only slowly. Primary exports, particularly wheat, boomed in the 1920s only to suffer severe setbacks in the 1930s. In short, in the first three decades of the twentieth century economic conditions were not conducive to the rapid expansion of port trade.

Although trade grew strongly after the Second World War, especially during the early 1950s and the mineral boom of the 1960s, the volume of port trade was still characterised by periods of feast and famine. Fremantle continued to experience a fall in its share of the value of trade but this was due to the expansion of other ports rather than diversion of trade. As the first and last port of call on the coast for vessels in the European trades, Fremantle had achieved some national importance as a bunkering port, but in the 1970s the reorientation of trade away from Europe towards Asia and the resultant loss of many passenger and cargo services led to a slump in sales of bunker fuel. Within Western Australia, Fremantle's dominance of trade values was never seriously challenged due largely to its proximity to the metropolitan area and the development of a basically Fremantle-centred transport system. However, Port Hedland and other regional ports dominated exports of mineral products. In the 1950s much interstate general cargo was lost to road and rail transport but shipping retained its competitive advantage for bulk cargo which provided a growing share of postwar trade.

The opening of the oil refinery at Kwinana led to the development of the Outer Harbour and was a major turning point in the history of the port. The Inner Harbour began to slowly wane as a centre of port activity as bulk cargo-handling operations were transferred to the Outer Harbour. The decline of the passenger trade after the Second World War only worsened the situation. By the late 1960s the Outer Harbour accounted for three-quarters of Fremantle's trade measured in tonnage terms. Perhaps the decision made at that time to locate container operations on the North Wharf in the Inner Harbour was influenced by the desire to stop it from becoming defunct as part of a commercial port. In the 1990s Victoria Quay (the south wharf) was still used for bunkering, unloading of cars, loading of live sheep and scrap metal, and visits by warships and the occasional passenger ship. Clearly, all of these changes had major implications for port operation and development. But they cannot be considered in isolation from the technological nature of the ships in which the cargo was carried. It is the task of the next chapter to examine alterations in the level and structure of ship flows at Fremantle.

Chapter 4
The Shipping of Fremantle

During the nineteenth century, Western Australia with its small population and consuming market offered only limited scope for the employment of shipping. In 1830, the first full year after settlement, thirty-nine vessels entered the Port of Fremantle, but until the gold rushes of the 1890s the average number of entries rarely exceeded seventy per year. Western Australia's significance to the British Empire and British shipping industry "was very little more than its red colour on the map."[1] The gold rushes were, however, a major turning point: by the turn of the century an average of more than 700 vessels per annum were using the new Inner Harbour.

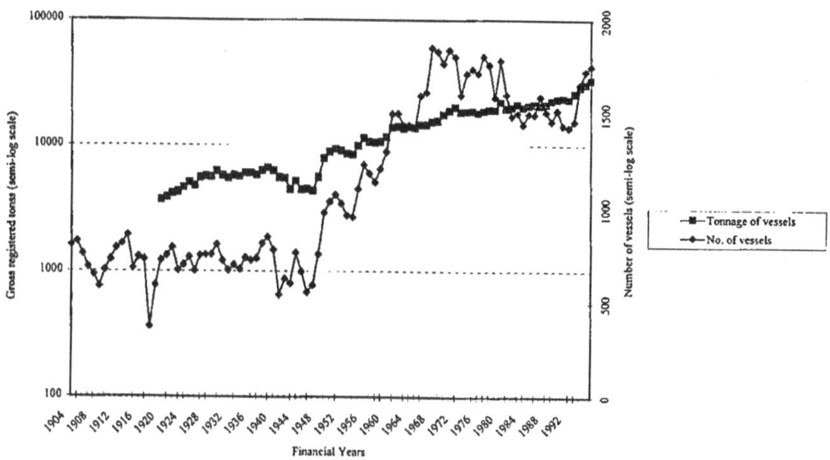

Figure 4.1: Ship Numbers and Tonnage Entering Fremantle, 1903-1904 to 1995-1996.

Source: Appendix A.

[1]F. Broeze, "Western Australia Until 1869: The Maritime Perspective, Part II, Early Days," *Journal and Proceedings of the Royal Western Australia Historical Society*, VIII (1983), 114.

Figure 4.1 illustrates the growth of ship numbers and tonnage entering Fremantle between 1903-1904 and 1995-1996. For about nine decades the number of ships calling grew at 1.3 percent per annum. The number of entries passed 1000 per annum in the 1950s and by the 1990s averaged 1500 per annum. The total tonnage of shipping calling at Fremantle did not exceed 100,000 tons until 1895. By 1919-1920 it had reached 3.7 million tons and by the outbreak of the Second World War had passed six million tons. The opening of the Outer Harbour in the mid-1950s led to a jump in shipping tonnages and in 1995-1996 a record 33.5 million tons of shipping called at the port.[2] Thus, commencing in the latter years of the nineteenth century, there was a major expansion in ship movements and the consumption of shipping services in Western Australia.

Table 4.1
The Composition of Fremantle's Trade, 1905-1995

Financial Years	Overseas		Coastal		Total	
	'000 tons	%	'000 tons	%	'000 tons	%
1905	635	43.4	828	56.6	1,463	100.0
1915	702	38.7	1,111	61.3	1,813	100.0
1925	1,257	40.5	1,849	59.5	3,106	100.0
1935	1,722	46.8	1,960	53.2	3,682	100.0
1955	2,935	51.2	2,799	48.8	5,734	100.0
1975	11,232	59.9	7,515	40.1	18,747	100.0
1995	28,347	90.7	2,918	9.3	31,265	100.0

Note: Tons and net registered tons until 1954-1955 and gross registered tons thereafter.

Source: FHT and FPA, *Annual Reports*

[2]In this chapter, unless otherwise specified, tonnage refers to gross registered tonnage (grt).

Ships calling at Fremantle can, in principle, be divided into two broad groups: overseas and coastal. Table 4.1 illustrates the composition of vessel arrivals between 1904-1905 and 1994-1995. One problem with interpreting the table is that many coastal vessels are overseas vessels trading via other Australian ports, blurring the distinction between overseas and coastal shipping. For these reasons, it gives only a rough indication of the geographical pattern of shipping services. Nevertheless, it is clear that coastal shipping has suffered a drastic decline. Prior to the Second World War it accounted for over fifty percent of vessel arrivals but by 1995 its share had plummeted to less than ten percent.

Clearly, there were major changes in the level and pattern of ship movements at Fremantle between the 1890s and 1990s. As we will see, alterations in ship movements called for substantial adaptation on the part of the port. In this discussion of ship movements we must deal not only with ship movements measured in terms of tonnage but also with the nature of ships. This is because the implications of ship movements for the port depended on factors such as the types, sizes and technology of vessels calling. Shipping and port technological alterations are closely connected, as subsequent discussion will demonstrate. In order to understand the pattern of ship movements at Fremantle it is necessary to provide a brief overview of types of ships and the organisation of international shipping services.

At the outset it should be emphasised that Australia as a whole poses some special problems for shipowners. It is a geographically isolated island situated at the end of what was, for historical reasons, one of the world's largest trade routes: Fremantle, for example, is 9537 miles from London (via Suez). Australia's primary exports such as wool, wheat and fruit fluctuate considerably on both a seasonal and annual basis. The long sea voyage to and from Australia means that shipping services need to be planned months in advance, well before the exports are "harvested" and detailed shipping requirements are known.[3] In addition many exports have special requirements for shipping capacity: meat and dairy produce, for example, require refrigerated shipping space and prompt delivery to overseas markets. The import trade, which comprises general cargoes and a few bulk cargoes such as crude oil, requires frequent and reliable shipping services. Until the 1960s there was also a major demand for regular and fast passenger services. The different requirements of the

---

[3]K. Burley, *British Shipping and Australia 1920-1939* (Cambridge, 1968), 13.

export and import trades force many vessels to arrive or leave less than fully loaded. Clearly Australia's onerous requirements for shipping services have significant implications for the level of freight charges paid by exporters and importers.

Ship Types and Organisation

The commercial vessels that call at Fremantle can be divided into three main types: liners, tramps and tankers.[4] The port also caters for a variety of other commercial vessels including fishing vessels and livestock carriers. From time to time the port has played host to special ships. For example, in 1954 Queen Elizabeth and the Duke of Edinburgh spent six days in port on the Royal Yacht *Gothic*. In 1962 a fleet of passenger ships arrived for the Commonwealth Games. The America's Cup defence held between October 1986 and February 1987 briefly made Fremantle the focus of international attention as the port played host to the contesting yachts and crews. Although such visits and events are spectacular they are only a brief interlude in the life of a busy commercial port. Furthermore, although until the establishment of HMAS *Stirling* in 1978 Fremantle was not a major naval port, it has always serviced the needs of naval vessels. We will consider both naval and commercial vessels but it is necessary to devote most attention to the latter because, except perhaps during wartime, they have by far the greatest impact on the port.

Liner Services

Liners are vessels which offer a regular service over specified routes. The fact that they are committed to offering regular services means that liner companies do not expect their ships to travel fully loaded on every trip. Liners normally carry general cargo that can range from small packages to bulky items such as railway locomotives. Thus in order to maintain an adequate service, liner companies need to provide vessels of varying types and speeds to suit the requirements of each individual trade. For example, the Australian/Europe trade required fast vessels with refrigerated space for carrying perishable cargoes such as meat and butter.

---

[4]For a clear discussion of different ship types and organisation, on which this discussion draws, see A.E. Branch, *Elements of Shipping* (5th ed., London, 1981).

Liners are usually organised by conferences. A conference is an association of shipowners who operate liners on specific routes and adopt common policies to customers.[5] In economic terms, conferences are cartels which regulate competition and enjoy varying degrees of monopoly power. Some conferences are governed by formal agreements and run by secretariats while others are organised on a more informal basis. Conferences fix freight rates that can be charged by members, thereby preventing competition through rate cutting. This tends to lead to competition in services and in order to regulate this conferences allocate sailings and ports of call and even pool trade and earnings amongst members. A crucial aspect of the conference system is the use of deferred rebates that are designed to tie shippers to a particular conference. The above practices are typical of "closed" conferences that admit new members only with the agreement of existing members. "Open" conferences, which do not restrict membership, are mainly confined to routes to and from the USA. This is because "closed" conferences would violate American anti-trust laws. Conferences often enjoy a virtual monopoly on routes, with the result that the bargaining power of shippers is relatively weak unless they are organised into associations.

The first major conference was the United Kingdom/Calcutta conference developed in 1875 to combat cut-throat competition which followed the opening of the Suez Canal in 1869. The introduction of deferred rebates in 1877 ensured its success and conferences were rapidly adopted on other routes. By 1939, "practically every liner trade or route of any importance was governed by conference agreements."[6]

The exact details of many conference arrangements are difficult to discover because of the traditional secrecy surrounding the shipping industry, but a conference was introduced on the United Kingdom/ Australia run as early as 1884. A homeward conference was slower to

---

[5]For detailed discussion of shipping conferences see D. Marx, *International Shipping Cartels: A Study of Industrial Self-Regulation by Shipping Conferences* (Princeton, 1953); S.G. Sturmey, *British Shipping and World Competition* (London, 1962); K. Trace, "Australian Overseas Shipping 1900-1960" (Unpublished PhD thesis, University of Melbourne, 1965); Burley, *British Shipping*, ch. 6; B.M. Deakin and T. Seward, *Shipping Conferences. A Study of Their Origins Development and Economic Practices* (Cambridge, 1973); J. Bach, *A Maritime History of Australia* (Melbourne, 1976); K.A. Moore, *The Early History of Freight Conferences. Background and Main Developments Until Around 1900*, (London, 1981).

[6]Branch, *Elements of Shipping*, 187.

develop largely because tramp shipping offered the cheapest way of transporting Australia's predominantly bulk exports. The advantages of liners, such as regular sailings, did not compensate for the higher freight rates charged by conference liners. But the introduction of refrigeration, which required more costly vessels and greater service reliability, led to a number of agreements amongst shipowners. By the eve of the First World War formal homeward conferences existed for both refrigerated and non-refrigerated cargoes.[7]

The above arrangements were mainly concerned with trade between Britain and eastern states ports; until the 1960s, the West Australian trade was controlled by a combination of local merchants and shippers, organised into the West Australian Shipping Association (WASA), and British shipowners.

WASA was established in 1884 by local merchants to counter their dependence on British shipowners and brokers for their shipping between Fremantle and London.[8] Even after the opening of the Inner Harbour, Fremantle merchants complained that liner companies still charged the same rates for Fremantle cargo as they had done when they called at Albany, despite the fact that they no longer had to absorb the cost of transferring the cargo from Albany to Fremantle. Generally speaking conferences serving Australia adopted pan-Australian rates, that is, uniform freight rates for all Australian ports and the persistence of the differential between Fremantle and eastern states' ports, which was claimed to be as high as twenty-five percent, was a serious bone of contention between merchants and the shipping lines.[9]

After a rate war lasting two years WASA negotiated an agreement with the British shipowners giving it a share of the trade on the condition that they charged agreed freight rates. In the early 1900s William Marden,

---

[7]Burley, *British Shipping*, 222-224; and F. Harcourt, "P&O and Orient: A Cool Partnership, 1886-1914," *The Great Circle*, XVII (1995), 73-94.

[8]This discussion draws on two articles by F. Broeze, "Merchants from Sail to Steam: The West Australian Shipping Association and the Evolution of the Conference System, 1884-1910," in L.R. Fischer (ed.), *From Wheel House to Counting House: Essays in Maritime Business History in Honour of Professor Peter Neville Davies* (St. John's, 1992), 273-301; and "'A Great Frankenstein:' The West Australian Shipping Association 1884-1906," *Studies in Western Australian History*, XIII (1992), 49-62.

[9]FPA 31/03, W. Sandover (in England) to Perth Chamber of Commerce, 21 November 1902; Fremantle Chamber of Commerce to Acting Premier, 22 April 1903.

the WASA's London manager said "the Association is not regarded as a fighting power, but as a very powerful body for maintaining peace...It is not our policy to start an opposition if it can be avoided."[10]

Between 1889 and 1904 WASA made average profits of over £18,300 per annum. The 1905 Royal Commission identified WASA as the main cause of the high freight rates to Western Australia.[11] Clearly, until it was wound up in the late 1960s, WASA, rather than minimising freight costs to consumers, served as a conduit to provide Fremantle merchants with a share of the monopoly profits generated in the shipping trade. Thus WASA provides a clear example of the triumph of private over public interest or, as Adam Smith said, people of the same trade seldom meet together without the conversation ending in a "conspiracy" against the public. It is no coincidence that Patsy Brown, who has studied the social history of Fremantle's merchant class, concluded that they "were guided by three principles...the broad tenets of nonconformism...the ethos of the British public school...and...Social-Darwinism."[12]

Liners developed the practice of doing a "milkround" of the Australian coast, beginning and ending at Fremantle. They "topped-up" with cargoes in each port:

> Liners, especially those engaged on the European route, spent a week or more after reaching Fremantle in circling the continent from west to east, discharging cargo en route. On reaching the east and completing discharge they began loading once more. They retraced their route, loading at each port before clearing the Commonwealth at Fremantle.[13]

In the 1920s considerable excess capacity, especially in refrigerated ships, forced liners to spend more time on the "milkround." But the

---

[10]Cited by Broeze, "Merchants from Sail to Steam," 273.

[11]Australia, *Royal Commission on Ocean Freights* (Perth, 1905), 7-17.

[12]P. Brown, "'Rich Men In Their Castles, Poor Men At Their Gates:' Status And Paternalism of a Colonial Elite 1870-1900," *Studies in Western Australian History*, XIII (1992), 39.

[13]Burley, *British Shipping*, 188-189.

"milkround" was costly as the shipowners had to pay multiple port and handling charges and this led to complaints about the level of Australian port charges. Following several years of losses, the Conference Lines raised freight rates in the outward trade to Australia in 1928.[14] It is, perhaps, not entirely a coincidence that freight rates were raised the year after the sale of the government-owned Australian Commonwealth Line. Australian shippers feared a similar rise in the homeward trade and asked the federal government to intervene. In 1929 the government called a conference of shipowners and representatives of producers, importers and exporters. As a result of this conference these groups formed the Council of the Australian Overseas Transport Association (AOTA). During the 1930s AOTA negotiated agreements and freight rates for general cargo, wool, refrigerated cargo, dairy produce and fruit. The Australian Industries Preservation Act, which had been passed in 1906 to stop deferred rebates in the coastal trade, was amended to allow such practices to continue legally. However, rationalisation of tonnage proceeded only slowly and not all shippers were happy with the new arrangements. In the early 1930s Westralian Farmers Co-operative Ltd. formed the West Farmers Line in order to fight the conference. The West Farmers Line was a chartering rather than ship-owning organisation and remained outside the conference until 1937.[15] The conference system continued without any major changes until it was brought to a halt by the outbreak of the Second World War.

The conference system was revived in the 1950s. In 1955, after increases in freight rates by the Australia/Europe conference, and mounting public hostility to the conference lines, the Liberal-Country Party government reluctantly intervened in the organisational structure of the overseas trade.[16] The government established a formula for freight rate increases based on voyage costs. This system continued, with some modifications, until 1968. The following year the government allowed the state-owned Australian National Line to compete in the overseas trades for the first time. In 1967 Australian shippers on the UK/Europe route formed

---

[14]The following discussion draws on Bach, *Maritime History,* ch. XIII.

[15]For details, see J. Sandford, *Walter Harper and the Farmers* (Perth, 1955).

[16]T. Sheridan, "Public Image of a Cartel: The Australia/UK-Continental Conference, 1950-1965," *Australian Economic History Review*, XXXIV (September 1994), 24-58.

the Australia/Europe Shippers' Association to replace AOTA but similar bodies failed to develop in most other trades. In 1972 the federal government established the Australian Shippers' Council to represent all shippers in negotiations with the conference lines.

The conference system has proved one of the most controversial aspects of the shipping industry. Concern about its effects led to the appointment of a number of governmental and other public investigations, the most well known being the British Royal Commission on Shipping Rings, which reported in 1909. The majority report favoured the conference system and declared that deferred rebates were acceptable but a minority report (significantly it was signed by Australia and New Zealand) identified major defects, including the creation of monopoly power, high freight rates and damage to the prospects of tramp shipping.[17] A West Australian Royal Commission (1905) and an Australian Royal Commission (1906) condemned various aspects of the conference system, and Australian Royal Commissions on the Navigation Bill (1906) and the Navigation Act (1924) argued that conferences hindered the development of an Australian shipping industry.[18] Public hostility to overseas shipping lines appears to have peaked in the 1950s when, as we have seen, it forced the government to intervene.

The emergence of Japan as a major trading partner in the 1960s led to few changes because, after some initial opposition from European lines, Japanese liner companies were admitted into the system of closed conferences. However, since the 1970s, the growth of other Asian economies, many of them with their own fleets, has led to increased competition from non-conference lines on many routes. Between 1983-1984 and 1991-1992, non-conference lines increased their market shares by about half in the inward trades and two-thirds in the outward trades.[19] It has been argued that because most liner trades are characterised by

---

[17]See Great Britain, *Report of Royal Commission on Shipping Rings*, 1909 (Cd 4668). From 1916 deferred rebates, fighting ships (used by conferences to undercut non-conference vessels) and similar practices were outlawed in the USA.

[18]See *Royal Commission on Ocean Freights*. The Commonwealth reports were as follows: *Report from the Royal Commission on Ocean Shipping Services* 1906 (No. 36); *Report of the Royal Commission on the Navigation Bill* 1906 (No. 30); *Report of the Royal Commission to the Navigation Act 1924* (No. 103).

[19]P. Brazil, H. Kolsen and J. Evans, *Liner Shipping Cargoes and Conferences. Review of Part X of the Trade Practices Act* (Canberra, 1993), 74.

freedom of entry and exit they are inherently "contestable," that is, subject to the threat of considerable competition. Under these circumstances, it is unlikely that conferences are inimical to the public interest.[20] In 1993 a government review recommended the continued exemption of conferences from the normal prohibition of cartels in the *Trade Practices Act 1974* (Part X - Overseas Cargo).[21]

For the majority of Fremantle's history the major liner service has been the one between the United Kingdom and Australia. This route was serviced by the vessels of many leading liner companies which, following the opening of the Inner Harbour at the turn of the century, called at Fremantle instead of Albany. The first British mail steamer to call was the Orient Line's *Ormuz* on the 13 August 1900 and it was followed a week later by the P&O's steamer *India*. At that time P&O steamers sailed from Tilbury to Marseilles, Port Said, Suez, Aden, Colombo, Fremantle, Adelaide, Melbourne and Sydney.[22] By the late 1930s at least ten British lines were servicing the United Kingdom/Australia route and about two-thirds of all shipping entering the port was flying the Red Ensign.[23] In

---

[20]See K. Trace, "Contestable Market Theory Applied to Australian Overseas Liner Shipping Arrangements," *Maritime Studies*, No. 22 (January/February 1985), 1-11; and J. Davies, "The Role of Contestability Theory in the Economic Analysis of Liner Shipping," *Maritime Studies*, No. 22 (March/April 1985), 2-8.

[21]See Brazil, Kolsen and Evans, *Liner Shipping Cargoes*.

[22]J.M. Maber, *North Star to Southern Cross* (Prescot, 1967), 17. Maber's book has been used as a general source of information on shipping companies and vessels servicing the Australian coast.

[23]The major services were as follows: P&O Steam Navigation Co. Ltd., monthly passenger and cargo service via Suez; P&O Branch Service (William Lund's Blue Anchor Line taken over by P&O in 1910), monthly passenger and cargo service via South Africa; Orient Steam Navigation Co. Ltd. (fifty-percent interest acquired by P&O in 1919), monthly passenger and cargo service via Suez, alternating with the P&O Line; Blue Funnel Line (Alfred Holt & Co. Ltd.), monthly passenger and cargo service via South Africa; Cunard Steamship Company, monthly cargo service via Suez; Federal Steam Navigation Co. Ltd. (acquired by P&O Group in 1916), monthly cargo service via Suez; Ellerman and Bucknall Steamship Co. Ltd., monthly cargo service via Suez. Homewards only: Aberdeen Line (George Thompson and Company), monthly passenger and cargo service via South Africa; White Star Line (Oceanic Steam Navigation Company; in 1926 the White Star, Aberdeen and Shaw Savill, and Albion Lines were transferred to the Royal Mail Packet Company under Lord Kylsant), monthly passenger and cargo service via South Africa; Clan Line (Cayzer, Irvine and Company), monthly cargo service via Suez; Scottish Shire Line (Turnbull, Martin and Company Ltd; acquired by Clan Line in 1918), irregular

addition, between 1916 and 1927, the Commonwealth Government Line of steamers (restructured as the Australian Commonwealth Line in 1923) provided a monthly service of passenger and cargo steamers to the United Kingdom via Colombo and Port Said and a fortnightly service to the United Kingdom via Suez.[24] The British lines also carried trade between Australia and Europe as did vessels of European lines, such as the Messageries Maritimes, Lloyd Sabaudo, Holland-Australia Line and Wilh. Wilhelmsen.

In order to obtain adequate cargoes and passengers at Fremantle liner companies either opened branch offices or employed the services of a shipping agent. At the turn of the century, at least ten overseas and six interstate steamship lines called at Fremantle, a considerable number given the fact that Western Australia's population was only about 213,000.[25] By the mid-1930s two British liner companies and four Australian ones operated branch offices at Fremantle. Due to the limited volume of business most overseas liner companies preferred to rely on one of the nine shipping agents then operating at the port.[26] However, many of the agents were intimately linked with shipping lines. For example, MacDonald Hamilton and Company acted as agents for the P&O, the British India Steam Navigation Company, the Australasian United Steam Navigation Company Ltd. and Messageries Maritimes. MacDonald Hamilton and Company and the first three lines all formed part of Lord

---

service via Suez and South Africa. See Australian Archives (AA): Department of Trade and Customs, CP 703/5, Papers of the Secretary, Commonwealth Board of Trade, 1917-1925, Australia's Overseas Shipping Connections, Bundle 3, undated.

[24]For a history of the Commonwealth Government Line, see R. McDonell, *Build a Fleet Lose a Fleet* (Melbourne, 1976); and F. Brennan, *The Australian Commonwealth Shipping Line* (Canberra, 1978).

[25]Western Australia, *Yearbook, 1903-04* (Perth, 1906), 1128-1148.

[26]The British shipping companies were the Aberdeen and Commonwealth Line and the Orient Line; the Australian ones were the Adelaide Steamship Company, McIlwraith, McEacharn Ltd., Melbourne Steamship Company and the State Shipping Service. The following firms acted as shipping agents: Burns Philp and Company, Dalgety and Company Ltd., Elder Smith and Company Ltd., George Wills and Company Ltd., H.J. Wigmore and Company, Johnson and Lynn Ltd., MacDonald Hamilton and Company, West Australian Shipping Association and W.M. Crosby and Company Ltd. See FPA 20/35/1, "Port Facilities and Charges at Fremantle," typescript prepared by the Department of Overseas Trade, London, 7 March 1934.

Inchcape's P&O group of companies, and Messageries Maritimes was a long-standing ally of the P&O.

Liner ships travelling between Europe and Australia travel via the Suez Canal, the Panama Canal or the Cape route.[27] The few sailing ships that remained after the First World War all took the latter route. The Panama Canal handles shipping travelling to and from Europe via New Zealand, as well as trade with North America, and is not usually used by ships calling at Fremantle. The Suez Canal, opened in 1869, did not have an immediate impact on the Australian run as the Canal route was not much shorter than the route round the Cape. As late as the early 1930s only about one-quarter of the steamships reaching Fremantle used the Canal. However, as far as Fremantle was concerned, the opening of the Canal was beneficial as it reduced the advantage of Albany's location on the Cape route. Vessels tended to make more use of the Canal on the homeward than outward voyage due to the need to deliver primary exports such as wool, meat and fruit as rapidly as possible to the European market.[28]

The majority of trade between Fremantle and Asia follows two routes: one from Fremantle to India, Ceylon (now Sri Lanka) and Burma; the other from Fremantle northwards to the Dutch East Indies (now Indonesia) and the Straits Settlements (now Singapore and Malaysia).[29] The Port of Singapore, located between the Indian and Pacific Oceans, grew in importance as an entrepot and coaling station following the opening of the Suez Canal and continues to provide a focal point for shipping lines trading with the Far East.[30]

Tramp and Tanker Services

Tramp shipping is very different from liner shipping. It operates in a world market, where the forces of supply and demand work freely.

---

[27]Burley, *British Shipping,* 40.

[28]W. Woodruff, *The Suez Canal and the Australian Economy* (London, 1957), 10.

[29]Burley, *British Shipping,* 41.

[30]Wong Lin Ken, "Singapore: Its Growth As an Entrepot Port, 1819-1941," *Journal of Southeast Asian History*, IX (1978), 70.

Tramps do not keep to a fixed schedule but trade wherever there is cargo. Tramp owners generally aim to carry full cargo loads and negotiate freight rates, routes and ports of call in order to achieve this. Tramps usually carry bulk cargoes and although the average tramp is designed to carry a wide range of bulk cargoes specialised vessels are built for the carriage of cargoes such as grain and ore. The owner's broker through the Baltic Mercantile and Shipping Exchange in London usually arranges the chartering of tramps. Tramps may be chartered for a single voyage or for a certain period of time. In the latter case the owner's responsibility is usually limited to the manning, provisioning and maintenance of the vessel. Tramp owners do not need to maintain branch offices to organise local cargoes and normally use shipping agents only to handle paperwork while in port.

In the 1920s and 1930s tramps suffered severe competition from liners which took "parcels" of wheat and other cargoes usually carried by tramps. The liners did this to suit the convenience of shippers and to help ensure fuller use of their shipping capacity on a chronically depressed market. One consequence of this was that tramps became less frequent visitors to Australian ports during the inter-war years than otherwise would have been the case.[31]

Since the late 1950s there has been a trend away from general purpose tramp vessels to bulk carriers specially designed for the carriage of specific commodities such as iron ore, coal and wheat. The entry of multi-national companies in these areas has led to them either purchasing their own vessels or signing long term contracts with shipping companies. As a result, by the 1960s, liners were no longer competing in the bulk minerals and food trades.[32]

The tanker trade is a specialised one that arises from the demand for the carriage of oil by sea. Following the drilling of the first successful well in Pennsylvannia in 1859, oil began to be carried by ordinary dry cargo ships in drums, cases and barrels. This was both cumbersome and hazardous and specialised vessels were gradually developed for the carriage of oil. The first steam tanker was the *Gluckhauf* built by the

---

[31]Burley, *British Shipping,* 100-116.

[32]Australia, Bureau of Transport Economics, *A Study of Liner Shipping Services Into and Out of Australia* (2 vols., Canberra, 1986), II, 16-17.

British for a German shipowner in 1886.[33] In 1938 the world tanker fleet totalled about 16.6 million dwt or ten percent of world shipping; by the mid-1980s it had leapt to 240 million dwt and accounted for about forty percent of world shipping.

The world's tanker fleet is divided between "free" operators, which charter ships to oil companies, usually on a long-term basis, and oil companies which operate their tankers on regular routes between production, refining and consumption centres. For example, by the eve of the Second World War, the Anglo-Iranian Oil Company (now known as British Petroleum), owned ninety-two tankers totalling 964,000 deadweight tons.[34] The first cargo of bulk petroleum arrived at Fremantle aboard the *Radix* on 8 April 1927.

It is apparent that bulk cargoes such as wheat or oil had different requirements for shipping capacity than general cargoes. Due to the pattern of Australia's trade more general cargo capacity was required in the import trade than in the export trade, making excess capacity a persistent problem for shipowners on routes to and from Australia. Shipowners are keen to fill their ships for each leg of a journey if possible because a high proportion of vessel costs is fixed regardless of the volume of cargo carried. Thus average cost per unit of output (cargo carried) falls as output increases. However, because the demand for shipping is a derived demand, the most important factor is probably the extent to which the commodity shipped can bear freight charges, since shipowners can set freight rates to take account of the possibility of excess capacity on one leg of a journey. According to Kevin Burley, in the inter-war period full cargoes to or from any Australian port were "extremely rare" except for tramps carrying bulk cargoes.[35] But tramps coming to pick up Australia's exports were usually forced to arrive in ballast: in the early 1930s ninety percent of vessels that loaded full cargoes of wheat arrived in ballast.[36]

---

[33]A.C. Hardy, *Bulk Cargoes* (London, 1926), 35-36.

[34]R.W. Ferrier, "The Oil Company as a Shipowner - The Case of British Petroleum" (Unpublished paper presented to the conference on "The Shipowner in History," Greenwich, September 1984).

[35]Burley, *British Shipping*, 188-189.

[36]Australia, Tariff Board, *Report and Recommendations on Bunker Coal - Imposition of Duty or Payment of Bounty* (Canberra, 1932), 8.

Table 4.2
Ship Entries at Fremantle Classified by Cargo Characteristics, 1974-1975 and 1994-1995

Class	1974-1975 Gross Average			1994-1995 Gross Average		
	No.	Tons (000)	Per Ship (000)	No.	Tons (000)	Per Ship (000)
Break Bulk/General						
Carrier	598	5,815	9.7	58	636	11
Container	124	2,336	18.8	473	9,627	20.4
Multi purpose				51	193	3.8
Roll-on/Roll-off	12	197	16.4	37	1,088	29.4
Vehicle Carrier				54	2,142	39.7
Livestock						
Carrier	34	206	6.1	103	1,624	15.8
Passenger	110	1,598	14.5	9	186	20.6
Tankers	174	3,486	20.0	213	6,668	31.3
Dry Bulk-Grain	131	1,864	14.2	186	3,536	19.0
Dry Bulk-Other				203	3,887	19.1
Bunkering only				37	955	25.8
Other (fishing, tenders, etc.)	362	166	0.5	307	723	2.4
Total	1,742	18,747	10.8	1,731	31,265	18.1

Note: Excludes naval vessels.

Source: FPA, *Annual Reports*.

At Fremantle, however, ballast entries have never made up a large proportion of *total* entries. Prior to the Second World War total ballast entrances never exceeded more than about six percent of tonnage. The low proportion of liners entering in ballast is a reflection of Fremantle's status as the first and last port of call on the Australian coast. Prior to the development of containerisation in the 1960s, liners tended to unload or load relatively small quantities of cargo. During the 1930s, for example, only between twelve to fifteen percent of the average vessel's cargo was discharged or loaded at Fremantle.[37] Thus over eighty-five percent of each ship's cargo was brought into the port and taken out again, reflecting the port's role as a first port of call on a "milkround" rather than as a single terminal port. In 1975-1976, 4.3 percent of liners, 12.3 percent of tankers and 57.5 percent of tramps entered Fremantle in ballast.

Table 4.2 illustrates ship entries (excluding naval vessels), classified by cargo characteristics in 1974-1975 and 1994-1995. Compared to the early years of the twentieth century, the port now caters for a diverse range of specialised vessels, including container ships, livestock carriers, passenger ships, tankers, dry bulk carriers and fishing vessels. In view of its importance, the post-Second World War trend towards the development of specialised bulk carriers and container ships will be discussed in detail later in the chapter. At this stage we will comment only on trends in passenger and fishing vessels.

As we saw in the previous chapter, after the war the Australian government's migration programmes led to a brief revival of passenger shipping. The traditional British lines were joined by others such as the Italian owned Lloyd Triestino and Sitmar Lines and the Greek owned Chandris Line.

The shortage of shipping meant that many old and sometimes unreliable vessels with spartan accommodation facilities were pressed into service. The Swedish vessel, *Anna Salen*, arrived at Fremantle in December 1950 with 1522 refugees aboard. It had been converted to an aircraft carrier during the war and the hangar spaces that had held aircraft were turned into makeshift sleeping quarters, with men separated from their families. Many years later Agnes Kovacs recalled sleeping in a noisy room which housed 300 other women in double bunk beds.[38] The Panamanian registered *Liguria* was towed ignominiously into Fremantle in 1951 after breaking down and running low on food and water. By the late 1950s the quality of shipping had improved but competition from air

---

[37] Tydeman, *Fremantle*, III, appendix 11.

[38] J. Fraser, "The 1950 Voyage of the Anna Salen," *BIMPR Bulletin* (March 1996), 26-27.

transport was affecting the trade. Some companies attempted to revive it by building new 40,000 ton plus passenger liners. The first of these to arrive at Fremantle was the P&O Orient Line's SS *Oriana* (41,923 tons) on 23 December 1960. The gleaming white hull of the P&O's SS *Canberra* (45,270 tons) attracted great attention when it berthed in the Inner Harbour in June 1961. But these vessels failed to revive the UK-Australia trade and they were diverted into cruising where they proved popular with passengers. On 7 August 1963 the P&O's *Strathmore* left Fremantle on its final voyage to London; it was followed by the *Stratheden* on 23 September 1963. These were the last of the "Strath" ships which, since the 1930s, had regularly carried passengers and cargo between the UK and Australia. In May 1964 the Blue Funnel Line's diesel motor ship *Charon*, berthed for the 250th and last time on her return to Europe. In 1963 Lloyd Trestino introduced two new gleaming white liners, the *Galileo Galilei* and the *Gugliemo Marconi*, into the liner trade between Italy and Australia, but these were also switched to Caribbean and Mediterranean cruising in the 1970s. The golden era of passenger ships was over.

Although fishing boats make only a minor contribution to shipping tonnage and commercial port activities, fishing has long been of importance to the local economy. In the nineteenth century whaling and pearling (in the northwest of the state) were important activities but the last whaling station at Cheynes Beach, near Albany, was closed in 1978. Until the 1940s, general fishing (the capture of scale fish, crustaceans and molluscs) was characterised by low levels of output, employment and earnings. A fish market was set up on South Beach in the 1890s but prices received by fishers were low. The port authority was not unsympathetic to the plight of fishers and, to the chagrin of the Fremantle Council, allowed them to sell fish direct to the public on Victoria Quay.[39] No special facilities were provided for fishing boats and they had to compete with other shipping for space in the Inner Harbour. After the Second World War, the industry was transformed by the development of export markets for high value seafoods such as rock lobsters and prawns.[40]

---

[39]FPA, Minutes, 29 July 1921 and 18 May 1923.

[40]See M. Tull, "Profits and Lifestyle: Western Australia's Fishers," *Studies in Western Australian History*, XIII (1992), 92-111; and Tull, "The Development of the Australian Fishing Industry: A Preliminary Survey," *International Journal of Maritime History*, V (June 1993), 95-126.

Today, the industry generates substantial income through activities such as the processing, marketing and distribution of the catch, and boat construction and servicing. It has also provided an important avenue of employment for migrants and has helped Fremantle develop a cosmopolitan atmosphere. The expansion of the industry in the 1950s led to some overcrowding in the Inner Harbour and the Harbour Master expressed concern that fishing boats were impeding the movements of larger commercial vessels. There were some communications difficulties as many of the fishers, while "first-class" skippers, were migrants with limited command of English.[41] In 1959 work started on the construction of a separate fishing boat harbour south of the river mouth.[42]

As the industry expanded, fishing boats became increasingly sophisticated, although they remain small by the standards of deep-sea vessels. Sailing vessels were still in use for inshore fishing in the early postwar period but in the 1950s were superseded by faster motor boats. Mr. G. Bass, a rock lobster fisher, sums up the march of technology:

> Yes well it's a far cry to the old days where we had on the original boat a compass, which was an aircraft compass so you had to read back to front, and a clock. And you set the throttle by the sound of the engine, because there was no rev counters on the engines those days and you steamed for four or five hours on a set course and then started looking for your gear. Today we have compasses with automatic pilots. We have sun logs, which actually measure distance through the water very accurately and to back all that up we have satellite navigators including GPS systems, which are accurate to within metres of a destination. [43]

---

[41]FPA 426/37, "Control and Manning of Fishing Boats," Manager Harbour and Lights Department to FHT, 3 June 1948.

[42]FPA 87/489, "Fishing Boat Harbour - Extension of."

[43]George Bass, interview by Jack Darcey for the FIRDC Oral History Project on the Western Australian Fishing Industry, 7 November 1989, available from the Battye Library, Perth, OH 2266.

Table 4.3
Ship Visits to Fremantle by Flag, 1964-1965 and 1994-1995

	1964-1965		1994-1995	
Country	No.	Percent	No.	Percent
Australia	269	18.8	176	10.2
Bahamas	*		108	6.2
China	*		39	2.3
CIS (USSR)	15	1.0	33	1.9
Denmark	28	2.0	17	1.0
France	16	1.1	9	0.5
Germany	45	3.1	41	2.4
Greece	64	4.5	96	5.5
India	12	0.8	11	0.6
Indonesia	*		27	1.6
Italy	61	4.3	7	0.4
Japan	85	5.9	252	14.6
Kuwait	6	0.4	20	1.2
Liberia	31	2.2	63	3.6
Malaysia	*		68	3.9
Netherlands	92	6.4	48	2.8
Norway	136	9.5	61	3.5
Panama	23	1.6	208	12.0
Philippines	*		102	5.9
Singapore	*		40	2.3
Sweden	24	1.7	3	0.2
United Kingdom**	506	35.4	65	3.8
United States	9	0.6	10	0.6
Others	7	0.5	227	13.1
Total	1,429	100.0	1,731	100.0

Notes: * = Data not available or insignificant. ** = 1964-1965 includes a small proportion of tonnage registered in parts of the British Commonwealth not separately identified in the table, principally New Zealand. Where percentages do not add to 100, this is due to rounding.

Sources: FPA *Annual Reports*, 1964-1965 and 1994-1995 and unpublished data supplied by the FPA.

Apart from Australian fishers, the port also caters for foreign fishing vessels needing to replenish fuel and supplies. In 1937 a Japanese whaling fleet comprising the factory ship SS *Tonan Maru*, and eight catcher boats called for bunkers and stores while enroute to the Antarctic. The increasing threat of war meant that on security grounds the crews of about 350 had their movements restricted and were banned from bringing cameras and binoculars ashore.[44] During the Cold War visits by vessels from Communist countries posed similar concerns. Since 1968 Japanese long-line tuna fishing vessels have been permitted to call at Fremantle under the terms of a fishing agreement between the two countries.[45] In the first half of the 1980s an average of 270 Japanese boats visited the port each year and each boat generated the FPA about $1500 in revenue.[46] Since 1945 alterations in Australia's trade patterns and the expansion of the Japanese shipping industry, has led Japanese vessels of all types to become more frequent visitors to Australia's ports. We will now turn and examine the changing nationality of shipping using the port.

The Nationality of Shipping Calling at Fremantle

Despite being an island nation, Australia has never had a strong tradition of maritime enterprise and has relied on foreign shipping to handle its overseas trade. In 1912 the Commonwealth government passed a Navigation Act to introduce cabotage provisions (reserving the coastal trade for vessels which met Australian wages and manning conditions) but, at the request of the British government, the act was not implemented until 1921, by which time British shipping companies had a dominant control of coastal services.[47]

There have been a number of attempts to establish state owned shipping companies to provide a measure of countervailing power against the conference lines. In 1916 Prime Minister Hughes established the Commonwealth Government Line to carry Australia's primary exports which were piling up on the wharves due to the war-time scarcity of

---

[44]FPA 3471/91, NEM 57, Whaling Fleet.

[45]FPA 3468/88/119/A, PM Fraser to Premier Court, 4 November 1976.

[46]FPA 5341/88/07/09/F, FHT to Minister Grill, 29 March 1985.

[47]McDonell, *Build a Fleet*, 216-220.

shipping. The Line was retained after the war but was the centre of considerable controversy. In 1923 S.M. Bruce's National Country Party Government restructured the Line and it became known as the Australian Commonwealth Line of Steamers but it made continual losses and was sold to the Royal Mail group in 1927. Another state venture came in 1956 when the Australian Coastal Shipping Commission (re-named the Australian Shipping Commission in 1974) was formed to manage ships acquired by the federal government during the Second World War. Trading as the Australian National Line (ANL) it has accumulated an impressive record of loss making. In 1993-1994, for example, it recorded a loss of A$120 million. Not surprisingly, in view of the trend towards privatisation of public enterprises, there has been talk of selling the Line, but considerable controversy surround its financial performance and value -- very reminiscent, in fact, of the fracas that accompanied the sale of the Commonwealth Shipping Line in the 1920s.[48]

Frank Broeze, in a broad survey of the role of merchant shipping in Australia and New Zealand between 1788-1992, demonstrates how seamen's unions and shipping companies were keen to prevent competition from cheaper foreign lines but the result was high cost levels and a lack of international competitiveness.[49] However, since the Second World War the desire by shipowners to escape the taxation, employment and safety requirements of many countries has led to the expansion of flag of convenience (FOC) shipping, where vessels are registered outside the flag state of a shipping company. It is difficult for Australian and other non-FOC shipping operators to compete with the lower wages and other costs enjoyed by FOC vessels. Unfortunately, FOC vessels have accounted for a large proportion of maritime and ecological disasters. For example, the Panamanian registered *Sanko Harvest* struck an underground pinnacle near Esperance in February 1991 and its cargo of fertiliser caused serious pollution. The loss of six bulk carriers off the Western Australian coast

---

[48]*Australian Financial Review*, 30 January 1995. For a detailed but dated discussion of the ANL, see P. Stubbs, *Australia and the Maritime Industries* (Melbourne, 1982).

[49]F. Broeze, "Private Enterprise and Public Policy: Merchant Shipping in Australia and New Zealand, 1788-1992," *Australian Economic History Review*, XXXII (1992), 8-32. See also Broeze, "Western Australia," 108-109; and C. Hartley, "Western Australia: The Decline of the Colonial Merchant Shipping Industry 1870-1890" (Unpublished BA Hons. thesis, Murdoch University, 1982).

between January 1990 and August 1991 led to a federal government inquiry into these "ships of shame."[50]

Nevertheless, the majority of economists agree that, despite the ecological threat posed by "ships of shame," Australia does not possess a comparative advantage in the provision of shipping services and is probably better off remaining as a consumer rather than a supplier of shipping services.[51] Currently, Australian ships carry only about three to four percent of overseas trade.

For most of the port's history the lion's share of shipping services have been provided by British ships; as late as the mid-1960s they still accounted for about one third of entries. As we will see in the chapters that follow, British shipping lines exerted a considerable influence on port operation and development. In 1926-1927, for example, Fremantle had fifty-one visits by P&O mail steamers that paid about £4482 in port and pilotage dues alone.[52] The FHT could not lightly disregard the wishes of such an influential customer (that, moreover, controlled several other major companies calling at Fremantle).

The fleets of many other countries apart from Britain, of course, provide shipping services. In the first decade of the twentieth century German ships accounted for about sixty percent of non-British tonnage entering Fremantle. The main German company involved in the trade was Norddeutscher Lloyd, whose ships began calling at Fremantle in 1902 on their run from Bremerhaven to Sydney. In 1908-1909, for example, the passenger-cargo steamer *Friedrich der Grosse* (10,536 tons) and the three 8000-ton sister ships *Roon*, *Gneisenau* and *Seydlitz* visited Fremantle. These were all modern vessels and offered strong competition to the

---

[50]Australia, Parliament, *Inquiry into Ship Safety. Report from the House of Representatives Standing Committee on Transport, Communications and Infrastructure* (Canberra, 1992). It was chaired by the Hon. P. Morris. Of course, not all accidents involve FOC vessels. For example, on 21 July 1991 the bow section fell off the Greek-registered *Kirki* off the Western Australian coast near Cervantes. The vessel was saved from sinking but its cargo of crude oil caused serious pollution.

[51]See K. Trace, "Revitalisation of Australian Shipping:" A Critique of the Crawford Report," *The Great Circle*, IV (1982), 125-130; and Trace, *Towards Efficient Transport* (Perth, 1986). See also R.O. Goss, "The Revival of Australian Shipping - A Review Article," in Australian Centre for Maritime Studies, *Issues in Australian Shipping* (Canberra, 1983).

[52]FPA 20/27/2, Return Showing Payments Made by Peninsular and Oriental Company During Year Ending 30th June 1927.

British lines. German tonnage was, of course, disrupted by the First World War, and never returned to its pre-war level. The Norddeutscher Lloyd was not able to resume services to Australia until 1925. The German-Australian Steamship Company (Deutsche-Australische Dampfschiffs Gesellschaft) of Hamburg entered the Australian trade in 1889 and built up a major position in the freight traffic. In 1926 it was taken over by the Hamburg America Line. In 1930 the latter line and Norddeutscher Lloyd agreed to run the Australian service on a joint basis and this arrangement continued until the outbreak of the Second World War. The joint service was restored after the war.

By the late 1930s the Norwegian vessels accounted for about one third of all non-British tonnage entering Fremantle. The major line was the Norwegian Africa and Australia Line, established in 1910 by Wilh. Wilhelmsen and Fearnley and Eger. It provided a Europe/Australia service which went via the Cape on the outward run and via Suez on the homeward run. In 1938-1939 sixteen vessels belonging to Wilh. Wilhelmsen called at Fremantle, including the *Tricolor* (6850 tons), the *Tamerlane* (6778 tons), and the *Talleyrand* (6732 tons). All were motorships designed to carry cargo and a small complement of passengers. As we shall see, the Scandinavian lines led the world in the adoption of the diesel motorship.

After the opening of the Inner Harbour the French company, Messageries Maritimes, included Fremantle as a port of call on its run from Marseilles via Suez to Sydney. From Sydney it offered a regular service to Noumea. Vessels belonging to Messageries Maritimes which visited Fremantle before the First World War included the *Australien* (6365 tons), *Behic* (6397 tons), and *Dumbea* (5809 tons). The First World War disrupted these passenger-cargo services and the Suez route was not reopened until 1920. It was abandoned at the end of the 1920s as an economy measure and by 1938 French vessels accounted for less than one percent of foreign shipping entering Fremantle. Messageries Maritimes was reconstructed after the war and opened an intermittent service to Australia via Suez in 1947.

Before the Second World War Dutch shipping lines were mainly concerned with the trade between the Netherlands and the Dutch East Indies (now Indonesia) and the Holland-Australia Line (one of the eight lines of the Vereenigde Nederlandsche Scheepvaart Maatschappij established in 1919) was the only Dutch line whose vessels regularly called at Fremantle. In 1923-1924, for example, the Holland Australia Line's *Aagtekerk*, *Abbekerk*, *Almkerk* and *Arendskerk*, averaging 7500 tons, made a total of fourteen calls at Fremantle. The Dutch share of Fremantle shipping grew substantially in importance in the 1920s, mainly due to the import of oil from the Dutch East Indies that was largely carried on Shell tankers. The end of Dutch rule in the East Indies in 1949 led to the collapse of the direct Netherlands/East Indies traffic, and a number of lines, searching for new business, decided to participate in the migrant trade to Australia. The Nederland Line (NV Stoomvart Maatschappi), for example, operated the *Johan Van Oldenbarnevelt* and the *Oranje* in the Europe/Australia migrant trade between 1950-1959. In 1959 they were placed on a round-the-world service between Europe and Australia via the Suez and Panama Canals but this ceased in the early 1960s.

After the First World War Italian emigration to the USA declined and larger numbers of Italians chose Australia as a place to settle. Consequently, Italian lines, such as Lloyd Sabaudo and the Navigazione Generale Italiana entered the passenger and migrant trade to Australia. In 1923-1924 the former line's *Principessa Giovanna* and *Principessa Maria* called briefly at Fremantle en route to the eastern states. These vessels, both around 8300 tons, provided fairly basic accommodation for up to 400 emigrants, and were typical of those engaged in this trade. The depression led to the collapse of the emigrant trade but the Italian Government ensured the maintenance of the service by paying an increased subsidy and arranging the merger of the Lloyd Sabaudo and Navigazione Generale Italiana into the Italia Line in 1932. This line operated the Australian service in conjunction with the Cosulich Line. A further reorganisation four years later left the Australian service in the hands of yet another Italian line, Lloyd Trestino. The Second World War halted the service and the company was not able to resume it until 1948.

Japan took advantage of the disruption caused by the First World War to expand the services offered by its shipping lines. Aided by subsidies and the depreciation of the yen, Japanese shipping began to make substantial gains, mainly at the expense of British and Dutch shipping.[53] However, liner services between Japan and Australia offered by Nippon Yusen Kaisha, Osaka Shosen Kaisha and other leading Japanese companies terminated at eastern states' ports and did not call at Fremantle. By the late 1930s Japanese shipping dominated trade between

---

[53]For a general survey of the development of Japanese shipping ,see T. Chida and P.N. Davies, *The Japanese Shipping and Shipbuilding Industries. A History of Their Modern Growth* (London, 1990).

Australia and the Far East and in 1938 the Australian government intervened to establish an agreement on cargo-sharing between the Japanese lines and the Eastern and Australian Steamship Company (significantly, another member of the P&O Group). All shipping links with Japan were cut during the Second World War and liner services to Australia were not re-opened until 1952. The bulk of Japanese shipping visiting Fremantle has always been engaged in the tramp trade and has come to pick up cargoes like wheat and flour. Vessels owned by companies such as Kawasaki Kisen Kaisha, Kokusai Kisen Kaisha and Kawasaki Zosen Kaisha (the three operated jointly as the "K Line" until 1927) and Yamashita Kisen Kaisha called at Fremantle. A major restructuring of Japanese shipping companies in 1964 led to many mergers including Kawasaki Kisen Kaisha with Iino Kisen and Yamashita Kisen with Shin Nihon Kisen.

Table 4.3 shows the proportion of ships entering Fremantle in 1964-1965 and 1994-1995 classified by their country of registration. It is necessary to stress that registration is not necessarily an indication of the origins or destinations of cargoes carried because the fleets of many countries, such as Norway and Greece, are primarily engaged in cross-trading.

Table 4.3 reveals that by the mid-1990s the ship nationalities, which dominated the first fifty years of the port's history, had declined significantly. While this decline was partly due to the changing trade patterns discussed in the previous chapter, especially the reorientation of trade away from Europe towards Asia, it was also caused by the changing pattern of ownership in the world shipping industry. Between 1970 and 1983 the share of world tonnage registered in OECD countries fell from sixty-five percent to forty-five percent.[54] United Kingdom-registered shipping entering Fremantle had dwindled to four percent of the total and visits by some other European fleets including Italy, the Netherlands and Norway had also declined. By contrast, the number of entries by FOC ships had increased. Entries by the two major FOC fleets, those of Panama and Liberia, had grown from four percent to sixteen percent of the total, while in 1994-1995 the FOC fleet of the Bahamas accounted for six percent of entries. Another major change was the increase in Japanese registered vessels, which increased from four percent to nineteen percent of entries. The spectacular postwar growth of the Greek shipping industry

[54]E.G. Frankel, *The World Shipping Industry* (London, 1987), 20.

is not reflected in entries into Fremantle because Greek vessels averaged only about five to six percent of entries.[55] Visits by vessels registered in Singapore, Malaysia and South Africa have increased significantly. The growth of the livestock trade has also led to regular visits by vessels registered in countries such as Kuwait, Iran, and Qatar. The number of Australian registered vessels visiting the port fell from nineteen percent to ten percent of the total. The majority of Australian vessels were engaged in the protected coastal trades where, ever since the end of the Second World War, shipping had been fighting a losing battle with land and air transport for passengers and general cargo.

Coastal Shipping Services

The coastline of Western Australia stretches for over 12,500 kilometres and covers more than one-third of the total coastline of Australia; a voyage from Fremantle to Darwin and back is about 7000 kilometres or one-half of the distance from Fremantle to the United Kingdom. The large tidal range in the north western ports and the primitive port facilities meant that vessels had to be specially designed to withstand the strain of resting on the seabed at low tide. Given these factors and the sparse population, the cost of providing coastal shipping services was high and regular services were slow to develop.

The first regular steam shipping services in Western Australia were developed as feeder routes for passengers and cargo to and from Albany, where they linked up with the Imperial and inter-colonial trunk lines.[56] The Adelaide Steamship Company entered the Western Australian trade in 1883 when it took over a local shipping company. It dominated the coastal trade until the gold rushes of the 1890s attracted other companies into the trade: McIlwraith McEacharn Ltd., the Australian United Steamship Navigation Company and the Melbourne Steamship Company were offering regular services between the eastern states and Western Australia before the end of the nineteenth century. Huddart Parker Ltd. soon followed with a service from Sydney steaming via

---

[55]For details see G. Harlaftis, *Greek Shipowners and Greece 1945-1975* (London, 1993); and Harlaftis, *A History of Greek-Owned Shipping. The Making of an International Tramp Fleet, 1830 to the Present Day* (London, 1996).

[56]This paragraph draws on B. Pemberton, *Australian Coastal Shipping* (Melbourne, 1979), 23 and 140.

Melbourne, Albany, Hamelin, Vasse, Bunbury, Fremantle to Geraldton. The Adelaide Steamship Company had a slight advantage over these companies because it obtained the mail contract for the north-west coast in 1893. The contract was renewed in 1896, 1901, 1907 and 1910. By the latter year the subsidy from the government was worth £5000 per annum.[57] Initially, the other companies competed strongly for the general cargo, passenger and coal trades. But in 1899 the interstate shipowners formed the Australasian Steamship Owners' Federation and this "combine" was accused of charging excessive freight rates and providing inadequate services. There was certainly considerable evidence of collaboration amongst the interstate companies before the First World War, particularly in the coal trade.[58] Feeling against the companies was so strong that the West Australian manager of the Adelaide Steamship Company told the 1906 Royal Commission on the Navigation Bill that "it is almost an indictable offence to belong to an interstate shipping company."[59]

In 1884 Trinder, Anderson and Company in partnership with Charles Bethell and Company, introduced a steamship service between Fremantle and Singapore, calling at north-west ports and Batavia en route. The *Natal* (618 tons) connected with the P&O's steamer service, enabling passengers and goods to be trans-shipped for carriage to and from the United Kingdom. In 1886 the West Australian Steam Navigation Company (WASN) was formed to take over this service and was to continue operating until 1936. Alfred Holt's Ocean Steamship Company was also keen to secure a share of this "connecting trade" and in 1889 reached an agreement with the WASN Company whereby Holt's vessel *Saladin* (1,990 tons), carried the WASN Company's trade from Singapore to Australia, while the latter Company acted as West Australian agents for Holt's vessel.[60] The *Sultan* (2062 tons), a steamer jointly owned by both companies, joined the trade in 1894 and was the first ocean going vessel to enter Fremantle's Inner Harbour. By 1895 their ships were calling every three weeks at Geraldton, Shark Bay, Carnarvon Roads, Ashburton

---

[57]AA Prime Minister's Department, CRS A461, correspondence files, 1934-1950, I418/2/6 Pt. 2, "NW Coast (WA) Mail Contract," 6 May 1937.

[58]Burley, *British Shipping*, 22.

[59]Australia, *Report of the Royal Commission on the Navigation Bill 1906* (No. 30), minutes of evidence, 575, cited by Bach, *Maritime History*, 211.

[60]See F.E. Hyde, *Far Eastern Trade 1860-1914* (London, 1973), 168-171.

Roads, Roebuck Bay Roads, the Pearling Grounds and Derby, providing a valuable service to the isolated communities in the northwest of Western Australia.[61]

In 1912, in an attempt to provide competition for Alfred Holt and Company and the eastern states' lines, the Scaddan Labor Government established the State Shipping Service (SSS). The SSS is of special interest because it is the only shipping line to have used Fremantle as a homeport. As we saw in chapter 2, it was administered by the FHT between 1913 and 1919 after its financial affairs got into disarray under its first manager. In 1913 the government awarded the northwest mail contract to the SSS and the Adelaide Steamship Company withdrew from the northwest route.

The SSS's first ships were the *Una* (178 tons) and the *Eucla* (564 tons), both of which were mainly employed on the south coast route to Eucla. By 1915 the fleet had expanded to include the *Western Australia* (2937 tons), the *Kwinana* (2425 tons), the *Bambra* (3302 tons) and the *Kangaroo* (4434 tons). The latter vessel was the first Australian owned motor vessel and only the second motor ship built by a British shipyard. By the outbreak of the First World War the SSS called regularly at Geraldton, Shark Bay, Carnarvon Jetty, Ashburton Roads, Cossack Roads, Balla Balla Anchorage, Port Hedland, Broome, Derby and Wyndham. The service was extended to Darwin in 1920 and Java and Singapore in 1921. The WASN Company withdrew from the northwest coast service in the mid-1930s leaving the trade to Alfred Holt and Company and the SSS.

In 1926 the federal government agreed to amend the Navigation Act to allow British vessels to operate on the coast under a permit system. In 1935 this permit system was placed on a statutory basis. Alfred Holt and Company took advantage of this to operate unlicensed ships on its service along the coast of Western Australia. Although the Western Australian service was only a minor part of Holt's operations, it was consistently profitable, averaging net earnings of £20,605 per annum

---

[61]Pemberton, *Australian Coastal Shipping*, 29-31.

between 1922 and 1939.[62] Attempts by the state government to drive Holt and Company from the trade were resisted by the federal government.[63]

For Holt and Company, the SSS and other shipping lines engaged in the coastal trades, the outbreak of the Second World War ushered in an era of decline. The federal government requisitioned many coastal vessels and the resulting shortage of shipping capacity forced much cargo to be diverted to road transport. In 1947 the surviving vessels were returned to their owners but the coastal trade failed to regain most of the diverted cargo. By 1949-1950, interstate cargoes carried by sea around Australia had fallen to 15.6 million tons, compared to 18.0 million tons in 1938-1939.[64] By the late 1950s Australia's six capital city ports together only handled 2.4 million tons of interstate general cargo. Between 1938-1939 and 1958-1959 the total tonnage of interstate cargoes handled at Fremantle increased from 0.4 million tons to 1.1 million tons but this was due to the bulk cargoes handled in the Outer Harbour; significantly, general cargo traffic plummeted from about 165,000 tons to 37,000 tons, a fall of seventy-eight percent.

A major reason for the demise of coastal shipping was the growing competitiveness of land transport and civil aviation. In the 1950s road forwarding companies were experimenting with door-to-door services and other measures to improve the quality of service while in the shipping industry goods were sent by local carriers to the ports and collected by the consignees on arrival with no one assuming overall responsibility for the movements of the goods.[65] In 1954 the legislation levying charges on interstate road transport was declared invalid, giving a further stimulus to road haulage. The shipowners, by contrast, were plagued with waterfront disputes and problems of excess capacity.[66] Many of the vessels were obsolete, with small holds and limited handling gear. This excess capacity and rising costs led to pressure to raise freight rates,

---

[62]M. Falkus, *The Blue Funnel Legend. A History of the Ocean Steam Ship Company, 1865-1973* (Basingstoke, 1990), 219.

[63]AA, I418/2/6 Pt. 2, "NW Coast (WA) Mail Contract," 6 May 1937.

[64]Australian Stevedoring Industry Authority, *Annual Reports*.

[65]For a discussion of these developments, see P.J. Rimmer, *Freight Forwarding in Australia* (Canberra, 1970).

[66]For an account of their problems see Bach, *Maritime History*, ch. XVII.

further driving away trade. Between 1939 and 1950 interstate freight rates almost quadrupled, whereas the retail price index increased less than twofold. In 1957 motor bodies could be transported from Melbourne to Adelaide by rail at fifty-five percent of the cost by sea or sixty-seven percent of the cost by road. The cost of transporting motor car tyres between Melbourne and Adelaide by rail was only nineteen percent of the cost by sea.[67] In April 1957 the FHT complained that wool transported from Melbourne to Western Australia cost seventy-one shillings per bale by sea compared to sixty-two shillings by rail. This was despite the fact that the wool had to be transhipped three times due to breaks of railway gauge. The shipping companies agreed to reduce the rate to fifty-nine shillings but the FHT estimated it had lost 200,000 tons of cargo to the railways.[68] Given the cost and quality advantages of land transport it is hardly surprising that sea transport's share of the freight market declined.

In an attempt to revitalise the Singapore-Fremantle trade, Holt and Company introduced a specially designed vessel, the *Centaur*, into the run in 1964. Despite some initial success, the service lost money, but the vessel was not withdrawn until 1981. The SSS survived only due to the continued willingness of Western Australian governments to subsidise its operations on the grounds that it provided an essential service to the isolated communities of the northwest. But as road and air links to the northwest improved this argument became harder to sustain. Between 1968 and 1978 the proportion of freight carried between Perth and the north-west by sea fell from about sixty-four percent to twenty-five percent.[69] A major problem was finding sufficient cargo for the south-bound voyage to Fremantle. The SSS was carrying only about one third of the northwest wool clip as pastoralists preferred to use road transport. Moreover, schedules and operations were subject to political pressures. A vessel once called into Point Samson to pick up a pensioner who was travelling on his annual free trip, although it would have been cheaper to send him to Perth by taxi![70] Despite such farcical incidents, passengers

---

[67]Data is from Tariff Board, *Annual Report,* 1956-1957; Australia, Parliament, *Debates* (1957-1958), IV, 1313-1371.

[68]FPA, Minutes, 12 April, 21 June, and 12 July 1957.

[69]Bureau of Transport Economics, *A Study of Western Australian Ports* (Canberra, 1981), 128.

[70]*The West Australia*, 5 February 1964.

were carried until 16 March 1973 when the last passenger stepped off the *Kangaroo* at Fremantle. The service (which was restructured and renamed the Western Australian Coastal Shipping Commission in 1965) struggled on until 1995 when it was finally closed by the state government. A detailed history of the line is yet to be written.[71]

There is no doubt that, to some extent, competition between shipping and land transport was distorted by government policy. In view of the railways record of loss-making shipping interests complained that the railways received "hidden" subsides because their losses fell on state finances. Similarly, it was argued that road hauliers did not make sufficient contribution to the upkeep of the road system and were also being subsidised.[72] In Western Australia a 1966 Act limited the transport of imported cargoes by road to a forty miles radius from the centre of Perth; beyond that distance it had to be transported by rail.[73] However, the heavily subsidised State Shipping Service boosted Fremantle's trade, so the subsidies were far from one-sided.

In Australia, the large distances between the capital cities has made air transport as well as land transport a force to be reckoned with, especially for high valued cargoes and, obviously, for passenger traffic. In the previous chapter we saw that by the late 1960s air transport had won the battle for passengers, but, as late as 1989-1990, shipping still accounted for about eighty percent of Australia's overseas trade by value and ninety-nine percent by weight. As far as the shipping industry is concerned, technological change is a double-edged sword, for while it has ensured the continued viability of shipping as a mode of transport, it has also made land and air transport more efficient than shipping for some transport tasks.

Technological Change in Shipping

It is widely recognised that by the outbreak of the First World War the world's shipping industry had been revolutionised by a number of

---

[71]For a brief in-house history, see A.M. Stephens, *The Stateships Story* (Perth, 1977).

[72]J.P. Williams, "The Problems Facing Australian Shipping in the Next Decade" (Unpublished paper presented to the Economics Society of Australia and New Zealand, Victorian Branch, Melbourne, 1960).

[73]FPA 87/976 Pt. 1, *Road and Air Transport Commission Act* of 1966.

technological innovations. These included the change from wooden to iron and then to steel ships, the replacement of sail by steam and the introduction of the compound and triple-expansion engines. These innovations contributed to increased productivity in ocean transportation and were a major factor in the expansion of world trade and the emergence of an integrated world economy.[74] Although Australia benefited from these developments, Geoffrey Blainey has suggested that the steamship did not make a major contribution to the growth of overseas trade until the early years of the twentieth century. According to Blainey it was from the 1920s onwards that shipping was most successful in overcoming the "tyranny of distance:"

> The cost of crossing the ocean was pared down by the increasing size of the average ship, the shift from coal to oil or diesel fuel, the adoption of bulk carriers for many cargoes ranging from sugar to oil, the cheaper tolls charged by the Suez Canal, and the more frequent use of the Panama Canal which saved 3,500 miles between Sydney and New York.[75]

However, Frank Broeze has suggested that cheap ocean freight rates and the increasing efficiency of steamship services had already done much to reduce Australia's isolation in the second half of the nineteenth century: "where it counted, the ocean was no tariff wall but a cheap and commodious highway."[76] It is not our intention to discuss the development of shipping technology in detail; we merely focus briefly on those developments of importance for Fremantle.

---

[74]See D.C. North, "Ocean Freight Rates and Economic Development 1750-1913," *Journal of Economic History*, XVIII (1958), 537-555; and K.M. Gwilliam, "The Development of the World Transport Market," in T.I. Williams (ed.), *A History of Technology*, VII, part 2 (Oxford, 1978), 692.

[75]G. Blainey, *The Tyranny of Distance* (Melbourne, 1966), 287-288.

[76]F. Broeze, "The Tyranny of Distance: A Flawed Paradigm," in A. Markus and M.C. Ricklefs (eds.), *Surrender Australia? Essays in the Study and Uses of History* (Sydney, 1985), 67. See also D.C. North, "The Role of Transportation in the Economic Development of North America," in *Les grandes voies maritimes dans le monde, XVe-XIXe siècles* (Paris, 1965), 209-246.

Graeme Henderson has shown that the transition from steam to sail in Western Australia was very rapid due largely to the advanced state of steam technology by the time it was first introduced into Western Australian waters.[77] The first steamship to enter the coastal trade was the *Xantho* in the early 1870s.[78] By the late 1890s sail traffic was confined to bulk cargoes such as timber and coal. On the eve of the First World War sailing vessels accounted for a mere one percent of the vessels entering Fremantle. By the early 1920s only a few sailing ships were calling and during the 1930s they virtually disappeared from all Australian ports.[79]

Apart from the switch from sail to steam, there were other important changes in engine technology. The original steamers were coal burners but in the interwar years their efficiency was improved by the adoption of oil-firing and the use of turbines instead of the original reciprocating engines. In 1912 the first diesel powered ocean-going liner, the *Selandia*, was built for the Danish East Asiatic Company. Diesel powered motorships offered significant advances over steamships including greater fuel economy, but in the inter-war years were more costly to run at speed and not as reliable. Diesel engines appear to have been less economic than steam propulsion on vessels larger than about 10,000 but they proved popular with shipowners in the Australian trade. In 1939, for example, less than a quarter of world tonnage was equipped with diesel engines but about one-third of the tonnage entering Sydney and Melbourne was diesel-powered. The Scandinavian lines led the way in the adoption of the motorship: by 1939, for example, sixty-two percent of the Norwegian fleet consisted of motor tonnage, whereas only forty-five percent of the British fleet and about five percent of the American fleet comprised motor tonnage.[80] The leading British lines were relatively slow to adopt motorships (except for the members of the ill-fated Royal Mail group) and most motorships that visited Fremantle before the Second

---

[77]G. Henderson, "From Sail to Steam: Shipping in Western Australia 1870-1890" (Unpublished MA thesis, University of Western Australia, 1977).

[78]See M. McCarthy, "Charles Edward Broadhurst (1826-1905): A Remarkable Nineteenth Century Failure" (Unpublished MPhil thesis, Murdoch University, 1989).

[79]This and the following paragraph draw on Burley, *British Shipping*, 92-96.

[80]K. Petersen, *The Saga of Norwegian Shipping* (Oslo, 1955), 84.

World War belonged to non-British lines.[81] As we saw in the previous chapter, the change from coal to oil as a fuel had major implications for Fremantle's bunkering trade. By the late 1930s coal bunkering had virtually ceased.

Turning to the size of vessels, there were steady increases in the first three or four decades of the twentieth century. Between 1910 and 1927 the average gross tonnage of the twenty largest vessels afloat increased from 28,000 to 35,800 tons.[82] Anxious port authorities the world over wondered how to provide adequate facilities for such "leviathans:"

> A race between engineers: such might describe the condition of affairs in the maritime world of to-day in regard to two of the most important branches of civil engineering. On the one hand, we have the ship designers turning out larger and larger vessels; on the other is the harbour engineer, striving vainly to provide a sufficient depth of water in which to float these large steamships. It is a tremendous struggle. The former has set the pace, and the latter finds it hot, so much so that he is hard put to it to keep on his rival's heels.[83]

The world's largest ships, however, were engaged in the Trans-Atlantic trade and did not visit Australia. As late as 1939, the largest commercial vessel to visit Fremantle was the *Dominion Monarch* of 27,155 tons. She was built for the Shaw, Savill and Albion Line and was a fast passenger-cargo ship, with accommodation for 525 first class passengers only. In

---

[81]See G.R. Henning and K. Trace, "Britain and the Motorship: A Case of the Delayed Adoption of New Technology," *Journal of Economic History*, XXXV (1975), 353-385; and A.S. Mallett and A.M.B. Bell, *The Pirrie-Kylsant Motorships 1915-1932* (Coltishall, 1984).

[82]FPA 108/28/1/2, "Some Notes on Harbour Engineering," lecture given by F.W.H. Stileman to Sixth Interstate Harbour Conference, 1928.

[83]FPA 90/12/3, cited in "Notes on Harbour Engineering," by H.D. Walsh, Engineer-in-Chief, Sydney Harbour Trust.

fact, in 1939 ships of less than 6000 tons still accounted for fifty-seven percent of world tonnage.[84]

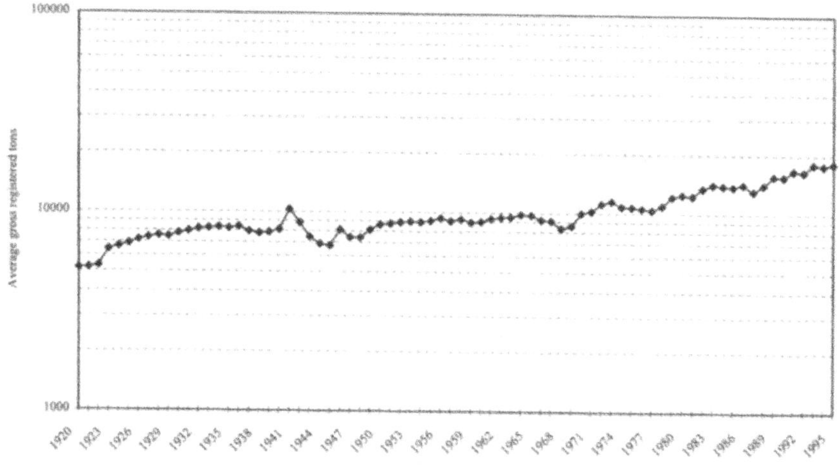

Figure 4.2: The Average Size of Ships Calling at Fremantle, 1919-1920 to 1995-1996.

Source: Calculated from data in Appendix A.

Figure 4.2 shows that the average size of ships calling at Fremantle grew steadily at about 1.2 percent per annum between 1919-1920 and 1995-1996. By 1995-96 the average visitor was 19,000 tons compared to only 5200 tons in 1919-1920. Of course, averages give no indication of the largest ships entering and therefore of the extreme demands on port facilities. In 1908-1909 almost ninety percent of ships calling were less than 5000 tons and no vessel over 10,000 tons entered port; by 1938-1939 vessels of 10,000 tons and over accounted for over one-quarter of entries. In the 1990s the port was catering for vessels of up to 130,000 tons in the Outer Harbour.

When planning port facilities the port authority is not just interested in the size of ships measured in terms of tonnage, but also in their length, beam and draught. In 1939 the average length of ships visiting Fremantle was 450 feet and the longest about 658 feet. In normal conditions the narrow curved entrance to the harbour limited ships to 750 feet in length but in fact longer ships were occasionally berthed. For

[84]G. Alexandersson and G. Norstrom, *World Shipping* (London, 1963), 30.

example, in 1924 the battle cruiser HMS *Hood*, 861 feet long and drawing thirty-three feet, was safely berthed in the Inner Harbour.[85] However, in 1922 the Orient Line expressed doubts about whether its lengthy 20,000 ton steamers could be safely handled in adverse weather conditions.[86] The *Hood's* record was not surpassed until February 1985 when the *Queen Elizabeth 2*, of 294 metres in length and 67,140 tons berthed at the passenger terminal. Generally speaking, until the 1950s, the length and beam of ships did not pose any major problems at Fremantle.

The draught of ships is another matter. It is costly and time consuming to provide deep-water berths. The decision to deepen Fremantle's Inner Harbour from thirty feet to thirty-six feet in 1916 eventually doubled the capital cost of the port.[87] Moreover, even one of the largest passenger liners took a relatively short time to construct when compared to the time required to cut channels and construct docks and wharves. The deepest draft vessel to call at Fremantle before the Second World War was the whale factory ship *Terje Viken* of 20,638 tons. She arrived in March 1939 and after taking on bunker fuel left drawing thirty-four feet nine inches of water. However, given that in the same year almost ninety percent of ships using the port drew twenty-eight feet or less, it is debatable whether the decision to deepen the harbour was justified. The decision had been influenced by the recommendations of the Dominion's Royal Commission (1913-1917) for deepening of the Suez Canal. In chapter 5, where harbour deepening is discussed in detail, we shall see that the FHT's desire to cater for the top spectrum of liner shipping frequently led them to neglect economic considerations. Moreover, as most port revenue came from cargo rather than ships the large liners did not make a proportionate contribution to the cost of establishing and running the port.

After the Second World War, technological advances and the search for economies of scale, caused ship size to "take-off." The closure of the Suez Canal during the Suez crisis in 1956 accelerated the tendency for bulk carriers to increase in size because shipowners needed to offset the higher cost of steaming around the Cape of Good Hope. By the early

---

[85]FPA 109/23/1, "Visit of Special British Service Squadron."

[86]FPA 60/23/2-3, T. Day, Manager, Perth Branch of the Orient Line, to FHT, 29 December 1922.

[87]Tydeman, *Fremantle*, II, 48.

1970s bulk carriers and oil tankers in excess of 200,000 dwt traversed the world's oceans. Bulk carriers of over 40,000 dwt accounted for twenty-three percent of the world fleet, compared to only four percent a decade earlier.[88] Fremantle, along with Australia's other capital city ports, was increasingly becoming swamped by industrial, commercial and residential development and was finding it difficult to provide adequate depths and space for the largest bulk carriers and tankers. This was a major factor in the port's decision in the 1950s to break out of the confines of the river and develop new port facilities in Cockburn Sound. The Outer Harbour offered natural anchorages with up to sixty-foot depths but extensive dredging was necessary to provide access to the Sound. In 1954 the channels through Success and Parmelia Banks were dredged to thirty-eight feet, and in 1967 to forty-five feet, enabling vessels of up to 70,000 dwt to use the port. However, as we have seen, in the 1990s the average ship calling was an 18,000 tonner rather than a "giant" of 100,000 tons or more. This is not just due to depth limitations but is a reflection of the nature of the port's trade which includes general cargo where the tendency to increased size has not been as marked as in the bulk cargo trade. The major changes in the general cargo trade were in cargo-handling techniques rather than ship size.

The post-Second World War period has seen the introduction of revolutionary new innovations in cargo-handling technology which have made shipping and port operations much more capital intensive. Bulk cargoes, because of their homogenous nature, presented less obstacles to the development of mechanical handling than the more heterogeneous general cargoes, and consequently the potential benefits of mechanisation were realised earlier for bulk cargoes than for general cargoes.

The world's first bulk carrier was probably the *John Bowes*, which was introduced into the coaling trade on the northeast coast of Britain in 1852. This ship had basic features that went unchanged for many years. These included a single deck, large hatches, water ballast spaces and machinery placed aft.[89] Around the turn of the century bulk carriage spread into the overseas trades, but until the Second World War few ships were designed purely as bulk carriers. However, in the 1950s

---

[88]FPA 88/1/6/9, "Port Development in Australia."

[89]G.R. Smith and I.L. Buxton, "The Development of the Bulk Carrier" (Unpublished paper presented to a conference on tanker and bulk carrier terminals, Institution of Engineers, London, November 1969).

a new era of specialised ships, incorporating major technological refinements, began. By the 1960s, for example, many new ships incorporated a bulbous bow, which reduced the hull's water resistance, especially when the vessel was in ballast. In 1968 a major review of the loadline standard, the first for over thirty years, permitted a reduction in freeboard, especially on larger vessels. This meant shipowners gained an immediate increase in capacity at virtually zero cost. The development of self-trimming, whereby bulk cargoes such as coal could be loaded by gravity, avoiding the need to trim cargo into the corners of the hold, greatly speeded up handling. Fremantle saw the first of these vessels in 1961 when the *Tresfonn* loaded bulk wheat into its one million cubic feet of hold space and the *Ringulv* loaded a cargo of pyritic ash for Japan, both using self trimming hatches. Increasingly, bulk carriers were not provided with ship board cargo-handling gear, relying instead on the provision of specialised handling facilities in the ports.

The post-Second World War trend towards specialisation in the tramp and tanker trades can be illustrated by the history of the Indian owned Great Eastern Shipping Company Ltd. This was established in 1948, a year after India gained independence, and was forced to specialise in the tramp trade because India's liner trades were dominated by foreign shipping lines. After the Second World War the USA sold off cheaply many liberty ships (the standardised vessels turned out in large numbers to combat the huge shipping losses during the war) and the company purchased a number of these as they "were the perfect work horses for the bulk cargo trades."[90] By the early 1950s the Company owned sixteen general purpose tramp vessels, ranging in size from the MV *Jag Ganga* and MV *Jag Jamna* (both 2008 dwt), to the MT *Jag Jyoti* (13,125 dwt). Its vessels were engaged from time to time in the carriage of wheat from Australia to India. For example, the company's first vessel, the ex-liberty ship, *Jag Vijay* (10,670 dwt), loaded 9750 tons of wheat at Fremantle in June 1953 and another, the *Jag Shanti* (9395 dwt), loaded 8,720 tons of wheat at Fremantle in March 1955. By the early 1990s the Company's fleet comprised forty-four specialised bulk carriers, tankers and offshore supply vessels. The largest tanker was the MT *Jag Laadki*, (144,993 dwt) and the largest bulk carrier the MV *Jag Leela* (124,100 dwt).

By the mid-1960s non-bulk cargoes had shrunk to about a quarter of the total volume of world trade but still cost more to transport than bulk

---

[90]S.N. Sanklecha, *Tramping to Success. Story of the Great Eastern Shipping Company Limited* (Bombay, 1994), 16.

cargoes.[91] This was basically due to the labour intensive nature of the operations. The conventional general cargo operation involved lifting cargo in units of two to five tons, with extensive manhandling in the ship's hold, on the shore and in the transit sheds.[92] Some idea of the inefficiency of general cargo operations can be gauged from the fact that Blue Funnel vessels engaged in the Australian trade spent up to sixty percent of their time in port; moreover, only fifteen percent or so of the time in port was actually spent working cargoes, the remainder was taken with waiting for clearances, delays caused by weekends, night-time, industrial action and other factors.[93] The escalating cost of handling these cargoes eventually forced shipowners to introduce radical technological innovations -- so radical in fact, that they have been likened in their effect to the transition from sail to steam.

The first innovation that occurred was in the coastal trade where shipowners were battling to regain trade lost to land transport. In 1959 the Australian National Line's (ANL) roll on/roll off (RO/RO) vessels *Princess of Tasmania* and *Bass Trader* were introduced into the run between Melbourne and Tasmania. RO/RO vessels represented an extension of ferry operations whereby the cargo was rolled on and off via stern doors. They provided for faster turnround times in port and did not require extensive berthing facilities so they could be operated in smaller ports. Some vessels were equipped with their own loading ramps while others relied on shore based ones.

The introduction of unitised cargo further improved efficiency. Unitised cargo is cargo that is pre-wrapped and packed on standard pallets and evolved from the use of forklift trucks with pallets in the Second World War. This is an intermediate technology in the sense that unitised cargo could be handled by conventional ships, yet the use of large standardised units speeded up cargo-handling and the experience gained helped pave the way for the more revolutionary container concept.

The container system involves the transport of cargo in standard boxes in specialised ships, with a highly mechanised handling process.

---

[91]R.O. Goss, *Studies in Maritime Economics* (Cambridge, 1970), 153.

[92]S. Gillman, "An Investigation into Some Effects of New Handling Technologies on the Structure of Maritime Transport Systems," *Maritime Studies and Management,* II (1975), 166.

[93]Falkus, *Blue Funnel,* 358. See also Goss, *Studies in Maritime Economics*, 153.

The technique was revolutionary in the sense that it offered a great technological opportunity for improved efficiency in transport.[94] For many years some cargo, such as fragile goods had been shipped in boxes but no attempt was made to ship large amounts of cargo this way until the 1950s. In 1957 Malcolm McLean's Company, Sea-Land Service Inc., built cells for holding containers into six conventional ships in the eastern seaboard trade in the USA. This experiment was so successful that by the mid-1960s eighty-five percent of general cargo in the protected coastal trade was carried in containers.[95]

In 1964 Associated Steamships Pty. Ltd. introduced the *Kooringah* on the route between Fremantle and Melbourne. This ship was the first purpose built cellular container vessel in the world and its arrival at Fremantle on 19 June 1964 marked the beginning of a new era in Australia's protected coastal trades. In 1969 the company introduced two more vessels to provide a service around the coastline between Brisbane and Fremantle. In 1970 ANL introduced the *Darwin Trader*, a combination cellular/bulk cargo vessel into their fleet. It carried general and refrigerated cargo northwards to Darwin in containers and returned southwards loaded with manganese ore from Groote Eylandt. Such hybrid vessels helped shipowners obtain full loads on both legs of a voyage and provided a hedge against the uncertainty of trends in world trade.

One of the most striking characteristics of container ships is that they are usually "gearless," that is, they depend on shore terminals with gantry cranes to handle the containers, rather than ships' gear. By avoiding the need to include on-board handling gear considerable economies in ship construction are possible.

Container vessels were, however, slower to appear in the international trades because, unlike the coastal trades, these were not protected and the risks of innovation were far greater. The first major innovation was the introduction of Skandia-type vessels, which are wide-hatched open-decked vessels with cranes that can handle palletised and container cargo. The first of these ships to visit Fremantle was the MV *Waitara* in December 1966. By the late 1960s Skandia-type vessels were frequent visitors to Australian ports.

---

[94]K.M. Johnson and H.C. Garnett, *The Economics of Containerisation* (London, 1971), 39.

[95]A.A. Evans, *Technical and Social Changes in The World's Ports* (Geneva, 1969), 8.

In March 1966 the world's first fully integrated container service was introduced into the North Atlantic trade by Sea-Land Service Inc. which enjoyed the security of a long term contract supplying the US Army in West Germany. It was not until three years later that the first overseas container vessel, *Encounter Bay*, tied up at Fremantle. By the early 1970s about fourteen container vessels were regularly engaged in the Australia/UK/European trade. In February 1993 the *Encounter Bay* visited Fremantle for the 100th time.

The shipowners scheduled a turnaround time of 100 hours on the Australian coast compared to three to four weeks on the coast for conventional vessels. It was estimated that this would reduce the total voyage time between Europe and Australia from 146 to sixty-three days, a saving of about forty-three percent.[96] However, teething problems with the ships and containers plus delays caused by industrial disputes, meant that the full potential of containerisation was not immediately realised. The first frozen cargo of meat landed at Fremantle in March 1969 was tainted by styrene used in the insulation of the containers and all refrigerated containers had to be replaced.[97] The successful handling of containers requires efficient land transit facilities and extensive areas for cargo-handling and storage: facilities not easily provided in cramped metropolitan ports.

The implications of containerisation were as momentous for the port as for the shipowners. At a simple physical level, the port skyline was altered by the presence of the giant skyscraper cranes located on the container terminal at the North Wharf. The luffing cranes used to handle general cargo gradually fell into disuse and straddled the wharves, idle and unsaleable; wooden wharves began to crumble; and most of the cargo sheds echoed only with the memory of bustling stevedoring activity. The new bulk handling facilities in the Outer Harbour attracted trade away from the Inner Harbour and by the 1970s the river port and, to some extent, the City of Fremantle, had acquired a "decaying" image. The size of the stevedoring workforce at Fremantle fell from about 1800 persons in the 1950s to about 370 in the early 1990s. It is clear that the port was forced to adapt to enormous changes imposed externally. The impact of

---

[96]P.E. Stonham, "Conferences and Competition in Australia's Overseas Liner Trades," *Economic Record*, XLVI (1970), 203.

[97]Falkus, *Blue Funnel*, 366-367.

naval shipping on the port, especially during wartime, provides another example of a compelling external force for change.

Naval Shipping at the Port of Fremantle

Fremantle has never been a major naval port but has some strategic importance due to its location on the eastern shores of the Indian Ocean. The decision by the British to establish an outpost at Albany in 1826 was based on the desire to prevent the French from occupying the coastline. The founder and first governor of the colony of Western Australia, James Stirling, was a naval officer, although the colony was established for commercial rather than strategic reasons. The visit of HMS *Driver* in 1846 caused some alarm as it was the first steamship to call at Fremantle and, as the lookout at Rottnest had never seen a steamer before, he thought it was on fire and declared an emergency. Between 1829 and 1914 Fremantle was visited by about fifty naval vessels but none were permanently stationed in Western Australia; their visits were primarily "flag waving" exercises.[98] By the beginning of the twentieth century, with British colonies scattered around the Indian Ocean and the sea policed by the powerful Royal Navy, the Indian Ocean was effectively "a British lake."[99]

In 1911, the year the Royal Australian Navy (RAN) was created, Admiral Sir Reginald Henderson recommended the establishment of a naval base at Cockburn Sound, south of Fremantle. The Commonwealth acquired a strip of land along the edge of the Sound but little work was done and plans for the naval base were dropped in 1921. The First World War had little direct impact on the port. A convoy carrying the Anzacs to Europe left from Albany in November 1914 and did not call at Fremantle. In 1924 the battle cruiser HMS *Hood* (45,000 tons) became the largest vessel to ever enter the Inner Harbour. Its record was not surpassed until the arrival of the aircraft carrier HMS *Ark Royal* (57,000 tons) in 1962. During the 1930s Australia became increasingly anxious about Japanese

---

[98]F. Broeze and G. Henderson, *Western Australians and The Sea. Our Maritime Heritage* (Perth, 1986), 53.

[99]K. McPherson, *The Indian Ocean. A History of People and The Sea* (Oxford, 1993), 252; and Rear Admiral A. Robertson, quoted in *The Weekend Australian*, 7-8 March 1987.

expansionism but trusted British reassurances that their naval base at Singapore guaranteed Australia's security.

The outbreak of war in 1939 did not immediately lead to attacks on Australian ports and cities. In 1939 two eight-inch guns were established on Rottnest Island to protect the approaches to Fremantle. Luckily the guns never had to fire a shot in anger and, together with their associated buildings and tunnels, they have been preserved as an historic site. In July 1943 the Navy took over the operation of the Rottnest signal station; it was returned to the FHT at the end of the war but it was closed in 1949 as improved wireless communications had rendered it obsolete.[100]

As far as Fremantle was concerned, one of the first impacts of the war was the withdrawal of the interstate passenger vessels *Kanimbla, Manoora* and *Westralia* which were requisitioned by the RAN in October 1939 and commissioned as armed merchant cruisers. Although the weekly mail services to and from Europe were disrupted, initially there was little effect on the volume of traffic as the harbour had to cope with the arrival of warships, troop transports, hospital ships and other war-related vessels. The first Australian and New Zealand troop convoy of eleven transports, escorted by the RAN cruisers *Australia* and *Canberra* and the RN battleship *Ramillies*, berthed in January 1940. On 10 May 1940, a convoy including the passenger liners *Queen Mary* and *Aquitania* arrived, but both of these vessels were too large to enter the Inner Harbour and had to be refuelled and reprovisioned in Gage Roads. The same convoy included the *Empress of Britain*, (42,348 tons) which at that time was the largest merchant vessel to enter the Inner Harbour. By the end of March 1943 the liners *Queen Mary* and *Aquitania* had visited the port nineteen and twenty times respectively in their role as troop carriers. The world's largest liner the *Queen Elizabeth* called on nine occasions between February 1941 and April 1942. While numerous RAN vessels visited the port on patrol and convoy escort duties, only one old cruiser, HMAS *Adelaide* and some corvettes, patrol boats, minesweepers and small naval craft were based at the port.[101]

---

[100]FPA, Minutes, 7 September 1945.

[101]V. Jeffrey, "A History of the Navy in the West," in Royal Australian Navy, *Australia's Navy, 1993-94* (Canberra, 1994), 58. For a discussion of general strategy during the war, see D. Stevens (ed.), *The Royal Australian Navy in World War II* (St. Leonards, NSW, 1996).

During the war years the control of the port was in the hands of the District Naval Officer who could over-ride normal port regulations. In September 1939 Western Australians lost their privilege of free access to the wharves on security grounds for the duration of the war. A defensive boom was erected at the entrance to the Inner Harbour in December 1940 and was closed between sunset and sunrise, effectively restricting shipping movements to daylight hours. A boom defence system was later installed in Cockburn Sound. In 1942 reports of sabotage in overseas ports and shipyards led to security being stepped up on the wharves.[102] Initially, FHT patrolmen and soldiers provided all the security guards but in June 1942 the federal government appointed special officers to man the wharf gates.[103] Anti-aircraft defences were erected in 1942. In the same year the chief officer of the State Fire Brigade Board warned that the harbour was inadequately equipped to deal with a major fire and, fortuitously in view of a later fire, the federal government agreed to make available two 1000-gallon-per-minute fire pumps.[104]

The outbreak of war with Japan in December 1941 and, in particular, the surrender of Singapore to the Japanese on 15 February 1942 brought the threat of military action close to the Australian mainland. Prime Minister John Curtin described the fall of Singapore as "Australia's Dunkirk," marking the start of the "Battle for Australia" just as the evacuation of Dunkirk preceded the Battle of Britain.[105] The strategic importance of Fremantle and other ports increased significantly. Many vessels crowded with refugees steamed southwards to Fremantle. In one fortnight in March 1942 a total of 103 vessels arrived and up to four vessels were tied alongside each other in the Inner Harbour.[106]

In his famous speech Prime Minister John Curtin declared that "Australia looks to America, free of any pangs as to our traditional ties or kinship with the United Kingdom" and the American armed forces, which arrived under the leadership of General Douglas MacArthur in 1942, were

---

[102]FPA 3471/NEM 74, District Naval Officer to FHT, 10 January 1942.

[103]FHT, *Annual Report* (1944-1945), 11.

[104]FPA, Minutes, 19 June 1942 and 20 August 1943.

[105]D. Lowe, "Australia in the World," in J. Beaumont (ed.), *Australia's War 1939-45* (St. Leonards, NSW, 1996), 165.

[106]FHT, *Annual Report* (1944-1945), 10.

welcomed as saviours. Troops and munitions flooded into the country - the first convoy of US troops arrived at Fremantle on 18 February 1942. In the first six months of 1943 alone more than 200 Liberty ships called at Fremantle, though most remained only long enough to load stores and water.

All this activity created unprecedented congestion in the ports.[107] The situation was worsened by major industrial unrest: between 1940 and 1945 about 180,000 man-days were lost through wharf strikes at Australian ports.[108] To a great extent this militancy was a legacy of the pre-war waterfront that had been a dismal place, characterised by irregular employment, poor working conditions and turbulent labour relations.[109] In large part, this was a result of the system of casual employment whereby men were hired by the hour or by the day; prior to the Second World War they faced a precarious struggle to earn a living wage. Cargo-handling was, moreover, a highly physical task as only limited amounts of labour-saving equipment were used, and the accident rate was high. The dismal employment conditions provided a fertile breeding ground for union militancy.

After the outbreak of war, labour became scarce and the Communist leadership of the Waterside Workers' Federation seized the opportunity to claim improved wages and working conditions for their members. The employers' power to discipline workers with the threat of sacking was weakened due to the scarcity of labour. The American forces complained that Australian wharf labourers were lazy and were smoking, stealing and even fishing during working hours. The German invasion of Russia in June 1941 caused the leadership of the WWF to change their attitude to the war but they had trouble controlling the rank-and-file. James Healy, the Communist leader of the WWF, made a radio broadcast in which he pleaded for an end to unofficial stoppages because "they are harmful to the Union, and to the Nation."[110]

---

[107]FPA 3471/91, NEM 98, Congestion on waterfont.

[108]Bach, *Maritime History,* 377.

[109]This discussion draws on M. Tull, "American Technology and the Mechanisation of Australian Ports, 1942-58," *Journal of Transport History*, VI (1985), 79-90.

[110]FPA, Minutes, 9 April and May 1943. The broadcast was made in December 1942.

The waterfront situation was posing a threat to the war effort and in 1942 the federal government established the Stevedoring Industry Commission (SIC) to try and improve turnround times and labour productivity, and the Port Equipment and Development Committee (PEDC) to advise on the provision of port facilities. In 1943 the SIC introduced the roster system whereby gangs of wharf labourers were rostered to particular jobs, irrespective of the preferences of employers or employees. This was designed to stop workers picking the least arduous jobs and favouring the higher paid night shift work. It also had the effect of spreading work more evenly, much to the dismay of employers such as the FHT, which preferred to pick men and gangs it knew to be reliable.[111] One problem was that even though wharf labouring was a reserved occupation, large numbers of young men were joining the Armed Forces and the burden was falling on older and less fit men. In other industries women stepped in to fill the gaps but they were not welcomed on the wharves. In 1943 the FHT was employing only three women in work normally done by males and this was as temporary clerks; of course, the women were all paid less than the male rates. The FHT firmly informed the manpower authorities that "work connected with the wharf is not suitable for women."[112]

The PEDC recommended improvements at Fremantle, including the deepening of the Inner Harbour and the construction of a new cargo store. The FHT provided improved washing and eating facilities for the workers. The construction of a 2000-ton slipway at the seaward end of Victoria Quay had commenced in 1940 but construction work was accelerated and the design altered to cater for the needs of naval vessels. On 22 September 1942 the *Chungking*, a merchant vessel, became the first ship to use the slipway and the first American submarine, the USS *Salmon*, was slipped a week later.[113] The slipway is still in use although it is now known as Swan Dock. On 3 March 1944 the US Navy's floating dock ARD 10, with a lifting capacity of 3,000 tons arrived and was

---

[111]FHT, Minutes, 21 May and 9 April 1943.

[112]FPA 3471/91, NEM 157A, National Security Manpower Regulations, FHT to Public Service Commissioner, 5 January 1943 and FHT to Deputy Director General of Manpower, Perth, 29 January 1943.

[113]For technical details of its construction see E. Smith, "Swan Dock Fremantle Harbour. Its Origin and Construction," *Maritime Heritage Association Journal*, VII (1996), 5-8.

moored at the eastern end of the Inner Harbour. This dock was designed to relieve pressure on the slipway and was able to cater for larger vessels than the slipway. It stayed at Fremantle until September 1945.[114] A Priority Committee was established to decide on the order in which ships should be handled. The Fremantle committee met at 4:30 pm every day and naturally gave first priority to naval vessels and ships carrying war materials.[115]

In 1942, along with Coca-Cola and other consumer products, the Americans brought new port equipment, including forklift trucks and pallets. The latter speeded up cargo-handling and led to savings of up to forty percent in turnround time. The federal government was impressed and requested 100 forklift trucks from the Americans under the Lend-Lease agreement. Unfortunately, despite a request that some be allocated to Fremantle they all went to Sydney and Brisbane, because these were the two most important ports for military cargo.[116] Fremantle had to wait until after the war to obtain this valuable equipment.

Between 1942 and 1945 Fremantle was the largest submarine base in the Southern Hemisphere but, according to Lynne Cairns, its strategic importance was "one of the best kept secrets of World War II."[117] Over 170 Allied submarines, mostly American but also including some Royal Navy and Dutch boats, were based at the port and completed a total of 416 patrols. Apart from actions against enemy shipping the submarines also carried commandos on secret missions. The most famous was the ill-fated Z-force mission, *Rimau*, which left in September 1944 to attack Japanese shipping in Singapore harbour.

The American forces had an enormous impact on the life of people in Western Australia. The United States Navy took over wharf sheds, warehouses and other buildings in Fremantle. American servicemen were billeted in scattered locations in Fremantle and Perth and taxi drivers, publicans, brothel owners and others in the entertainment industry welcomed their free spending. But Australian troops resented their success

---

[114]FPA 3471/91, NEM 133, "US Floating Dock."

[115]FPA 3471/91, NEM 99, Australian-American Co-operation Movement Committee.

[116]FPA 3471/91, NEM 146, Mr. Angus, Administrator of the Allied Material Handing Standing Committee, to FHT, 23 October 1944.

[117]L. Cairns, *Fremantle's Secret Fleets* (Fremantle, 1995), 3.

with the local females and complained that they were "over-sexed, over-paid and over here." The regular brawls and other disputes involving servicemen of all nationalities gave Fremantle a reputation of being a violent city.[118]

On 17 January 1944, a day when the harbour was crowded with shipping, the *Panamanian*, an old ship taken from the scrap heap for war service, was loading cargo when a discarded cigarette butt set a piece of hessian sacking alight.[119] The sacking was thrown overboard but the surface of the water was covered with oil, probably spilt while refuelling submarines, and instead of being extinguished the flaming sack started a major conflagration. The *Panamanian* was engulfed in flames and the blaze threatened to spread to HMS *Maidstone*, a tender vessel moored nearby which was loaded with explosives and fuel. The *Maidstone* had no steam up and had to be dragged out of harms way by tugs. The ship was moved just in the nick of time because its paintwork had caught alight. One seaman died of injuries sustained while fighting the fire and it took six days to finally extinguish it.[120]

Once the war ended the American forces left fairly quickly and Fremantle slipped back into obscurity as far as naval operations were concerned. The only RAN vessels kept in Western Australia were small training vessels, although the oceanographic survey ship HMAS *Diamantina* was based at Fremantle for twenty years from 1959.[121] In 1960, however, a training base for junior naval recruits was established at HMAS *Leeuwin*, north of Fremantle. In the early 1960s the federal government even offered to sell Garden Island back to Western Australia but the state government did not accept the offer.[122] The port authority had long term plans for the development of Garden Island for port use but, in the early 1970s, the federal government asked the state to restrict

---

[118]See A.J. Barker and L. Jackson, *Fleeting Attraction. A Social History of American Servicemen in Western Australia during the Second World War* (Nedlands, WA, 1996).

[119]*The West Australian*, 12 April 1949.

[120]FPA 422/1, Outbreak of Fire at Berth 7 and Aboard *Panamanian*.

[121]Jeffery, "History of the Navy," 60.

[122]*The West Australian*, 29 April 1966.

development of commercial shipping in Cockburn Sound because it planned to provide repair and maintenance facilities for US submarines.[123]

Photo 9: US Submarines Based at Fremantle, 1945.

Source: *The West Australian*.

Until the Second World War the main focus of Australia's strategic interests was on the trade routes to and from the United Kingdom and Europe. However, since the war the focus has gradually shifted towards North America and Asia and this has led to changes in maritime defence strategy. One outcome has been a growing awareness of the strategic importance of the Indian Ocean. The view that "a base would be a symbol of power and efficiency on a lonely coast" eventually led to the decision to establish a naval base, HMAS *Stirling* (also known in the navy as Fleet Base West), on Garden Island.[124] A 4.2-kilometre causeway linking the Island to the mainland was completed in 1973 and the base was officially opened on 28 July 1978. Garden Island had developed into a popular holiday spot and was covered with holiday cottages; much to the

---

[123]FPA, Minutes, 15 March 1973; *The Sunday Times*, 26 December 1971.

[124]The quotation is from *The Sunday Times*, 14 August 1969.

dismay of many Western Australians these were removed and the government proposed to close the Island to the public. After a public outcry, public access was allowed to the northern part of the Island during daylight hours.[125] HMAS *Stuart* arrived in January 1984 and became the first destroyer to be home-ported at HMAS *Stirling*.

Photo 10: The Fire on the Merchant Ship *Panamanian*, January 1944.

Source: Battye Library 3314B/25.

The development of the "Two Ocean" concept in 1987 led to a decision to locate more warships and submarines permanently at HMAS *Stirling*. In September 1987 HMAS *Oxley* became the first submarine to be home-ported at HMAS *Stirling*; HMAS Orion later replaced her. A submarine escape-training facility was built in 1988. In addition, HMAS *Stirling* is now the home to the guided-missile frigates *Adelaide* and *Darwin*, the destroyer escorts *Derwent*, *Swan* and *Torrens*, the hydrographic survey ship *Moresby*, as well as numerous smaller naval craft.[126]

---

[125]*The West Australian*, 24 February 1972.

[126]Jeffery, "History of the Navy," 61.

By the year 2000 it is planned to have half of the RAN home-ported at HMAS *Stirling*, including all six of the new Collins-class submarines.

The opening of the *Stirling* Naval Base and the growing strategic importance of the Indian Ocean has led to an increase in the number of visits by naval vessels. Between 1980 and 1995 an average of eighty naval vessels called every year. Numbers increased on special occasions such as the visit of the Tall Ships in December 1988 for Australia's bicentennial celebrations. The same year the USS *Midway* became the largest ship to ever enter the Inner Harbour, breaking the record held by the *Queen Elizabeth 2* since 1985. In February 1992 many thousands of Western Australians flocked to the port to welcome HMAS *Sydney* on her way home after six months in the Arabian Gulf. The launch of the replica of Captain Cook's bark *Endeavour* on 9 December 1993 provided a reminder of an earlier chapter of naval history. Units of the US 7th Fleet are frequent visitors to Fremantle. In October 1986 the battleship USS *Missouri,* a veteran of the Second World War, anchored in Gage Roads. In 1994-1995 five US naval groups visited Fremantle, with a total of sixteen ships and about 18,000 personnel.

The American visits have led to controversy because some of the vessels are nuclear powered. The danger of fallout from nuclear tests has long been a cause of concern. The *Koolinda* was steaming from the northwest to Fremantle at the time of a British atomic test at the Monte Bello Islands in 1956. Seventy-five cattle died on the voyage and when the ship arrived in Fremantle the crew refused to unload the surviving cattle because it was feared that the deaths were caused by radiation sickness. To everyone's relief it was later found that they had died from red water fever a tick-transmitted disease.[127] Clearly, a major radiation leak in the port would have devastating effects on the population of Fremantle but there is no record of an accident leading to the escape of nuclear radiation. In the early 1960s the port authority admitted that while ships carrying radioactive materials were allowed in the Inner Harbour it had little knowledge of the hazards associated with radioactive materials. Apparently monazite was loaded in bags for several years before the

---

[127]Australia, Department of Resources and Energy, *A History of British Atomic Tests in Australia* (Canberra, 1985), 357. My thanks to Paul Weaver for drawing my attention to this reference.

wharf manager became aware of its radioactive nature.[128] There is now a Port Safety Scheme administered by the State Emergency Service which includes daily radiation checks of visiting nuclear ships and operational counter measures.[129] The fire on the *Panamanian* during the Second World War provides further evidence that there have always been risks with locating ports close to metropolitan areas. It is, of course, important not to overlook the fact that the city has expanded partly due to port related economic activity and that the proximity of the port and city provides benefits which have helped to offset these risks.

Conclusions

This chapter has shown that there were important changes in the level and pattern of ship movements at Fremantle between the turn of the century and the 1990s. Shipping calling at Fremantle falls into two broad groups - overseas, and coastal - although, as we have seen, the distinction between the two groups is blurred. Coastal shipping declined drastically after the Second World War as both passengers and general cargo was lost to land and air transport. The United Kingdom's dominance of Fremantle's overseas shipping declined after the war, due to shifts in Australia's trade patterns and growing competition from the shipping fleets of other nations, including "flag of convenience" vessels. During the Second World War Fremantle was a major submarine base and the opening of HMAS *Stirling* at Garden Island in 1978 has further increased the port's strategic importance. However, from the viewpoint of the commercial port, the most striking changes were undoubtedly the trends towards increased ship size and specialisation in vessel design, both of which accelerated after the Second World War. The average vessel calling increased from about 5200 tons in 1919-1920 to 19,000 tons in 1995-1996, but much larger vessels, especially bulk carriers of 100,000 tons and above, became frequent visitors. These large ships required costly deep-water channels and berths and the need to service such vessels was a major factor in the decision to develop the Outer Harbour.

---

[128]FPA 87/1066, "Dangerous Goods," General Manager of FHT to Deputy Director Fremantle Marine Branch of the Commonwealth of Australia, 25 July 1961; and Wharf Manager to Harbour Master, 6 December 1963.

[129]FPA 5341/88/01/09/01/9, Hon. G. Troy to Hon. P. Pendal, 8 May 1986.

The extension of mechanisation to the handling of both bulk and general cargoes made shipping and port operations more capital intensive. Bulk handling was first developed for more homogeneous cargoes such as grain and oil and general cargo handling remained a basically labour intensive activity until the 1940s. Fork lifts and pallets, roll on/roll off ships and, finally, containerisation: all offered to obtain the benefits of mechanised handling for general cargo operations. The port was required to provide a wide range of depths and port facilities in response to externally imposed demands. However, as subsequent chapters will show, it is an over-simplification to see the port simply as a technology-taker; the relationship is essentially two-way. The tension between what "a modern port should have" and what Fremantle could realistically provide, led to numerous conflicts and delays in port planning.

Photo 11: The Inner Harbour at Fremantle, 1996.

Source: See photo 1.

Chapter 5
A Century of Port Development, 1897 to 1997

In chapters 3 and 4 we examined the growth and changing composition of port activity at Fremantle between the 1890s and 1990s. The volume of cargo grew from about 0.7 million tons in 1903-1904 to 20.2 million tons in 1995-1996; over the same period shipping tonnage increased from 1.4 million tons to 33.5 million tons and passenger movements dropped from about 46,000 to less than 10,000. Fremantle was called on to make provision for a wide range of cargoes and ship types. Passenger liners, tankers and bulk carriers, in particular, placed heavy demands on the port for increased depths and rapid turnround. The objective of this chapter is to trace the physical evolution of the port in response to these demands.

The changes to the port were the outcome of a complex process of decision-making and adjustment in which a large number of actors played a part, amongst whom the most important were the Fremantle Harbour Trust (renamed the Fremantle Port Authority in 1964), government, shipowners and consignees. Moreover, in Western Australia's small community the port served as a visible symbol of progress, and plans for port development were a matter of widespread public discussion and debate. Over the years a number of "battles" occurred over the appropriate port facilities and their locations - "battles" which even a succession of "expert" reports failed to completely resolve. As we will see, Fremantle's development (or non-development) in consequence was not merely a mechanical response to trends in trade and shipping; it was the result of a complex interaction between a multitude of social, political and economic influences.

We commence with a schematic, bird's-eye view of the physical growth of Fremantle, based on J. Bird's "Anyport" model. A brief discussion of the advantages and (limited) disadvantages of C.Y. O'Connor's port follows this. We next chart the major endeavours to make Fremantle a "first class port:" the provision of increased depth of water; the ill-fated dock; the battle of the plans in the 1920s; the development of bulk grain handling in the 1930s; Tydeman's plan for post-Second World War port development and how it was constrained by metropolitan landuse activities; the development of the Outer Harbour and containerisation. Finally, we consider the issues affecting the survival of the Inner Harbour as a commercial port over the next century.

An Overview of Port Development, 1897 to 1997

In order to provide a preliminary overview of Fremantle's physical growth and to place it in a broader perspective, it is useful to consider James Bird's "Anyport" model of seaport development. Bird argues that all major ports experience similar stages of eras of physical development because they exist to serve essentially the same world shipping fleets.[1] Bird suggests that there are six eras of port development, although he stresses that the eras are not clear-cut as installations from earlier eras can continue in use. The "Anyport" model was based on the experience of British ports and, of course, there is no guarantee that all ports followed a similar sequence of development. Table 5.1 shows how Fremantle fits into the "Anyport" model.

The first or primitive era of port development began in 1829 with the foundation of the colony of Western Australia by Captain James Stirling. The second era of marginal quay extension did not occur at Fremantle but the third era of marginal quay elaboration began with the construction of a small jetty near Arthur's Head in 1832. The fourth era, of dock elaboration, was not necessary at Fremantle owing to the small range of tides (two feet nine inches at ordinary spring tides). The fifth era of simple lineal quayage commenced with the opening of the Inner Harbour in 1897. As we saw in chapter 1, the latter development was conceived, designed and mainly carried out by C.Y. O'Connor. It involved the removal of the rock bar at the mouth of the Swan River, the building of two moles at the mouth, dredging the harbour to thirty feet below low-water mark, building about 7000 lineal feet (2135 metres) of timber wharves and equipping them with sheds and cargo-handling appliances. Fremantle was the first Australian port to enter Bird's era of simple lineal quayage: Melbourne and Sydney, for example, did not enter this era until 1917 and 1929, respectively.

The success of C.Y. O'Connor's scheme, at least in a physical sense, is underlined by the fact that Fremantle's layout remained basically unchanged throughout the first half of the twentieth century. The southern quay of the harbour, Victoria Quay, had a length of 5055 feet (1542

---

[1] J. Bird, *Seaports and Seaport Terminals* (London, 1971), 67.

metres) and was mainly used for mail steamers and general cargo traffic. Work on North Quay commenced in 1901 and by 1903 it had reached about 2000 feet (610 metres) in length. The completion of North Quay in 1916 brought the total length of wharfage in the harbour to 9875 feet (3012 metres). North Quay was mainly used for the handling of bulk cargoes such as wheat, coal and oil. The total length of wharfage remained about 10,000 feet (3050 metres) for many years. By the early 1990s the port had 3859 metres of wharfage in the Inner Harbour. Thus comparing 1903-1904 and 1995-1996, while the tonnage of cargo increased by 2700 percent the length of wharfage increased by only seventy-nine percent. At first sight these statistics imply that port capacity was outstripped by the demands of trade. But this comparison takes no account of technological change and the opening of the Outer Harbour and is not a reliable guide to the port's capacity to efficiently service the needs of port users.

Prior to the Second World War port engineers used the tons of cargo handled per lineal yard of quay as a rough guide to the physical adequacy of port capacity. In 1927, Mr. Stileman, the Engineer-in-Chief, suggested that 500 tons per yard of quay per annum was a reasonable target for Fremantle.[2] According to this benchmark, it was not until the late 1920s that the port began operating anywhere near its maximum sustainable capacity. The depression of the 1930s reduced trade levels and consequently pressure on port facilities was also reduced, increasing again only in the late 1930s. Between 1903-1904 and 1938-1939 cargo handled per yard of quay averaged only 347 tons, well below the 600 tons per annum considered the norm in European ports. But Fremantle's performance was comparable to that of other Australian ports such as Melbourne and Sydney, which, after the First World War, averaged 297 tons and 338 tons, respectively.

These low throughputs indicate, of course, the presence of substantial excess capacity. In fact, C.Y. O'Connor provided Fremantle with an infrastructure that was so far in advance of immediate needs that, with some improvements, including the introduction of mechanical cargo-handling equipment, it was able to serve the needs of port users until the 1950s when a new era of specialised quayage and Outer Harbour development began. Unlike most British ports, which evolved in a

---

[2]*Report on Fremantle Harbour and Cross River Communications by the Engineer-in-Chief* (Perth, 1917), 8; and M. Tull, "The Development of the Port of Fremantle, Australia's Western Gateway," *The Great Circle*, VII (1985), 121-122.

piecemeal fashion over the centuries, Australia's capital city ports were constructed from "greenfield sites" in the nineteenth century and were provided with considerable excess capacity to cater for future growth.[3] In this respect Australian ports were not unique and possibly illustrate a general pattern for colonial ports. For example, when Indian ocean ports such as Madras and Colombo were constructed in the nineteenth century, engineers had to overcome considerable physical obstacles and provided extensive facilities at one go, even if such facilities were in excess of the short-term needs of trade and shipping.[4]

The relationship between port development and changes in trade and shipping technology is normally regarded as a "chicken and egg" one.[5] One might have expected the ports to dominate the relationship because they require investment in long lasting infrastructure while ships, with a life span of twenty to thirty years, are relatively short-term investments. So ships would tend to adapt to existing facilities at Fremantle and other Australian ports. However, in the long run, it is the ports that adapt to demands generated by shipping companies and port users. Containerisation, in particular, has facilitated the movement of cargo across different modes of transport and led to the development of door-to-door cargo services. Shipping lines whose operations are global in scale control much of this trade. This has led to increased inter-port competition and the weakening of the monopoly powers ports have enjoyed over their hinterlands. A clear example is the concept of landbridging where feeder services carry containers from Singapore to Fremantle for distribution to the eastern states by rail. Thus ports have increasingly become pawns in a global game of commerce.[6]

---

[3]For an excellent survey of the development of British ports see G. Jackson, *The History and Archaeology of Ports* (Tadworth, 1983).

[4]F.J.A. Broeze, K.I. McPherson and P.D. Reeves, "Imperial Ports and the Modern World Economy: The Case of the Indian Ocean," *Journal of Transport History*, VII (1986), 1-20.

[5]Bird, *Seaports and Seaport Terminals*, 87-88.

[6]See B. Slack, "Pawns in the Game: Ports in a Global Transportation System," *Growth and Change*, XXIV (Fall 1993), 579-588.

Table 5.1
Major Eras in the Development of the Port of Fremantle

Era	General characteristics of each era	Evidence for each era at Fremantle
1. Primitive	Establishment of port on an estuary. The port develops lineally along the waterfront, with storage and handling facilities being established.	Ships anchored off-shore; cargo lightered ashore
2. Marginal quay extension	The lineal development of the ports begins to outstrip the areal growth of the town	Nil
3. Marginal quay elaboration	The construction of jetties and hythes (cuts in the river bank) which increase port capacity without greatly increasing the area of the port	Jetties provided for Fremantle shoreline, with lighterage continuing for larger vessels
4. Dock elaboration	The opening of wet docks	Not required due to small tidal range
5. Simple lineal quayage	Over 1,500 feet of uninterrupted quayage, with at least 26 feet of water alongside	Commenced with the opening of the Inner Harbour in 1897
6. Specialised quayage	Provision for large-scale industry and bulk cargoes, with deep water berths	Commenced with provision of deepwater access to the Outer Harbour in 1955

Source: Adapted from J. Bird, *Seaport Gateways of Australia* (London, 1968), 6-12, 96.

Although still assured of a captive market for a large proportion of Western Australia's trade, the port authority has never attempted to exploit its monopoly power and disregard the needs of port users. Support for harbour deepening and a dry-dock was, as we will see, based largely on the notion that such facilities were part of the equipment of a "first class port." It was recognised that "port facilities must therefore be kept not only abreast but rather in advance of average requirements; otherwise serious congestion and economic waste will be inevitable."[7] There was, as we will see, a tendency to plan far in excess of demand and disregard financial criteria. In this respect, ports were probably no different from other public enterprises in the early years of this century.[8]

A sound physical infrastructure, with considerable excess capacity, is not Fremantle's only asset: the port enjoys a minimal tidal range removing the need for expensive wet-docks; the port is free of strong currents and fog although strong winds can cause problems with larger ships; and only minimal maintenance dredging is required to maintain channel depths. As we saw in chapter 3, these advantages, combined with her geographical position and favourable railway connections, helped her become Western Australia's "premier" port.

Did C.Y. O'Connor's port have any disadvantages? One problem was that the harbour bottom consisted of mixtures of sand, clay and calcareous sandstone. This soft type of bottom made the construction of solid concrete wharf walls extremely costly. Thus Fremantle's original wharves were built on less durable timber piles. These were subjected to the ravages of seaworms (*Teredo Navalis*) which can affect jarrah piles within eight weeks. Fremantle's wharves had a life of only ten to fifteen years and by 1911 some parts of Victoria Quay had collapsed, threatening to topple cranes into the water. The FHT was forced to undertake renovations that cost £65,725 up to 1911-1912. The FHT wanted to use more durable concrete piles but was pressured by the government to continue using jarrah piles in order to protect the local timber industry.[9] It was eventually allowed to encase the piles in ferro-concrete sleeves as a preventive measure. In 1923 it was again necessary to begin replacing the timber quays; this time the FHT was allowed to use reinforced

---

[7]Battye Library of West Australian History, Public Works Department Archives Deposit (PWD), 460/30, Stileman, Engineer-in-Chief, to Under-Secretary for Works, 7 March 1930.

[8]See W.A. Sinclair, "Capital Formation," in C. Forster (ed.), *Australian Economic Development in the Twentieth Century* (London, 1971), 16-26. For general discussions of public investment see N.G. Butlin, *et al.*, *Government and Capitalism* (Sydney, 1982); and R. Mathews, *Public Investment in Australia* (Melbourne, 1967).

[9]PWD, 1481/13, J. Ramsbotham, "The Port of Fremantle: A Report on Suggested Improvements and General Extension," typescript dated 31 January 1913; FPA, Minutes, 5 October 1910 and 30 June 1911; and FHT to Colonial Secretary, 25 March 1911.

concrete piles. The work was completed at South Quay in 1938 and at North Quay in 1943. The harbour bottom was also to pose massive obstacles to the construction of a dry-dock, an issue we consider in detail later in the chapter.

Problems caused by the harbour bottom were, however, less serious in the long run than those posed by the presence of road and rail bridges upstream of the port site. Captain Stirling's decision to place the capital Perth and the port, Fremantle, on opposite banks of the Swan River, meant that cross-river communications were essential. As we will see later in the chapter, numerous plans for up-river development of the port foundered on the difficulty and cost of bridge re-location. In fact the bridges proved a more formidable constraint on Inner Harbour development than did the rock bar in the nineteenth century. Therefore, port development was not simply a passive response to externally imposed changes in trade and shipping technology; it was shaped by a complex interaction between forces originating from within as well as outside Western Australia.

The Deepening of the Inner Harbour

Between 1903-1904 and 1913-1914 the tonnage of cargo grew by about fifty percent to over one million tons; over the same period the net tonnage of shipping grew by about eighty percent to 2.6 million tons. Cargo tonnage handled per yard of quay reached a record of 347 tons in 1913-1914. In July 1912, Frank Stevens, Secretary of the FHT, had expressed concern that the accommodation in the fifteen-year-old harbour "was not coping with the trade of the port."[10] The main problem was the tendency of the ship "to beat the quay;" that is, to discharge the cargo faster than it could be cleared from the wharves, causing bottlenecks on the shore side. As a result, ships were often forced to queue in Gage Roads while they waited for a berth.[11] The solution was to improve shore facilities, including cargo-handling equipment and road and rail access, but this aspect tended to receive less attention than the need to provide deep-water for the larger ships that were calling.

The average ship calling in 1913-1914 was 3000 tons, compared to only 1800 tons in 1903-1904. But the port needed, on occasion, to cope

---

[10]FPA, Minutes, 23 July 1912.

[11]*Ibid.*, 5 January 1912.

with much larger vessels, usually mail steamers or passenger liners. By the mid-1920s "leviathans" of 10,000 tons and over accounted for about twenty percent of port entries. Such vessels required deep-water berths and could not be catered for only by improving shore facilities. As we saw in chapter 4, port authorities the world over struggled to cope with these "leviathans."

The interest in harbour expansion was increased by the decision of the Commonwealth in 1911 to establish a naval base at Cockburn Sound south of Fremantle. In February 1912, Mr. G.F. Pearce, Commonwealth Minister for Defence, predicted commercial as well as naval development of Cockburn Sound. He also raised the possibility of Fremantle being "the port of the great Australian continent and not of a State."[12] The possibility of Fremantle being a port of call for giant steamers, from which cargo and passengers would be transhipped by smaller vessels or (after the opening of the Trans-Continental Railway in 1917) by rail to the eastern states, was a tantalising prospect, periodically surfacing throughout the port's history, but, unlike the idea of an outer-harbour, slow to reach fruition.

Mr. Fanstone, Director of Naval Works, also supported the development of a commercial outer-harbour in March 1912. He argued that up-river development would involve pulling down the road and rail bridges, resuming urban land and extensive dredging - all very costly. In his view Cockburn Sound offered "the only adequate means of supplying the necessary deep-sea shipping accommodation," but Sir John Forrest declared that Fanstone was trying "to ram down their throats his opinions about a commercial harbour."[13] While Frank Stevens, Secretary of the FHT, later described Cockburn Sound as "a magnificent sheet of deep water, measuring eight miles long by four miles wide, all entirely protected from ocean influence," at the time the FHT strongly favoured up-river expansion.[14] The FHT boldly declared that the river offered sufficient space "to take all the shipping of Australia for all time with ease

---

[12]*The West Australian*, 28 February 1912.

[13]*Ibid.*, 4 and 11 March 1912.

[14]F. Stevens, "History of the Harbour," in J.K. Hitchcock (ed.), *The History of Fremantle: The Front Gate of Australia 1829-1929* (Fremantle, 1929), 143.

and in perfect safety."[15] Stevens, who had worked as C.Y. O'Connor's secretary before he came to the FHT, argued that the founder of the harbour had always favoured up-river expansion. Moreover, the development of the outer-harbour would harm existing businesses including the Swan River lighterage trade.[16] Commercial interests generally favoured up-river expansion. The Perth Chamber of Commerce suggested that the Cockburn Sound proposal was merely a ploy "to lure the State into bearing some of the cost of their [the Commonwealth's] naval harbour."[17] There was even opposition on environmental grounds to bringing ocean shipping up-river:

> The city does not want it; the country, as much interested as the port or capital, would refuse assent to a scheme that would turn the waters of the banks into a wilderness of dingy wharves and factories, with perpetual volumes of smoke from shipping driving over the city.[18]

Nevertheless, the final decision was for up-river expansion and harbour deepening: development of the Outer Harbour had to wait until the 1950s.

Prior to the First World War, the deepest draft vessel to visit Fremantle was the Scottish Shire Line's *Argyllshire* of 6610 tons. She entered in April 1912 drawing twenty-nine feet five inches and, after taking on 500 tons of bunker coal, left drawing thirty feet one and a half inches. But several months later the Trust was alarmed when the Blue Funnel Line's steamer *Nestor* of about 15,000 tons and drawing thirty-one feet was diverted from Fremantle to Albany, ostensibly because of a lack of adequate deep-water berths at Fremantle.[19] News of plans for deepening of the Suez Canal confirmed the FHT's fears that vessels drawing

---

[15]*The West Australian*, 13 March 1912.

[16]FPA, 90/12/4, FHT to J.F. Ramsbotham, Resident Engineer, Fremantle Graving Dock Construction, 12 December 1912; and FPA, 90/12/2, Stevens to Chairman FHT, 7 March 1912.

[17]*The West Australian*, 22 March 1912.

[18]*Ibid.*, 15 October 1912.

[19]FHT, *Annual Report* (1912-1913), 14.

thirty-three to thirty-five feet would soon become frequent visitors to Fremantle. In 1913 the FHT pressed the government to deepen the port to thirty-six feet, stressing that "they do not intend to shoulder the blame for inadequacy in an important national institution like Fremantle Harbour."[20] In 1914 the Royal Commission on the Dominions urged Australian authorities to consider deepening their harbours and suggested that "a first class harbour should provide a working depth of not less than 40 feet."[21] The SS *Ulysses* ran aground just south of the harbour entrance in March 1916, and this appears to have helped convince the government to deepen the harbour to thirty-six feet. But the FHT was provided with such a meagre trickle of loan funds that work proceeded very slowly. By 1923-1924 the FHT had finished dredging of the entrance channel and about five-sixths of the Inner Harbour; the work was finally completed several years later. The outbreak of the First World War, however, had caused a dramatic slump in trade and shipping: by 1917-1918 shipping tonnage and cargo throughput had plummeted by about sixty percent. In 1915-1916, owing to the wartime scarcity of shipping, a record wheat crop had piled up on the wharves. There was clearly no urgency for port expansion.

The determination of the FHT to cater for the top spectrum of liner shipping left an enduring legacy: it almost doubled the capital cost of the port. In 1927, Mr. Stileman, the Engineer-in-Chief, argued that the deepening was unnecessary because thirty-two feet would have been sufficient to float ninety-five percent of ships calling at Fremantle.[22] By that date the deepest draft vessel handled was the White Star Line's *Ceramic* (18,600 tons) which drew thirty-three feet ten inches. As a result of the deepening, Fremantle provided a depth in excess of that then available in the Suez Canal. It would have made more sense to provide a range of depths to match the spectrum of shipping, rather than deepen the whole harbour to cater for the largest liners, but the FHT does not appear to have seriously considered this option. The result was that in 1925 the

---

[20]FPA, 90/12/4, FHT to Colonial Secretary, 10 October 1923.

[21]Great Britain, *Royal Commission on Dominions: Second Interim Report*, 1914 (Cd. 7210), 57-58. The final report of the Commission (Cd. 8462) advocated thirty-eight feet for a first class port. See J. Bach, *A Maritime History of Australia* (Melbourne, 1976), 342-343.

[22]F.W. Tydeman, *Report on the Port of Fremantle* (3 vols., Perth, 1949), II, 48; and PWD, 1163/27, Stileman to Under-Secretary for Works, 28 November 1927.

capital debt per lineal foot of berthage at Fremantle was £217 compared to £182 at Sydney, £203 at London, £169 at Liverpool, £128 at Glasgow and £200 at Bristol.[23] Although these statistics were affected by numerous factors, including differences in port facilities and variations in accounting practices, they suggest that Fremantle was over-capitalised by the mid-1920s. The need to service a large capital debt goes a long way towards explaining the level of port charges and debt at Fremantle, an issue we explore more fully in chapter 7.

The Dock That Never Was

In May 1906 a visiting ship's captain declared that "Fremantle as a port is a very pretty arch without a keystone until it gets a dock."[24] All seemed to agree that a dock was essential if Fremantle was to be a first class port.[25] Little consideration was given to the financial viability of the dock, although it was recognised that it was unlikely to operate at a profit.

The problem is that Fremantle is only an intermediate port for most of its shipping. Shipowners tended to concentrate repair work at terminal ports where their own technical staff can supervise the work. In 1907 Mr. Day, local agent of the Orient Company stated that as long as his company's vessels could scrape back to their terminal ports they would not use a dock at Fremantle.[26] Even interstate vessels treated eastern states ports as their terminals and Melbourne and Sydney were already equipped with graving docks. Thus the only regular users would have been the small vessels engaged in Western Australia's coastal trade. Tramp shipping went where costs were lowest, usually to an Asian port. Approaches to the federal government and British Admiralty for subsidies on the grounds that the dock would strengthen the defences of the region were unsuccessful. Naval experts contended that the dock facilities at

---

[23]FPA, 679/21, Stileman to Engineer for Harbours and Rivers, 3 December 1929.

[24]*The Morning Herald*, 15 May 1906. The quote is from Captain Marchbank of the SS *Dongola*.

[25]See *The West Australian*, 2, 22 and 23 March; 4 April; 3 and 11 May 1906.

[26]WAPD, .XXXII (1907), 1333.

Singapore were adequate for the need of shipping in the region.[27] The FHT estimated that a dry-dock would be used only twelve times per year, with an average stay of seven days.[28] In short, there was no justification for extensive ship repair facilities at Fremantle. The only function a dry-dock would have performed was as a symbol of the community's achievements but, as we will see, even as a symbol, it was to be a costly failure.

Mr. Dillon Bell, Engineer for Harbours and Rivers, made the first proposal for a dock in Fremantle Harbour in 1895.[29] He proposed that a wooden dock be constructed at Arthur's Head but C.Y. O'Connor, the Engineer-in-Chief, considered this to be impractical. The following year the government appointed Mr. C.N. Bell, a consulting engineer from New Zealand, to design a dock for Fremantle. Bell considered the following sites suitable for a dry-dock: Arthur Head, Rous Head, the north and south sides of the harbour between the road and railway bridges, Preston Point and Rocky Bay. He recommended the choice of Rous Head on the grounds of its accessibility. However, the government took no action until 1904 when, under pressure from public opinion, it requested Mr. T.W. Keele, Engineer for Harbours and Rivers in New South Wales to prepare another report on the site for a dock. Keele examined the sites considered by Bell and concluded that Rocky Bay was best. However, he thought that Butler's Hump, in Freshwater Bay (the site currently occupied by the Royal Freshwater Bay Yacht Club) was preferable as the Bay could be developed into a full-scale harbour. Both the Rocky Bay and Butler's Hump sites would have required relocation of the existing rail and road bridges across the river. The proposals for constructing port facilities in Perth created alarm in Fremantle circles. A representative of the Fremantle Citizen's League urged the government to build the dock in Fremantle "as an assurance that the permanency of the Port was no longer

---

[27]PWD, 476/11, Agent General of WA, London, on meeting with Representative of Admiralty, 5 May 1910. See also *The West Australian*, 27 June 1935.

[28]PWD, 563, C.S.R. Palmer, "Report on Size and Description of the Proposed Dock at Fremantle," Engineer-in-Chief, 1 December 1904; and FPA 62/10, memo to Engineer-in-Chief, 12 March 1910.

[29]PWD,1472/24, typescript summarising history of Fremantle Dock proposals, 18 August 1933.

in doubt."[30] However, the government baulked at the cost of re-locating the bridges across the river and this sealed the fate of Keele's proposals. Thus the "battle of the sites" continued with only two contenders, Arthur's Head and Rous Head. The Engineer-in-Chief, Mr. Thompson, favoured the latter site, but before going ahead the government called for yet another report from a British engineer, Sir Whatley Eliot.

Eliot favoured Rous Head but expressed fears that the porous nature of the rock could make exclusion of water during the construction process somewhat difficult. He suggested the use of a diving bell to aid in laying the concrete floor. His proposed graving dock was 560 feet by ninety-four feet and was estimated to cost £325,000 plus £28,000 for subsidiary works such as alterations to railway tracks and existing port facilities. The dock was to have an entrance at each end and be divisible into two compartments so two vessels could be dealt with simultaneously.

Dredging and excavation work commenced in 1908. In November 1910, Mr. Ramsbotham, an English engineer experienced in dock construction, was appointed to take charge of the dock works. Mr. Ramsbotham reported that the diving bell technique was unsuitable and suggested that the difficulties were so great the site should be abandoned or used for berthing a floating dock. Sir Whatley Eliot was consulted again and he agreed that the diving bell method was unsuitable and that cofferdams be used instead. But this increased the estimated cost to £422,000. On 30 May 1912, drilling operations revealed the existence of a large cave only fourteen feet below the steel sheet-piling dam built to allow construction of the north wall of the graving dock. In a vain attempt to fill the cave, 171 barrels of cement and six tons of ashes were tipped in.[31] Several caves were eventually discovered, the bottom of one being sixty-seven feet below low water mark. The plan had been to construct the dock in the dry by pumping the area behind the piling dam dry. But the sea flooded in through the caves in such volume that it was impossible to pump the area dry. Ramsbotham estimated that construction in the wet would increase the cost of the dock to £725,000. He recommended abandonment of the scheme.

On 27 June 1912 the Minister for Works, Mr. W.D. Johnson, announced the dropping of the scheme. The work already carried out

---

[30]*The West Australian*, 28 April 1906.

[31]A.T. Bonds, "Early History of the Port of Fremantle," *Port of Fremantle Quarterly*, III (1969), 22.

would be used for a concrete quay for deep draft vessels. However, even this project was eventually abandoned on the grounds of cost and only timber wharfage built. The only other benefit derived from the work put into the dock was the dredging to thirty-six feet. The government stated that the final cost of the dock work up to abandonment was £207,417.[32] This represented over one fifth of total loan expenditure on harbours and rivers between 1908 and 1912. Such a waste of public money was a serious matter for the small Western Australian economy but, surprisingly, plans for a dock resurfaced again.

In 1925 a deputation representing the Fremantle Council and local business interests approached the Labor Premier, Collier, with another request for a dock. The deputation was somewhat taken aback when the Premier read them a letter from the local representative of the Overseas Shipowners' Representatives Association which said that a dock "must involve a very large expenditure of public money for a very occasional and disproportionate advantage to shipping or to the public."[33] The then Engineer-in-Chief, Mr. Stileman, recognised that a dock was uneconomic but still considered one to be "part of the necessary equipment of a first class terminal port."[34] Some proposals for a dock were made to the government in the 1930s, mainly with the aim of boasting local employment.[35] The economic feasibility of a dock was investigated on a number of occasions after the war. As late as 1981 the state government rejected a proposal for a dock when it was informed that it would need an annual subsidy of approximately $2 million.[36]

The only dock ever available at Fremantle was a small floating one operated within the harbour by the American Navy during the Second World War. But, to this day, one legacy of the dock fiasco remains: in 1910 Pietro Porcelli was working on a statue of C.Y. O'Connor and

---

[32]WAPD, XLVI (1913), 860.

[33]PWD, 1472, OSRA (Perth Branch) to Premier, 12 August 1925; and *The West Australian*, 15 August 1925.

[34]PWD, 1472, Stileman, "Fremantle Harbour Docking Facilities," 19 December 1927.

[35]*The West Australian*, 25 July 1933 and 27 January 1934.

[36]See FPA, 5341/88/106/04, development of dockyard and naval base; and FPA 88/1/6/4.2, development of docking facilities.

included on the statue four plaques depicting O'Connor's engineering projects. Aware of the work in progress on the dock Porcelli decided to include it in the plaque of Fremantle Harbour. Visitors to the port can still see the dock that never was.

The Battle of the Plans: Schemes for Port Development in the 1920s

Port trade and shipping underwent a burst of activity in the 1920s: by 1924-1925 cargo tonnage was just over double and shipping tonnage three times their respective levels in 1917-1918. Not surprisingly, this increased activity led to revived calls for port expansion. Numerous plans for port expansion were proposed but the "Battle of the Plans" focused on three major schemes of port development: the Buchanan Scheme (1927), the Stileman Scheme (1927) and the Gibb Scheme (1929).

Table 5.2 summarises the basic features of the three schemes. All three initially envisaged up-river development even though this involved pulling down bridges, resuming expansive land and extensive dredging. The number of up-river berths ranged widely, from eleven to fifty-four. Only the Stileman and Gibb schemes provided for seaward development. Interestingly, the cost estimates suggest that there was little difference in cost between major up-river development (Buchanan's scheme) and minor up-river development followed by seaward development (Stileman and Gibb's schemes). Up-river development had the attraction of being cheaper, at least initially. However, a thorough re-costing of the schemes in the late 1940s found that their cost had increased threefold; this increase was more than double the increase in the general price level.[37] This suggests that the greater part of the increase in costs was due to omissions and errors in the original estimates, rather than increases in the prices of labour and materials. In particular, the cost of land resumptions required for port facilities and adequate road and rail access appear to have been understated in the original estimates. The "Battle of the Plans" exemplifies the pre-war approach to port planning: the focus of attention was on structural excellence rather than economy; costing procedures were often rudimentary. This laxity of costing and investment procedures appears to have been a common feature of public investment in the early years of the twentieth century.[38] We will consider each in turn.

---

[37]Tydeman, *Fremantle*, 84-85.

[38]Sinclair, "Capital Formation," 16-26.

Sir George Buchanan, a leading British expert on ports, included his proposal for the development of the Port of Fremantle in a general review of harbour facilities in Australia. He also recommended that Fremantle should get a dry or floating dock as this was "part of the necessary equipment of any first class port."[39]

Table 5.2
Summary of Schemes for Port Development in the 1920s

Key Features	Buchanan	Stileman	Gibb
Length of quay (in feet)			
Up-river	28,000	6,100	6,200
Seaward		26,700	20,000
Number of berths			
Up-river	54	11	11
Seawards		45	30
Estimated cost (£million)			
Up-river	13.5*	3.2	4.0
Seawards		12.8*	12.0
Total	13.5	16.0	16.0

Notes: * Gibb's estimates. Buchanan's own estimate was £6,750,000 and Stileman gave no estimate of the cost of seawards development.

Source: F.W. Tydeman, *Report on the Port of Fremantle* (3 vols., Perth, 1949), II, 76-85.

In 1927 Stileman, the then-Engineer-in-Chief, put forward a different scheme for up-river development. He proposed re-siting the road and rail bridges at Point Brown, far enough up-river to provide room for an additional eleven berths. Further development of the port was to be seawards, north of the river mouth. Stileman's limit of eleven berths for further up-river development arose from his concern about the need to

[39]George Buchanan, *Report on Transport in Australia with Special Reference to Port and Harbour Facilities* (2 vols., Canberra, 1927), II, 53.

maintain adequate cross-river communications. As early as 1917 the FHT had alerted the government to the need for removal of the road and rail bridges.[40] Heavy floods in July 1926 caused the collapse of part of the railway bridge and focused attention on the need to replace these ageing structures. Stileman assumed that Buchanan wanted a combined road-rail bridge at Blackwall Reach and argued that "a harbour having a total length of nearly three miles, with no communication between the wharves on the two sides, other than by a bridge at one end, is very seriously handicapped."[41] He was also opposed to opening span bridges which tended to lead to long delays as vehicles and shipping waited to pass. If land and shipping traffic was to flow smoothly, high-level bridges or tunnels were required. However, these were extremely costly: the Sydney Harbour Bridge, for example, cost the New South Wales government in the region of £9 million. Hence Stileman's scheme, proposing seawards expansion in the long-term, appears to have been fundamentally sound.

The FHT agreed with Stileman that expansion was necessary but strongly opposed his plan for seaward development. The FHT's pilots noted that modern mail boats are built up to seventy feet above the water level and "when knocked dead are like great bladders utterly unable to be held without four or five tugs and, if possible, shore capstans."[42] They considered a sheltered up-river harbour was essential for such ships. Stileman proposed that the width of the channel be only 800-900 feet, compared to 1400 feet in the existing harbour; also, that it was wasteful to provide thirty-six feet throughout the harbour, thirty-two feet would be adequate in the new extensions. The FHT maintained that 1400 feet was necessary in order to swing ships safely but Stileman retorted that "the 1400 feet width is, in my opinion, a fetish;" and the FHT's opposition to an Outer Harbour was "based on a prejudice which admits of no alternative to up-river extensions."[43] Not surprisingly, the President of the Perth

---

[40]FPA, Minutes, 20 February 1920.

[41]*Report on Fremantle Harbour and Cross River Communications by the Engineer-in-Chief* (Perth, 1917), 9.

[42]FPA, 114/27/2, Harbour Master and Pilots to Secretary of FHT, 8 December 1927.

[43]PWD, 1163/27, Stileman to Under-Secretary for Works, "Fremantle Harbour - Improvements and Extensions," 28 November 1927; and "Comments by Engineer-in-Chief on Harbour Extension Proposals Put Forward 8 June 1928 by the Secretary Fremantle

Chamber of Commerce shared the "prejudice" for up-river development, claiming that the FHT was "unfairly expected to abide by the decision of engineers."[44] The Premier, Collier, however, strongly supported Stileman and criticised the Commissioners of the FHT, claiming that some "attended a meeting of the trust for an hour, and that is all they see of the harbour." He supported the opinions of a professional engineer, rather than those of a man like Stevens (the Secretary of the FHT), "who has had only a clerical training."[45]

In September 1928 the Leader of the Country Party, Mr. A. Thomson, called for the appointment of a select committee to inquire into Stileman's scheme. In the course of his reply, the Minister for Works, the Hon. A. McCallum, rallied to Stileman's defence and took the opportunity to criticise Sir George Buchanan's proposals. McCallum pointed to defects in Buchanan's cost estimates, and claimed that none of his suggestions in a similar report on ports in South Africa had been acted on. Moreover, he made the unfounded claim that Buchanan had been struck off the role of the Institute of Civil Engineers for "unprofessional conduct."[46]

The government's antipathy to Buchanan was due to criticisms he had made of government interference in the running of the port. Buchanan claimed that the Premier's remark that "it is for them (the FHT Commissioners) to administer the harbour as they find it, not to consider extension schemes," was a "damning indictment" of port administration in Western Australia. No responsible English politician, he suggested, would use such language about, say, the port authority of Liverpool. He also accused the government of using the port as a "tax-collection organisation."[47] Although Buchanan was undoubtedly right to deprecate government interference in port administration, in Western Australia's small community it was

---

Harbour Trust," 10 September 1928.

[44]*The West Australian*, 31 August 1928.

[45]*Ibid.*, 6 September 1928. See also WAPD, LXXIX (1928), 582; and PWD, 1163/27, copy of government reply to a parliamentary question asked by Mr. Brown, 12 September 1928.

[46]Hon A. McCallum, MLA, *Fremantle Harbour. Proposals for Extension. Schemes Outlined and Compared* (Perth, 1928), speech given in Legislative Assembly, 12 September 1928.

[47]Buchanan, *Report*, I, 99; and *The West Australian*, 27 April 1928.

unrealistic not to expect government, business and the general public to take a keen interest in port affairs. Such interest, of course, did not always contribute to sound decisions. As Mr. McCallum pointed out, the graving dock provides an example where, "instead of the advice of engineers being openly sought without restriction, and that advice of engineers being accepted, politics were brought in and local agitation was listened to, with the result that over a quarter of a million of the people's money now lies at the bottom of the ocean."[48] The motion for the select committee was defeated but the government, bowing to political pressure, agreed to yet another inquiry into the port's development.

In February 1929 Mr. Rustat Blake, of Sir Alexander Gibb and Partners, arrived in Western Australia to examine the plans for the development of the port. In July 1929 the final report (henceforth referred to as the Gibb Report) was presented to the government. The Gibb Report declared that "Harbour extensions on the general lines of the recommendations contained in the Report of the Engineer-in-Chief, Public Works Department, are calculated to give results which are in the best interests not only of the Port, but of the State as a whole."[49] In particular, the Gibb Report sided with Stileman rather than with the FHT on the question of channel depth and width. Thus the FHT, striving for the best possible port facilities, had clearly not paid enough attention to economic realities.

All three plans overestimated the expansion of port trade. The Gibb Report, for example, predicted that, given past trends, trade would reach 2.6 million tons by 1932-1933. But the onset of depression meant that the predicted trade flows failed to materialise and this, with the accompanying financial stringency, led to the shelving of plans for port expansion. The "Battle of the Plans" was finally resolved not by technical experts or even by political force but merely by the dismal power of economics.

The Development of Bulk Handling

The depression years, although years of relative quietude in port development, were not devoid of change. Cargo handled per yard of quay averaged 490 tons during the 1930s, about forty percent above the level

---

[48]McCallum, *Fremantle Harbour,* 14.

[49]Alexander Gibb and Partners, *Report on the Fremantle Harbour* (Perth, 1929), 8.

of the 1920s. This improvement in cargo throughput was mainly due to the growth of bulk handling.

Cargoes such as coal and phosphates were handled in bulk using shore cranes by the end of the first decade of the twentieth century. In 1920 the Anglo-Persian Oil Company (now known as British Petroleum) erected oil storage tanks at North Fremantle and built a pipeline to carry oil from Victoria Quay to their tanks. The first ship to use the new facilities was the tanker *British Fern* that arrived on 8 October 1920 and put 7536 tons of oil into the tanks.[50] There was little oil bunkering done that year but, as we saw in chapter 3, oil bunkering increased rapidly from the mid-1920s onwards. In 1925 Sir Robert Wylie Cohen, Managing Director of the British Imperial Oil Company, visited Fremantle and observed that the "cumbersome handling of petrol in tins and cases was costing the consumer a large amount of money."[51] His company (now known as Mobil Oil) and the Vacuum Oil Company laid pipelines to North Quay to carry petrol and kerosene. These facilities commenced operation on 8 April 1927 when the tanker *Radix* discharged the first bulk cargoes of petrol and kerosene. The FHT observed that this was "another mark in the steady progress of the state."[52] About two years later the Texas Oil Company (Australia) Ltd. installed a bulk pipeline and shortly before the outbreak of the Second World War Commonwealth Oil Refineries Ltd. followed suit.[53] However, the major landmark in the progress of bulk handling at Fremantle was undoubtedly the introduction of bulk grain handling, and we now turn to, and consider, this in detail.

On 23 August 1904, the steamship *Essex* left Fremantle for England with 262 tons of locally grown wheat, the first recorded wheat shipment from Western Australia.[54] The first wheat export of any magnitude occurred in 1908-1909 when 14,774 tons was shipped from Fremantle. From these humble beginnings wheat exports grew to become

---

[50]PWD, 4432/21, FHT to Engineer-in-Chief, 7 February 1927.

[51]FPA, Minutes, 9 January 1925.

[52]*FHT, AnnualReport* (1926-1927), 16.

[53]*Ibid.* (1937-1938), 7.

[54] Western Australia, *Yearbook* (1902-1904).

a mainstay of the port's trade, although, as we saw in chapter 3, the progress of the wheat trade was far from smooth and uninterrupted.

The record season in 1908-1909 caught the port unprepared: most of the wheat had to be sampled and weighed on Victoria Quay in the midst of the ordinary work of the port. Handling was slow because of a lack of proper equipment and the inexperience of the men; the railway system was not able to supply enough grain to enable ships to be worked continuously. Stevens, the Secretary of the FHT, admitted that there was a "want of system and confusion."[55] The FHT lost about 6d per ton of wheat handled as it underestimated the cost of the work. Faced with predictions of heavier crops to come, the FHT was forced to make urgent provision for the wheat trade.

At that time all wheat in Australia was handled in bags. Bulk handling had, however, been developed in the USA as early as the 1860s, and in 1905 Mr. Palmer, the Engineer-in-Chief, had made a detailed examination of American methods. He concluded that:

> there does not seem much doubt that, other things being equal, export in large quantities can be more profitably carried on in bulk than in bags, in order, however, to succeed the ships require to be specially suited to or fitted for bulk trade and a considerable amount of capital must be laid out in elevating machinery and storehouses.[56]

The advantages of bulk handling included: a saving in the use of wheat sacks, cheaper handling, faster ship turn round and potentially lower freight rates, better use of railway rolling stock and higher prices through improved grading and cleaning of the grain.[57] However, the FHT eventually decided to design facilities for handling wheat in bags rather than in bulk.

---

[55]FPA, 78/09/4, notes on interview with the Commissioner of Railways, 14 June 1909.

[56]FPA, 109/07/2, C.S.R. Palmer, "Report on Methods and Cost of Handling of Wheat in the United States of America," 19 July 1905.

[57]FPA, 92/10/1, copy of notes to Premier on reasons why Fremantle adopted bag handling (undated).

There were a number of reasons for the preference for bag handling. The development of bulk handling involved costly investment in handling equipment, silos, railway trucks and other facilities. But the volume of grain handled at Fremantle was still relatively small which limited the port's ability to reap the economies of scale offered by bulk handling. Even in the late 1930s, Sydney, Australia's leading wheat port, handled only 0.5 million tons per annum, compared to over four million tons per annum at leading Canadian ports.[58] Another problem was that shipowners were often reluctant to carry bulk wheat and, as late as the 1920s, asked for higher freight rates for bulk wheat than for bagged wheat.[59] Ships had to be specially equipped with "shifting boards" to stabilise the cargo.[60] Sailing ships were particularly vulnerable to shifting of cargo and few shipowners were prepared to risk carrying bulk grain around Cape Horn. Thus the development of bulk wheat shipments was slow until just before the First World War, when tramp steamers finally supplanted sailing vessels in the grain trade. For many years even ports which shipped wheat in bulk sent some in bags, purely for the sake of holding and binding the wheat.

Discharging at the other end also needed to be taken into consideration. In 1911 there were six ports in the United Kingdom equipped with facilities for discharging bulk wheat. But as late as the 1930s only two Japanese ports possessed bulk handling equipment and there was none in any Indian or Chinese port.[61] At ports without bulk handling equipment it was necessary to re-bag the wheat - an expensive operation. When tramp ships arrived to load grain in Australia the final destination was not always known; grain producers would be reluctant to risk loading them in bulk if they could end up going to a port with no

---

[58]K. Burley, *British Shipping and Australia 1920-1939* (Cambridge, 1968), 200-204.

[59]G.D. Snooks, *Depression and Recovery in Western Australia 1928/29-1938/39* (Perth, 1974), 43.

[60]FPA, 92/10/1, extract from a letter written by the London agents of Messrs. H.G. Barker and Co., 16 September 1910. See also Secretary South Australia Farmers' Coop. Union Ltd., to FHT, 27 December 1911. The following two sentences also drew on these two sources.

[61]Australia, *First Progress Report of the Parliamentary Standing Committee on Public Works* (Adelaide, 1934), 59.

facilities for bulk wheat. This problem illustrates the technical interrelatedness of port investments: if a developed country such as Australia was to obtain the maximum benefit from capital-intensive techniques then these techniques needed to be adopted in countries whose factor endowments might favour a more labour-intensive mode of handling.

The waterside workers correctly feared that bulk handling would lead to unemployment. According to one estimate, about two-thirds less men were required if grain was handled in bulk than in bags.[62] This was, of course, a point not lost on employers. The FHT, for example, optimistically declared that bulk handling would enable them to "rid themselves, once and for all, of one of the most troublesome of all the problems to be handled, *viz.*, the question of labour."[63] After the First World War Australian ports acquired a reputation for slow turnround mainly due to restrictive practices and industrial unrest by waterside workers, seamen and other maritime workers. But even when bulk handling was introduced men were still needed to trim the grain into the corners of the ships' holds - an arduous task that was not mechanised until after the Second World War.[64]

It is not surprising, therefore, that the FHT initially provided for the handling of bagged wheat only. By the end of 1910 the port had a large shed on North Quay equipped with five elevators for taking bags from trucks. The elevators carried the bags either into stacks in the shed or connected with conveyors, which carried them across the shed and wharf, and into the ship's hold. The appliances worked smoothly but bags bursting in all directions caused problems:

> Hundreds of bags reached the Port during the past year in a condition which made it practically impossible to handle them without damage; a number of bags which burst either on the elevators or in the stacks were found, on examination, to be superphosphate bags which had been turned inside out and filled with grain; many, too, were burned through coming in contact with phosphate or

---

[62]Australia, *Report of the Royal Commission on the Bulk Handling of Wheat* (Perth, 1935), xix.

[63]*The West Australian*, 26 September 1910.

[64]Burley, *British Shipping*, 197-215.

> lime, and many, again, were old or patched or with holes filled with grass, rags, paper, or whatever else seemed to have been handy to stuff them up with at the moment.[65]

However, the machinery worked well and in 1913-1914 the FHT reported that 75,140 bags were placed on one ship in forty working hours. Wheat handling, however, remained a hard physical task: wharf labourers had to manhandle bags of at least 200 lbs. and sometimes much more. Serious injuries were not uncommon.[66]

The FHT estimated that the 1913-1914 grain season brought in £18,300 in port dues and harbour charges; total expenditure by grain ships in Fremantle was estimated at £56,000.[67] It is little wonder that the Trust was somewhat alarmed when drought ruined the 1914-1915 season and no surplus was available for export. The following season produced the heaviest crop in the state's history, but, ironically, little could be exported owing to the scarcity of shipping caused by the outbreak of war. Wheat piled up on the wharves and the FHT took urgent steps to protect the bags from the winter rains. This problem was repeated throughout Australia; in the eastern states serious damage was caused to the grain by wet weather and by the actions of mice and weevils. The federal government intervened in the marketing and shipping of wheat in an attempt to improve the situation. Between 1915 and 1922 Western Australian wheat was marketed through a compulsory wheat pool, organised jointly by the federal and state government.[68] In 1916 the Commonwealth Line was established primarily to transport Australian exports to Europe. But according to one estimate it would have taken the Line's fifteen ships about eight years to shift the wheat surplus of 2.5 million tons![69] The federal government gave the New South Wales government money to aid the construction of storage silos in country areas in 1917. The following

---

[65]*FHT, AnnualReport* (1910-1911), 8.

[66]See M.T. Tull, "Blood on the Cargo: Cargo-Handling and Working Conditions on the Waterfront at Fremantle 1900-1930," *Labour History*, No. 52 (May 1987), 15-29.

[67]*FHT, AnnualReport* (1913-1914), 13-14.

[68]For a survey of wheat marketing in Western Australia see S. Glyn, *Government Policy and Agricultural Development* (Perth, 1975), appendix 2, 150-154.

[69]R. McDonell, *Build a Fleet Lose a Fleet* (Melbourne, 1976), 53.

year work started on a bulk grain terminal in the Port of Sydney. The latter, completed in 1922, made Sydney the first Australian port to provide bulk grain handling facilities.[70]

In Western Australia, the first experiment with bulk handling was undertaken by Westralian Farmers Ltd., a producer's cooperative, in July 1924.[71] The steamer SS *Arna* (3250 tons), was partly loaded in bulk. The wheat was sent on board in bags that were then slit and their contents emptied into the ship's hold. But the experiment cannot have been a great success, as it was not repeated. This was mainly because freight rates for bulk wheat were about two shillings a ton more than for bagged wheat. However, in the 1929-1930 season, Westralian Farmers Ltd. found that for the first time they could obtain vessels for shipping bulk wheat at lower rates than for bagged wheat. The experiment with bulk handling was repeated twice and found to be more profitable than in 1924. After 1930 rates for bulk wheat stayed lower than for wheat in bags.

The 1930s depression provided the final impetus for the introduction of bulk handling in Western Australia. In 1930-1931 there was a record wheat crop of 53.5 million bushels but the growers received less income than they had in 1920-1921 when the harvest was only a quarter of this size. Of the total value of the 1930-1931 crop, about thirty percent was paid out by growers for wheat bags, receiving at country sidings, railage and handling at mills and ports.[72] In evidence given before the Royal Commission on the Dominions in 1913, a leading representative of Western Australian grain producers put their financial position clearly:

> The price is regulated by London Market, and nothing the farmer here can do with his hatful of wheat, will affect it in the slightest. The only way, therefore, to improve the position is to effect savings in cost of production and transport.[73]

---

[70]C.R. Bickford, "The Handling of Bagged Wheat at Glebe Island, N.S.W.," *Journal of the Institution of Engineers (Australia)*, III (1931), 325-329.

[71]This paragraph draws on J. Sandford, *Walter Harper and the Farmers* (Perth, 1955).

[72]Snooks, *Depression and Recovery*, 43.

[73]FPA, 123/13/1, copy of evidence of Mr. W. Oliphant, manager of the Western Australian Producers' Union, 1913.

The depression starkly revealed the weakness of the farmers' position; the time was ripe for the introduction of bulk handling.

In July 1931 Westralian Farmers Ltd. submitted a proposal to the government for the installation of a bulk handling system, the government to provide port and railway facilities and the company country siding installations. Five country sidings were equipped with experimental wheat bins and in 1932 a limited quantity of wheat was handled in bulk from these sidings to the mills. The wheat bins differed from conventional silos in that they were made from timber and iron obtained from old storage sheds rather than from concrete and they used a cheap portable elevator. The FHT provided temporary bulk elevating equipment on North Quay.

In October 1932 Mitchell's National/Country Party Coalition Government introduced a Bill to establish a trust to operate a bulk handling system. The Bill proposed to give the trust a monopoly of wheat handling and it was to be financed by a loan to the Wheat Pool of Western Australia, repayment of the loan being guaranteed by the government. The Bill met with considerable opposition, particularly in regard to the granting of a monopoly and the financial arrangements. A Joint Select Committee of both Houses recommended passage of the Bill, subject to amendments, but the Bill was still not passed.[74] Following the defeat of the Bill, in 1933 Westralian Farmers and the Trustees of the Wheat Pool of Western Australia formed a company called Co-operative Bulk Handling to establish a bulk handling system. The company secured leases for storage bins at forty-eight railway sidings, bringing the total to fifty-three. The company wanted to build more but Premier Collier's new Labor Government (elected in April 1933) refused to grant any more leases pending a full inquiry into the whole question of bulk handling.

The government's concerns were twofold: first, some members of the Labor Party, mainly those representing port constituencies, were strongly opposed to the development of bulk handling.[75] They correctly feared the scheme would lead to a loss of employment for lumpers and others involved in the transport and handling of wheat. It was estimated that 500-550 lumpers would be displaced permanently; the loss of about

[74]See the record of debate in WAPD, LXXXIX (1932). The bill was introduced on 7 September 1932, the second reading passed on 11 October, and the report of the Select Committee received on 22 November.

[75]B.K. Hyams, "The Political Organisation of Farmers in Western Australia 1914-1944" (Unpublished MA thesis, University of Western Australia, 1964), 138.

£80,000 per annum in wages would hurt local businesses.[76] The timing was particularly embarrassing for the Labor Party as the depression had caused the rate of unemployment to soar to twenty-eight percent in the early 1930s, making it impossible for most of the displaced lumpers to find work. Second, the Collier Government had reservations about bulk handling being run by a monopoly outside of government control. The government favoured a board of management containing representatives of government, consumers, millers, merchants, railways and the FHT, but this was strongly opposed by the wheat producers.

The government finally appointed a Royal Commission, which reported in July 1935. It was estimated that a bulk handling system enabled one man hour of effort to shift 300 bushels of wheat; originally, one man hour of effort shifted only 105 bushels of bagged wheat.[77] Although this was a great improvement, achieved at only one-quarter of the cost of an orthodox system with concrete silos, the FHT considered the system as only "a bag eliminating method of handling wheat."[78] It was no substitute for an orthodox system of concrete silos, with ample terminal storage and rapid cargo-handling appliances. At Fremantle it took about twenty-four hours to load the amount loaded in one hour at Sydney.[79] The Royal Commission recommended that silos with a capacity of one and a half million tons be constructed, but Fremantle did not acquire an orthodox system until 1964. Nevertheless, the Royal Commission found that the Western Australian system was about 2.5 pence per bushel less expensive than bagged handling. In 1935 the total saving amounted to seven percent of the average price of wheat so this innovation made an important contribution to the wheat industry's recovery from the 1930s depression.[80] The Royal Commission recommended that Cooperative Bulk Handling be given a state-wide monopoly of wheat marketing and the government, influenced by the demonstrated advantages of bulk handling, agreed to the recommendation. One spin-off from bulk handling was that

---

[76]*The West Australian*, 25 October and 4 November 1932.

[77]FPA, 104/35/2, FHT to Chairman, Royal Commission on Bulk Handling, 2 April 1935.

[78]*FHT, AnnualReport* (1935-1936), 8.

[79]Burley, *British Shipping*, 203.

[80]Snooks, *Depression and Recovery*, 43.

it enabled the flow of wheat cargoes to be more evenly distributed over the year, eliminating the seasonal peak, which saw most of the port's eighteen berths occupied for a short period. In effect, it created four surplus berths, which reduced the need for any major expenditure on harbour works prior to 1939.[81]

In chapter 4 we saw that after the Second World War the increasing size of bulk grain and other carriers posed problems for the ports. The lack of adequate depths at some ports prevented vessels from taking on full loads and they had to "top-up" at ports with suitable depths of water. Shipowners responded by imposing a two-port surcharge on top of the freight rate. For example, in the mid-1960s the Fremantle terminal could only service vessels up to 40,000 dwt but much larger ones were scheduled to enter the trade.

The FPA responded by modernising the existing facilities but, eventually, was forced to relocate the grain terminal to the Outer Harbour. The new terminal was opened in 1977 and was capable of handling vessels up to 100,000 dwt and could load 5000 tons of grain per hour compared to only 1600 tons per hour at the old terminal. Nevertheless, as late as the 1980s, two-port loading frequently occurred at other ports in South Australia, Western Australia and Victoria and a two-port surcharge continued to apply in such cases.[82] A Commission of Inquiry into the Australian Maritime Industry, which reported in 1976, found that in general bulk cargoes were handled efficiently although all Australian ports suffered from problems of labour unrest and restrictive practices which slowed vessel turnround and reduced port efficiency.[83] In a later chapter we will examine these important issues in detail.

The Immediate Post-Second World War Years

Apart from the development of bulk grain handling the depression, as we have seen, led to the shelving of plans for port development and the port was not well equipped to cater for the strains of the war years. The

---

[81]FPA, 99/32/2, Mr. McCartney to Chairman of FHT, 27 October 1932.

[82]Australia, *Royal Commission into Grain Storage, Handling and Transport* (3 vols. Canberra, 1988), II, 16.

[83]Australia, Commission of Inquiry into the Maritime Industry, *Report on Adequacy of Australia's Ports* (Canberra, 1976), 1-21.

situation was worsened by the fact that during the war the port authority was able to undertake only limited maintenance work. As we saw in chapter 4, the state of the ports led to urgent attempts to improve output but these concentrated on labour efficiency since the improvement of port facilities was a longer term objective. The ports experienced difficulties in coping with post-war trade flows and in 1947 the West Australian government appointed Mr. Frank Tydeman to report on development plans for Fremantle.

Tydeman, born in 1901, was an English engineer with considerable experience of ports. From 1936 until the fall of Singapore to the Japanese he was the Chief Engineer of the Singapore Harbour Board. Tydeman served as a Colonel in the Royal Engineers during the war and afterwards decided to settle in Perth.[84]

Tydeman's report was completed in August 1948 and provided a remarkably detailed analysis of port efficiency and a thorough plan for port development into the twenty-first century. He proposed a five-stage scheme of port development:

1. Immediate improvements to existing facilities including the introduction of forklift trucks and pallets
2. Longer term improvements to existing facilities including the reconstruction of North and South quays and a new railway layout
3. Upstream extensions including the re-siting and renewal of the existing road and rail bridges and the creation of eleven new berths.
4. Seawards extension to the north including the provision of ten new berths
5. Seawards extension south including the provision of forty-one more berths.

The first stage and, to a large extent, the second stage, involved organisational and operational improvements designed to achieve maximum utilisation of existing capacity. The introduction of forklifts and pallets to handle cargo was the major innovation proposed. As we saw in chapter 4, during the Second World War the Americans introduced this method of handling cargo to Australia and it enabled general cargo to be handled at greater speed and lower cost. Stage three involved up-river development; stage four development north of the river mouth; and the

---

[84]*The West Australian*, 11 November 1948.

final stage development south of the river mouth (but not in Cockburn Sound). Thus Tydeman's scheme was not radically different than those of Stileman and Gibb, although it certainly cost more thoroughly.

The government adopted his plan and in May 1950 appointed him as General Manager of the FHT at a salary of £2770. He immediately set about implementing stage one including the increased mechanisation of cargo-handling. Within two years he had bought 133 forklift trucks, forty-five towmotors, and forty-five mobile cranes, making Fremantle one of the best equipped ports in Australia.[85] The other stages of Tydeman's plan proved more difficult to implement because the port was experiencing the constraints imposed by its close proximity to a large and growing city.

The Development of the Outer Harbour in the 1950s

The passage of time alters the viability of existing port locations. After the Second World War ship sizes increased rapidly and land intensive industries such as oil refineries sought out seaboard sites: suitable depths and areas were not easily provided in cramped metropolitan ports. Consequently, port authorities the world over were forced to search for alternative sites for new facilities. The decision to develop Cockburn Sound, some twenty kilometres south of Fremantle, as a deep water port, was partly a response to pressure on facilities in the Inner Harbour, where the depth limit of eleven metres was beginning to become a constraint, especially for oil tankers.[86] But a key reason was the state government's attempt to encourage the growth of manufacturing industry.[87] Prior to the Second World War Western Australia's economy was predominantly devoted to primary production. Secondary industry was limited to the supply of the local market and the processing of some primary products for export. In the early 1950s four oil refineries were built around Australia and, due partly to inducements offered by the Western Australian government, one was located at Kwinana on Cockburn Sound. Kwinana's attractions included the availability of deep water, ample

---

[85]J.K. Ewers, *The Western Gateway: A History of Fremantle* (2nd ed., Nedlands, WA, 1971), 151; and FHT, *Annual Report* (1959-1960), 20.

[86]FPA, Minutes, 11 May 1953.

[87]A.T. Bonds, "The Economics of Outer Harbour Development in the Port of Fremantle" (Unpublished MA thesis, University of Western Australia), 1969, 103-107.

supplies of cheap land (a legacy of the cancelled naval base) and access to the services and infrastructure of the metropolitan area.[88]

In 1955 the West Australian government published a plan for the development of the Perth metropolitan area produced by Professor Gordon Stephenson. In 1959 the Metropolitan Regional Planning Authority was created to administer it. The plan observed that

> There exists in the south-eastern part of the Cockburn Sound a vast hinterland capable of accommodating all the uses associated with a major port and industrial area without any of the restrictions on space, becoming more and more apparent, in the vicinity of the Inner Harbour[89]

The plan explicitly recognised the need to keep port traffic away from the central area of Fremantle and to guide the development of port, transport and public utility facilities in the Kwinana Industrial Area. In 1961 the Premier's Committee for the Development of Cockburn Sound and Kwinana was set up, with representatives of relevant government departments, to ensure that development proceeded in a coordinated manner. The Committee ensured that the growth of the port did not outstrip the capacity of the transport network. The movement of goods to and from the port was channelled into corridors that were designed to avoid conflicts with inner-city traffic. The major transport corridor (both road and rail) was located south of the Swan River, linking industrial areas to the port. Offers of cheap land and other inducements were used to attract industries to industrial parks such as Kewdale and Canning Vale, which were given good access to the port via the transport corridor. Thus the port and transport network was developed in an integrated manner; port planning did not take place in isolation from planning for the metropolitan area as a whole.

The government funded the dredging of channels to twelve metres at a cost of \$2.9 million, but the companies were required to build the necessary shore facilities. The refinery began operation in 1954 and in its first five years of operation exported petroleum products worth \$254

---

[88]Rendel and Partners, *Port and Urban Systems* (Canberra, 1976), 316.

[89]G. Stephenson and J.A. Hepburn, *Plan for the Metropolitan Development of Perth and Fremantle* (Perth, 1955), 136.

million or eleven percent of the total value of the state's exports.[90] The Outer Harbour was officially opened on 11 January 1955 when the tanker MV *British Crusader* cut a floating boom across the new channel through the Parmelia and Success Banks.[91]

The refinery sparked off an "industrial chain reaction" and was followed by an iron and steel works (1954), an alumina refinery (1964), a fertiliser plant (1969) and a nickel refinery (1970).[92] The Premier, Albert Hawke (the uncle of ex-Prime Minister Bob Hawke) opened the steelworks jetty on 30 May 1956 and the first vessel to use it was the *River Hunter* which discharged 1800 tons of steel billets.[93]

There is no doubt that the government's policies were a success but the inducements offered by the state had significant implications for the Fremantle Port Authority. In particular, the port authority lost control over land which it had owned since its inception in 1903, and the company was given exemption from port charges until the year 2000 with an option to extend this arrangement for a further twenty years. Similarly, when the steel plant was established, Broken Hill Proprietary Ltd. was given control over about a mile of foreshore and reduced wharfage charges. The FPA was not consulted about the wharfage concessions.[94] In 1956, after an increase of over sixty-six percent in wharfage rates, shipowners complained that the "increases represent the first step to balance the price Western Australia is paying for the advantage of an oil refinery at Kwinana."[95] Due to these and other concessions, by 1969-1970 full wharfage was paid by only sixteen percent of imports and one percent of exports, a situation that led to a highly uneven incidence of charges and financial problems for the FPA.[96] It was later estimated that between

---

[90]J. Hutton, *Manufacturing Industry and Western Australia Development* (Nedlands, WA, 1966), 78.

[91]FPA, Minutes, 11 January 1955.

[92]Ewers, *Western Gateway*, 162.

[93]FPA, Minutes, 29 May 1956.

[94]*Ibid.*, 24 July 1959.

[95]FPA, 87/1006, OSRA and ASOF to FHT, 10 July 1956.

[96]Bonds, "Economics of Outer Harbour Development," 220-222.

1955-1972 the exemptions granted to BP for oil shipped at Kwinana cost the FPA almost $95 million![97] Thus in a very real sense the port was merely a pawn in a larger game.

The Development of Containerisation since 1964

In chapter 4 we saw that containerisation offered enormous potential to improve cargo-handling efficiency. The first specialised container vessel was introduced into Australia's coastal trade in 1964 and two British consortia, Overseas Containers Ltd.(OCL) and Associated Container Transportation Ltd. (ACT) introduced the container service on the United Kingdom/ Australia route five years later.[98]

Following the shipowners decision to adopt containerisation the FPA began the construction of container facilities in Fremantle's Inner Harbour. Two berths were provided downstream from the new Railway Bridge at a cost of almost $5 million and were ready by late 1968. The land at the rear of the berths was leased to private container operators as a location for cargo depots for loading and unloading containers. Seatainer Terminals, a subsidiary of OCL, leased eight acres of land for a cargo depot and also took over operation of the terminal. ACT established an additional cargo depot in conjunction with Container Terminals Fremantle Pty. Ltd. The FPA retained control of the wharf, the container crane, and an area extending 138 feet back from the wharf face and all roadways. The main reason for this was to ensure that other (non-OCL and ACT) shipowners would not be excluded from using the facilities. The container terminal was provided with direct access to the main highway system to allow for speedy movement of containers.

By 1974-1975 container movements reached 64,000 TEUs (a TEU is a "twenty foot equivalent unit" and represents a standard 20ft. x 8ft. x 8ft. container), of which just over one-half were accounted for by interstate traffic. But in 1975 Associated Steamships Pty. Ltd. withdrew from the trade and the bulk of interstate container traffic had to be carried

---

[97]FPA, 5431/88/0109/02, text of Parliamentary reply for Hon. Treasurer to Hon. Mr. Jones, 7 August 1972.

[98]ACL was formed by Alfred Holt and Co., British and Commonwealth Shipping Co. Ltd., Furness Withy and Oriental Steamship Navigation Company. ACT was formed by the Port Line, Cunard Steamship Company, Blue Star Line, Ellerman Lines, Ben Lines and the Harrison Line.

by rail. This was a severe blow to the port because it meant that the container terminal was greatly under-utilised. It was not until 1984-1985 that container traffic reached 100,000 TEUs per annum. Thus commercial decisions effectively downgraded the port's status as a container port; once again it was a pawn in a global game of commerce.[99]

A Commission of Inquiry into the Maritime Industry reported in 1976 that there were serious problems with container handling in Australia. Shipowners complained that container-handling rates were well below the twenty-five per hour which they achieved in ports such as Rotterdam, Tilbury, Oakland and New York. The low productivity in Australian ports was attributed to a variety of factors including the state of the physical infrastructure and problems with the workforce, including industrial disputes and restrictive work practices. However, Fremantle was by no means the worst performer, although another container crane was needed.[100] But it took until June 1982 before another container crane was commissioned. At that time Fremantle Cargo Services Ltd. (made up of two overseas shipping companies and a local stevedoring company) and the FPA agreed to a build a new container terminal behind berths four and five on North Quay. In 1985 Fremantle Cargo Services Ltd amalgamated with Seatainer terminals Ltd. to form Fremantle Terminals Ltd.[101]

The huge capital required to establish a container system and a desire to reap economies of scale forced the operators to join consortia but this led to fears of monopoly. In the late 1960s a Select Committee on Containerisation dismissed this as a serious threat but containerisation certainly strengthened the economic power of the conference lines serving Australia.[102] Concern about the P&O's domination of container handling at Fremantle led to a proposal for a joint venture involving Stateships,

---

[99]Slack, "Pawns in the Game," 579-588.

[100]*Report on Adequacy of Australia's Ports,* 505-506.

[101]FPA, 5341/88/07/F, FPA to Minister for Transport, "Developments Since the Government Took Office," 29 May 1985.

[102]Australia, Senate Select Committee, Report on the Container Method of Handling Cargoes (Canberra, 1968), Part 1, 67-70; and F.D. Gallagher, *Options for Western Australia-Europe Container Traffic* (Perth, 1977), 19.

Patricks Stevedoring, the FPA and the Australian National Line but this never came to anything.[103]

Since the 1980s the Australian waterfront has been the target of microeconomic reforms designed to combat market power and improve productivity and efficiency. The process of reform at Fremantle will be considered in detail in the next chapter but included new capital investment and radical labour market reforms.

By the 1980s the carriage of containers was increasingly being concentrated in large ships of more than 4000 TEU's capacity which called at a limited number of ports. The containers were then distributed to smaller ports by feeder vessels carrying up to 1000 TEUs.[104] The FPA has attempted to promote a land-bridging service whereby a feeder service carries containers from Singapore to Fremantle for distribution to Adelaide by rail. This move, which threatens the market shares of eastern states' ports, would make Fremantle more of a "Gateway to Australia."

Fremantle's container terminals have long been handicapped by a lack of space. For example, Seatainer Terminals had two berths with fifteen acres compared to Rotterdam which had five berths with 121 acres.[105] In 1996 container operations on North Quay were consolidated into a single continuous length of deep-water berth instead of having containers handled over three separate areas. P&O Ports operates from berths four to six and Patrick's Stevedoring from berths seven to ten. Berths 1 to 2 and 11 to 12 have been reserved for common user berths. The FPA spent about $7.2 million upgrading North Quay and the two container operators have agreed to spend $60 million on new equipment such as cranes. The FPA estimates that the Inner Harbour will be able to accommodate trade growth until 2020 but has undertaken preliminary planning to provide extra container facilities in the Naval Base/Kwinana area.

---

[103]FPA, 88/1/15/64.4, proposed joint venture.

[104]FPA, Future Port Options Auxiliary Study, *Final Report* (Fremantle, 1991), 3.

[105]FPA, 88/1/6/2-2A, Fremantle Sub-Regional Centre Study Technical Committee, Acting Port Engineer to Metropolitan Regional Planning Authority, 26 June 1979.

The Port and Urban Environment: The 1890s to 1990s

Fremantle, in common with Australia's other capital city ports, developed in close proximity to the metropolitan area. Western Australia was unusual in the sense that the port (Fremantle) and administrative capital (Perth) were originally physically distinct, although from the mid-1890s suburbanisation began to link the two towns.[106] However, despite "the relentless spread of the greater Perth conurbation," Fremantle has, to this day, retained many of the distinctive characteristics of a port city.[107]

Although the gold rushes caused rapid population growth in the 1890s, by 1901 Western Australia's population was still only 184,000. Of this total, approximately 56,700 or thirty-one percent lived in Fremantle and Perth.[108] Urbanisation in Western Australia increased rapidly in the 1910s and 1920s but was checked in the 1930s with the revival of gold mining.[109] By the late 1940s Western Australia's population had grown to about half a million of whom about fifty percent lived in Perth. After the war, Western Australia's population grew rapidly, especially during the mineral boom in the 1960s. By the 1990s the state's population had reached 1.5 million of whom over seventy percent lived in the metropolitan area.

As population increased, so did the pressures on city land use: port operations began to hamper and be hampered by metropolitan land use activities. There were three main areas of potential conflict between port and city: first, over the provision of transit and long term storage facilities; second, over the provision of road and rail access to the port; and third, over the general environmental impact of port operations. We will consider each in turn.

Prior to the advent of containerisation, large numbers of transit sheds were required on the wharves because of the tendency of the ship

---

[106]C.T. Stannage, *The People of Perth* (Perth, 1979), 240-251.

[107]R. Reece and R. Pascoe, *A Place of Consequence. A Pictorial History of Fremantle* (Fremantle, 1983), xi.

[108]B.J. Shaw and J.T. Jackson, "A Comparative Study of Residential Development in Perth and Fremantle in 1880: Some Initial Findings," *Australia 1888*, Bulletin No. 5 (September 1980), 151.

[109]G.D. Snooks, "Development in Adversity 1913 to 1946," in C.T. Stannage (ed.), *A New History of Western Australia* (Nedlands, WA, 1981), 257.

to beat the quay, that is, for the rate of ship discharge to exceed the rate of wharf clearance and because of the need to assemble export cargoes. When it was created in 1903, the FHT inherited three transit sheds on Victoria Quay but quickly decided that these were inadequate and within a year had added four larger ones. Road and railway access was provided to the waterfront side as well as to the land-side of the sheds, enabling about one-half of cargo to be handled directly between ships and railway or road vehicles, avoiding double handling in the transit sheds.[110] By the 1920s there were ten transit sheds on Victoria Quay but the FHT found that they were becoming inadequate for the larger ships and larger cargoes being handled. At a cost of almost £1 million, the sheds were lengthened and widened and the timber floors were replaced with a harder wearing surface of reinforced concrete topped with bitumen. Although the number of sheds was reduced from ten to eight, storage capacity was increased from 260,000 to 340,000 square feet.[111]

The introduction of containerisation in the late 1960s made conventional wharf sheds obsolete. Containers require specially strengthened wharves, specialised mechanical equipment and open areas for stacking and storing containers. Although some conventional wharves and wharf sheds continued to be required for the dwindling proportion of non-containerised cargoes, most were under-utilised. The FPA, faced with the task of finding alternative uses for its empty cargo sheds, has made them available for various non-port uses. In 1987 "B" shed was converted into an historic boats museum and the following year "A" shed was transformed into an art gallery and restaurant. The Boom Defence Building at the southern end of Victoria Quay which was constructed during the war to make and repair torpedo nets was used as a Media Centre during the America's Cup defence in 1986-1987. In 1989 it was converted into a campus for the Maritime Studies Department of TAFE. "E" shed has been dismantled and relocated to a new position east of the FPA administration building. The development was handled by Fini Properties and includes restaurants, shops and a market; it was officially opened on 20 September 1996. The adaptive use of historic structures is an alternative to complete

---

[110]Estimated from FHT, *Annual Reports*, which give data on cargo handled directly between ships and land transport, between ships and lighters and through the sheds, but unfortunately the data do not distinguish between cargo travelling by rail and by road.

[111]Stevens, "History of the Harbour," 150.

redevelopment and helps preserve the port's maritime heritage, an issue we return to later in the chapter.

Warehouses and bond stores are normally provided in the vicinity of ports to meet the need for long term storage. A bond store is a warehouse supervised by customs officers and used for goods on which duty has not been paid. Free stores or warehouses are used for the storage of goods on which customs duty has been paid. Bond stores were developed in Britain during the eighteenth century to store imports such as tea and coffee until they could be sold at a favourable price. Previously, merchants were forced to pay customs dues when the cargo was landed, which often forced them to sell their goods immediately, even if prices were low, in order to pay customs duty.

The need for warehouses and bond storage varies from port to port. Fremantle lacks a significant entrepôt trade and so has never required extensive bond and warehouse facilities. After the turn of the century the decline of the gold industry and the removal of the railway workshops to Midland in 1904 caused Fremantle to stagnate, and the locus of economic activity switched to the capital Perth. A number of warehouse operators including Harris Scarfe, George Wills, Charles Atkins and P. Falk moved their headquarters to Perth.[112] Fremantle never regained its ground and by the mid-1930s there were five bond and free stores in Perth but only one in Fremantle.[113] Consequently, importers sometimes decided to leave their goods in the transit sheds on the wharves, rather than pay the cost of transhipment to Perth. In a sense, the FHT encouraged this practice by providing the first three days storage free of charge and levying only modest storage charges thereafter. The Trust also took sub-orders from merchants for delivery of goods direct to the merchants customers, who were then able to take delivery direct from the wharf sheds saving intermediate handling and carting. This use of transit sheds for longer term storage, while a convenience to importers and their customers, caused problems when the port was busy as the sheds could be littered with cargo from several vessels, leading to delays in cargo sorting and delivery. In the late 1940s it was estimated that the eight

---

[112]T. Joll, "1901-1930," in P. Firkins (ed.), *A History of Commerce and Industry in Western Australia* (Nedlands, WA, 1979), 50.

[113]See *Trade and Professions Directory of Western Australia* (Perth, 1933-1934).

wharf sheds on Victoria Quay would still be adequate for the port's needs if the FHT enforced the three-day transit storage period.[114]

Regardless of the type of storage, at some stage all cargoes had to be transported to or from the port. A variety of methods of transport can be used including, rail, road, lighters and pipelines. Before the opening of the Inner Harbour there was a bustling lighter traffic on the Swan River between Fremantle and Perth. This trade continued until September 1938 when the stiff competition offered by motor transport forced the last two firms to cease operations.[115] By that time almost one-half of the port's cargo was moved by rail, about one-quarter by road and about one-quarter by pipeline. The fact that almost one-half of the port's trade was carried by rail helped reduce pressure on the road system. By contrast, in Sydney, where the topography made the provision of rail access costly and difficult, only about thirteen percent of port trade was carried by rail, putting considerable strain on the road network.[116]

Fremantle was provided with railway connections to the old sea jetty in 1891 and, as we saw in chapter 1, the wharves were actually administered by the Railways Department before the formation of the FHT. The railway system, which was narrow gauge (three-feet six-inches), developed in two directions: northwards, via Perth, which was the major route, and southwards, via Robbs Jetty. The northward route crossed the Swan River immediately upstream of the port and connected with the Midland Railway at Midland Junction and, after 1917, provided a connection to the eastern states via the Trans-Continental Railway. However, rail access between Victoria Quay and the North Quay was via the main line only and both the mainline and the port system operated in a restricted land area behind the wharves. In the late 1940s it was observed that the system had "grown up over half a century into a cramped lay-out, barely adequate to meet the trade of the moment, not

---

[114]Tydeman, *Fremantle*, 115.

[115]Battye Library, Harbour and Lights Department Deposit 335, Chief Harbour Master to Under-Secretary for Works, 5 October 1921; Inspecting Accountant to Under Treasurer, 10 November 1939.

[116]C.R. Bickford, "The Development of the Port of Sydney," *Journal of the Institution of Engineers (Australia)*, XXIX (1957), 121. See also P. Proudfoot, *Seaport Sydney. The Making of the City Landscape* (Sydney, 1996).

capable of overload, and inefficient in operation."[117] A major reason for this was the limited land areas available for railway access, especially on Victoria Quay.

Photo 12: Bulk Grain Being Loaded at the Grain Jetty in the Outer Harbour, September 1966.

Source: See photo 1.

The majority of the port's road traffic went via Victoria Quay because North Quay specialised in bulk cargo that was normally transported by rail. When the FHT was formed in 1903 it found Cliff Street, the main approach to Victoria Quay, was crooked, uneven and poorly lit. It was used by all types of city traffic and was criss-crossed by railway lines; every week between 4000 and 5000 vehicles travelled along the road to and from the port and about 600 lines of railway trucks were shunted backwards and forwards across the street. The result was a congested and "highly dangerous thoroughfare." By the end of 1905 the

---

[117]Tydeman, *Fremantle*, 130.

FHT had spent £2133 on the road and could claim that it was "a fine, straight, well-built roadway," with adequate lighting and a broad footpath for pedestrians.[118] The relocation of the railway station in 1907 also improved access to Victoria Quay.

Tydeman, in his 1947 report, had advocated the removal of the road and rail bridges to provide space for extra berths but the development of the Outer Harbour removed the need for this expensive operation. However, a new railway bridge was built in 1964 upstream of the existing site and the land released was used for the port's first container terminal. At the beginning of the 1970s the main line marshalling yards were transferred to South Fremantle releasing land for port uses on Victoria Quay. It is clear that the provision of adequate road and rail access is vital to the smooth functioning of a port. In the 1990s the standard gauge railway line which winds around Fremantle City makes it difficult to upgrade rail access to North Quay. There is little point in making improvements to port facilities if the land transport system cannot cope with the increased cargo flows but the FPA considers that land transport links will be adequate to cater for trade growth until at least the year 2020.

Over a generation ago, L.E. Klimm wrote that "port and harbour works, being protective and local in effect, have a rare distinction among man's activities in changing the face of the earth; they are almost universally beneficial and it is seldom possible for their effect to be harmful."[119] It is unlikely that in the latter part of the twentieth century many would share this starry-eyed assessment. Port activities affect the environment in a variety of ways, for example, dredging and land reclamation can destroy the habitats of marine species and pollution, noise and congestion often accompanies port operations. The development of specialised container and bulk handling facilities with their intensive high-speed operations has also affected the environment.

Prior to the Second World War, environmental pressures were probably less of a concern in Western Australia than in the more densely populated and heavily industrialised eastern states, but problems did arise from time to time. Earlier in this chapter we saw that concern about the effect of port operations on the Swan River led to some opposition to

---

[118]FHT, *Report for the Half-Year Ending 30 June 1905*, 12-15.

[119]L.E. Klimm, "Man's Ports and Channels," in W.L. Thomas (ed.), *Man's Role in Changing the Face of the Earth* (Chicago, 1956), 539.

further up-river expansion. In 1928 the Minister for Public Works also opposed development south of the river mouth on the grounds that it would spoil Fremantle as a seaside resort, turning it into "a mere mass of wharves and boats."[120] The advent of oil bunkering and bulk oil handling in the early 1920s increased the dangers of fire and water pollution. In 1911 the Marine Underwriters' Association of Western Australia requested separate facilities for oil ships and a tighter control of inflammable cargoes. The FHT agreed to make them berth on the north side of the harbour and provide an inspector to prevent smoking and other fire hazards.[121] In the early 1920s further regulations governing night working were introduced.[122] However, these seem to have been mainly directed against the threat of fire because in 1926, when the Orient Steam Navigation Company's *Orama* collided with the quay and burst an oil pipe, there were no regulations or appliances to guard against oil spills. As a consequence, about thirty tons of oil escaped into the harbour.

In 1918 the SS *Polgowan,* which was reputedly carrying sufficient TNT on board to blow up Fremantle, caught fire at the North Wharf. The ships' crew and the local fire brigade brought the fire under control. Two of the crew received Sea Gallantry medals for their courage in fighting the fire.[123] The serious fire on the *Panamanian* during the Second World War also highlighted the potentially hazardous nature of port operations.

A horrific accident at the Canadian Port of Halifax on 6 December 1917 provides an indication of the catastrophe that could have occurred. The *Mont Blanc*, a French munition ship carrying a full cargo of explosives, collided with another vessel and blew up. The massive explosion instantly killed 1600 people, injured more than 9000 and left 25,000 homeless. It was reputedly the largest man made explosion in history until the detonation of the first atomic bomb. The shattered city

---

[120]McCallum, *Fremantle Harbour*, 9.

[121]FPA, 80/12/1, FHT to Secretary of Marine Underwriters' Association of WA, 5 December 1911.

[122]*FHT, Annual Report* (1923-1924), 12.

[123]City of Fremantle, *Victoria Quay and Its Architecture. Its History & Assessment of Cultural Significance* (Fremantle, 1991), 98.

took many years to recover. The Australian government gave $250,000 in financial aid.[124]

Photo 13: *Queen Elizabeth 2* entering Inner Harbour, February 1995.

Source: See photo 1.

In the early 1950s there was opposition from local councils to upriver development due to fears of pollution. At that time the government was still officially in favour of upriver development as advocated by the port authority, but there was growing support for development of the Outer Harbour.[125] An agreement made in 1972 between the FPA and Cockburn Cement Pty Ltd to remove sand from the Parmelia and Success sandbanks for use in the manufacture of cement and lime has proved controversial due to damage to seagrasses. In 1968 the Cockburn Sound Conservation Committee was established to advise on problems caused by

---

[124] J.F. Kitz, *Shattered City: The Halifax Explosion and the Road to Recovery* (Halifax, 1989).

[125] *The West Australian*, 3 and 18 February, and 23 May 1950; and 14 October 1954.

pollution.[126] In 1979 a controversial study by Dr. Graham Chittleborough identified serious water quality problems in the Sound but these were not primarily due to port operations.[127] In chapter 4 we saw that issues such the safety of visiting nuclear ships and the smells associated with live sheep shipments have also led to criticisms of port operations. The FPA, however, attempts to maintain high environmental standards and control pollution. One measure of its success is the fact that dolphins can regularly be seen swimming in both the Inner and Outer Harbours. It is hard to imagine a truly "green port" and, clearly, the environmental costs of port operations have to be weighed against the considerable economic benefits.[128]

In summary, our discussion of storage facilities, road and rail access and environmental problems suggests that competition between port and metropolitan land use activities increased with the passage of time. However, it was less serious than in older port cities such as Sydney.[129] A breakout from the confines of the Inner Harbour was not necessary until the mid-1950s, when Fremantle was able, at last, to exploit the deep-water and extensive land areas of Cockburn Sound.

The Future of the Inner Harbour

Since the development of the Outer Harbour the locus of bulk cargo-handling has been shifting southwards, away from the Inner Harbour. However, the Inner Harbour retained the lion's share of high valued general cargoes. By the 1990s Victoria Quay, originally the main centre of port activity, was divided into two sections: the Western End, which is no longer used for commercial port purposes, and the Victoria Quay

---

[126] FPA, 88/1/15/24A, Cockburn Sound Conservation Committee.

[127] Department of Conservation and Environment, *Cockburn Sound Environmental Study, 1976-1979* (Perth, 1979).

[128] A.C. Burdall and H.J. Williamson, "A Green Port: An Engineer's View," in C.R. Ford (ed.), *Ports into the Next Century* (London, 1991), 247-248.

[129] See A. Roberts, "Planning Sydney's Transport 1875-1900," in M. Kelly (ed.), *Nineteenth-Century Sydney. Essays in Urban History* (Sydney, 1978), 24-36; M. Tull, "The Development of Port Administration at Sydney, 1901 to 1936," *The Great Circle*, IV (1982), 92-104; G. Wotherspoon (ed.), *Sydney's Transport. Studies in Urban History* (Sydney, 1983); Proudfoot, *Seaport Sydney.*

Operational Area.[130] The Western End comprises South Mole, Berths "A" and "B" and includes a variety of maritime related activities including ship repairs and maintenance, a maritime college, port service activities, the port administration building, a cafe and art gallery, maritime museum and home-port facilities for the sail training ship *Leeuwin*. We have already seen that "E" shed was relocated to a new position east of the FPA administration building and now operates as a tourist facility. The berths would require extensive repairs to render them useable by trading ships.

The Victoria Quay Operational Area incudes berths "C" to "H," tug berths and the facilities for the pilot and work boats, transit sheds, and the passenger terminal. Non-trading ships such as fishing boats and naval vessels usually tie-up in this area. Within the Inner Harbour, although general cargo is still handled on Victoria Quay, the bulk of cargo activity now takes place on North Quay.

In 1989 the entrance channel and about two-thirds of the harbour were deepened to thirteen metres. The dredged material was used to provide reclaimed land for a new commercial boat harbour at Rous Head on the north side of the North Mole. The Rous Head Industrial Park was completed in August 1990 at a cost of about $30 million. A downturn in the economy made it hard to obtain tenants for the Park and three years later only about seventy percent of the land was leased or under options. By 1996 the land was fully leased.

In 1989 the government set up a future port options study.[131] The study concluded that the existing facilities on North Quay have the capacity to accommodate projected trade levels at least until the year 2020. Beyond that period, road and rail access are likely to constrain growth more than the state of port facilities. If the landbridging concept takes off rail facilities will need to be upgraded. The Fremantle Council has supported continued use of the Inner Harbour as a commercial port but concern has been expressed about the impact of higher levels of rail traffic associated with landbridging on the urban area. There has been some discussion of developing container facilities at regional ports such as Bunbury but because most containers are destined for the metropolitan area it would be inefficient to transport them over the large distances from regional ports.

---

[130]This paragraph draws on FPA, *Victoria Quay Study Report* (Fremantle, 1993).

[131]See FPA, *Future Port Options*.

The *Future Port Options* Study recommended three options for long term development of the port: first, an extension of the Inner Harbour to the north of north mole; second, a new harbour at Catherine Point about three kilometres south of Fremantle; third, a new harbour at Naval Base/Kwinana. The cost of each option, including rail and road works, was estimated at $173 million, $254 million and $279 million respectively. While a new container terminal is not required for twenty years or so it will be necessary to plan ahead otherwise possible port sites might be lost to other uses. The Catherine Point and Naval Base sites offered potential for creating more of a "textbook" port with good rail connections and ready availability of potential industrial land. In 1996 the government approved the Naval Base/Kwinana site for developments beyond 2015.

The Inner Harbour contains many buildings or areas worthy of retention and conservation because of their historic and architectural merits. In 1990 the Institute of Engineers listed Victoria Quay as a national engineering landmark. A 1991 study by the Fremantle Council found that the historical value of Victoria Quay has three components: first, the influence the port has had on the growth of Fremantle and the state; second, its association with historical personalities such as Sir John Forrest and C.Y. O'Connor; and, third, the changes in operations and physical form of the Quay.[132] Although obsolete as part of the commercial port, some cranes, wharf sheds and other structures survive as physical links with the past. Two vital links to the state's past, Arthur's Head and the Round House, the colony's first prison, were originally under the control of the port authority, which was understandably reluctant to maintain these non-port structures. In 1982 the Round House was transferred to the Fremantle City Council and Arthur's Head made an "A"-class reserve; they have since become popular tourist sites. In 1984 when the Challenger Boat Harbour was being constructed for the America's Cup Races the few remaining piles of the historic Long Jetty were left in place after a public outcry. However, the Council's study was not so complimentary about the port's administration building. It was built in 1963 in order to consolidate administrative staff, who previously were scattered around the port in eight existing buildings, under one roof. It was far larger than needed as the intention was to generate income by

---

[132]Fremantle, *Victoria Quay*.

leasing areas to commercial interests and it dwarfs the townscape of the port and the West End of the city.

In 1994, in response to requests from customs and complaints from importers about damage to motor vehicles, the FPA erected a security perimeter fence around the cargo-handling areas on Victoria Quay. Many Western Australians who had been used to free access to the wharves greeted this with dismay. However, the withdrawal of port functions provides an opportunity to restore some of the historic links between people and the waterfront. But conflicts exist between socially and commercially motivated uses of the waterfront space. In some overseas ports waterfront areas have been overwhelmed by high-income developments at the expense of open space and lower-income housing. A well-known example is found in the Port of London, where the old docks, stretching from Stepney to Woolwich, were made redundant by new facilities downstream at Tilbury and Felixstowe. The London Docklands Development Corporation redeveloped the area for high-income commercial industrial, residential and recreational use.[133] There is also potential conflict between conservation of historic structures and higher intensity redevelopment. However, public attitudes towards heritage issues have changed enormously in the last thirty years or so and urban residents and tourists now appreciate the adaptive use of historic structures such as warehouses and wharf sheds.[134] In this respect, the redevelopment of E Shed provides a good example of a workable compromise between heritage and commercial interests. In 1993, the Premier, Richard Court, declared the government's intention to create a maritime precinct in Fremantle. This move plus the intention to house *Australia II*, the yacht which won the America's Cup, in a new Museum on Victoria Quay, all help reinforce the historic importance of the area.

In the longer term, similar issues will arise in relation to North Quay, although it possesses few buildings of historical interest. The old silos used for grain storage are to be demolished before the end of the century. Container vessels are likely to continue to increase in size, as may the containers themselves. The trend to automation and reduction in manning levels will continue. These developments and problems with road

---

[133]C.J. Evans, "New Ports for Old," in Ford (ed.), *Ports*, 225.

[134]For a useful overview see P.R. Proudfoot, "A Model for Government Control in Urban Waterfront Renewal," *International Journal of Maritime History*, VIII (June 1996), 183-198.

and railway access will probably increase the pressure to relocate port facilities outside the confines of the river port. The waterfront land currently occupied by port facilities has high value for alternative uses such as housing. However, it is much harder to find suitable sites for port development than it is for residential housing and the relocation of port facilities would impose substantial costs on the port authority, other providers of port services and port users. The resolution of these competing claims for land use goes well beyond the ambit of the port authority and will involve many actors including politicians, heritage groups and other state bureaucracies.

Conclusions

With the opening of the Inner Harbour in 1897, Fremantle became the first Australian port to enter James Bird's era of simple lineal quayage. The first four decades of the twentieth century saw the harbour progressively deepened to thirty-six feet, an abortive attempt to provide a dry-dock, modest extensions of wharfage, the provision of more cargo-sheds and handling equipment, and the development of bulk oil and grain handling. The improvements and extensions that were made before the Second World War had only a limited impact on the port's physical geography; the same cannot be said of post-war developments. The changing requirements of trade and shipping and the constraints imposed by the port's proximity to the metropolitan area placed severe pressures on the port. The port authority responded in two ways: first, by rehabilitating the Inner Harbour by further dredging, demolishing old sheds and buildings or finding alternative uses for them and introducing specialised facilities such as container berths and cranes; second, by gradually relocating bulk cargo handling to a new Outer Harbour which provided ample depth of water and land areas suitable for both port and industrial purposes. The pressures of city growth make it increasingly difficult to adapt to changing demands within the confines of the existing river port. While some consider it unlikely that the Inner Harbour will celebrate another century as a fully-fledged commercial port, there are others who see the Inner Harbour as vital to the economy and heritage of Fremantle and strongly support the retention of its existing role.

The port's development (and non-development) was the result of a complex process of decision-making and adjustment in which a large number of interests, including the port authority, government and port users played a part. The FHT (and its successor the FPA), anxious to make Fremantle "a first class port," strove to gain the depths and other facilities required to service the world's largest ships. Considerations of port prestige tended to lead to building well in excess of demand. In 1934, Mr. McCartney, then Manager of the FHT, gave an interesting insight into the port authority's thinking:

> I feel we are over-efficient mechanically as compared with what we are called upon to do. You may query the necessity for that condition of affairs, because that must represent expenditure which is not earning. The overplus of power is a splendid standby for the farming or shipping community, in as much as if they were behind in deliveries on one day, and it were necessary to hasten up on some following day, the surplus of machinery would enable that to be done.[135]

The "overplus of power" was undoubtedly a splendid standby, especially with the trend towards larger and deeper draught ships; it was also an expensive one with major implications for port charges and budgets. In the 1980s the FPA faced a financial crisis which led to a major restructuring and a more commercial approach to port operation and development.

[135]South Australia, Committee on Public Works, *Minutes of Evidence* (Adelaide, 1934), 119.

Chapter 6
Cargo-Handling Technology, Working Conditions and Industrial Relations on the Fremantle Waterfront

In previous chapters we have seen that the structural transformation of the waterfront industry from a labour intensive to a capital intensive one did not begin until the 1940s when forklifts and pallets were introduced by the American armed forces. However, the most dramatic changes occurred in the late 1960s with the introduction of containerisation. This technology placed increased pressures on the ports to improve efficiency and labour productivity and had far-reaching implications for the workforce. The objective of this chapter is to examine the evolution of cargo-handling practices, working conditions and employment on the waterfront at Fremantle.

Cargo-Handling Technology and Working Conditions on the Waterfront

Stevedoring, that is, the physical handling of ships' cargo, is unique to the ports industry. By the late 1930s most ports in developed countries handled homogeneous cargoes such as grain, coal, and oil in bulk using mechanical devices such as conveyors, elevators and pipelines. But the handling of general cargo remained primarily a manual task, requiring "a mighty arm, a hard muscle, and a large strong back."[1] In the case of imports, for example, cargoes were usually loaded into slings or onto wooden platforms and discharged using ships' gear or wharf cranes. The wharf labourers, or lumpers as they were known at Fremantle,[2] would

[1]H. Jerome, *Mechanization in Industry* (New York, 1934), 154.

[2]The *Macquarie Dictionary* defines a "lumper" as a colloquial expression for wharf labourers. According to the *Oxford English Dictionary*, lumpers were people who contracted to unload ships; the earliest reference to the term appeared in 1785. Mr. Bill Latter has suggested that the term was used in the West Country to denote those who handled timber and was taken up at Fremantle because timber was a major cargo in the early years of the colony.

transfer the contents of the sling or platform to the wharf shed. Usually, the only piece of mechanical equipment used was a two wheeled sack truck, equipped with a blade or other load support which was prised beneath the cargo, but at some ports, including Fremantle, four-wheeled platform trucks and trolleys operated by manpower were also used.[3]

By means of the "bull" system stevedores achieved high handling rates from the men. Foremen selected men for work at the daily pick-up. Strong men known as "bulls" were used to set the pace of work and, with the ever present fear of unemployment, the men could be relied on to work feverishly. Competition for work was so great, especially during the 1930s depression that it was difficult for even regular followers of the industry to earn a living wage.[4] Inexperienced casuals, who were employed only after all the experienced workers had been employed, became known as "seagulls," as they fought for work like birds fighting for titbits of food. At many Fremantle hotels workers would contribute their small change to a pot on the bar which was collected by the foreman. When picking his workers it was hoped he would favour those who contributed. It was even rumoured that some men seeking work on the higher paid nightshifts left their key under the door mat so he could "visit" their wives.[5]

The job was often arduous and hazardous; some cargoes were very unpleasant to work. Jim Clarke recalled that on the pre-war waterfront at Fremantle:

> The usual shift if you got work, was eight in the morning until eleven at night. It was a long shift, and if you didn't do your job, it was no use turning up the next day because you didn't get a job. It was just slave labour. In those days it was digging coal, bunkering ships, necking

---

[3]*Commonwealth Arbitration Reports,* XXVI (1928), 881.

[4]See M. Tull, "Blood on the Cargo: Cargo-Handling and Working Conditions on the Waterfront at Fremantle, 1900-1939," *Labour History* (May 1987), 26-29.

[5]*Daily Commercial News,* 13 April 1991. The article "Violent Times that Changed the Wharves" by Evelyn Duffy draws on the memories of Mr. Fred Wayman.

> wheat, digging sulphur, super, you name it; all the real hard slushy work, hard slogging work.[6]

Another worker, Norm Pickles, remembers the backbreaking work:

> Everything was physical down in the hold; there were no forklifts...Loading wool - Fremantle has always been a big wool port - was very, very heavy work in the ships, particularly when you were getting to the top of the holds. They still required the wool to be packed so tight, you would lift three bales high...And if you didn't do it, there was one thing you could do: you could finish.[7]

Handling wheat was a particularly arduous task:

> A man has to carry, for a period of eight hours, bags weighing anything from 180 to 200 lbs., and sometimes more than 200 lbs... The men have to work out in the sun at times, with the thermometer at 100, 107 or perhaps 108 degrees, without any covering ... A man wants a cast iron constitution to stand it. At any rate, speaking of men who have been following the trade for some time, and who are supposed to be good workers you will often hear it stated "so and so is getting broken up; he will not last much longer."[8]

Men could be picked-up to work in a freezer ship and be expected to work in freezing temperatures clad only in shirts and shorts.[9] The long shifts worked -- twenty-four hours and longer -- increased the risks of accidents. Injuries such as cuts and bruises, strains and fractures were

---

[6]B. Griffiths, *Wharfies. A Celebration of 100 Years on the Fremantle Waterfront 1889-1989* (Perth, 1989), 50-51.

[7]*Ibid.*, 53.

[8]Australian National University (ANU), Noel Butlin Archives (NBA), Waterfront Workers' Federation (WWF), Federal Deposit, T62/52/33, transcript of evidence before Justice Beeby, 23 August 1928, 408-410.

[9]*Ibid.*, 714.

common. Mr. W.E. Miller, who worked on the wharves for forty-five years, witnessed a number of bad accidents: one of his work mates was almost decapitated by a grab, two were killed by falling derricks, one got wrapped around a capstan used for pulling wheat trucks and another had a leg sliced off by falling timber.[10] The accident rate climbed from about eight accidents per 100 unionists in 1904-1905 to nineteen per 100 unionists in 1924-1925, to thirty-nine per 100 unionists in 1927-1928. The union attributed the increases to a faster pace of work.[11]

Injured workers were entitled to benefits under the *Workers' Compensation Act* 1912. The maximum weekly payment was set at £2 in 1912 and increased to £3 10s in 1924. It was unchanged in 1944-1945 when the FHT had 391 claims (340 for wharf labourers and fifty-one from other workers). The FHT's insurer, the State Government Insurance Office, paid out six lump-sum settlements for permanent disability to fingers, totalling almost £274. A few years earlier the Manager of the FHT had claimed that the workers "owe allegiance to no one, the prospects of their future employment are so nebulous as not to be worthy of consideration, and there is therefore the tendency on their part to make the most of their injuries, and generally to magnify their disabilities." After pressure from the State Government Insurance Office, men with a history of making claims were black listed.[12]

In 1943 Dr. Ronald McQueen was asked to examine Sydney waterside workers who were suspected of being malingerers. To his astonishment he found most were genuine cases:

> My chief impression of these men was that all of them were prematurely aged...I had examined men, who in the main, had been ruined physically by the intolerable anxieties of the depression years. The endless search for the infrequent job, which would keep them and their families from the precarious borderline of malnutrition, had take its devastating toll. The feverish, high tension

---

[10]Memoirs of Mr. W.E. Miller. Undated typescript supplied by his son Terry Miller, of Spearwood, WA.

[11]Tull, "Blood on the Cargo," 24.

[12]FPA, 3467/178V1, Insurance-Workers Compensation, Manager to Head Foreman, 16 September 1940.

> work performed when the job was secured, in order to ensure its repetition had been paid for at the shocking price of premature old age and physical calamity.[13]

One traditional way of reducing the strain of wharf work was to introduce restrictive work practices. Restrictive practices have a long history on waterfronts throughout the world.[14] A restrictive practice may be defined as "an institutional arrangement requiring the employer to hire more labor than he would have hired in the absence of compulsion, at a given wage rate."[15] The ability of unions to impose restrictive practices depends on two main factors: first, the extent of union control over the workforce and productive process; second, the willingness of employers to resist strikes and stoppages.[16]

Written and unwritten rules of the union led to disagreements over issues such as manning, sling weights and "smoke-ohs." In 1914 Mr. Justice Higgins had complained that each branch of the WWF tried to make its own rules, with maximum sling weights varying from twenty cwt at Sydney to fourteen cwt at Melbourne. But he concluded that many restrictive practices, "which seemed to me to be most arbitrary and unreasonable at first, turn out to be expedients, crude and clumsy, for securing a better distribution of work among the labourers."[17]

In the 1920s the FLU increased restrictive practices, which adversely affected turnround of vessels. For example, it insisted that barrowmen handling general cargo were not permitted to assist in unloading their barrows meaning additional men had to be employed for that purpose. Extra men were forced into wheat loading gangs with no

---

[13]R. McQueen, "Report on the Medical Examination of Sydney Waterside Workers with Disability Cards" (1943), typescript in National Library.

[14]See, for example, A. Green, "Spelling, Go-slows, Gliding Away and Theft: Informal Control Over Work on the New Zealand Waterfront 1915-1951," *Labour History*, LXIII (1992), 100-114.

[15]P.T. Hartman, *Collective Bargaining and Productivity: The Longshore Mechanization Agreement* (Berkeley, CA, 1969), 42.

[16]E. Mansfield, *The Economics of Technological Change* (London, 1969), 153-154.

[17]*Commonwealth Arbitration Reports*, VIII (1914), 76.

increase in output. The union resolved to get the practice of "Hookey-on" established (the task of simply attaching and removing the crane hook from a sling of cargo) in order to provide work for older lumpers. These, and other practices, increased the costs of cargo-handling.[18] Frank Stevens, Secretary of the FHT, echoed all employers when he wrote that:

> The restrictions placed upon output by the waterside workers have had a most important bearing both on the pace and the cost of the work, and it is a fact that the employers have little success in combating [sic] the continual effort being made by the men to increase their earnings and to spread these increased earnings among a larger and still larger number of men without a commensurate increase in output.[19]

However, Stevens must have relented because in 1931 he was accused of allowing the introduction of many domestic rules for "the sake of peace and harmony."[20] In the late 1930s breaches of the award increased as the union became more militant and the FHT threatened to prosecute the union. For example, the union told the men that when handling goods from lorries they were not to go on the lorries.[21] But the union's gains were only modest: in 1938 the wage rate rose from two shillings and one half penny per hour to two shillings and nine pence per hour, but this only restored it back to the level of 1921.[22]

Although many restrictive practices were designed to protect workers from the deleterious effects of the system of casual employment, they were also used to protect the workers from the effect of technological change. In 1926 Stevens observed that the men pushing trolleys across the wharf were "often all in by the time the stacks were reached and wanted

---

[18]FHT, *Annual Report* (1924-1925), 10; ANU, NBA, WWF, N28/7, Fremantle Branch Records, Minutes, 13 October 1924.

[19]FPA, 106/25/1, internal memo on cargo-handling by F. Stevens, 24 August 1925.

[20]FHT, Minutes, 4 August 1931.

[21]*Ibid.*, 11 and 15 August 1933; 9 October 1934; 5 and 29 January 1937.

[22]*Ibid.*, 4 and 18 November 1938.

a spell while someone else stacked their cargo." He offered to introduce horses to pull the trolleys but the men resisted even this, as they feared it would mean less work.[23] As we saw in the previous chapter, the introduction of bulk grain handling was viewed with alarm by the lumpers, the more so because it occurred in the depths of the 1930s depression. In other countries, when machinery was first introduced on the wharves, it was sometimes sabotaged or driven into the sea.[24] After the Second World War, when mechanical equipment was introduced, the WWF would insist on maintaining gangs at the same size, irrespective of actual requirements. In addition, safety issues were sometimes used as a cover for overmanning and other restrictive practices.[25]

Although safety has improved enormously over the years, wharf work remains a relatively risky occupation and the union has often had legitimate reasons for concern. In the 1950s and 1960s large quantities of blue asbestos were shipped to Fremantle from the northwest. It was stowed in individual bags and these often leaked; when the bags were lifted out of the ship's hold, blue asbestos would rain on the workers below. The asbestos that did not immediately go onto rail trucks was stacked in the wharf sheds so that many people who worked at the port were exposed to the deadly dust. Spillages were swept up and it was only in the 1980s that vacuum cleaners were used. The workers were provided with a piece of cheese cloth to wear over their faces when handling asbestos, but this was ideal for cleaning car windscreens and was often used for this purpose rather than for the purpose for which it was provided. After one worker lost an eye as a result of getting asbestos in it, they were issued with plastic glasses but were not made aware of the dangers of asbestos. The result was a number of deaths from asbestos related diseases such as asbestosis (an incurable disease which causes scarring of the lungs and leads to shortness of breath) and mesothelioma

---

[23]FPA, 105/26/2-3, F. Stevens and J. Taylor, "The Port of Fremantle in Comparison with the Ports of Adelaide, Melbourne, and Sydney," 1 March 1926.

[24]Jerome, *Mechanization,* 356; and P.N. Stearns, *Lives of Labour* (London, 1975), 126.

[25]FPA, 87/840/1-2, Wharf Manager to General Manager, 15 November 1951; and Secretary, FHT, to Branch Manager, AEWL, 15 October 1965.

(a rare and highly malignant cancer of the outer covering of the lung).[26] In 1972 the FPA introduced an accident prevention scheme but despite this reported numerous injuries due to workers slipping on the icy floors of freezer trucks and hurting their hands while handling cartons of frozen meat. The FPA paid out more in premiums for workers' compensation than any other government department, with the exception of the Forestry Department, which administered another traditionally risky occupation.[27]

The early years of the twentieth century saw only modest technological improvements in general cargo-handling throughout the world. Platform trucks powered by electric batteries began to appear around 1910 and after the First World War petrol-engined versions appeared.[28] But these were rare in Australian ports: as late as the mid-1920s, Fremantle, for example, had only one petrol trolley.[29] During the 1920s mobile cranes were introduced to speed up the movement of cargo and aid stacking operations in wharf sheds. The FHT purchased its first one in 1927 and, remarkably, the following year was described as having one of "the best equipped wharves in the Commonwealth," a revealing commentary on the state of affairs in other Australian ports.[30]

Australia was not the only country in which stevedoring was technologically backward. A sample of American industries taken in 1925 showed that stevedoring had the lowest proportion of machine to hand-workers: only twelve percent of workers operated or contributed to machine operation. Of the remainder, eighty percent were handworkers and eight percent were supervisors.[31] Nevertheless, by the beginning of the 1930s the high-lift platform truck, the forerunner of the modern forklift truck, had appeared on some American wharves. But, as we saw in chapter 4, Australia did not see any until the American forces brought

---

[26]Statutory Declaration by Cyril Martin, Assistant Wharf Superintendent, FPA, 3 February 1995. Copy supplied by Mr. Martin.

[27]FPA 3468/88/119-A, Personnel Officer to General Manager, 12 March 1973.

[28]K.E. Booth and C.G. Chantrill, *Materials Handling with Industrial Trucks* (London, 1962), 2.

[29]FHT, *Annual Report* (1926-1927), 15.

[30]*Commonwealth Arbitration Reports*, XXVI (1928), 881.

[31]Jerome, *Mechanization*, 275.

them in 1942. Most stevedoring companies possessed minimal mechanical equipment: before the Second World War a man could buy himself a coil of rope and a hook and call himself a stevedore. An analysis of stevedoring costs between 1948-1954, based on a large sample of Australian stevedoring companies, showed that direct labour costs still accounted for seventy percent of total costs.[32]

The slow progress of technology on the wharves was due to five main factors: first, the irregular nature of shipping and trade which meant that it was more economical to hire casual labour, even at relatively high hourly rates, than use mechanical equipment which could not be laid off when demand was slack. Second, profits were calculated as a percentage of direct costs and this system of cost-plus charging gave stevedores little incentive to reduce costs by introducing machinery or improved working methods. A study of American stevedoring concluded that such charging practices had "made for slow and glacier-like changes in methods of cargo-handling over the past 50 years."[33] Third, technical factors such as limitations in the design of machines, wharves and sheds, also help explain the slow spread of mechanisation on the waterfront. Many ports had narrow finger piers and sheds with forests of pillars both of which made it difficult to operate mechanical equipment. However, only the latter was a problem at Fremantle. Of course, these difficulties could have been overcome if port authorities had been willing to scrap existing facilities but most port infrastructure is relatively long-lived and once paid for can be maintained in operational condition at relatively little cost. Therefore, many port authorities were unwilling to replace wharves and sheds until they reached the end of their economic lives; this was especially the case at Fremantle where, as we shall see in the next chapter, port profits were siphoned off by the government. Fourth, the stevedoring industry was made up of many small companies, which lacked both the volume of work, and the capital required to purchase machinery. Finally, the workers often opposed the introduction of machinery, even though it would reduce the physical strain of wharf work. Thus economic, technical and social factors combined to reduce the progress of mechanisation prior to the Second World War.

---

[32]*Report of the Committee of Inquiry into the Stevedoring Industry* (Canberra, 1957), 111.

[33]H.M. Levinson (ed.), *Collective Bargaining and Technological Change in American Transportation* (Illinois, 1971), 275.

Figure 6.1: The Productivity of Waterfront Labour at Fremantle, 1949-1950 to 1982-1983.

Source: See appendix C.

Although the structural transformation of the industry from a labour intensive to a capital intensive one began in the 1940s, the major transformation was delayed until the late 1960s when containerisation was introduced. This technology required substantial investments in port infrastructure and equipment, the training and retraining of waterside workers and led to massive losses in port employment.[34] Some work, such as the loading and unloading of containers, was transferred to depots outside the existing port areas, further increasing job losses on the waterfront. In the mid-1960s conventional general cargo vessels still required gangs of fifteen to twenty-one men to handle about 500 tons of cargo per shift; while container ships required only two small gangs to move up to 6000 tons per shift.[35] In 1955-1956 the Fremantle workforce peaked at 1873 men and 1.1 million tonnes of general cargo was handled; by 1982-1983 664 men handled 3.6 million tonnes of general cargo. In the latter year seventy-three percent of general cargo was handled in containers. The reductions in port employment, were, however, accompanied by substantial increases in output per worker. Figure 6.1 shows that

[34]International Labour Organization, *Social and Labour Problems Caused by Structural Adjustments in the Port Industry* (Geneva, 1996), 5-6.

[35]ASIA, *Annual Report* (1966-1967), 23.

increased capital intensity, with or without improvements in labour skills and organisation, led to steadily rising output per worker up to 1974. The decline in 1975 was due to the loss of interstate container services; however, the volume of trade and the growth of labour productivity recovered in the late 1970s. As we shall see, the changes in technology posed considerable challenges for the maritime unions and the existing culture of work in the industry.

The Organisation of the Fremantle Waterfront

Historically, there are three main groups that have been involved on the waterfront: workers, employers and government authorities. We shall consider each in turn.

Waterside Workers

A wide range of people derive employment opportunities from port operations at Fremantle: the port is composed of congeries of trades, rather than one single type. Workers employed in the port area include waterside labourers, port authority employees, crews of pilot boats and tugs, shipwrights, carpenters, electricians, engineers, plumbers, painters, clerks, maintenance and construction workers and government officials.

By the twentieth century waterfront workers were organised into a number of different unions. Skilled craftsmen belonged to the relevant craft union, such as the Amalgamated Engineering Union, the Australian Institute of Marine and Power Engineers, the Amalgamated Society of Carpenters and the Plumbers' Union.[36] But the most important unions on the Fremantle waterfront were the Fremantle Lumpers' Union (FLU) (later to become a branch of the Waterside Workers' Federation of Australia), the Seamen's Union and the Coastal Dock, Rivers and Harbour Works Union (renamed the Maritime Workers Union in 1968).[37] Wharf labourers, or lumpers as they were known in Western Australia, historically have provided the most important labour input to cargo-handling and will be the focus of attention in this chapter.

---

[36]See R. Broomham, *Steady Revolutions. The Australian Institute of Marine and Power Engineers* (Kensington, NSW, 1991).

[37]S. Macintyre, *Militant. The Life and Times of Paddy Troy* (Sydney, 1984), 66-69.

The first lumpers were members of the ships' crews, but in the 1890s the expansion of trade created the need for a regular workforce to ensure that sufficient labour was available to avoid delays to shipping.[38] Until 1967, lumpers were hired on a casual basis, by the hour or by the day. This system of hiring evolved to cope with the wide daily fluctuations in trade flows. In 1950-1951, for example, the FHT employed an average of 537 wharf labourers on each day shift but on some days needed only 200-300 men and on others 700-800 men.[39] From the point of view of the employers, the problem was to maintain a labour reserve sufficient to cope with peak demands but to avoid as far as possible the costs of maintaining such a reserve. As long as there was a plentiful supply of labour this was possible, since the employer hired labour only for as long as he needed it and there were always men willing to work when required.

Over one quarter of a century ago Raymond Miller argued that the conditions of dockwork produced a universal dockworker sub culture.[40] His views are summarised in table 6.1.

These endemic features were all present in varying degrees in the workforce at Fremantle. In particular, before the Second World War, irregular earnings made life difficult for lumpers and their families; restrictive practices reduced labour efficiency; industrial relations were usually turbulent; and "class war was seen at its most ferocious on the waterfront."[41]

---

[38]See T. Fletcher, "Stevedoring Efficiency at Fremantle, 1829-1903. The Problems Experienced by a Waterfront Industry in a Developing Port," *The Great Circle*, XVII (1995), 22-38.

[39]T. Sheridan, "Shipowners, Stevedores and Foremen: Divergent Management Attitudes to Waterfront Labour in the 1950s," *Journal of Industrial Relations*, XXXVIII (1996), 420.

[40]See also C. Kerr and A. Siegal, "The Interindustry Propensity to Strike - An International Comparison," in A. Kornhauser, R. Dubin and A. Ross (eds.), *Industrial Conflict* (New York, 1954).

[41]See W. Mitchell, "Home Life at the Hungry Mile: Sydney Wharf Labourers and Their Families, 1900-1914," *Labour History*, No. 33, (1977), 86-97; Tull, "Blood on the Cargo," 15-29; W. Lowenstein and T. Hills, *Under the Hook. Melbourne Waterside Workers Remember: 1900-1980* (Melbourne, 1982), 6.

Table 6.1
The Main Conditions of Dockwork and Waterfront Culture

Main Conditions of Dockwork

- The casual nature of employment
- The exceptional arduousness, danger, and variability of the work
- The lack of an occupationally stratified hierarchy and mobility outlets
- Lack of regular association with one employer
- Continuous contact with foreign goods, seamen, and ideas
- The necessity of living near the docks
- The belief shared by longshoremen that others in the society consider them a low-status goup

Main Characteristics of the Subculture

- Extra solidarity and undiffused loyalty to fellow dockworkers
- Suspicion of management and outsiders
- Militant unionism
- Appearance of charismatic leaders from the ranks
- Liberal political philosophy but conservative view of changes in work practices
- "Casual frame of mind" (free men or irresponsible unionists)

Source: R.C. Miller, "The Dockworker Subculture and Some Problems in Cross-Cultural and Cross-Time Generalizations," *Comparative Studies in Society and History*, XI (1969), 304-305, 308.

The Fremantle Lumpers' Union, formed in July 1889, was the first union of unskilled workers in Western Australia and "its formation was a significant milestone in the development of unionism in Western Australia."[42] During a strike in 1899, the employers had successfully defended their right to employ non-union labour but significantly they did so only if labour was short, giving the FLU effective control of the workforce.[43] Thus from a small nucleus of 136 members it expanded rapidly: by the turn of the century it had 841 members. Subsequently, membership stagnated because in 1918 it had only 843 members. This was due to members leaving to join the armed forces and the introduction of

---

[42]I.A. Vanden Driesen, "The Evolution of the Trade Union Movement in Western Australia," in C.T. Stannage (ed.), *A New History of Western Australia* (Nedlands, WA, 1981), 355.

[43]For an account of the strike see I.A. Vanden Driesen, "Confrontation and Reconciliation on the Waterfront: The Fremantle Lumpers' Strike - 1899," *Labour History*, No. 40 (May 1981), 29-48.

the rival National Workers in 1917. In 1929 there were 1624 members but by 1936 the depression had taken its toll and membership had fallen to about 1150.[44]

The Waterside Workers' Federation of Australia (WWF) was formed in 1902 but the FLU appears to have been fearful of losing its independence and did not join until 1910. By the eve of the First World War the WWF had over forty branches but had problems ensuring branches adhered to national policy, especially in the outlying states. The wide distribution of branches across the country made it hard for the federal leadership to maintain contact with them; the telephone was in occasional use only in the late 1920s and, except in emergencies, when the telegraph was used, most communication was still by letter.[45] Relations between the FLU and the federal exceutive reached breaking point in 1933 and the FLU left the WWF. It did not rejoin until 1946 when it officially became the Fremantle Branch of the WWF.[46]

Fremantle's waterside workers shared two common characteristics with their brethren the world over: first, the overwhelming majority of members lived in Fremantle and adjoining suburbs; second, sons tended to follow fathers into the industry. Until the 1950s about fifty percent lived within two miles of the wharves.[47] Such proximity to the work place was essential in an industry where work was so uncertain; before the Second World War regular attendances at the pick-ups were the only way to ensure a chance of earning a living wage. After the war the introduction of attendance money and the growing availability of the motor car, meant that waterside workers were not forced to live close to the wharves and they began to gradually migrate to the suburbs. By the 1990s the

---

[44]ANU, NBA, WWF Federal Deposit, T62/39, Membership Books - Western Australian Branches, 1902-1948.

[45]M. Beasley, *Wharfies. A History of the Waterside Workers' Federation of Australia* (Rushcutters Bay, NSW, 1996), 61.

[46]ANU, NBA, WWF, N28/2, Minutes, 11 May 1903 and 6 November 1910; and Federal Deposit, Z55, Box 43, J. Healy, "Brief History of the Australian Waterfront and the Waterside Workers' Union," typescript, 1954.

[47]ANU, NBA, WWF Fremantle Branch Records, N28/303, Lists of Members, 1935-1950; and N28/206, transcript of evidence by O.W.T. Cook, Vigilante Officer, before Justice Beeby, 11 March 1936.

inner-city areas once dominated by waterside workers were home to the families of middle class professionals.

The tendency for sons to follow fathers into the industry and the clustering of the workforce undoubtedly contributed to the strength and solidarity of the union. An illustration of this solidarity is provided by the rules introduced in the era of casual employment to ensure a more even distribution of work amongst members. They were designed "to curb the ravenous appetites [sic] for work of some of the 'stars' who have little consideration for their less favoured comrades." In August 1930, John Small, one of the "stars," worked continuously from 7pm on the 26th to 6:30am on the 27th. According to union rules he should then have stood down for eight hours to allow other men a share of the work but he attended another pick-up at 1pm on the 27th. The union fined him and when he refused to pay expelled him from the union. In that year the union fined a total of twenty-two men for breaches of the rules.[48]

Stevedoring, together with coal mining, gained a reputation as being one of Australia's most strike prone industries. Rather than attempt a tedious chronology of every dispute, it is proposed to discuss only a few key ones that illustrate the general pattern of waterfront conflict.

In 1917, a strike, fanned by the workers' dissatisfaction with the war and the increasing cost of living, flared into a major dispute.[49] On 13 August the lumpers at Fremantle refused to load the *Minderoo* with flour for export, ostensibly because proper precautions had not been taken to prevent the flour falling into the hands of the enemy. Prime Minister Hughes was determined to keep the ports open and decided to recruit a national volunteer workforce. The Arbitration Award was amended to give volunteers or National Workers, as they became known, preference of employment over members of the existing unions. The employers set up Employment Bureaux to ensure that work was allocated to the Nationals. The Fremantle Bureau opened on 24 August but the dispute continued until the 3 October when the FLU announced that its members would return to work the next day.

---

[48]ANU, NBA, WWF Federal Deposit, T62/11/6, Secretary of the FLU to General Secretary of the WWF, 1 April 1930; and Fremantle Branch Records, N28/142, Fines Receipt Book, 13 January 1924-5 May 1934.

[49]This account draws on P. Hopper, "The 1919 Fremantle Lumpers' Strike" (Unpublished Honours Dissertation, University of Western Australia, 1975).

After the strike the lumpers and Nationals worked side by side, with the Nationals getting first preference for any work. In December 1917 a group of Nationals complained to the government that the best jobs were going to lumpers and that they were suffering from intimidation. It was claimed that "old lumpers" deliberately dropped coal, bolts and other objects on them when they were working in the holds. Some employers preferred to employ "old lumpers" as they were more experienced.[50]

In 1919 the divisions between the lumpers and the Nationals flared up again: the result was "Westralia's Eureka."[51] After the war ex-servicemen and members of the FLU returned to the wharves. Ex-servicemen were supposed to be guaranteed preference of employment before any one else including Nationals, but many failed to obtain work and this added to the volatility of the situation. An outbreak of influenza in January 1919 in the eastern states led Hal Colebatch, the Acting-Premier, to quarantine all people arriving by land. The rail link with the eastern states was closed leading to shortages of food in Western Australia. A seamen's strike had cut shipping with the eastern states but in April the *Dimboola* arrived with urgently needed food supplies; she also had several people with influenza on board.

The first attempt to berth the ship succeeded only in alienating public opinion; the lumpers refused to work the ship until the seven days period of quarantine had expired. However, the *Dimboola* was fumigated at anchor and brought in for unloading by the Nationals. The lumpers who picketed the wharf prevented this. The FHT's carpenters, acting under instructions from the Trades Hall, refused to help erect barriers to enclose the wharves and protect the Nationals.

The government was somewhat preoccupied, as Hal Colebatch had just succeeded Sir Henry Lefroy as Premier. It was hoping that the federal government of Prime Minister Hughes would intervene in the wharf crisis but the federal government refused to become involved. On Sunday 4 May Colebatch and a group of "scabs" proceeded by boat from Perth to Fremantle to unload the *Dimboola*. As they passed under the bridges at Fremantle a barrage of missiles greeted them. When they reached the wharf, armed police on horseback and foot were able to push

---

[50]FPA, 126/17/2, Colonial Secretary H. Colebatch to FHT, 14 December 1917; and Captain Cleary, Wharf Manager, to Secretary, 20 December 1917.

[51]This account of the 1919 strike draws on B.K. de Garis "An Incident at Fremantle," *Labour History* (May 1966), 31-37.

back the lumpers but one, Thomas Edwards, was severely injured in the fracas. The situation deteriorated rapidly: some shots were fired from the crowd, the Riot Act was read and the Police Commissioner, Robert Connell, gave instructions for ammunition to be issued to the police. However, the Officer in Charge at Fremantle, Inspector W.C. Sellenger, doubtless fearing that the use of firearms would only exacerbate the situation, did not comply with the instruction.[52] Colebatch, alarmed at the way things were developing, called an emergency conference between himself, the Police Commissioner and union officials. It was agreed that the police and volunteers would withdraw. The lumpers had clearly come off best, "and for some days Fremantle continued to bubble over with excitement; successful rioting was a heady diet for the sleepy community of the West."[53] The state government appealed for military assistance from the federal government but, once again, the federal government refused to become involved. The dispute was finally resolved on the 7 May when the Nationals agreed to withdraw from the waterfront, partly out of fears for their safety. After some political wrangling the government found the Nationals alternative employment or gave them financial compensation. The government paid 215 Nationals compensation totalling £17,929.[54] "Westralia's Eureka" was over and the FLU had won a monopoly of the supply of wharf labourers at Fremantle. The episode contributed to the downfall of Colebatch, who lasted only a month as Premier.

On 7 May Thomas Edwards died from his injuries received on the wharf. To trade unionists be became a martyr in the fight for worker rights and his funeral was attended by about 7000 unionists. A memorial plaque was constructed to commemorate his memory but the FHT refused to allow it to be erected at the entrance to the port because "it would remind people of events best buried in oblivion."[55] It was eventually placed on the Trades Hall building where it remained for many years; it

---

[52]I am indebted to Bill Latter for this point. His source was Battye Library of Western Australian History, Perth, AN5, Police Department Accession No. 430, file 2400, 1919

[53]De Garis, "Incident at Fremantle," 35.

[54]Australian Archives (AA): Prime Minister's Department, CRS A1606, Correspondence Files, Secret and Confidential Series, Third System, 1926-1939; B26/1 Fremantle Volunteer Wharf Labourers - Question of Compensation, 1919.

[55]FHT, Minutes, 23 May 1919.

is now located in King's Square. However, according to Brian de Garis, Edwards' was soon forgotten and the lumpers' victory "has never assumed the place in the mystique of the trade union movement that contemporary references to 'Westralia's Eureka' attempted to confer upon it."[56]

The port was disrupted by industrial action again during the British Seamen's strike of 1925.[57] The seamen went on strike in protest against a wages cut of £1 per month and the British shipowners decided that their vessels would not visit Fremantle while the strike was on. Fremantle was singled out for attention partly because it was the first port on the United Kingdom/Australian run but possibly also because the leading British shipowner, Lord Inchcape, disliked Australians and, in particular, Western Australians. The Perth retailer, Harry Boan, who was returning home from England, was forced to travel on to Melbourne even though he offered the Captain £100 to put him and other Western Australian passengers ashore by launch. As an act of international solidarity, the striking seamen received strong support from the local port workers. On 2 November the tensions erupted in a violent confrontation between hundreds of strikers and police. However, by the end of November the strike had petered out and the shipowners enjoyed a complete victory.

A major reason for the failure of the seamen's strike was that unemployment in the inter-war period placed the balance of industrial power firmly in the shipowners favour. In 1914, when presenting the first uniform wages award for the Australian waterfront industry, Mr. Justice Higgins had observed that "the weaker side complains of tyranny; and often becomes a tyrant itself, when occasion offers."[58] After the outbreak of the Second World War the employment situation on the Australian waterfront swung rapidly from one of labour surplus to labour shortage. The "weaker side became the tyrant" and the WWF exploited its monopoly of the labour supply to win vastly improved wages and conditions for its members. Although the unions adopted a "Win-the-War" policy in June 1940, strike activity increased substantially.

---

[56]De Garis "Incident at Fremantle," 37.

[57]This paragraph draws on P. Gifford, "The Effects of the British Seamen's Strike of 1925 on Fremantle," *The Great Circle*, XIV (1992), 73-87.

[58]*Commonwealth Arbitration Reports*, VIII (1914), 76.

As we saw in chapter 4, because the situation on the wharves was hampering the war effort, in 1942 the Stevedoring Industry Commission (SIC) was established to try and improve turnround times and labour productivity. Within two years it had introduced many improvements, including a roster system of employment. Under this system the wharf labourers were organised into gangs who were engaged as a unit. The gangs were rostered to particular jobs regardless of the preferences of the workers or the employers. This scheme met with opposition from both employers and employees.[59] The FHT argued that the roster gave all labourers work irrespective of their merit; workers tended to slow down to the rate of "bludgers" and foremen became disheartened; it was reluctant to introduce mechanisation "until management of labour is...restored to employers."[60] Many men regarded the roster system as an infringement of individual liberty; to some extent, casual labour appears to have bred the casual labourer; the failure to get regular work eventually reduced the capacity to work regularly. However, as Margo Beasley has observed:

> The gang system became a core feature of WWF strength because of the deep and personal relationships which flourished within it. The element of choice involved in gang selection allowed groups of men to form around political allegiances (militants, moderates and others) or around more personal relationships (fathers, sons, brothers and friends). Many gangs were like extended families in which the members were aware of, and shared in, important events in each others' lives; births, deaths, illnesses and hard times. The gang system was a key factor in intense union loyalty, of which the WWF was a beneficiary.[61]

The introduction of attendance money and other benefits meant that the industry was only nominally casual. In the early 1950s the government agency regulating stevedoring commented that

---

[59]FHT, Minutes, 9 April 1943 and 12 December 1944.

[60]FPA, 87/509.v2, criticisms of the Trust.

[61]Beasley, *Wharfies*, 118.

> On present indications it would seem that the shipowners are in favour of maintaining the labour force at full strength, even at the cost of increased attendance money payments. This is said to be on the basis that "attendance money payments are an insurance against slow turn-round."[62]

This change of attitude can be attributed to increased awareness by shipowners of the cost of slow turnaround.

Between 1946-1947 and 1956-1957 manhours lost through disputes at all Australian ports averaged 4.5 percent of manhours worked.[63] Fremantle, however, enjoyed a better industrial relations record than the major eastern states' ports. For example, between 1949-1950 and 1969-1970 manhours lost through disputes averaged only 2.3 percent of manhours worked compared to four percent at Sydney.[64] Strikes were due to local and national issues but national ones dominated. A nation-wide strike in 1956 over wage margins led to the loss of 190,000 manhours at Fremantle, which almost equalled the total number of manhours lost over local disputes between 1950-1957.[65]

In order to place industrial unrest in perspective it is interesting to note that between 1949-1950 and 1966-1967 manhours lost through rain averaged 2.8 percent of manhours worked at Fremantle and 5.5 percent at Sydney.[66] Thus at both ports, on average, manhours lost through rain exceeded manhours lost through disputes; union actions were not the only source of disruption to waterfront work.

As well as being rather strike prone, the WWF had a tendency to ignore the established arbitration procedures for consultation and

---

[62]ASIB, *Annual Report* (1951-1952), 12.

[63]Inter-State Commission, *Waterfront Investigation: Preliminary Findings and Discussion Papers*. III: *Employment Arrangements* (Canberra, 1988), 191.

[64]Calculated from data in ASIB and ASIA, *Annual Reports*.

[65]See J. Vance, "Some Aspects of Industrial Relations and Economics of the Western Australian Waterfront Industry" (Unpublished MA thesis, University of Western Australia, 1960).

[66]Calculated from data in ASIB and ASIA, *Annual Reports*. Data on rain loss were not published after 1966-1967.

settlement of industrial disputes. In May 1963 Mr. Justice Ashburner complained that:

> members of the Waterside Workers Federation wish to have their claims dealt with by the Commission when it is reasonably anticipated that they might be successful but if they have no such anticipation they neglect to use the established machinery and attempt to obtain their claims by direct action. The Commission cannot tolerate this "heads I win, tails you lose" attitude.[67]

The WWF also had a long tradition of supporting international causes by boycotting ships of the nations concerned. Such activity was much criticised because it was not specifically directed towards winning material gains for union members. In October 1937 members of the FLU refused to provide coal bunkers for a Japanese whaling ship. In a well-known incident in December 1938 waterside workers at Port Kembla refused to load pig iron bound for Japan on the grounds that it would be used for war purposes. The Attorney General, Mr. Robert Menzies, attempted to force them to load it but the workers refused until the government agreed to end shipments. Menzies' efforts earned him the nickname "Pig Iron Bob." Later, as Prime Minister, Menzies is reputed to have contemptuously described the WWF as "those experts on foreign affairs down on the waterfront."[68] Between 1945 and 1949 the WWF imposed black bans on Dutch shipping in support of Indonesian independence. The union has also taken industrial action on a variety of other social and political issues, ranging from apartheid in South Africa, the Vietnam War to improving conditions for the crews of flag of convenience vessels.

The militancy of the waterside workers was reflected in their selection of Communist leaders. In 1937 the Communist Jim Healy was elected as national Secretary, a position he held until his death in 1961. But his successor, Charlie Fitzgibbon, who served until 1983, was a member of the Australian Labor Party. Members of the Australian Labor

---

[67]Cited in Association of Employers' of Waterside Labour (AEWL), "The Stevedoring Industry in Australia: Submission to the Commonwealth Government in Connection with the Industrial Situation and Employment Arrangements," December 1964.

[68]*Tribune*, 28 July 1965.

Party dominated the leadership of the Fremantle Branch although its membership included Communists.[69] In 1948 a Communist, Paddy Troy, became Secretary of the Western Australian Coastal, Dock, Rivers and Harbour Works Union which covered a diverse group of workers including crews of tugs, lighters, pilot boats, and general labourers employed on the Fremantle waterfront.[70] Through militant leadership the waterfront unions obtained major gains in wages and working conditions for their members.

While the mass media highlighted the role of the Communists, in retrospect it seems that the workers elected them primarily for their ability to obtain improved wages and working conditions, rather than from any great desire to fight a revolutionary war on the wharves.[71]

The WWF certainly acted as a pacesetter in relation to wages and conditions of employment. By the 1960s wage rates and earnings were above those in other industries and waterside workers enjoyed numerous benefits such as sick pay and long service leave. The thirty-five-hour week was introduced in 1972, as was a formal no compulsory redundancy agreement. By 1987 waterside workers involved in conventional stevedoring at Fremantle worked an average of 26.9 hours per week and earned about $604.[72] By contrast, average weekly earnings for Australian males were only about $482.

Once the union had succeeded in raising its members from their "no-hopers" status of the 1930s, there were signs of a change in outlook: in the 1960s manhours lost through disputes averaged only 2.5 percent of manhours worked compared to 4.5 percent in the 1950s.[73] The discussions that preceded the introduction of permanent employment in 1967 took

---

[69]Griffiths, *Wharfies*, 47.

[70]See Macintyre, *Militant*, 69.

[71]See F. Crowley (ed.), *A New History of Australia* (Melbourne, 1974), 494; and T. Sheridan, "Australian Wharfies 1943-1967: Casual Attitudes, Militant Leadership and Workplace Change," *Journal of Industrial Relations*, XXXVI (1994), 258-284.

[72]Inter-State Commission, *Waterfront Investigation*, III, 88.

[73]Data on strikes in this paragraph are from *ibid.*, 191.

place "in an atmosphere of goodwill probably unparalleled in the history of the industry."[74]

The employers had two major reasons for supporting permanent employment. First, and most importantly, containerisation required fewer but more highly skilled workers, and the introduction of the necessary training programs was difficult to implement with casual employees. Second, the casual nature of waterfront employment meant that a worker's employer could change from day to day; under these circumstances the worker tended to owe his first allegiance to his union, rather than his employer. It was hoped, somewhat naively given the long history of icy industrial relations in the industry, that permanent employment would lead to the development of greater employee loyalty.

Permanent employment was introduced in Sydney in November 1967 and by August the following year had been extended to Melbourne, Port Kembla, Adelaide, Fremantle, Brisbane and Newcastle. By 1970 over three-quarters of Australia's waterside workers were permanent employees; they received a guaranteed minimum weekly wage of $50.50 and penalty rates for night and weekend work. The balance of waterside workers worked at minor ports where trade volumes were insufficient to support a permanent workforce. These workers received attendance money and a guaranteed minimum wage. A key feature of the permanent employment scheme was the development of a system of centralised labour allocation. The WWF and Association of Employers of Waterside Labour (AEWL) allocated labour to stevedores and ports through coordinating committees. A number of industry-wide levies were used to fund leave, idle time payments, pensions and redundancy payments. A quota of workers was calculated for each employer based on the volume of cargo handled. In theory, at the end of each quarter the quota was adjusted and if necessary some workers were redeployed to other companies. In practice, however, companies tended to hang onto workers because the cost of idle time was funded by an industry-wide levy and thus spread across all employers. This gave stevedores little incentive to improve efficiency. Thus although manhours lost through disputes fell to two percent of manhours worked between 1977-1978 and 1986-1987,

---

[74]*General Report of National Stevedoring Industry Conference* (April 1967), 4.

permanent employment did not bring all of the expected improvements in industrial relations and productivity.[75]

The task of achieving industrial peace was complicated by the technical changes that swept the industry after the Second World War. Mechanisation drastically reduced the demand for waterfront labour and posed a challenge to the WWF's control of waterfront employment. From a peak of about 26,400 in the mid-1950s the Australia-wide membership of the WWF had shrunk to 8300 by the early 1980s. In order to strengthen its position the WWF attempted to poach workers from other unions, especially the Amalgamated Metal Workers' Union, the Federated Clerks Union and the Australian Workers Union (AWU). This led to numerous demarcation disputes as other unions opposed the WWF's "body snatching" activities.

In 1951-1952 members of the WWF had handled sixty-three percent of total tonnages in Australian ports; by 1983-1984 they were handling only twenty-two percent. This was because, due to pressure from employers, the 1956 *Stevedoring Industry Act* had prescribed that bulk handling was to be done by non-WWF workers. In the 1970s the WWF tried to recruit this group of workers. The management of Co-operative Bulk Handling Ltd, which employed members of the AWU at its grain handling operations at Kwinana, feared the flow-on of the WWF's premium wages and conditions and strongly supported the AWU's fight to retain grain workers.[76] But in 1982 the WWF was successful in persuading the Arbitration Court to change the definition of waterside workers and won coverage of some grain workers the following year. However, the struggle ended in a "draw," because while grain workers won the right to join the WWF they failed to obtain the flow-on of the WWF's more generous conditions of employment.[77]

---

[75]See S. Deery, "The Impact of the National Stevedoring Industry Conference (1965-1967) on Industrial Relations on the Australian Waterfront," *Journal of Industrial Relations*, (June 1978), 202-222.

[76]FPA, 4804/03/8/3. Statement by Mr. J. Green, General Manager Co-Operative Bulk Handling Ltd., 6 August 1979; and 88/1/15/72F, "One Union on the Waterfront," paper prepared by the Industrial Section, April 1982.

[77]G. Harcourt, "Bulk Grain Handling Facilities at the Port of Fremantle and the Development of a Work Culture 1933-1977" (Unpublished Honours thesis, Murdoch University, 1991), 83.

In the 1980s technological change and micro-economic reform (to be discussed later) led to further reductions in waterfront employment and, despite the WWF's efforts to recruit more workers, by 1987 the national membership had plummeted to about 5400 and the Fremantle Branch membership to less than 400. In 1988 the federal Labor government announced that within five years unions had to have at least 10,000 members to retain registration under the Industrial Relations Act; this move was designed to put pressure on the WWF and other small unions to amalgamate. In 1989 the WWF saw the writing on the wall and merged with the Seaman's Union to form the powerful Maritime Union of Australia.

Waterside Employers

Against this diversity of labour and unions engaged in cargo-handling stood a similar diversity of employers and employers associations. Shipping companies, shipping agents, stevedoring companies and bunkering contractors were all involved in cargo-handling. The shipowners usually contracted out stevedoring operations to specialist companies.

In the discussion that follows the words stevedore, employer, and shipowner will be used more or less interchangeably. This is because of the high degree of vertical and horizontal integration in the industry. In the mid-1950s, there were forty-nine major stevedoring companies in Australia, only eight of which were completely independent of shipping interests. In the same year, overseas shipping companies held all the shares or a predominant interest in fifteen companies and interstate shipowners controlled a further seven companies.[78] In effect, although separate companies undertook stevedoring operations, shipowners controlled most of the stevedoring industry.

After the Second World War technological change led to concentration in the provision of stevedoring services. At Fremantle, as we saw in chapter 2, the FHT had acquired a monopoly of cargo-handling on the wharves in 1904 and quickly became the largest stevedoring concern at Fremantle. In the 1930s, in addition to the FHT, there were

---

[78] *Report of the Committee of Inquiry into the Stevedoring Industry*, 28-29.

eight private stevedoring companies operating at Fremantle.[79] The port authority remained the sole wharf-side stevedores until 1968 when Stateships took over all stevedoring of their own vessels. In 1969 Seatainer Terminals Ltd. (STL) started handling containers and it was joined by the Peninsular and Oriental Steam Navigation Company's (P&O) controlled Fremantle Cargo Services (FCS) in 1983. An inquiry by the Prices Justification Tribunal in the mid-1970s found that there was no real competition for terminal services in Sydney or Fremantle and that the profits of stevedoring companies were very high.[80] This suggests that they were exploiting their monopoly powers and enjoying economic rents. STL and FCS merged in 1985 to form Fremantle Terminals Ltd. and as a result the P&O Group gained a monopoly of container operations. In 1986 Stateships and James Patrick and Company Ltd. entered a joint venture to provide some competition to FTL but this was shortlived as Stateships folded in 1995; Patrick's has, however, continued to provide container-handling services. As part of its own restructuring programme, the FPA withdrew from stevedoring on 21 January 1991, although it retained a handful of men to operate a depot for packing and unpacking containers until this was closed in June 1995. By the early 1990s a series of mergers and rationalisations had effectively left all stevedoring in the hands of only two private companies, Conaust (now P&O Ports) and Patrick, the Australian Stevedore.[81] In 1995 a company owned by a colourful entrepreneur, Mr. Len Buckridge, attempted to enter the industry but failed because he insisted on employing only non-union labour. However, in April the following year a new company, Western Stevedores, run by John Peraldini an ex-FPA employee, started opera-

---

[79]FPA, 20/35/1, "Port Facilities and Charges at Fremantle," Report by the Department of Overseas Trade, London, 7 March 1934. The companies were Robert Laurie and Company Ltd., Fremantle Stevedoring Company, Federal Stevedoring Company, Nicholls and Company Ltd., Ocean Stevedoring Company Ltd., Adelaide Steamship Company, McIlwraith McEacharn Ltd., and the West Australian Stevedoring Company.

[80]Cited in Australian Shippers' Council, *Annual Report* (1976-1977), appendices C and E.

[81]By the early 1990s James Patrick and Company Ltd had merged with F.G. Strangs and National Terminals Australia Ltd.; and another company, Mercantile Stevedores, had become part of the Conaust (P&O) Group. Port Warratah Stevedores, a company owned by BHP Pty. Ltd.., continued to provide stevedoring at the company's wharf in the Outer Harbour.

tions. Industry rumours indicate that Buckridge backed it. While Western Stevedores offers competition for non-containerised cargoes, container handling continues to remain in the hands of a duopoly.

Shipowners are not a homogenous group and, while they have always attempted to present a united front to the unions, their attitudes to the workforce have been affected by their respective cost structures. Stevedoring costs represented only ten to fifteen percent of total operating costs for overseas shipowners and rather than delay ships in port overseas owners were often willing to grant concessions to maritime unions, particularly as the increased costs could be passed on in the form of higher freight rates. However, stevedoring costs represented thirty-five to forty percent of total operating costs for interstate shipowners and consequently they were less willing to follow a policy of appeasement after the Second World War.[82]

Overseas and interstate shipowners each formed their own representative organisations.[83] By the 1880s there were coastal shipowners' associations in Fremantle, Sydney, Melbourne and Adelaide. The West Australian association was called the West Australian Steamship Owners' Association. A national organisation, the Steamship Owners' Association of Australasia, was established in 1884 (though it did not include the West Australian Steamship Owners' Association), and in 1899 the Australasian Steamship Owners' Federation (ASOF) was formed. The Head Office was located in Melbourne and by 1922 it had established branches in Sydney, Brisbane, Adelaide and Fremantle. In 1905 the Commonwealth Steamship Owners' Association (CSOA) was formed to allow the members of the ASOF to register under the Commonwealth Conciliation and Arbitration Act. The overseas conference lines formed the Overseas Shipping Representatives Association (OSRA) in 1913. This powerful organisation, dominated by the P&O and the Orient Steam Navigation Company, generally protected the interests of overseas shipowners as well as dealing with industrial matters. In 1927 interstate and overseas shipowners formed the Central Committee to represent their interests at the national level.

---

[82]K.F. Walker, *Industrial Relations in Australia* (Cambridge, MA., 1956), 278-279.

[83]This discussion draws on J. Bach, *A Maritime History of Australia* (Melbourne, 1976), 206; K. Buckley and K. Klugman, *The History of Burns Philp* (Sydney, 1981), 36-37; Inter-State Commission, *Waterfront Investigation*, III, 5-15.

These organisations survived until the collapse of coastal shipping in the 1950s which led to a drastic reduction in the number of interstate shipping companies. The Association of Employers of Waterside Labour (AEWL) was created in 1963 to include all stevedoring employers in one umbrella organisation.

According to Tom Sheridan, in the pre-container era stevedoring management "was handicapped by a common, anachronistic mind-set resting on a pervasive seagoing culture that defined stevedoring as a mere second-rate derivative of the real industry-shipping."[84] The title "Captain" was common amongst the ranks of stevedores but the traditionally authoritarian approach adopted at sea was not so effective on land. Many stevedores refused to bargain realistically with the unions but, at the same time, undermined the authority of foremen by pressuring them to make on-the-job concessions to keep the ships moving. There is considerable evidence that management was inefficient in the coordination of labour and, with the exception of the Australian owned James Patrick & Company Proprietary Ltd., slow to use mechanisation to improve productivity.[85] The mindset of many employers was created in the pre-war era of abundant casual labour and they failed to adjust to the changed circumstances after the war.

Given the backward looking outlook of some senior management, it is not surprising that the development of containerisation led to a division of interests between conventional stevedoring companies, which conducted labour intensive operations, and container terminal operators whose activities were capital intensive. The latter broke away from the AEWL to form the Terminal and Depots Employers Federation in 1969 but it was short lived and its members were reabsorbed into the AEWL in 1978. The influence of the AEWL, described as "a cosy little club" was greatly reduced in November 1990 when one of the two major container operators, Conaust (now P&O Ports), left in order to develop its own

---

[84]Sheridan, "Shipowners, Stevedores and Foremen," 412-413.

[85]See M. Tull, "American Technology and the Mechanisation of Australian Ports, 1942-58," *The Journal of Transport History*, VI (1985), 79-90; and T. Sheridan, "Baggage Taken Ashore: The Outlook of Senior Waterfront Management in the 1950s," *Journal of Industrial Relations*, XXXVII (1995), 562-586.

agreement with the WWF.[86] As we will see later in the chapter, in the 1990s reform of the industry led to the cessation of industry based employment, funding and administration arrangements. The AEWL became redundant and it was wound-up in 1994.

Government Authorities

The third and final group concerned with stevedoring, are the government authorities. Attempts to control strikes and achieve greater efficiency on the waterfront have led to a long history of government involvement in the industry. The Commonwealth government has the constitutional power to intervene due to its responsibility for interstate trade and commerce and this led to intervention of a more extensive character than in other industries. In 1914 the Commonwealth Court of Conciliation and Arbitration provided the first award covering wages and conditions in the industry. In 1928, after a waterfront strike, the federal government introduced a system of licensing of labour that worked on the waterfront. This became known as the "Dog Collar Act" because the cost of a licence was the same as the cost of a dog license and the workers thought they were being treated with contempt.[87] The Act was, in effect, a political move against the WWF and resulted in the loss of its effective monopoly of waterfront employment. However, the Act was not applied at Sydney where members of the WWF had offered for work and its application at Fremantle was withdrawn in 1929. As a result of the Act, the smaller Permanent and Casual Wharf Labourers Union (PCWLU) gained a foothold in some ports. There were many violent clashes between the WWF and PCWLU members who were regarded as "scabs." Tensions continued even after 1950 when the last members of the PCWLU were absorbed into the WWF.[88]

As we have seen in 1942 the SIC was created to improve the situation on the waterfront. After the war the employers demanded its abolition but in 1949 Prime Minister Chifley's Labor government created

---

[86]H. Dick, "Progress and Frustration: Restructuring of Coastal Shipping and Ports," in P. Forsyth (ed.), *Microeconomic Reform in Australia* (St. Leonards, NSW, 1992), 217.

[87]See R., Morris, "Australian Stevedoring and Shipping Labour under the Transport Workers Act 1928-47," *The Great Circle*, XI (1989), 17-31.

[88]Beasley, *Wharfies*, 85-86 and 133-134. The Act was suspended in 1941.

the Australian Stevedoring Industry Board (ASIB), which was given extensive powers to control and regulate the performance of stevedoring operations. These powers were anathema to employers who saw them as interfering with their right to control the employment of their workers.

The ASIB tried to improve working conditions on the wharves by encouraging the provision of first aid facilities, lavatories, clean dining rooms and tea water. Workers carried their own billies for brew-ups and obtained boiling water from coppers kept for this purpose on the wharf.[89] Jim Clark recalls that at Fremantle in the early 1950s:

> There were no such things as amenities room or things like that. When you had your smoko or your lunch break you sat on a bale of wool. There were no toilets, only underneath the wharf. There used to be an old story - you don't need to take toilet paper with you, because the waves would clean you up.[90]

The ASIB complained that there was "a wide belief that a garden tap, plugged into a water pipe on a shed wall, constituted a satisfactory washing facility."[91] A measure of the time taken to change traditional attitudes to working conditions in this industry was that it was not until 1963 that the authority could report that there was no complacency over the provision of welfare facilities.

The FHT complained that the ASIB gave workers what they wanted "on the wishful thinking basis that it would produce peace in the industry;" Frank Tydeman, the General Manager, sarcastically described it as "a workers 'benefit society.'"[92] In 1956 Prime Minister Menzies' Liberal Country Party government bowed to the wishes of the employers and replaced it with the Australian Stevedoring Industry Authority (ASIA), an organisation with considerably reduced powers.

---

[89]FPA; and Fremantle City Library Oral History Project, Interview of Michael Donnes by M. Howroyd, 7 November 1988.

[90]Griffiths, *Wharfies*, 48.

[91]ASIB, Annual Report, (1952-1953), 19.

[92]FPA, 87/840/1-2, Wharf Manager to General Manager, 15 November 1951; and FPA, 87/840/1, Frank Tydeman, "Address to Members of AOPA," undated.

Both the ASIB and the ASIA had the task of regulating the numbers of waterside workers, which was difficult due to the conflicting aims of stevedores and waterside workers. From the employers point of view it was important to have labour where and when they wanted it at the price they wished to pay. But the WWF which had a monopoly of recruitment to the waterfront, desired to protect members' incomes and tried to restrict the supply of labour so as to ensure maximum employment to its members. The authorities often found that if they enlarged employment quotas the WWF was very tardy in recruiting new workers, sometimes holding out against quota increases for six months or more.[93] The number of registrations did not come close to the quotas until the mid-1950s illustrating the difficulty of obtaining labour in the post-war full employment economy. The difficulty of attracting workers meant that the average age of the workforce was high and the ASIB remarked on the need to remove a large amount of "deadwood."

One way of increasing the labour supply, of course, is to use overtime. In 1949-1950 about eighty percent of time worked was paid at ordinary rates; by 1969-1970 the figure was sixty-two percent.[94] As the capital intensity of stevedoring operations increased overtime became more common. Container terminals are usually worked on a twenty-four-hour basis.

Labour shortages were, as we have seen, exacerbated by restrictive practices. At some ports, including Fremantle, foremen belonged to the WWF, which made it hard for them to combat labour inefficiency because they were subject to discipline from the men they were meant to supervise![95] Frank Taylor, secretary of the Foremen's Association, complained bitterly to the Tait Inquiry in 1954 that:

> The coronation of job control has been affected at Fremantle, where all foremen are members of the [Federation], and a situation exists wherein before a foreman will carry out the orders of his employer [he] will ring up the [Federation] Branch Secretary and ask if

---

[93]ASIB, *Annual Report* (1950-1951), 23.

[94]Calculated from data in ASIA, *Annual Reports.*

[95]ASIB, *Annual Report* (1951-1952), 14.

> it is all right to do as he is told - and if the answer is No, then he just does not issue the instruction.[96]

There were occasions when the foremen were fined by the union for carrying out the FHT's orders.[97] The Fremantle foremen remained with the WWF until 1960 when the Foremen's Association (founded in Sydney in the 1930s) was finally able to achieve coverage.[98]

The problems were complicated by the icy climate of industrial relations in the industry. While the WWF exploited its job control to win gains for its members, employers tended to maintain pre-war attitudes to the workforce and did not adopt the positive approach of trying to improve productivity with mechanisation or seek greater cooperation from their employees.[99] Thus the scene was set for some bitter industrial disputes.

In some respects, responsibility for efficient cargo-handling rested with the port authorities. The FHT was singled out in the early 1950s as one of the most resistant of employers to efforts to improve supervision of workers.[100] In the mid-1960s the ASIA introduced a comprehensive training scheme for waterside workers' in an attempt to improve productivity.

By the 1970s there were signs of splits in the ranks of employers regarding the role of the ASIA. The WWF and the AEWL favoured abolition of the ASIA and the withdrawal of the government from the industry but others, including port authorities such as the FPA, favoured the retention of a statutory body between employers and employees. They feared that the laissez-faire approach of meeting power with power - a strong union bargaining with a strong employer group - was not in the interests of shippers and port authorities. The Western Australian government also shared this view.[101] In view of the willingness of

---

[96]Cited in Sheridan, "Shipowners, Stevedores and Foremen," 438.

[97]FHT, Minutes, 29 November 1957.

[98]Sheridan, "Shipowners, Stevedores and Foremen," 432-433.

[99]Sheridan, "Baggage," 571.

[100]Sheridan, "Shipowners, Stevedores and Foremen," 437.

[101]*Australian Financial Review,* 16 February 1977.

shipowners to make concessions to unions rather than delay ships in port, and their ability to pass increased costs on in the form of higher freight rates, it was suggested that government withdrawal amounted more to "an exercise of 'buck passing' than responsible policy-making."[102] Nevertheless, despite these fears, the government bowed to the wishes of the main players and abolished the ASIA in 1976.

Microeconomic Reform on the Waterfront

In 1975, following continued complaints about the adequacy of Australia's ports, the federal government appointed a Commission of Inquiry into the Maritime Industry. It found that, on the whole, the bulk ports performed well and that the major problems were in container handling. Shipowners claimed that container handling was slower and more costly in Australia than any other country they served. This was attributed to the attitude of the labour force, unauthorised stoppages, the large number of unions, demarcation disputes, labour disputes by non-waterfront unions affecting delivery of cargoes, labour shortages, insufficient training and restrictive work practices.[103]

Another problem that has long concerned shipowners and port authorities is the pilfering of cargo. There was a saying on the waterfront that wharf labourers' wages were "twenty quid a week and half the cargo."[104] It is hard to find firm evidence of pilfering but in 1920 a Royal Commission estimated that pillaging led to the loss of cargo valued at £21,760 at Fremantle.[105] The presence of a police station on Victoria Quay undoubtedly helped to keep pilfering down, but this was closed in July 1984 as an economy measure and the security on the wharf was left in the hands of the FPA's watchmen at the gates. Mr. W.E. Miller, a wharf labourer, recalled that "there were the specialists in some gangs with the inborn dexterity for opening and closing anything, they had noses like

---

[102]S. Deery, "Industrial Relations on the Australian Waterfront: A Policy of Laissez-Faire," *Journal of Industrial Relations*, XIX (1977), 97.

[103]Commission of Inquiry into the Maritime Industry, *Report on the Adequacy of Australia's Ports* (Canberra, 1976), 5-6 and 21-22..

[104]Lowenstein and Hills, *Under the Hook*, 16.

[105]Australia, *Report of Royal Commission into Pillaging of Ship's Cargoes* (Canberra, 1921), 16-24.

ferrets for anything tasty or removable."[106] Some thieves foiled the best efforts of the police and watchmen for years. "Old Bill," a maintenance worker, was long suspected of being a thief, and the police regularly whipped off the canvas cover of his wheel barrow as he passed through the gates in the hope of catching him. They never did. After he retired the Harbour Master visited him at his home and asked, out of curiosity, what he had been stealing: "with a smile he said, Wheelbarrows."[107]

A Royal Commission in 1976 highlighted another problem, that of corruption. The fitting out and cleaning of foreign vessels had tended to be done by ships' crews. This led to numerous disputes until the mid-1960s when the painters and dockers obtained the right to compensation pay. Under pressure from the Maritime Workers' Union (which acted as the Western Australian Branch of the Painters and Dockers Union), local firms submitted bills to ships agents for work that was not done. The FPA was involved because it was responsible for administering the roster and the levies paid by employers to fund the payment of attendance money and other benefits. The administrative machinery of the FPA was used to have some of the payments made by ships agents paid as wages to workers. The practice of paying workers for work not performed was known as "ghosting." Between January 1971 and July 1975 shipping agents paid over $42,000. His Honour Justice Sweeney concluded that:

> There were quite immoral demands by the union, that there was in some cases ready participation in those demands by the two ship repair firms, that the agents in a number of cases were quite willing to capitulate, that the Port Authority charged with the administration of the port was quite happy to see what was going on continuing to happen - and, frankly that seems to me an appalling picture.[108]

---

[106]Miller, "Memoirs."

[107]Captain J. Adams, *A Pinch of Salt* (Perth, 1996), 109.

[108]Australia, *Royal Commission into Alleged Payments to Maritime Unions* (Canberra, 1976), 77. See also FPA, 87/1035, IX, Industrial Matters - Ship Painters and Dockers; and *The West Australian*, 26 May 1976.

As a result of the outcry, the FPA tightened up procedures but the practice of "ghosting" appears to have declined only slowly.[109]

In the 1980s the federal government turned to microeconomic reform in an attempt to improve the competitiveness of the Australian economy.[110] According to Howard Dick, there were few industries "more in need of but less amenable to microeconomic reform than Australia's long notorious shipping and ports."[111] Most observers agreed that the main problem was the lack of effective competition. This was due to two main factors: first, as we saw in chapter 3 Australia's geography has meant that the major capital city ports have long enjoyed a degree of monopoly power over their hinterlands; second, given the scale of cargo tonnages handled at Australian ports the attempts to take advantage of the economies of scale in shipping and cargo-handling technology have inevitably led to concentration. The anti-competitive bias has been reinforced by institutional characteristics of the industry, including the monopoly power of the WWF, the public ownership and operation of ports, and the role of various regulatory authorities such as customs and quarantine.

Table 6.2 summarises the findings of a report by the Inter-State Commission in 1989 which found that the waterfront industry was also characterised by:

> high costs, endemic unreliability, a high level of industrial disputation, inappropriate manning levels and work practices, poor discipline, poor motivation throughout the industry, and a pervasive lack of competition.[112]

It was agreed that the Australian waterfront was close to the bottom of the pile in international comparisons of efficiency and that this was not the fault of the unions or any other single group.

---

[109]FPA, Minutes, 18 September 1975.

[110]Microeconomic reform refers to measures taken at the firm or industry level to increase efficiency in the use of inputs and so improve economic performance and incomes. See Forsyth (ed.), *Microeconomic Reform in Australia,* for a detailed discussion.

[111]Dick, "Progress and Frustration," 204.

[112]Inter-State Commission, *Waterfront Investigation: Conclusions and Recommendations* (Canberra, 1989) I, xv.

Table 6.2
The Main Characteristics of the Australian Waterfront

- Ineffective management
- Poor workforce training
- Introspective industrial attitudes
- Poor response to user needs
- Poor information flows to users and between links in the transport chain
- Lack of supply and demand balance, often reflected in congestion and queues or in under utilisation of expensive facilities
- Abuse of monopoly power, reflected partially in port authority pricing and investment policies
- A tendency for matters to improve while under investigation but to lapse once the pressure is removed

Source: Inter-State Commission, *Waterfront Investigation: Conclusions and Recommendations*, I (Canberra, 1989), xv.

The ISC recommended a radical programme of reform that included a change from industry based to company employment, improvements in the efficiency of port authorities and the creation of a more competitive commercial environment. In the labour area, it recommended the creation of career structures, and training and incentive arrangements. The size of the workforce was to be reduced by 3000 voluntary redundancies but 1000 younger workers were to be recruited to improve the age profile of the industry. Awards were to be restructured and the number of unions reduced. The ISC estimated that savings from reforms could amount to nineteen percent of all waterfront costs. The government accepted the main recommendations and the Waterfront Industry Reform Authority (WIRA) was created in July 1989 to oversee the changes.

After some difficulties the ACTU, stevedoring employers, unions and the federal government reached an In-Principle Agreement (IPA) in 1989 on a three-year programme of waterfront reform. Following the completion of the programme in October 1992, a study by the Bureau of Transport and Communications Economics (BTCE) concluded that "waterfront reform has been successful in achieving substantial benefits for the waterfront industry and its customers." Table 6.3 summarises the BTCE's main conclusions on the national programme.

Table 6.3
Main Outcomes of the WIRA Reform Process, 1989 to 1992

- The workforce had been reduced by fifty-seven percent and was younger by about ten years.
- Enterprise agreements (EA) had been established making the industry more dynamic and competitive.
- The EA system has resulted in a company ethos developing, although attitudinal change has been particularly slow in Sydney and Melbourne.
- Integrated port labour force agreements have resulted in much lower port costs, and idle time dropping to zero, while minor ports elsewhere continue to experience high levels of idle time.
- Ship time lost through industrial disputes is down by seventy-five percent despite time lost per employee continuing to be as high as before the WIRA process.
- Time lost through accidents has decreased by eighty-eight percent.
- The most significant stevedoring performance improvements have occurred in container and bulk terminals.
- Container crane productivity increased by fifty percent and net ship working rates by sixty-four percent.
- For bulk cargoes, labour productivity improved by about sixty percent.
- For non-containerised general cargo stevedoring, tonnes per person-shift doubled for dry cargoes, and increased by about seventy percent for refrigerated cargoes.
- National average cost to the stevedore of loading or unloading containers declined by $76 per TEU or twenty-nine percent between 1990 and 1993.
- Container stevedoring prices paid by vessel operators decreased by a national average of $61 per TEU, or twenty-four percent, between 1990 and 1993. Vessel turnaround times also improved.
- Competition has forced vessel operators to pass forward to shippers most of the savings received from reductions in stevedoring prices. Reductions in freight rates and terminal handling charges have exceeded the reductions in stevedoring charges in most trades.
- The BTE estimates that the value of benefits to all shippers in 1993 totalled $276 million, of which $200 million accrued to Australians.

Source: BTCE, *Review of the Waterfront Industry Reform Program* (Canberra, 1995), xvii-xviii.

Turning to the situation at the FPA, at the beginning of the 1990s there were seventeen unions representing about 750 workers with twenty-two industrial awards in place. This led to numerous demarcation problems and inefficient work practices. For example, trades persons moving from one area of the port to another could not drive themselves but had to be driven by a transport worker. By the end of the WIRA period there was only one main union (the MUA) and seven enterprise agreements covering all workers; 225 waterside workers had been made redundant.[113] Flexibility in the use of labour has been improved and training for multi-skilling provided. For example, traditionally mooring gangs did only the one task and insisted on numerous restrictive practices that reduced efficiency. These included travelling to and from the Outer Harbour in a convoy of three vans when one would have done the job; and having all their lunch and tea breaks in their own room on Victoria Quay even if they were working in the Outer Harbour. Such practices were labelled the "Fremantle disease" because they gave the impression that the unions and not FPA management was running the port.[114] As a result of the reforms hours of work became totally flexible except for a requirement for a minimum six-hour break between shifts; the mooring gangs were trained in the use of small cranes and to make the water connections to ships tied up in port; and the pay structure was changed from a basic wage plus overtime to an aggregate wage. The reforms have enabled the gang numbers to be reduced from twenty-three to sixteen and allowed the port to offer a twenty-four-hour mooring service.[115]

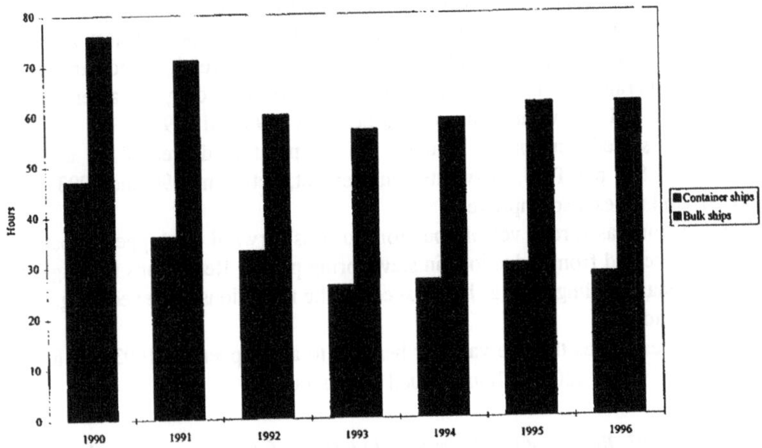

Figure 6.2: Turnaround Times at Fremantle, 1989-1990 to 1995-1996.

Source: FPA, *Annual Reports*.

[113]FPA, Box B557, CMS.005V03, AEWL to WIRA, 14 November 1989.

[114]"Review of the Fremantle Port Authority for the Minister of Transport, Final Report," (March 1991), 48-49, typescript in FPA Library.

[115]C. Rees, "Microeconomic Reform and the Waterfront. A Case Study of the Fremantle Port" (Unpublished Honours thesis, Murdoch University, 1995), 34.

By the 1990s there were, however, signs that technological and social changes had altered the traditional culture of the waterfront. Ships were more sparsely crewed and spent less time in port, leading to the decline of taverns and other service industries catering for itinerant sailors. This was one reason why commercial interests welcomed increased visits by American naval vessels for "R and R" purposes. Container crane operators are isolated in their cabs thirty metres in the air and with fewer workers around there is less opportunity for the rank and file discussions that used to occur.[116] These changes altered the links between port and city and reduced the militancy and cohesiveness of the workforce.

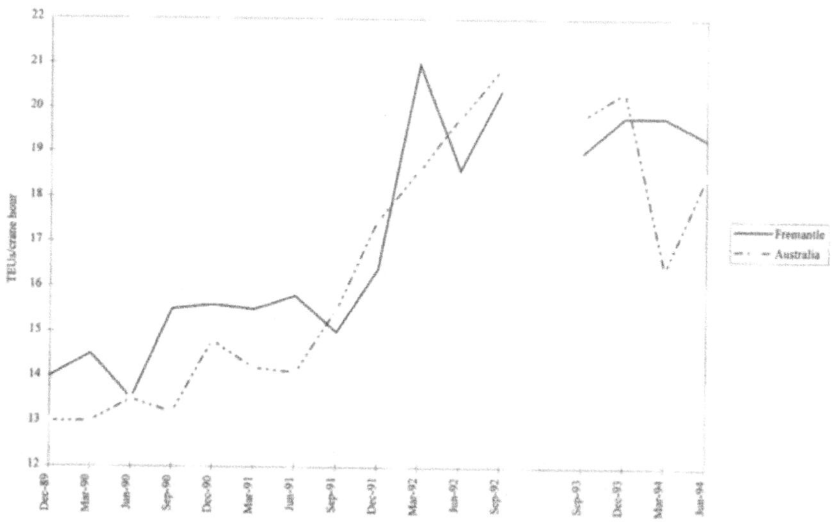

Figure 6.3: Container Crane Productivity at Fremantle, December 1989 to June 1994.

Source: BTCE, *Review*, appendix IV.

Even the male dominated culture of the waterfront has changed: in the past the role of women was as loyal wives and mothers. The first time women took an active role in a dispute was in 1919, when they

---

[116]This paragraph draws on Beasley, *Wharfies*, 180, 229 and 256-257.

pelted the police with horseshoes, nuts, bolts and stones.[117] For the most part women provided background support during strikes, operating canteens and circulating leaflets. The Fremantle's women's committee made history in January 1956 when it became the first to attend a WWF stop-work meeting. A leaflet issued by the women declared that "we are solidly behind our menfolk in their struggle for wage justice." In 1975 the union's rules were altered to allow women to join. The first women to do so were some tally clerks who transferred to the Whyalla branch in 1976; the first woman to work as a wharf labourer was Sandra Elliman who joined the Townsville branch, aged twenty-one, in 1989. Significantly, she was following a family tradition as her grandfather, father and brother were also wharf labourers.

As part of the reform process, port authorities and other agencies began to compile performance indicators, such as ship turnround times and crane handling rates. Figure 6.2 illustrates the trend in turnround times at Fremantle between 1989-1990 and 1995-1996. Slow turnround in port is extremely costly for shipowners due to the high capital costs of their ships. Thus the speed of turnround is of great interest to shipowners and influences their willingness to send ships to Fremantle. In the early 1990s turnround times for container ships improved by about forty percent and for bulk ships by about eighteen percent, suggesting that there were substantial gains in efficiency. Figure 6.3 compares the productivity of container cranes at Fremantle with the average for the five main Australian ports between December 1989 and June 1994. Fremantle's crane rate, defined as the number of TEUs moved per crane per hour of gross time, increased from an average of around fourteen TEUs per hour in the early 1990s to an average of around twenty TEUs per hour in early 1994, an increase of forty-three percent.[118] This was in line with the national trend. However, crane intensity, which refers to the average number of cranes used to simultaneously work each vessel, was almost constant, while nationally there was a rise of about 6.5 percent.[119] This was probably due to deficiencies in the physical layout of the port together with an accident

---

[117] J. Williams, *The First Furrow* (Perth, 1976), 76.

[118] A TEU is a twenty-foot equivalent unit based on the standard shipping container of 20 feet x 8 feet x 8 feet.

[119] Crane intensity is calculated as follows: crane intensity = TEUs per net hour/TEUs per crane hour. The source for the data is BTCE, *Review of the Waterfront Industry Reform Program* (Canberra, 1995), appendix IV.

that destroyed a container crane, which was not replaced until the latter part of 1996. In 1996 the FPA also rectified the physical deficiencies by consolidating container operations on North Quay and upgrading facilities. Clearly, there is still scope for further improvements although Fremantle's position as a first and last port of call will always make it difficult to achieve the productivity levels of ports where ships routinely discharge their total cargo. In the mid-1990s the average number of container moves per hour on ships of the Maersk Line, which discharged full cargoes from Singapore, was about twelve percent higher than on other vessels handled at the P&O's container terminal.[120] This gives an approximate indication of the impact of the bias towards partial cargoes.

Conclusions

Before the Second World War, waterside workers at Fremantle faced a precarious struggle to earn a living wage, their labour was inefficient and they were a source of persistent industrial unrest: these were the general consequences of the system of casual employment. Wartime labour shortages swung the balance of power in the workers' favour and, with a militant leadership, they were not slow to press for changes in their working environment. The waterfront was notoriously strike prone and external intervention by the government failed to counteract the divisive forces in the industry. There is no doubt that the task of achieving efficient stevedoring and equitable wage and working conditions was a formidable one; it was further complicated by the technological changes that swept the industry.

By the 1980s waterside workers throughout Australia enjoyed permanent employment and wages and conditions beyond the wildest dreams of the pre-war workforce but the waterfront was plagued by restrictive practices and low productivity. In the late 1980s the federal government began a radical programme of microeconomic reform which led to substantial gains in efficiency. But in the mid-1990s container handling rates at Australian ports still lagged behind world best practice and there were claims that inertia was setting in on the wharves.[121]

---

[120]Calculated from data kindly provided by Captain D. Ravn of P&O Ports. The data were for 1995, 1996 and the first three months of 1997.

[121]See *Australian Financial Review*, 28 February and 5 June 1997.

A problem with maintaining the momentum for reform is that responsibility for waterfront activity is split between a large number of public and private agencies. Almost half a century ago, the ASIB claimed that:

> The major turn-round problems boil down to problems of co-ordination. The fact is that restrictive working hours, labour shortages, and space problems existing throughout the industry, including the waterfront, are all climaxed at the wharves...The whole wharf-sea transport process is broken into many parts - there are spheres of Commonwealth responsibility, State responsibility and no responsibility. It presents a knotty problem in co-ordination.[122]

The ports are controlled by state government instrumentalities and outside the direct control of the federal government. Yet, as we saw in table 6.1, the ISC had identified port authority pricing and investment policies as a major cause of concern. These issues of microeconomic reform were on the national agenda when, in 1990, the FPA registered a record $14 million operating loss. This, as we shall see in the next chapter, was the catalyst for a major programme of restructuring that was designed to turn the port authority into a dynamic, commercially orientated enterprise.

[122]ASIB, *Annual Report* (1950-1951), 29.

Chapter 7
From Port Authority to Strategic Manager: The Transformation of the FPA

In different circumstances and at different times, the appropriate form of port administration varies. So it was at Fremantle. In chapter 2 we discussed the formation of the Fremantle Harbour Trust and the establishment of an institutional framework which survived relatively intact for over ninety years. The Fremantle Port Authority, which was created in 1964, exercised substantially the same powers and functions as its predecessor.[1] However, as we saw in the previous chapter, in the late 1980s, as part of the wider process of waterfront reform, ports were required to improve their efficiency and operate more commercially. At Fremantle and many other Australian ports the 1990s were marked by the introduction of major institutional reforms that led to the development of a new commercially-orientated port culture.

It is commonplace to historians that changes in social and economic conditions alter the viability of institutions; but it is also true that the quality of the staff counts as much as the institutional framework in which they have to operate. Thus, it is also necessary to give due attention to the organisation and performance of the staff. Before discussing port staffing and changes in port administration, it is proposed to use some yardsticks developed in the 1920s by a British engineer, Sir George Buchanan, to evaluate port administration at Fremantle.

The Efficiency of the Administrative Framework

Buchanan's yardsticks, which have often been cited with approval by world experts on ports, are listed below:[2]

---

[1]*Fremantle Harbour Trust Amendment Act 1964* (No. 35).

[2]See Commission of Inquiry into the Maritime Industry, *Report on Adequacy of Australia's Ports* (Canberra, 1976), 12-13, which repeats many of Buchanan's yardsticks without mentioning him by name. J. Bird, *Seaport Gateways of Australia* (Oxford, 1968), 234, cites Buchanan's work with approval.

1. The whole of the foreshores within the port area should be under the absolute control of the state, either directly or by delegation of power to a public corporation or trust.
2. Administration of the port should be free from political influence.
3. The port authority should include representatives of organisations interested in the port's welfare.
4. The port should be self-contained financially and revenues should be applied solely to its maintenance and development, any surplus being used to build up reserve funds, reduce port charges or extinguish capital debt.
5. Port charges should be uncomplicated, easily collected and levied so that there is an even distribution of taxation on port users. No portion of the community should be taxed for the benefit of another section and everything using the port must make a reasonable contribution towards its upkeep.
6. Capital charges should be adjusted so as to avoid undue burden either in the present or the future, and adequate arrangements should be made for the ultimate liquidation of the capital debt.
7. Development should invariably be kept ahead of actual trade requirements, as a growing port is never really completed.[3]

We will consider each yardstick in turn but it is necessary to give greater attention to capital funding, port charges and profitability, as these issues have not been considered in detail in previous chapters.

Area of Jurisdiction

The FHT was "given" control over the Inner Harbour, an area of about 152 acres (sixty-two hectares) of land and 250 acres (101 hectares) of water, and also control over an Outer Harbour, which covered a vast area of 114,000 acres (46,154 hectares) of water. Thus the FHT satisfied Buchanan's first yardstick, but, of course, this tells us more about the framework within which it operated, than about administrative performance.

---

[3]George Buchanan, *Report on Transport in Australia with Special Reference to Port and Harbour Facilities* (2 vols., Canberra, 1927), I, 69.

Freedom from Political Interference

When Buchanan stated that port administration should be free from political influence, he was presumably referring to day-to-day administration. It would have been unrealistic to expect governments to remain aloof from major planning decisions that had the potential to affect the well-being of all West Australians. In chapter 5 we saw that discussions over developments such as the proposed dock, bulk grain-handling, the opening of the Outer Harbour and containerisation involved the port authority, government, business and the community at large. However, even day-to-day administration has not been entirely free from government intervention.[4] In particular, governments intervened to preserve revenue and to protect rural interests. For example, in 1907, to help local producers, the government ordered the FHT to exempt primary products and goods manufactured locally from wharfage charges; in order to compensate for the lost revenue, higher charges had to be levied on imports. As one contemporary complained, "the consumer pays for the pastoralist." Such practices were consistent with the policy of protection all round, that is, compensating primary producers for the increased costs they incurred as a result of the protection given to manufacturing. Due to this deeply entrenched practice, the FPA was not able to restore wharfage charges on exports until 1965. Other examples of interference include pressure in the early years of the century to use jarrah rather than concrete wharf piles in order to protect the local timber industry; and the introduction of a "temporary" surtax of twenty percent during the First World War which, despite repeated requests by the FHT for its removal, survived until 1956. The FPA has often been encouraged by government to take on apprentices, especially during times of significant unemployment, but the FPA complained that there was a limit to the number of apprentices it could take.[5] It is apparent that Fremantle failed to satisfy Buchanan's requirement that port administration should be free from political interference.

---

[4]This discussion draws on M.T. Tull, "The Financial Performance of the Fremantle Harbour Trust, 1903 to 1939," *Australian Economic History Review*, XXVII (1988), 26-29.

[5]FPA, *Annual Report* (1976-1977), 17.

User Representation

Buchanan's view that the port authority should include representatives of organisations interested in the port's welfare was undoubtedly based on his experiences of the public trusts which ran many British ports. For example, the Mersey Docks and Harbour Board, which had been established in 1857, had twenty-one members, of whom eighteen were elected by dock ratepayers (shipowners and merchants) and three were government nominees.[6] In the words of a port manager, such trusts were "run by shipowners, traders, and merchants, for shipowners, traders, and merchants."[7] But these groups have never had formal representation on the Board that controls the Port of Fremantle. The government appoints the five part-time Commissioners. However, they usually come from organisations involved with the port, including unions and, given that they are appointed only on a part-time basis, undoubtedly give *de facto* representation to user interests. Nevertheless, port users lack the direct representation that Buchanan considered essential if a port were to be run efficiently.

Port Charges

When the FHT was created it inherited a scale of charges devised by the Department of Railways and the Harbour and Lights Department. As at most ports, charges fell into two main groups: those levied on ships and those levied on cargoes. Dues on ships were based on the tonnage of vessels, a system dating back to the Middle Ages and generally accepted throughout the British Empire. Dues on cargoes were based on the freight ton (2240 lbs.) or the measurement ton (forty cubic feet).

The distribution of port charges at Fremantle and other Australian ports was very uneven. In 1928 for every £100 received in revenue from ships the cargoes paid £239.[8] Between 1948-1949 and 1969-1970, sixty-

---

[6]A. Jarvis, "The Port of Liverpool and the Shipowners in the Late Nineteenth Century, *The Great Circle*, XVI, (1994), 3.

[7]T.H. Hawkins, "Ports and Harbours," in J.A. Todd (ed.), *The Shipping World* (London, 1934), 233.

[8]A.G. Whitlam, "Australian Port Charges," *Economic Record*, Supplement (1930), 212.

three percent of the FPA's revenue was derived from charges on cargoes and only thirty-two percent from charges on ships.[9] This discriminative pattern of charging may have been the result of a series of rule-of-thumb pricing decisions but it seems likely that it reflected the relative lobbying powers of shipowners and consignees. The desire to attract shipping, mollify the powerful conference lines, and keep freight rates low, has meant that charges on ships have tended to be lower than those on cargoes.

In addition, there was, as we have already seen, discrimination between import and exports, with primary exports being exempted from wharfage charges after 1907. In chapter 5 we saw that exemptions were granted to cargoes using the Outer Harbour when it opened in 1955. Faced with a shrinking revenue base and rising costs, the port authority was forced to increase rates substantially in 1956, the first major increase since 1918. The inward wharfage rate, for example, was increased by 170 percent to $1.35 per ton of cargo and remained at that level until 1970. The government usually approved increases only after the port had experienced deficits.[10] The authority complained it had to:

> Increasingly depend on diminishing import trade for its essential wharfage revenue and saturation point has been reached in so far as the levying of wharfage on imports is concerned. It is the firm opinion of the Commissioners that all cargoes, whether import or export, should contribute commensurately towards the revenue of the port.[11]

However, nothing changed and by 1959-1960, due to the exemptions, about seven percent of port trade contributed about sixty-one percent of wharfage revenue.[12] The incidence of charges remained highly uneven

---

[9]Calculated from data in FHT and FPA, *Annual Reports*. The balance of revenue was accounted for by other minor charges.

[10]A.T. Bonds, "The Economics of Outer Harbour Development in the Port of Fremantle" (Unpublished MA thesis, University of Western Australia, 1969), 164.

[11]FHT, *Annual Report* (1957-1958), 6.

[12]Bonds, "The Economics of Outer Harbour," 135.

until 1965, when, after several years of deficits, the government relented and allowed the FPA to levy charges on primary exports.

From an economic point of view such practices led to a rather arbitrary distribution of costs to port users. Regarding Australian ports in general, P. Stonham has observed that:

> In many cases...the rates are set according to the "custom of the port" and are rarely related to the marginal or average private or social costs of port investment in static facilities. The custom of the port may embody all sorts of historical and rule of thumb factors.[13]

Apart from historical inertia, port charges continued to be determined by a variety of pressures including revenue requirements, political bargaining, and state development policies. It was not until July 1990 that the pricing structure was redesigned so that charges more closely reflected the cost of providing services. By 1996-1997, under the new system, charges had fallen by 18.5 percent in real terms.[14]

In 1974, in clear violation of Buchanan's dictum that it is wrong to use the ports for revenue-collecting purposes, the government forced the FPA and some other statutory authorities to pay three percent of their revenue to the Consolidated Revenue Fund (CRF).[15] Since 1987 the FPA has been required to pay a dividend into the CRF, one of the first public authorities to do so.[16] The legislation provided for the dividend to be recommended by the FPA to the Minister of Transport, who jointly with the Treasurer determined the amount to be paid. The three-percent levy was not removed and the FPA was left paying the levy or dividend, which ever was greater. The levy was not abolished until 1996 when a dividend policy was finally agreed. The 1987 legislation also gave the power to the Minister to "give directions to the FPA with respect to the performance of its functions, either generally or with respect to a particular matter, and

---

[13]P.E. Stonham, "User Cost in Port: An Australian Study," *Australian Economic Papers*, VIII (1969), 180

[14]FPA, *Annual Report* (1995-1996), 12.

[15]*Public Authorities (Contributions) Act 1974 (No. 43).*

[16]*Acts Amendment (Port Authorities) Act 1987.*

the FPA shall give effect to those directions," signifying the intention of government to retain ultimate control over the port.

Capital Funding, Financial Performance and Profitability

The availability of capital funds is obviously a major factor in the port's ability to respond to change. *The Fremantle Harbour Trust Act 1902* instructed the FHT to pay surpluses to CRF after deducting operating costs, interest on borrowed funds and the cost of providing a sinking fund for the redemption of capital debt. But the act of formation failed to specify explicit financial objectives. An Amendment Act in 1906 created a Renewals and Replacement Fund to provide for the replacement of assets, but it appears that the government was not prepared to grant the port authority large discretionary powers in the area of finance because appropriations to the fund were limited to £2000 per annum.[17] Despite repeated requests from the port authority the limit remained unchanged until the late 1960s. In 1960 the FPA was given the power to establish a Reserve Fund and to borrow on the open market but was limited to maximum borrowings of $600,000 in any one year. Thus the new borrowing power did not represent "a vital change in the autonomy of the port."[18] In the late 1960s the FPA succeeded in increasing the proportion of investment funded from internal sources but was still forced to go cap-in-hand to the government every year to get sufficient funds for port reconstruction and development.[19]

Figure 7.1 illustrates the financial surpluses earned by the port authority between 1903-1904 and 1995-1996. It is necessary to stress that it gives only a crude approximation of the real surpluses earned because port charges do not measure all the benefits and costs of ports and because of deficiencies in the accounting data.

Port surpluses are closely related to the level of port activity. The port recorded its first ever deficit during the lean years of the First World

---

[17]*Fremantle Harbour Trust Amendment Act 1906.*

[18]Bonds, "The Economics of Outer Harbour," 124. The Act was the *Fremantle Harbour Trust Amendment Act 1960* (No. 75).

[19]From 1963-1964 State Treasury allowed the FPA to retain depreciation on capital works previously repaid to Treasury as special loan repayments and in 1968-1969 a special dredging reserve was created. In 1969-1970 total depreciation provisions amounted to $1.65 million, equivalent to about seventeen percent of revenue.

War and the 1930s depression also caused a sharp drop in profitability. By contrast, the 1920s was a golden decade of port activity and profitability, so much so, in fact, that the shipping lines complained that the port was being used as "a taxing machine" and that port charges were too high.[20] The Second World War reduced trade and hence revenue but after the war trade boomed and the port earned increasing surpluses. The introduction of import controls in 1952 reduced trade and helped to plunge the port into deficit in 1952-1953. In 1955-1956 there was a record deficit of about $333,000. The port authority blamed this on the concessions granted to users in the Outer Harbour. The extension of wharfage to primary exports in 1965 helped restore the port to profitability.

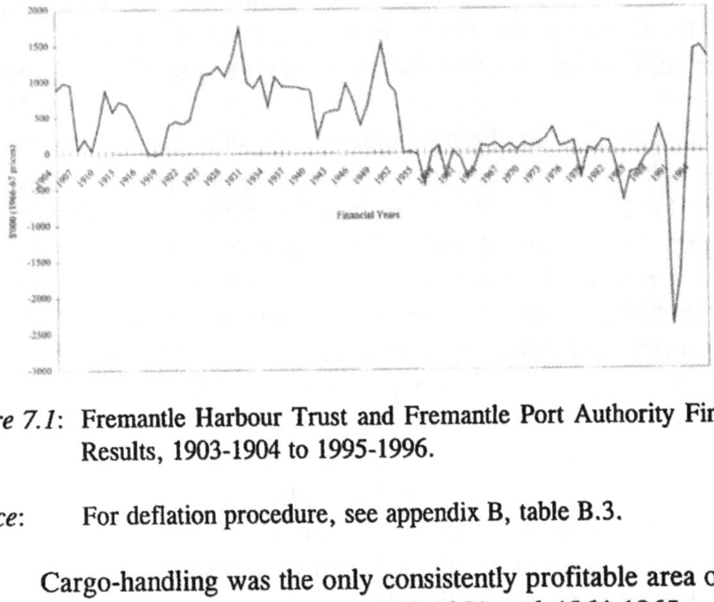

Figure 7.1: Fremantle Harbour Trust and Fremantle Port Authority Financial Results, 1903-1904 to 1995-1996.

Source: For deflation procedure, see appendix B, table B.3.

Cargo-handling was the only consistently profitable area of port operations. For example, between 1950-1951 and 1964-1965 revenue from sources other than cargo-handling was sufficient to meet all relevant operating costs only in 1950-1951 and 1951-1952.[21] The port became increasingly reliant on cross-subsidisation from cargo-handling in order to break even.

Apart from a deficit in 1978, the FPA was consistently profitable until the 1980s, when a succession of large deficits reduced it to a parlous

[20]Tull, "The Financial Performance," 29-35.

[21]Bonds, "The Economics of Outer Harbour," 179.

financial situation. In 1991 a government-appointed review (henceforth referred to as the *Review*) attributed the deficits to a number of factors, including a downturn in trade, sloppy budgetary and financial procedures and a non-commercial approach to port management.[22] A major cause was the cost of repaying the capital borrowed to finance the deepening of the Inner Harbour to thirteen metres, an expensive project begun in 1989 which was discussed in chapter 5. It was claimed that the FPA's exit from stevedoring in 1991 was poorly managed: it was slow to rid itself of redundant mechanical equipment and faced the heavy burden of paying out superannuation and leave entitlements. It is curious that the deficit ballooned in 1990-1991, the year that the new, supposedly cost-based, tariff policy was introduced, suggesting some miscalculations. The FPA was forced to use its reserves (leave and superannuation provisions) to meet financial obligations. The reserves stood at $13.02 million on 1 July 1990 but by 31 December 1990 had plummeted to $5.61 million. If nothing was done, it was estimated that by March 1991 all the FPA's reserves would have been exhausted and it would have had to borrow to pay wages.

Figure 7.2 illustrates the ratio of net profits (operating surplus less capital debt charges) to net fixed assets between 1906-1907 and 1995-1996. This measure provides an approximate check on managerial performance.[23] Between 1906-1907 and 1995-1996 the port earned an average rate of return of two percent per annum; over the same period the long term yield on government bonds averaged 6.3 percent.[24] This suggests that the port was not earning a "market" rate of return. Up to 1938-1939 the average rate of return was 3.6 percent per annum, but from 1945-1946 to 1995-1996 the average rate of return was only 0.9 percent. The deterioration in financial performance in the late 1950s was partly due

---

[22]"Review of the Fremantle Port Authority for the Minister of Transport. Final Report" (2 vols., 1991), I, 1 and 85, typescript in FPA Library.

[23]For a variety of reasons, including the fact that it is affected by managerial policies with regard to depreciation provision and profit declaration, this measure provides only an approximate indication of financial performance. For a detailed discussion see K.A. Tucker, "Interpreting Accounting Data and Business Records," in K.A. Tucker (ed.), *Business History. Selected Readings* (London, 1977), appendix I, 399-406.

[24]Calculated from data in M.W Butlin, *A Preliminary Annual Database, 1900/01 to 1973/74* (Canberra, 1977), table 4.16; and Reserve Bank of Australia, *Australian Economic Statistics, 1949-50 to 1994-95* (Sydney, 1996).

to the concessions granted to the users of the Outer Harbour, but other factors, including over-investment and over-staffing, undoubtedly played a role.

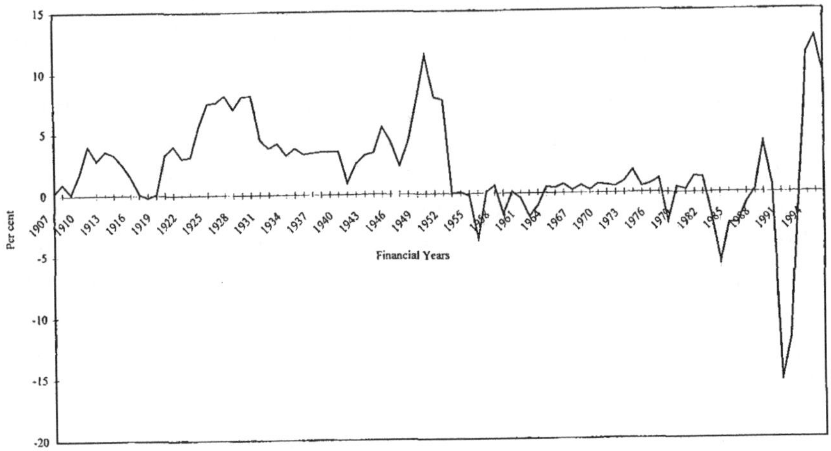

Figure 7.2: Fremantle Harbour Trust and Fremantle Port Authority Net Profits/Net Fixed Assets, 1906-1907 to 1995-1996.

Source: See figure 7.1.

It should be noted that our yardsticks of financial performance fail to capture the full economic impact of the port on the City of Fremantle and on the Western Australian economy. A comprehensive economic assessment needs to take into account all of the social costs and benefits of port operations and the connections between port and city development. A study undertaken by consultants in 1993 estimated that the port accounted for a total of 10,200 jobs, or 1.2 percent of state employment, and produced an annual output valued at over $700 million. Visits by naval ships were estimated to generate an additional $96 million per annum.[25] While such estimates are only very approximate, it is clear that the port plays a vital role in the Western Australian economy.

---

[25]Economic Research Associates Pty. Ltd., *Economic Impact Study. Port of Fremantle* (Nedlands, WA, 1993), iv-v.

Did the Port Keep Ahead of Trade Requirements?

It is difficult to assess whether or not port facilities kept ahead of trade requirements, except in a very approximate sense. Figure 7.3 illustrates indices of port investment and cargo tonnage (1909-1910 = 1000). It should be stressed that because no allowance is made for depreciation and obsolescence of the capital stock, the index of port investment is only a crude indicator of the state of port facilities.

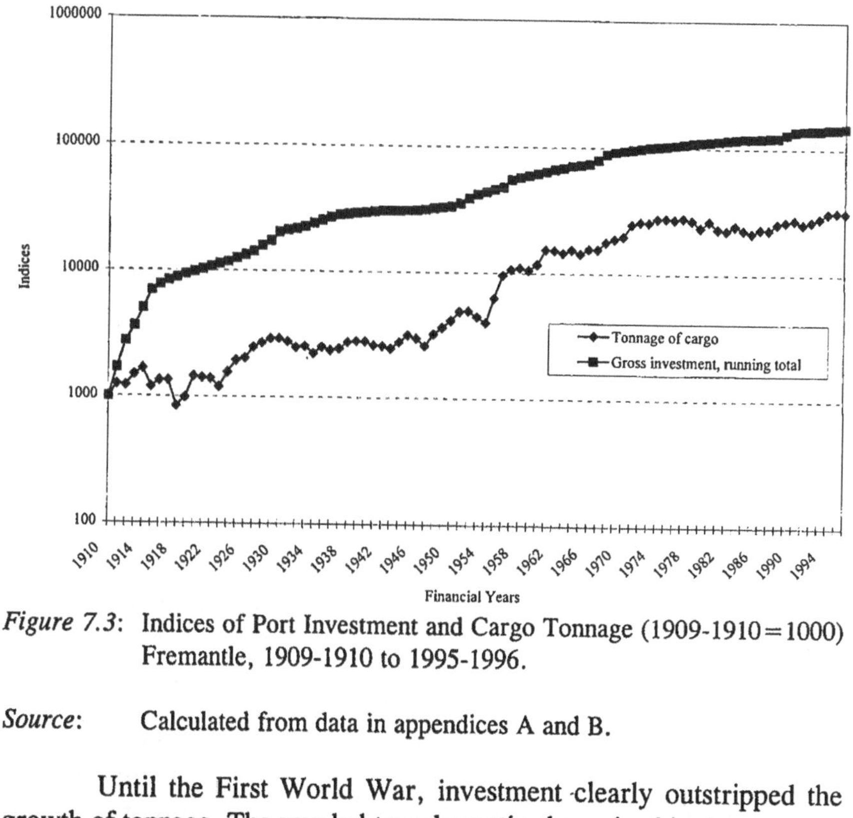

Figure 7.3: Indices of Port Investment and Cargo Tonnage (1909-1910=1000) Fremantle, 1909-1910 to 1995-1996.

Source: Calculated from data in appendices A and B.

Until the First World War, investment clearly outstripped the growth of tonnage. The war led to a dramatic slump in shipping tonnage and consequently reduced the need for further investment. The parallel growth of investment and tonnage in the 1920s suggests that port facilities were regularly adjusted to meet the needs of trade and shipping. But in the 1930s falling trade led to low-capacity utilisation and only about one-third of Fremantle's eighteen berths were usually in use at any one time.[26] The

[26]F.W. Tydeman, *Report on Port of Fremantle* (3 vols., Perth, 1949), II, 98.

outbreak of the Second World War led to an upsurge in port activity, while expenditure was cut to the bone. As result, during the war and the trade boom that followed, port facilities lagged behind the needs of trade and shipping. The port authority responded by expanding investment with peaks occurring in the mid-1950s due to the expenditure on the Outer Harbour; in the late 1960s due to the construction of container facilities; and in the late 1980s due to the deepening of the Inner Harbour and the construction of the Rous Head Business Park. The parallel growth of investment and tonnage from the mid-1950s suggests that port facilities kept pace with the needs of trade and shipping: as we saw in chapter 6, the port authority has always striven to provide an "overplus of power."

In summary, the FHT and its successor, the FPA, suffered from political interference in the day-to-day running of the port; the port commissioners failed to include direct representatives of port users; port charges were unevenly distributed; the government was siphoning off port profits; depreciation provisions and reserves were inadequate; and there was a tendency to "over-invest" in port facilities. Judged by Buchanan's yardsticks, it was far from an efficient administrative machine. Buchanan himself concluded that "in no State perhaps is the need for a reform in methods of administration more urgent than is the need in West Australia."[27] He is reported to have described Fremantle as "the best designed, the best equipped, and certainly the best administered port in Australia," so it is clear that he was really criticising the way the founders of the FHT had circumscribed its administrative powers, rather than criticising the way it had actually performed its administrative functions.[28] As an engineer, preoccupied with structural excellence, he naturally approved of the "overplus of power" provided by the authority and was less concerned with the implications of costly works for port finances and state budgets. In his eyes, the port's Commissioners were undoubtedly more sinned against than sinning. Buchanan recommended that the port authority be given greater independence so that it could run the port free from political influence. But it had to wait until the reforms of the 1990s to obtain a substantial increase in autonomy.

---

[27]Buchanan, *Report on Transport*, 97.

[28]FHT, Minutes, 27 August 1925.

Organisation and Staffing of the Port Authority

We now turn to examine the organisation and staffing of the FHT and FPA. The wide range of services provided by the port authority has meant that it has employed a correspondingly wide range of personnel, including professional engineers, pilots, administrative staff and wharf labourers. We discussed the wharf labourers in the previous chapter and here the focus is on the authority's Commissioners and permanent staff.

The Commissioners

The Fremantle Commissioners are appointed by the government for a three-year term and are eligible for reappointment at the end of that period. A list of Commissioners who served between 1903 and 1996 is given in appendix C.

Although the government appointed the Commissioners it was customary, at least until the 1920s, for the major interests involved in the port to nominate representatives. The Fremantle and Perth Chambers of Commerce and the Kalgoorlie Chamber of Mines nominated representatives until 1912 when the Scaddon Labor Government ended this practice.[29] The Labor Government appointed two public servants and a wharf labourer to the Trust. The public servants were the Engineer-in-Chief, J. Thompson, and the Chief Harbour Master, Captain Irvine. This move met with criticism on the grounds that the two men would be in the position of commenting on their own advice; instead of having a board dominated by public servants the government might as well abolish it and administer the port as an ordinary government department. The appointment of a wharf labourer, Mr. John Taylor, was criticised on the grounds that "there is no need for their representation on the Trust in order to protect them, any more than there is need to appoint a railway porter co-commissioner in order to protect the railway servants."[30] However, not all business interests were strongly opposed to the appointment of a lumper. In 1911, Mr. Moxon, the local manager for the Adelaide Steamship

---

[29]FPA, 35/18/1, J. Anderton, Acting General Secretary, Kalgoorlie Chamber of Mines, to H. Colebatch, Colonial Secretary, 28 September 1917.

[30]WAPD, XLIV (1912), 3068-3069, Criticism by Hon. J.D. Connolly speaking in debate over 1912 Amendment Act.

Company and President of the Fremantle Chamber of Commerce, stated that he was not opposed providing "a suitable man" could be found.[31]

The election of a Liberal Government in 1917 led to another change of policy in the appointment of Commissioners. Thompson and Irvine were instructed to resign "as a matter of policy."[32] The government revived the practice of requesting nominations for Commissioners and was flooded with requests for representation from bodies such as the Fremantle and Perth Chambers of Commerce, the Kalgoorlie Chamber of Mines, the Farmers and Settlers Association, the Chamber of Manufacturers and the Fremantle Lumpers Union. The Colonial Secretary, Hal Colebatch, pointed out that the FHT Act did not allow for the representation of special interests: "directly a man was appointed to the Trust, no matter who nominated him, his duty was to the Trust and the Trust only."[33] In 1908 the appointment of Frank Viles was not renewed because he actively campaigned for mining interests.[34] The government eventually appointed three men who had been nominated by the Perth Chamber of Commerce, which provoked protests from those groups whose nominations were ignored.

All commercial groups were, however, united in opposition to the re-appointment of the lumper, John Taylor. This was a legacy of the bitterness generated by the 1917 strike, which we discussed in chapter 6. The Fremantle Chamber of Commerce argued that if a labour representative were appointed he should be a member of the National Volunteers, who had worked during the strike. Colebatch replied that Taylor had served satisfactorily in the past and had been reappointed for that reason. During the labour difficulties in 1919 Taylor attacked the shipping companies for desiring "to starve into submission to their wishes the members of the Fremantle Lumpers' Union," but despite threatening to do

---

[31]FPA, 147/11, transcript of evidence given to Royal Commission on Wharves and Water Frontage (South Australia), 2 June 1911.

[32]FPA, 35/16/1, Colonial Secretary to J. Thompson, Chairman of FHT, 13 October 1916.

[33]FPA, 35/18/1, copy of Cabinet Submission by H. Colebatch, Colonial Secretary, on FHT, *circa* September 1917.

[34]FPA, 48/08/1-2, Minutes, 26 June 1908.

so, said nothing of this outside the confines of the FHT. Taylor's appointment was renewed until his death in 1931.[35]

From the 1920s onwards the practice of calling for nominees was dropped in favour of direct selection by the government. Commissioners appointed included businessmen, public servants, a member of the labour movement and an ex-Labor politician. W.C. Angwin, who had served as MLA for North East Fremantle between 1904 and 1937, was appointed to the Trust to replace H. Tanner, who died in January 1934. Tanner had "represented" primary producers and his replacement by a member of the Labor Party provoked a strong protest from the Primary Producers' Association. Angwin was later appointed Chairman of the Rural Relief Trust and did not re-nominate for the FHT. However, he was replaced in 1936 by Frederick Mann, Secretary of the Fremantle Trades Hall, a move that was attacked by Mr. Keenan, leader of the Country Party, on the grounds that rural interests were still not represented on the Trust.[36] Between 1924 and 1939 there were only three years (1930-1933) in which a non-labor coalition governed in Western Australia; thus the Labor Party had a dominating influence on appointments to the Trust. However, Mr. T. Carter and Mr. L. Bateman, both with business backgrounds, were re-appointed by Labor governments. Tom Carter served as Chairman from 1917 to 1944 and has the distinction of being the Trust's longest-serving Chairman.

The same pattern of appointments, both in terms of background, length of service and gender, continued after the Second World War. Examples include Mr. William Hughes, a businessman and past President of the South Fremantle Football Club, who served from 1957 to 1971; Mr. J. Manford, a businessman involved in the transport industry, who served from 1960 to 1974 and Mr. T. Lewis, Under-Secretary of the Public Works Department, who served from 1975 to 1987. A waterside worker, Mr. N. McKenzie, was appointed in 1957 by a Labor government but served for only two years before a Liberal government terminated his appointment.

---

[35]FPA, 35/18/2, Fremantle Chamber of Commerce to Colonial Secretary, 15 January 1918; Perth Chamber of Commerce to Colonial Secretary, 14 January 1918; Kalgoorlie Chamber of Mines to Colonial Secretary, 22 December 1917; Colonial Secretary to Kalgoorlie Chamber of Mines, 28 December 1917; FHT, Minutes, 2 May 1919.

[36]*The West Australian*, 10 January 1936; and *The Daily News*, 2 January 1936.

There were no females on the Board or in senior management until the 1990s, a reflection of the heavily male-dominated culture of the ports industry. On his retirement in 1917 Frank Nicholas declared that he would miss the usual Friday meeting with its convivial associations.[37] After the Second World War the Commissioners' wives joined them for an annual port inspection on the port authority's VIP boat, the *Challenger*. The first female to serve on the Board was Ms. Kerry Sanderson, who was appointed General Manager in April 1992 and to the Board in June the same year. Kerry Sanderson had extensive management experience, having worked for the State Treasury for seventeen years, the last five as Director, Economic and Financial Policy Division, and had served as Deputy Director General of Transport for Western Australia. Her arrival heralded a major change in the culture of the port authority because not only did she turn it into a more commercially orientated organisation but also other women were recruited into management positions.

Since Kerry Sanderson's arrival there has been a shift away from the notion of appointing people who are *de facto* representatives of port users to the appointment of people with business experience. This is seen as more appropriate for a commercially-orientated port authority. Nevertheless, someone with a union background was still appointed while the Labor government was in power (1983-1993). Mr. W. Pritchard, State Secretary of the Maritime Union of Australia, served on the Board between 1992-1995, but the Liberal-National Party government elected in 1993 did not appoint any new union representatives to the Board.

The reliance on part-time Commissioners meant that each member, "for a few hours in each week, must idealistically endeavour to suppress both his private interests in relation to the port, in addition to the internal clash of interests which arise between representation of various commercial sectors."[38] Not surprisingly, Commissioners were sometimes accused of lacking the necessary "idealism." For example, the first chairman of the FHT, Captain Laurie, also ran the port's main stevedoring business. It was claimed that when incoming steamers were competing for berths, Laurie gave preference to ships stevedored by his firm. Laurie complained that "the moment a man takes any public position in this State he has to put up with all the mud that may be slung by anyone in the

[37]FHT, Minutes, 28 December 1917.

[38]Bonds, "Economics of Outer Harbour," 126. By the 1990s the Board was meeting only monthly.

street."[39] No doubt the memory of the State's Chief Engineer, C.Y. O'Connor, driven to suicide in 1902 by public criticism, was still fresh in his mind.

Other Commissioners did not escape attack. One of the first actions of the Trust was to lease new premises from Dalgety and Company. One of the Commissioners, Mr. A. Leeds, was Dalgety's Fremantle manager, a fact which led to the claim that "the transaction...emits a powerful odour." Another Commissioner, Mr. W. Hudson, an insurance agent, was given the job of arranging accident insurance for the Trust's employees, and thus "experienced the material advantages of belonging to the Fremantle Harbour dis-Trust."[40] There is no doubt that part-time commissioners are particularly vulnerable to such criticisms, although in more recent times the laws of libel have protected Commissioners from unsubstantiated criticisms.

The permanent officers, responsible for day-to-day administration, were not always represented on the Board, which created some potential for internal conflicts. The General Manager attended Board meetings but was not made a voting member until the 1980s.[41] As Chief Executive Officer, the General Manager has enjoyed direct access to the Minister which, at times, has reduced the influence of the Board and led to confusion about the chain of accountability. Mr. Frank Tydeman, General Manager of the Trust between 1950 and 1965, claimed that the Board always backed him up and was merely "a rubber stamp."[42] Mr. Trevor Poustie, General Manager between 1985 and 1991, also served as Chairman of the Board for two years, a situation that he found unsatisfactory because he was effectively reporting to himself.[43]

---

[39]*The Sunday Times*, 14 June 1903; and WAPD, XXIX (1906), 1521.

[40]*The Sunday Times*, 14 June 1903.

[41]FPA, and Fremantle City Library Oral History Project, Interview with William Willis by M. Howroyd, 9 March 1989.

[42]Transcript of Interview conducted by the author with Mr. Tydeman, 17 February 1983.

[43]Transcript of Interview conducted by the author with Mr. Poustie, 26 March 1997.

The Permanent Staff

In 1903 the Trust employed fifty-six permanent staff; in 1918, 126; and by 1936 the number had grown to 232.[44] The number increased significantly after the Second World War, reaching 1125 in 1970. Figure 7.4 illustrates the trend of employment numbers between 1968 and 1996. Staff numbers were allowed to decrease by natural attrition in the late 1970s. In the early 1980s the state Labor government requested the FPA, along with other government agencies, to adopt a replacement ratio of one for two personnel in order to achieve an overall staffing reduction of two percent.[45] In 1986-1987 the FPA was told to reduce its workforce by a further three percent and in the 1990s staff numbers were drastically reduced as part of a radical programme of "down-sizing," an issue we discuss later in the chapter.

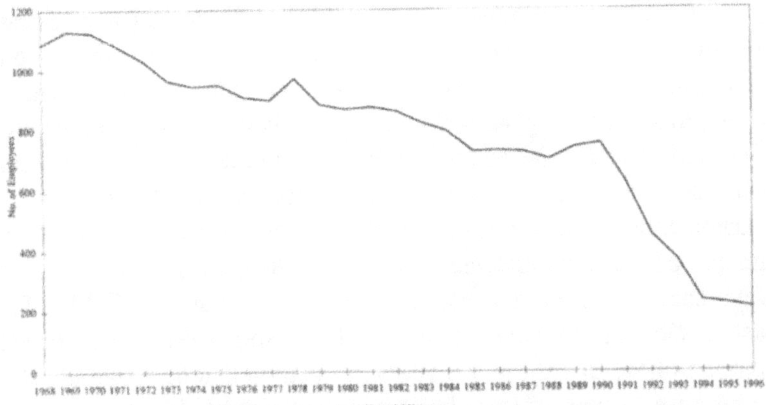

Figure 7.4: Fremantle Port Authority Employees, 1967-1968 to 1995-1996.

Source: FPA, *Annual Reports*.

Table 7.1 shows the numbers employed in 1918 and 1990 classified into four broad divisions. Between 1918 and 1990 the authority's permanent staff grew by about 428 percent and trade grew by 2400 percent in tonnage terms, implying that the productivity of the workforce

---

[44]FPA, 99/03, List of Staff at 1 April 1903; FPA, 126/17/1, List of Staff 1918; FPA (new series), 302/1/1, FHT to Under Secretary, 3 July 1936.

[45]FPA, 5341/88/01/09/01/6, General Manager of the FPA to the Minister for Transport, 1 August 1983.

increased.[46] However, as we shall see, over-staffing and restrictive practices reduced the gains from increased mechanisation.

Table 7.1
The Staff of the Port Authority in 1918 and 1990

Category of Staff	1918	Percent	1990*	Percent
Administrative	7	5.6	134.5	20.2
Engineering	70	55.6	374	56.2
Nautical	25	19.8	99	14.9
Wharf	24	19.0	57.75	8.9
Total	126	100.0	665.25	100.0

Notes: *Includes temporary and contract staff but excludes eighty-seven waterside workers. Due to the system of casual employment there is no firm data on the size of the waterside workforce in 1918 .

Sources: FPA, 126/17/1, List of Staff, 1918; *Review of the Fremantle Port Authority*, II, appendix H.

In both 1918 and 1990 the Engineering Division accounted for about thirty-six percent of the FPA's permanent staff. The proportion of general administrative staff has increased over time due to the expansion of activities such as marketing, public relations, finance and human resources. By contrast, the proportion of staff in the nautical and wharf divisions has declined. The decline in wharf staff was due to the general changes in waterfront employment discussed in the previous chapter; after 1991, when the FPA withdrew from stevedoring, the remaining staff were forced to choose between early retirement or redeployment. The changes in the Engineering and Nautical Divisions will be discussed in more detail below.

It is clear that for most of its history the Engineering Division has dominated the port authority. When the FHT was formed, the government insisted that the Public Works Department be responsible for construction works and that the Engineer-in-Chief act as consulting engineer for the

[46]The growth of trade was calculated from three-year averages centred on 1917-1918 and 1989-1990.

Trust. This saved the cost of a separate engineering department and in theory avoided conflicts over technical issues. However, the Trust was responsible for commercial decisions and, as we saw in chapter 5, had some major battles with Engineer-in-Chiefs over port development.

In the first year of its existence, the Trust had the loan of Mr. William Leslie, a Public Works Department Engineer. He was appointed Acting Engineer at a salary of £700 per annum from 27 January 1903. However, he did not "pull" with the Board and got into numerous disputes with the Commissioners.[47] The first major dispute occurred when Leslie advocated the use of departmental labourers for construction work while the Commissioners favoured putting it out to contract. Disputes also occurred over his wharf designs and their potential cost, and his desire for a separate engineering department within the Trust. The Commissioners complained to the government that he refused to go across the river in a rowing boat and urged the Trust to provide him with a special launch. His "arrogance and over-bearing conduct" was bad enough, but a secret report he made to the Premier on cargo-handling made him "guilty of gross disloyalty." Consequently, after about three months he was returned to the Public Works Department. Leslie stood for the Legislative Assembly seat of Swan in the general election of 1904 and further enraged the Trust by attacking it in an election speech. The FHT asked for a permanent engineer of its own over whom it could have full control. But the government insisted that works it paid for should be supervised by the Public Works Department and refused to agree to such a proposal. However, the Trust was eventually allowed to hire Mr. Carlin as a maintenance engineer and quickly built up an extensive engineering department.

By 1990 the FPA had a very high proportion of engineering staff compared to other port authorities because most contracted out their engineering work. The Division included such anachronisms as a joinery shop making furniture, a blacksmith's shop making bolts and small steel components, and a fibreglass shop producing customised items. In most cases, these items were produced at much greater cost than if they had been obtained from outside the FPA. Office furniture, for example, was sometimes 100 percent or more of the cost of equivalent furniture purchased from outside. The maintenance workshop was so overstaffed

---

[47]This paragraph draws on FPA, 127/03, "Notes for Interview with the Hon. Premier and Ministers," 25 June 1903; FPA, 34/04/1, "Mr. Leslie and the Fremantle Harbour Trust Notes for the Hon. Mr. Kingsmill," undated; FPA, 80/08/1, Premier to FHT, 25 July 1903.

that it performed excessive maintenance on cranes and other machinery. Rather than lay-off surplus staff in the vehicle maintenance workshop, they were employed servicing the private vehicles of FPA staff. The rationale was "it is better to get some revenue to offset the cost of retaining staff than to pay the staff to be idle."[48] Such overstaffing suggests that the employees had some ability to use the FPA as "a taxing machine" themselves and was undoubtedly one cause of the financial crisis experienced in the late 1980s.

Another important Division is the Nautical one, which is responsible for pilotage, port security and emergency services. The establishment and early history of the pilotage service has already been discussed in chapter 2. The Chief Harbour Master, who originally was Harbour Master for the whole state, not just Fremantle, controlled it. When Captain Irvine, the FHT's first Harbour Master, retired in 1917, the Trust attempted to obtain a separate Harbour Master for Fremantle but the government refused.[49] His successor, Captain Morrison, served until July 1921. After Morrison's retirement his duties were divided between Captain Nicholas (Wharf Manager and Berthing Master) and Captain Clack (Senior Pilot). Captain Nicholas was given the post of Harbour Master in addition to his other duties, while Captain Clack was given the title of Chief Pilot. In practice, however, Captain Clack acted as Harbour Master. The object of this reorganisation was to save the employment of an additional pilot because the Harbour Master's position did not include an obligation to pilot ships; as Chief Pilot, Clack was not exempted from piloting ships. In 1927 Captain Nicholas was relieved of responsibility for wharf administration and was able to devote more time to the duties of Harbour Master; the position of Chief Pilot was abolished. This arrangement lasted until 1938 when Nicholas died and Clack was finally promoted to the position of Harbour Master.

For many years the Trust's workers on Rottnest Island provided an important back-up to the pilots.[50] These were the signalmen responsible

---

[48]This paragraph draws on "Review of the Fremantle Port Authority," 31-34.

[49]FPA, 120/17, Under Secretary to FHT, 20 June 1917; and FHT, Minutes, 24 December 1935.

[50]FPA, 10/21, file entitled "Maintenance of Rottnest Signal Station;" 25/07/1, FHT to Comptroller General of Prisons, 10 April 1907, asking for services of a native prisoner; FHT, Minutes, July 1932.

for sighting incoming vessels and telephoning the details to the mainland. As early as 1921 they were using a homemade radio to pick up signals from ships. They were allowed the use of aboriginal prisoners for odd jobs such as painting, collecting firewood and tending the horses, until the Rottnest Board of Control stopped the practice in 1932. Doubtless, the depression led to pressure to use "free" labour.

Until just before the Second World War, all the pilots, the Harbour Master and the General Manager lived in houses on Arthur's Head so they could be readily available to meet the needs of shipping.[51] The availability of telephones and cars reduced the need for this and the pilots were allowed to live up to six miles from the port, although the General Manager and Harbour Master continued to live on Arthur's Head. An additional house was kept for the pilots' use while they were waiting to board ships.

In 1945 Clack was replaced as Harbour Master by Captain Trivett, a man who was so wedded to his job that he kept a board in his bedroom which he or his wife altered every time a ship berthed or sailed. In November 1949 Trivett abolished compulsory pilotage from the outer pilotage grounds (ten nautical miles from the port) and ships were allowed to go to Gage roads and pick up a pilot there. They notified their expected time of arrival by radio through the wireless station at Applecross. This made the signal station at Rottnest redundant and it was closed.

In order to learn the local conditions, new pilots had to accompany all of the experienced pilots in turn, which also gave them an opportunity to get to know their colleagues. Captain John Adams, who became a pilot in 1949, had some vivid memories of his fellow pilots: one "piloted as if he disliked handling ships. He would rush them into and out of port, often I thought dangerously fast." Another pilot, a tall thin man, (surprisingly nicknamed the long pilot rather than "shortie"), "handled ships very slowly and carefully." Yet another spent all his spare time sleeping: "he piloted ships, as he lived, very slowly and calmly." While he was still learning, Captain Adams had to move a Norwegian whale chaser across the harbour, but the helmsman was so drunk he fell onto the telegraph, knocking it to full-speed ahead. The ship crashed into the wharf and a worried Adams got the Captain to sign a paper exonerating him: "he signed, he had no idea what he was doing, he was so drunk." The incident

---

[51]This paragraph and the following two paragraphs draw on the very readable autobiography of Captain J. Adams, *A Pinch of Salt* (Perth, 1996).

did no harm to Adams' career because he was appointed Harbour Master in November 1968, and in July 1972 was promoted to the position of Divisional Manager Operations, a post he held until his retirement in 1977.

Captain Anthony Worthington joined the FPA as a pilot in 1966 after three years spent working at Singapore, then the world's fifth-busiest port. By comparison with Singapore, Fremantle had ancient tugs and a bureaucratic port authority where "innovation was a dirty word." The *Wyola*, the last coal-fired steam tug, was under-powered yet continued in service until 1970. Captain Worthington observed that while, by international standards, the pay was relatively poor, pilots enjoyed high status in the seaport town.[52] The position of Harbour Master, in particular, carried considerable prestige; he was usually made an honorary member of local yacht clubs and perks included the occasional bag of crayfish. Captain Adams recalls that he and the General Manager, Captain Noble, after a few drinks at a local hotel set off in different directions in their own cars but managed to crash into each other about a kilometre down the road. He claims that an Italian gentleman who witnessed the accident complained the men had been drinking but he was whisked away by the police for disturbing the peace. The accident was hushed up, "because in those days it was not what you knew but who you knew."[53]

A major change occurred in July 1994 when, as part of the commercialisation of the authority, the pilotage service was privatised by an employee buy-out with a five-year contract. The FPA supported the change despite the fact that it led to the loss of a profitable activity that had subsidised loss-making services: in 1990-1991, for example, pilotage generated a surplus of $1.32 million.[54] One pilot, Captain Bob Howell, remained with the FPA as Deputy Harbour Master. The change led to increase in pilot hours of availability about fifty percent.

The successful operation of the pilotage service has depended not only on the skills of the pilots but also on the skills of the men who crew the pilot boats. They venture out in all weathers and also work on a roster system to ensure twenty-four-hour availability of the pilotage service. The

[52]FPA and Fremantle City Library Oral History Project, Interview with Captain Worthington by M. Howroyd, 29 November 1988.

[53]Adams, *A Pinch of Salt*, 106.

[54]FPA, CMT, 076V08, Proposed Employee Buy-Out of Pilotage, 18 July 1991.

main pilot boat, the *Lady Forrest*, which had served the port since 1902, was replaced in 1964 by the *Lady Gairdner*, a faster and longer vessel. The *Paddy Troy* replaced her in turn in 1975. This boat was named after the well-known trade union leader and capable of a speed of twenty knots. In 1993 the FPA acquired the *FP Osprey*, a twin-hulled aluminium vessel capable of cruising at twenty-six knots. Alan Donnes, who started as a deckhand in 1938, recalled how the crew used to be at sea for many hours, but with the modern boats they could be out and back in as little as twenty minutes.[55]

Photo 14: A Container Crane at North Wharf Fremantle, 1996.

Source: Courtesy of the FPA.

The port authority's permanent staff has had a tradition of long and loyal service, with internal promotion to executive positions. Promotion was usually based on seniority rather than merit, which caused some ambitious staff to leave in frustration.[56] In 1910 Arthur Leeds, the

[55]FPA and Fremantle City Library Oral History Project, Interview with Michael Donnes by M. Howroyd, 7 November 1988.

[56]*Ibid.*, Interview with Alan Bonds by M. Howroyd, 24 November-1 December 1988.

Chairman of the Board, justified the preference for internal candidates on the grounds that "it was only in this way that valuable loyal staffs [sic] were built up."[57] For example, Mr. Frank Stevens, whom we discuss below, served as Secretary from the inception of the FHT in 1903 to 1929. Mr. G.V. McCartney joined the Railway Department as a cadet in 1900, transferring to the FHT at its inception in 1903. He worked in the wharf and cargo-handling section, eventually rising to the position of Wharf Manager in 1927. Following Stevens' retirement in 1929, he was promoted to Manager of the Trust and served in this capacity until his retirement in May 1950. In all, he had spent forty-seven years in the service of the Trust. When he joined the FHT in 1949, Captain John Adams was ushered in to meet him in the main office, an old weatherboard building with floors and furniture of polished jarrah:

> I saw a little old man, with glasses balanced on the end of his nose, sitting behind a beautifully polished desk...He questioned me about my sea experience and was interrupted by the harbour master who was rudely told to, "Shut up! I can talk to you anytime." The general manager's false teeth spat onto the table...I was shocked...and wondered whether I had made the correct decision in joining Fremantle pilots.[58]

Another man who joined the Trust in 1903 was Mr. L.A. Hancock; he eventually reached the position of Secretary three years before his retirement in 1948. In July 1944 Miss Letchford, a typist, retired at the age of sixty after thirty-three years of service.[59] Mr. William Willis joined as an office junior, "the lowest of the low," in 1941 and rose to the position of Secretary and Divisional Manager of Administration by the time he retired in 1985.[60]

---

[57]FHT, Minutes, 10 May 1910.

[58]Adams, *A Pinch of Salt,* 72-73.

[59]FPA, 3471/91/NEM 157.

[60]FPA and Fremantle City Library Oral History Project, Interview with William Willis by M. Howroyd, 9 March 1989.

As with the waterside workers, sons frequently followed fathers into the workforce. Mr. Len Wrightson's grandfather and father both worked for the FHT. In 1910 a train killed his grandfather, John Wrightson, while he was adjusting navigation aids on the Railway Bridge. The FHT paid his widow £400 as compensation. Len's father, Merv Wrightson, joined as a labourer in 1935 and rose to become Maintenance Supervisor. Len Wrightson worked as a carpenter until he lost two fingers in an accident and was transferred to the Wharf Department, where he served as a gatekeeper until his retirement in 1991.[61]

The personal relationships among staff helped to create a close and loyal workforce. In 1917 Mr. B. Lehmann, an engineer on the pilot boat, was posthumously awarded the Military Cross for action on the Hindenburg Line, an award noted with great pride by his colleagues and the Board.[62] By contrast, in December the following year the Board had to dismiss a clerk for stealing, the first in the history of the Trust.[63]

In 1990, 280 people who had served the port for more than ten years received small gifts to mark the occasion. Of the 280, 126 had worked for the port for more than twenty years. The tradition of lengthy service had the advantage that staff had a wealth of experience and, given that similar practices existed in the private sector of the port industry, there was a stable environment, with everyone "speaking the same language."[64] But such lengthy service meant that management tended to be conservative and inward-looking, not always an asset when the port was called upon to respond to substantial changes in port activity.

It is clearly unfair to single out the achievements of individuals in the port's history - the smooth running of the port has always required a team effort from Board member down to typist. Nevertheless, in order to give some insight into the personalities behind port management, it is proposed to give a brief biographical sketch of Frank Stevens, a man who was responsible for the day-to-day running of the port for over a quarter-century.

---

[61]*Ibid.*, Interview with Len Wrightson by M. Howroyd, 19 January 1989.

[62]FHT, Minutes, 21 September 1917.

[63]*Ibid.*, 13 December 1918.

[64]"Review of the Fremantle Port Authority," 108.

Frank William Buck Stevens was born in Wellington, New Zealand, on 16 December 1867.[65] At the age of seventeen he became a law clerk but after five years he switched to journalism, working for *The Evening Press*. He rose to become Chief of the Reporting Staff. In 1892, when he was only twenty-five, Stevens was offered the post of private secretary to C.Y. O'Connor, and arrived in Western Australia the same year. For the next ten years Stevens worked closely with O'Connor on his public works' programmes.

When the FHT was formed the government appointed Stevens, by then a well-known figure in the community, as Secretary. He was paid a salary of £400 a year for the onerous task of establishing this new organisation. One of Steven's first acts was to ask for guidance from a man he knew from his days as a pressman, William Ferguson, Secretary of the Wellington Harbour Board. Ferguson outlined administrative arrangements at Wellington where, significantly, the port authority was involved in cargo-handling. The New Zealand connection was to exert a considerable influence on Fremantle's administrative history. Unfortunately, Stevens left no diaries or personal papers and few clues to his personality emerge from the Trust's files. However, he appears to have been a stickler for detail. When Captain Cleary was appointed Wharf Manager, Stevens wrote a lengthy memo setting out his responsibilities. Cleary was told to always have "in view a fair deal to the public in conjunction with the protection of the interests of the Trust and the revenue of the country."

In 1911 a local newspaper, whose source was probably a disgruntled Trust employee, claimed that "the wharves are rotting, the secretary is utterly incapable of handling his responsibilities, the accountant is inefficient, and revenue is being lost, while nepotism and injustice is driving old hands out of the service." It was claimed that Stevens kept aloof from the clerical staff and that "he has not once during the past seven or eight years even walked through the office to make an inspection of what is going on." He reputedly reorganised the office without

---

[65]This survey draws on J.S. Battye, *The Cyclopedia of Western Australia* (Perth, 1912), 721-722; M. Tauman, *The Chief, C.Y. O'Connor* (Nedlands, WA, 1978), 244; FPA, 75/10, Stevens to Captain Cleary, 8 June 1910; *The Sunday Times*, 14 and 21 May, and 6 August 1911; FPA, 144/11/1, file entitled "Staff Annual Picnic;" FPA, 118/11/1, Mr. Toppin, Auditor-General, to FHT, 26 June 1911; FHT to Hon. Colonial Secretary, 27 June 1911; internal memo by Stevens for the Chairman and Commissioners entitled "Article in *Sunday Times* of Sunday, August 6th 1911," 10 August 1911; WAPD, XLIV (1912), 3068; *The West Australian*, 3 August 1934; FHT, Minutes, 3 August 1934.

consulting the staff, resulting in the resignation of seven long-serving clerks. Perhaps it was a desire to improve relations between staff and management that led Stevens to inaugurate an annual staff picnic in October of the same year. It was also claimed that Stevens' lack of supervision of the accountant, Mr. Glyde, reputedly enabled this man to secure a relative "inordinate increases and much promotion." Glyde was accused of spending too much time teaching at the Perth Technical School and neglecting his duties. However, the Auditor-General, Mr. Toppin, carried out an investigation that exonerated Glyde. The Commissioners expressed to the Colonial Secretary "their abhorrence at the publication of articles bristling with mis-statement and untruth, and aiming at belittling, in the eyes of the general public two valued officials." The following year, the Hon. J. Connolly MLC, declared that Stevens was "a most competent man," probably a fairer assessment of his performance.

Stevens was granted six months leave from 31 August 1929 and officially retired on 28 February 1930. He lived in retirement at Claremont where he died, after an illness, on 2 August 1934. At its next meeting the Board stood in silence for a minute as a mark of respect.

It had long been apparent that the Secretary shouldered an onerous workload and following Stevens' retirement the administrative structure was altered. Mr. G.V. McCartney, the Wharf Manager, was appointed Manager, and Mr. Cox, previously Treasurer, was appointed Secretary and Accountant. This reorganisation separated the managerial and secretarial functions that had previously been combined in the person of Stevens.

The port authority's permanent staff was employed on the same basis as public servants.[66] As already indicated, the majority of staff were male: single women were employed only at lower levels, such as typists and telephonists, and until the early 1970s they were expected to leave when they got married.[67] Formal discrimination ended when the *Western Australian Equal Opportunity Act* (1984) was applied to the port.

In common with other government departments, the FPA provided a subsidised canteen, and a staff gymnasium was established in March 1974. After the war, the practice of "FPA Relativity" evolved, which

---

[66]FHT, Minutes, 18 July 1911. This arrangement was introduced in 1991 and made retrospective from the inception of the FHT.

[67]FPA and Fremantle City Library Oral History Project, Interview with Alan Bonds by M. Howroyd, 24 November-1 December 1988.

meant that when waterside workers got an increase in wages or an improvement in conditions the FPA gave their own workshop and service staff a similar increase.[68] Thus in 1972 they gained a thirty-five-hour week, annual leave loading and sick-leave benefit. In July 1974 the Federated Clerks' Union achieved similar conditions for their members employed at the FPA.

Since the 1970s the nature of work has changed, with a trend away from unskilled and semi-skilled jobs; the port workforce has increasingly become a white-collar one.[69] In order to cope with this trend, staff were encouraged to gain education and time off was given to attend classes. However, training tended to be uncoordinated and usually only to meet specific needs. On at least one occasion the Engineering Department gave a training course to all staff even though demarcation agreements meant that there was no possibility of most ever being able to use the skills.[70]

In September 1980 the FPA began holding monthly meetings between management and shop stewards of all unions in an attempt to improve industrial relations. One problem was that management was not united in dealing with the unions; the latter tended to go from one level of management to another, and even to the Minister, in the hope of getting a favourable decision. But the FPA faced the difficult task of negotiating with at least seventeen unions. The largest (with 1990 FPA membership in brackets) were the Waterside Workers' Federation (218), Federated Clerks' Union (137), Australian Workers Union (82), Civil Services Association (77) and the Seaman's Union of Australia (62).[71] The desire to reduce the number of unions was, as we saw in the previous chapter, a major goal of microeconomic reform. The FPA itself was also to become a target for reform.

---

[68]FPA, *Annual Report* (1974-1975), 19.

[69]Australia, Industry Commission, *Port Authority Services and Activities* Report No. 31, (Canberra, 1993), 148

[70]"Review of the Fremantle Port Authority," 78.

[71]The other unions with members in the FPA, in addition to the eleven in the Combined Unions Association, were the Merchant Services Guild (35), Royal Australian Nurses' Federation (2), and the Australian Foremen Stevedores Association (1).

The Commercialisation of the FPA: The Late 1980s Onwards

In April 1985 Mr. Julian Grill, the Minister for Transport, recruited Mr. Trevor Poustie, Assistant General Manager at Cooperative Bulk Handling Ltd. to the position of General Manager of the FPA. Poustie had extensive experience in the commercial world and his brief was to ensure that the America's Cup Races, which were to be held in the summer of 1986/1987, proceeded smoothly and to improve efficiency and profitability. At the time it was not realised that the two objectives might conflict.

Poustie recalls that on his arrival it was suggested his first task should be to learn the regulations, a striking indication of the absence of a customer-focussed culture.[72] Mr. John Willinge, Chairman of the Bunbury Harbour Board, admitted that port authorities tended to be like "little empires."[73] In 1986 Poustie reorganised the FPA's management structure, and three years later introduced a corporate plan designed to turn the FPA into a more commercially-orientated business. But the corporate plan was later criticised due to a lack of definition of the FPA's role and the specific directions that it should pursue in the future.[74]

In 1985, to help ensure smooth industrial relations during the America's Cup, the government upgraded the position of Union Convenor of the Combined Unions Association. The Convenor represented eleven unions with a total of about 242 members employed in the port. He had previously been employed on a part-time basis by the unions, but was placed on the FPA's payroll as a full-time employee.[75] Numerous other concessions were made to the unions, including severe restrictions on

---

[72] Transcript of Interview conducted by the author with Mr. Poustie, 26 March 1997.

[73] J. Willinge, *Full Steam Ahead. Bunbury Port Authority 1909-1995* (Bunbury, 1966), 41.

[74] "Review of the Fremantle Port Authority," 133.

[75] The unions (coverage in 1990 in brackets) were the Australian Workers' Union (82), Seamen's Union of Australia (62), Construction, Mining and Energy Workers' Union (20), Transport Workers' Union (17), Painters and Decorators Union (13), Liquor and Allied Trade Employees (11), Plumbers and Gasfitters Union (10), Miscellaneous Workers Union (10), Australian Society of Engineers (8), Shop Distributive and Allied Trade Employees (5), and the Professional Divers Association (4).

outside contractors working in the port. These concessions increased the power of the unions over management and, after the America's Cup, any attempts to retrieve the situation were met with the threat of industrial action.[76] Negotiations were begun on enterprise agreements but little progress was made. Mr. John Peraldini, who was involved in the negotiations, claimed that the reform process "hit a brick wall" in the late 1980s. This was due to opposition from the unions and some FPA employees, and a weakening of state government support.[77]

The federal government's drive for microeconomic reform, discussed in the previous chapter, revitalised the reform process. Although the main focus was on the reform of the labour force, some of the reforms recommended by the Interstate Commission specifically targeted port authorities. It was recommended that they should become more commercially-orientated, withdraw from most direct service provision, and take a more strategic role in port management, planning and development. In 1990 the state government announced its intention to fully commercialise and eventually corporatise public trading enterprises, including port authorities, as part of its programme of microeconomic reform. The Minister of Transport, Mrs. Pam Beggs, set up a ministerial review "to examine the existing role, structure, financing, organisation and operations of the FPA with a view to maximising its efficiency."[78] It was chaired by Poustie and included Ms. Kerry Sanderson, who was then at the Department of Transport; Mr. Bruce Denham from the Public Service Commission; Mr. Neil Brown from the Treasury; and Dr. Mike Lisle-Williams from Consultants Deloitte Ross Tohmatsu.

The *Review*, which was completed in 1991, provided a devastating critique of existing management policies and practices. The FPA had provided many services on a "closed shop" basis and this had led to the development of inefficient practices, including overstaffing, restrictive work practices and a lack of customer focus. In addition, the FPA suffered "from a lack of cohesion at the Corporate Executive level." There was a unilateral pattern of decision-making with little critical discussion among the Executive; the Board was not always fully aware of the details of proposals it approved. Management was top-heavy with up to six levels

---

[76]"Review of the Fremantle Port Authority," II, appendix A.

[77]Transcript of interview by the author with John Peraldini, 25 March 1997.

[78]"Review of the Fremantle Port Authority," 1.

of management from the General Manager to workers in the workshops. Investment decisions, such as the deepening of the harbour to thirteen metres, tended to be made in an *ad hoc* way with little analysis of the economic costs and benefits. But, as we saw in chapter 5, this was a long-standing feature of port development. The *Review* recommended the immediate divestiture of all activities that could be performed more efficiently by the private sector, the creation of commercial business units, and the development of the strategic port manager role. It was estimated that there were 378 surplus staff and a voluntary redundancy programme was needed to reduce the size of the workforce. It is likely that the *Review* painted a rather bleak picture of existing management practices in order to strengthen the case for change, but there was clearly a strong case for reform.

Following the *Review*, there was a change of guard at the top, with Poustie taking early retirement. His successor, Kerry Sanderson, vigorously pursued the radical organisational change needed to transform the FPA into a profitable business enterprise. The FPA was reorganised into five divisions running the core businesses: business and strategic development, port maintenance, port operations, management service and human resources. The FPA adopted a Continuous Improvement Programme (CIP), which involved the bench-marking of port services to ensure conformity with world-best practice, an external customer survey, improvements to trade statistics and an employee development scheme. The first enterprise bargaining agreement was signed in 1992, and by the end of the following year virtually all employees were covered by an enterprise agreement. Due to extensive consultation during the negotiation process, these agreements were achieved without serious industrial problems. They eliminated the problem of demarcation disputes and provided for the contracting-out of services. The FPA began to contract-out construction, maintenance, pilotage and other activities, and it gradually withdrew from non-core activities, such as the maintenance of beaches and public access roads. The maintenance of Port Beach Road was transferred to the Main Roads Department in 1994 and, the following year the management of Port and Leighton Beaches was handed over to the City of Fremantle. The transformed FPA provides only core services such as shipping co-ordination, asset management planning, safety control, marketing, planning and liaison with port users.

In 1995 a study by consultants concluded that while efficient ports can operate in a wide range of structural frameworks, the best model for Fremantle was commercialisation and the strategic manager/coordinator role.[79] Under this model the publicly-owned port undertakes little operating activity but is responsible for the overall strategic planning and coordination of the port. Thus, unlike in Victoria, where the government began a programme of privatising regional ports such as Portland and Geelong, complete privatisation has not been pursued.[80]

In November 1995 for the first time in the history of the port the government spelled out the FPA's role, which is "to facilitate trade in an efficient and commercial manner." The government officially approved the commercialisation of the FPA from 1 July 1996. The relationship between the port and government is now primarily strategic, with the port having greater autonomy to work within an annual performance plan. Immediate benefits of commercialisation included the removal, in the interests of competitive neutrality, of the three-percent statutory levy on turn-over and the establishment of a dividend policy which allows the port to reduce debt and cater for future investment before dividends become payable. The government, however, retained the power of veto over tariff changes, suggesting that it was not keen to give the FPA complete autonomy. The FPA was restructured again, with a reduction in the number of divisions from five to three: Strategic and Commercial Development, Marine and Technical Services and Commercial Operations.

As part of the move towards commercialisation, the FPA produced a port charter, a strategic development plan, and a statement of corporate intent. The Port Charter is a long-term agreement (5-10 years) defining the government's relationship with and expectations of the port; the Strategic Development Plan is a medium-term agreement (3-5 years) detailing the economic and financial objectives of the port and the strategies and initiatives to be pursued to achieve these objectives; and the Statement of Corporate Intent is a short-term performance agreement (annual) which details the planned achievements for the forthcoming year. In its strategic plan the FPA defined its mission statement as "to facilitate trade and to maximise the competitive advantage available to customers using the Port of Fremantle."

---

[79] Symonds Travers Morgan Pty. Ltd. and Meyrick and Associates Pty. Ltd., *Fremantle Port Authority Review of Alternative Structural Models. Final Report* (October 1995).

[80] *The Australian*, 27 February 1996.

The size of the FPA's debt remained a major obstacle in the search for profitability: its debt equity ratio in 1993-1994 was 3.8:1 compared to an industry average of 1:1. The FPA has no real government equity because the capital is funded mainly from borrowings. Thus, a high proportion of operating cost continues to be made up of interest charges on the capital debt. Another major problem is unfunded superannuation liabilities, which stood at $32.6 million in 1996. In order to aid commercialisation the government has agreed to accept limited responsibility for past superannuation debts.

As a result of these changes, there were major cuts in staff numbers: in the six years between 1990 and 1996 staff numbers fell from 753 to 208. The loss of about three out of four staff was obviously fairly traumatic, but there was a widespread acceptance of the need for change. Many staff took early retirement or found employment elsewhere in the port, often with the private contractors providing services previously supplied by the FPA.

Conclusions

It is fair to say that for most of their history ports have not generally led the field in terms of management practices. The FPA, together with most other Australian port authorities, was an inward-looking organisation, prone to over-staffing and over-investment. While the emphasis on internal promotion to senior positions helped create a stable and loyal workforce, it also meant that the port was not always able to cope adequately with major changes. However, by the end of the first century of the port's history, technological change had caused a revolution in cargo-handling and commercialisation, as well as a revolution in port management. While the management "revolution" was not painless, especially for the workforce, there was a general consensus among management, the workforce, unions and port users that change was necessary if Fremantle were to be an efficient gateway for trade and shipping. The FPA now enjoys increased management autonomy and accountability and is more focused on the needs of port users. Judged by Buchanan's yardsticks, it should be an efficient administrative machine.

Photo 15: Bulk LPG Carrier in Outer Harbour, 1997.

Source: Courtesy of the FPA.

Appendices

Appendix A
Trade and Shipping Statistics

This appendix presents trade and shipping statistics for Fremantle between 1903-1904 and 1995-1996.

Trade Statistics

The financial year 1903-1904 was chosen as a starting date because this is the first full financial year for which port trade data are available. For most of the period covered by this book, Fremantle, in common with other Australian ports, measured cargo in revenue tonnes. This was a combination of measurement cargo at one cubic metre = one tonne (formerly 40 cubic feet = 1 ton) and weight or mass tonnes (formerly 2240 lbs. = 1 ton). The ports assessed cargo on the deadweight or measurement basis, depending on which yielded the greatest revenue.

In 1977, in order to increase uniformity between ports, the Council of the Australian Port Authorities Association decided that port statistics should be published in mass tonnes with the optional inclusion of revenue tonnes. The FPA commenced the collection of statistical data on both a revenue and mass basis from 1 July 1978. From the 1979-1980 financial year all data have been presented in terms of mass tonnes. In the FPA's *Annual Report* for 1979-1980 it stated that mass imports into and exports out of Fremantle approximated eighty-three percent and ninety-three percent, respectively, of their equivalent revenue tonnage. Thus while these data are not directly comparable to the years prior to 1979-1980, the effect is to only slightly reduce the measured level of port trade.

Strictly speaking, the resulting aggregate series of cargo tonnages are not meaningful for analysis because the unit of measurement is not constant. To establish a constant unit revenue tonnes calculated on a measurement basis must be converted to a deadweight basis or vice-versa. In practice this is impossible due to data limitations and it is necessary to use the combined weight/volume measure. In order to facilitate comparisons data have been converted from tons to tonnes on the basis that 1 ton = 1.02 tonnes.

Shipping Statistics

There are three main measures of merchant shipping tonnage: gross registered tonnage (grt), net registered tonnage (nrt) and deadweight tonnage (dwt). Gross registered tonnage is based on the total volume of enclosed ship space. Net registered tonnage is based on the total volume of enclosed ship space which can be utilised for passengers or cargo (1 ton = 100 cubic feet). Gross Registered tonnage are based on the difference in weight (1 ton = 2240 lbs.) between a loaded and empty vessel. Deadweight tonnage is usually regarded as the best measure of shipping capacity, especially for tankers, but the port's statistics show only a vessel's net registered tonnage and gross registered tonnage. The gross registered tonnage of vessels was only published in aggregate from 1919-1920 onwards. Throughout the book, shipping tonnage, unless otherwise specified, refers to gross registered tonnage.

Table A.1
The Growth of Trade at Fremantle, 1903-1904 to 1995-1996 (000 tonnes)

Financial Year	Exports	Imports	Total
1904	191	515	706
1905	171	597	768
1906	151	494	645
1907	103	481	584
1908	114	489	603
1909	114	399	513
1910	194	451	645
1911	177	627	804
1912	182	606	788
1913	283	675	958
1914	372	693	1065
1915	141	627	768
1916	245	617	862
1917	319	544	863
1918	211	332	543
1919	287	346	633
1920	520	411	931
1921	380	528	908
1922	431	463	894
1923	323	450	773
1924	456	546	1002
1925	554	684	1238
1926	635	658	1293
1927	753	824	1577
1928	856	857	1713
1929	873	985	1858
1930	852	1011	1863
1931	1175	580	1755
1932	1021	562	1583
1933	912	708	1620
1934	744	674	1418
1935	836	762	1598
1936	672	834	1506
1937	621	934	1555
1938	769	990	1759
1939	831	961	1792
1940	773	1008	1781
1941	796	868	1664
1942	716	922	1638
1943	631	938	1569
1944	819	951	1770
1945	1002	1021	2023
1946	926	990	1916
1947	673	982	1655
1948	993	1083	2076
1949	1036	1312	2348
1950	1072	1599	2671

Financial Year	Exports	Imports	Total
1951	1347	1812	3159
1952	1242	1950	3192
1953	1257	1629	2886
1954	859	1729	2588
1955	1421	2635	4056
1956	2743	3470	6213
1957	3281	3591	6872
1958	3193	3897	7090
1959	3064	3766	6830
1960	3573	4028	7601
1961	4800	5163	9963
1962	5005	4861	9866
1963	4326	5049	9375
1964	4644	5332	9976
1965	4149	5134	9283
1966	4781	5388	10169
1967	4861	5251	10112
1968	5764	5766	11530
1969	5798	6375	12173
1970	6082	6704	12786
1971	8089	7816	15905
1972	8709	7923	16632
1973	8886	7580	16466
1974	9309	8329	17638
1975	9640	8220	17860
1976	9831	7727	17558
1977	9390	8575	17965
1978	8810	8409	17219
1979	7839	7305	15144
1980	9847	7149	16996
1981	7652	7132	14784
1982	7616	6774	14390
1983	9287	6403	15690
1984	8516	6011	14527
1985	7910	5907	13817
1986	9370	5455	14825
1987	9027	5666	14693
1988	9698	6680	16378
1989	10263	6765	17028
1990	10207	7415	17622
1991	10337	5995	16332
1992	10659	6540	17199
1993	11019	7270	18289
1994	11792	8216	20008
1995	11834	8495	20329
1996	11647	8359	20006

Source: FHT and FPA, *Annual Reports*.

Table A.2
Number and Tonnage of Vessels Calling at Fremantle, 1903-1904 to 1995-1996

Financial Years	No. of Vessels	Gross Registered Tonnage of Shipping (000 Tons)
1904	801	
1905	821	
1906	754	
1907	687	
1908	648	
1909	586	
1910	672	
1911	726	
1912	786	
1913	810	
1914	857	
1915	681	
1916	741	
1917	727	
1918	376	
1919	593	
1920	721	3733
1921	747	3893
1922	789	4200
1923	671	4311
1924	698	4646
1925	739	5074
1926	669	4801
1927	748	5524
1928	751	5661
1929	752	5605
1930	805	6246
1931	720	5726
1932	672	5502
1933	698	5752
1934	677	5639
1935	735	6054
1936	722	6039
1937	732	5807
1938	810	6298
1939	847	6650
1940	776	6291
1941	543	5581
1942	627	5503
1943	603	4491
1944	762	5236
1945	665	4479
1946	557	4517

Financial Years	No. of Vessels	Gross Registered Tonnage of Shipping (000 Tons)
1947	592	4401
1948	754	5594
1949	978	7947
1950	103	8955
1951	1074	9371
1952	1027	9113
1953	964	8625
1954	956	8507
1955	1105	9978
1956	1232	11480
1957	1185	10685
1958	1140	10504
1959	1210	10755
1960	1300	11658
1961	1501	13937
1962	1504	14187
1963	1439	13633
1964	1440	14073
1965	1429	13852
1966	1600	14702
1967	1618	14690
1968	1856	15467
1969	1836	15790
1970	1772	17673
1971	1844	18869
1972	1808	20246
1973	1603	18471
1974	1718	18572
1975	1742	18747
1976	1719	18192
1977	1811	18801
1978	1765	19337
1979	1591	19456
1980	1790	22435
1981	1607	19844
1982	1490	20187
1983	1507	21274
1984	1446	20209
1985	1502	20803
1986	1498	21253
1987	1596	20918
1988	1512	21343
1989	1462	22905
1990	1520	23617

Financial Years	**No. of Vessels**	**Gross Registered Tonnage of Shipping (000 Tons)**
1991	1439	24006
1992	1429	23484
1993	1462	26248
1994	1661	29341
1995	1731	31265
1996	1758	33542

Note: Data on the grt of vessels is available only from 1919-1920. In the 1980s the FPA began including naval vessels. These have been removed to ensure consistency with earlier years.

Source: FHT and FPA, *Annual Reports*.

Table A.3
Fremantle's Share of the Value of Australian Trade, 1903-1904 to 1975-1976

Financial Years	Percentage Share
1904	16.8
1905	15.8
1906	13.2
1907	9.8
1908	8.2
1909	7.4
1910	6.0
1911	6.7
1912	7.3
1913	6.0
1914	5.4
1915	4.3
1916	4.6
1917	4.1
1918	2.9
1919	3.3
1920	6.8
1921	4.8
1922	5.2
1923	5.6
1924	6.2
1925	5.5
1926	5.8
1927	6.1
1928	7.2
1929	7.2
1930	8.1
1931	10.3
1932	9.7
1933	8.7
1934	9.2
1935	8.9
1936	8.8
1937	8.1
1938	8.3
1939	8.2
1940	--
1941	--
1942	--
1943	--
1944	--
1945	--
1946	--

Financial Years	Percentage Share
1947	--
1948	--
1949	6.5
1950	6.7
1951	7.1
1952	6.8
1953	7.1
1954	6.6
1955	6.1
1956	6.8
1957	7.5
1958	7.5
1959	6.9
1960	7.4
1961	8.7
1962	7.9
1963	7.0
1964	6.7
1965	6.1
1966	7.1
1967	7.0
1968	7.1
1969	6.9
1970	5.9
1971	6.2
1972	6.7
1973	6.8
1974	7.1
1975	7.9
1976	7.7

Note: -- = data not available.

Source: Calculated from data in Commonwealth Bureau of Census and Statistics, *Overseas Trade*. The series was discontinued after 1975-1976.

Table A.4
Coal and Oil Bunkers, Fremantle, 1923-1924 to 1995-1996 (000 Tonnes)

Financial Years	Coal	Oil	Total
1924	88	17	105
1925	70	53	123
1926	68	73	141
1927	79	101	180
1928	52	105	157
1929	38	131	169
1930	43	147	190
1931	23	113	136
1932	16	116	132
1933	16	123	139
1934	16	117	133
1935	22	122	144
1936	18	124	142
1937	19	113	132
1938	16	130	146
1939	11	126	137
1940	22	177	199
1941	27	225	252
1942	43	205	248
1943	49	222	271
1944	47	186	233
1945	40	219	259
1946	41	236	277
1947	41	223	264
1948	44	177	221
1949	43	283	326
1950	18	306	324
1951	18	344	362
1952	14	328	342
1953	10	287	297
1954	7	266	273
1955	6	324	330
1956	6	408	414
1957	5	430	435
1958	6	352	358
1959	4	333	337
1960	6	362	368
1961	7	438	445
1962	4	369	373
1963	6	321	327
1964	5	358	363
1965	4	351	355
1966	3	375	378

Financial Years	Coal	Oil	Total
1967	2	434	436
1968	1	583	584
1969		546	546
1970		612	612
1971		668	668
1972		879	879
1973		696	696
1974		695	695
1975		616	616
1976		514	514
1977		585	585
1978		632	632
1979		601	601
1980		509	509
1981		522	522
1982		327	327
1983		411	411
1984		316	316
1985		344	344
1986		252	252
1987		251	251
1988		286	286
1989		251	251
1990		251	251
1991		232	232
1992		224	224
1993		215	215
1994		179	179
1995		238	238
1996		246	246

Source: FHT and FPA, *Annual Reports*.

Table A.5
Passenger Traffic at Fremantle, 1962-1963 to 1984-1985

Financial Years	Transit passengers	Embarking passengers	Disembarking passengers	Total passengers
1963	21046	12737	136874	170657
1964	23428	15237	152873	191538
1965	23562	16813	156061	196436
1966	26247	17926	166343	210516
1967	28014	18460	155984	202458
1968	27987	19251	127034	174272
1969	28494	21205	122004	171703
1970	27740	23028	121570	172338
1971	24835	21448	93970	140253
1972	27310	26026	81257	134593
1973	26155	19230	72787	118172
1974	23901	18542	54349	96792
1975	19592	16182	31021	66795
1976	15982	14699	21437	52118
1977	15509	16111	17458	49078
1978	14204	14825	10008	39037
1979	11337	12309	7251	30897
1980	6048	6076	2461	14585
1981	4452	3149	462	8063
1982	4497	3824	977	9298
1983	1333	1122	1937	4392
1984	904	703	914	2521
1985	3302	3326	3485	10113

Source: FPA, *Annual Reports*.

APPENDIX B
Financial Statistics

Table B.1
Fremantle Harbour Trust and Fremantle Port Authority, Financial Results, 1903-1904 to 1995-1996 ($000)

Financial Year	Income	Expenditure	Net Surplus/Deficit
1904	168	68	100
1905	196	86	110
1906	188	80	108
1907	192	186	6
1908	232	208	24
1909	206	202	4
1910	268	220	48
1911	354	240	114
1912	340	258	82
1913	400	294	106
1914	408	308	100
1915	360	280	80
1916	374	324	50
1917	352	350	2
1918	326	332	-6
1919	372	368	4
1920	564	448	116
1921	604	462	142
1922	564	454	110
1923	564	448	116
1924	714	506	208
1925	842	560	282
1926	886	594	292
1927	1000	680	320
1928	1072	786	286
1929	1178	830	348
1930	1122	720	402
1931	846	612	234
1932	752	558	194
1933	798	580	218
1934	730	598	132
1935	862	646	216
1936	886	694	192
1937	946	748	198
1938	1022	818	204
1939	1024	824	200
1940	1068	866	202
1941	942	888	54
1942	1160	1012	148
1943	1230	1044	186
1944	1336	1140	196
1945	1560	1242	318

Financial Year	Income	Expenditure	Net Surplus/Deficit
1946	1420	1174	246
1947	1312	1178	134
1948	1566	1312	254
1949	2062	1594	468
1950	2486	1790	696
1951	2995	2501	494
1952	3847	3335	512
1953	3631	3634	-3
1954	4058	4046	12
1955	4429	4446	-17
1956	4112	4445	-333
1957	5030	5024	6
1958	5156	5084	72
1959	5020	5258	-238
1960	5513	5492	21
1961	6162	6225	-63
1962	5875	6160	-285
1963	6218	6381	-163
1964	6642	6550	92
1965	7334	7258	76
1966	7870	7750	120
1967	8045	8006	39
1968	9638	9520	118
1969	10009	9975	34
1970	9920	9761	159
1971	10832	10674	158
1972	10970	10821	149
1973	11388	11123	265
1974	13853	13329	524
1975	15509	15380	129
1976	18926	18740	186
1977	21453	21154	299
1978	19517	20224	-707
1979	19814	19705	109
1980	23160	23105	55
1981	27456	27062	394
1982	30561	30183	378
1983	32563	33171	-608
1984	31289	33311	-2022
1985	36358	37280	-922
1986	39325	40206	-881
1987	42688	42989	-301
1988	43071	43005	66
1989	49662	48172	1490
1990	54156	53895	261
1991	39364	50946	-11582
1992	33473	42221	-8748
1993	37737	37210	527

Financial Year	Income	Expenditure	Net Surplus/Deficit
1994	42353	33964	8389
1995	49527	40257	9270
1996	48044	39474	8570

Source: FHT and FPA, *Annual Reports*.

Table B.2
FHT and FPA Net Profits/Net Fixed Assets, 1906-1907 to 1995-1996

Financial Years	Percentage
1907	0.2
1908	0.9
1909	0.1
1910	1.7
1911	4
1912	2.8
1913	3.6
1914	3.3
1915	2.5
1916	1.5
1917	0.1
1918	-0.2
1919	0.1
1920	3.3
1921	4
1922	3
1923	3.1
1924	5.6
1925	7.5
1926	7.6
1927	8.2
1928	7
1929	8.1
1930	8.2
1931	4.5
1932	3.8
1933	4.2
1934	3.2
1935	3.8
1936	3.3
1937	3.4
1938	3.5
1939	3.5
1940	3.5
1941	0.9
1942	2.5
1943	3.2
1944	3.4
1945	5.5
1946	4.3
1947	2.3
1948	4.3
1949	7.8

Financial Years	Percentage
1950	11.4
1951	7.9
1952	7.7
1953	0
1954	0.1
1955	-0.2
1956	-3.7
1957	0.1
1958	0.6
1959	-1.7
1960	0.1
1961	-0.4
1962	-1.9
1963	-1.0
1964	0.5
1965	0.4
1966	0.7
1967	0.2
1968	0.6
1969	0.2
1970	0.7
1971	0.6
1972	0.5
1973	0.9
1974	1.8
1975	0.5
1976	0.7
1977	1.1
1978	-2.4
1979	0.4
1980	0.2
1981	1.3
1982	1.2
1983	-1.8
1984	-5.7
1985	-2.5
1986	-2.5
1987	-0.8
1988	0.2
1989	4.0
1990	0.5
1991	-15.3
1992	-11.9
1993	-0.2

Financial Years	Percentage
1994	11.5
1995	12.8
1996	9.8

Notes: The net fixed assets were taken from the FHT's and FPA's balance sheets. 1906-1907 is the first year that data on the value of the assets are available. Until 1929-1930 only assets purchased from revenue were depreciated. It was assumed that sinking fund payments were an approximate substitute for historic cost depreciation, and the cumulated totals of sinking fund payments were used to derive estimates of net fixed assets prior to 1929-1930. Net fixed assets were taken at the beginning of the period concerned, that is, the 1995-1996 rate of return was calculated on the basis of assets at the end of 1994-1995.

Source: FHT and FPA, *Annual Reports*.

Table B.3
Gross Investment by the FHT and FPA, 1909-1910 to 1995-1996

Financial Years	$000	$000 (1966-1967 prices)
1910	86	682
1911	60	460
1912	102	713
1913	90	612
1914	140	943
1915	212	1299
1916	112	544
1917	102	432
1918	86	333
1919	94	365
1920	92	311
1921	96	299
1922	100	371
1923	88	346
1924	80	321
1925	128	502
1926	154	587
1927	162	615
1928	292	1102
1929	270	1031
1930	452	1959
1931	134	571
1932	78	367
1933	126	625
1934	188	927
1935	204	1009
1936	214	1047
1937	174	815
1938	66	300
1939	78	349
1940	46	201
1941	110	431
1942	88	323
1943	7	22
1944	6	17
1945	44	135
1946	70	207
1947	108	308
1948	188	492
1949	186	450
1950	200	439
1951	692	1345
1952	1418	2329
1953	1415	2112
1954	786	1157
1955	1054	1507
1956	1017	1350
1957	3747	4834

Financial Years	$000	$000 (1966-1967 prices)
1958	1164	1481
1959	1125	1405
1960	1235	1500
1961	1400	1659
1962	1609	1854
1963	1093	1262
1964	1637	1835
1965	880	943
1966	1156	1206
1967	3652	3652
1968	6317	6105
1969	2717	2527
1970	1982	1559
1971	2363	1221
1972	1732	1363
1973	2295	1671
1974	1286	826
1975	1632	981
1976	2280	1283
1977	2805	1476
1978	3223	1588
1979	2270	1046
1980	1232	531
1981	3083	1243
1982	4661	1759
1983	2437	861
1984	3463	1143
1985	1037	320
1986	2136	617
1987	3252	879
1988	2125	537
1989	22741	5376
1990	22909	5068
1991	6971	1443
1992	3512	681
1993	2928	530
1994	8148	1381
1995	5242	831
1996	8615	1357

Notes: Prior to 1909-1910 new investment appears to have been funded from revenue and in 1908-1909 the accumulated value of gross expenditure was only about $16,000. The series was deflated using the implicit deflator for public gross fixed capital expenditure in M.W. Butlin, *A Preliminary Annual Database 1900/01 to 1973/74* (Canberra, 1977). For years after 1973-1974, Butlin's series was spliced with a series based on 1989-1990=100 in Reserve Bank of Australia, *Australian Economic Statistics, 1949-1950 to 1994-1995* (Sydney, 1996).

Source: FHT and FPA, *Annual Reports*.

APPENDIX C
Labour Statistics

Table C.1
The Number of Waterside Workers and Tons Handled Per Waterside Worker at Fremantle, 1949-1950 to 1989-1990

Financial Years	No. of Registered Labourers	General Cargo 000 Tons	Tons Per Worker
1950	1298	1267	976
1951	1494	1343	899
1952	1652	1383	837
1953	1656	1024	618
1954	1698	1250	736
1955	1819	1238	681
1956	1873	1105	590
1957	1862	1109	596
1958	1835	1104	602
1959	1795	1137	633
1960	1752	1306	745
1961	1830	1549	846
1962	1803	1501	833
1963	1708	1582	926
1964	1667	1688	1013
1965	1712	1871	1093
1966	1693	1980	1170
1967	1615	1980	1226
1968	1481	2092	1413
1969	1521	2611	1717
1970	1417	3066	2164
1971	1350	3274	2425
1972	1229	3187	2593
1973	1138	3518	3091
1974	1116	3758	3367
1975	1111	3463	3117
1976	1148	2978	2594
1977	1155	3015	2610
1978	1015	2522	2485
1979	885	2730	3085
1980	858	3134	3653
1981	830	3009	3625
1982	750	3035	4047
1983	664	3575	5384
1984	536		
1985	481		
1986	468		
1987	326		

Financial Years	No. of Registered Labourers	General Cargo 000 Tons	Tons Per Worker
1988	405		
1989	397		
1990	373		

Note: The number of registered workers does not measure actual labour effort. This is because it includes workers who are not active because of illness or some other reason. Cargo tonnages are revenue tonnes (cargo measured on a deadweight or measurement basis, depending on which yields the greatest revenue) not mass tons. The measure of tons per worker is not continued after 1982-1983 because after that date data on general cargo are available only in mass tonnes and are not directly comparable with data measured in revenue tons. The table gives only a crude indication of the trend in productivity.

Sources: ASIB and ASIA *Annual Reports*; FPA, 88/01/09/01/D, Wharf Manager, "Stevedoring Port of Fremantle," 11 August 1983; FPA, Per 0071, Personnel-A Register - Labour Redistributions & Transfers.

APPENDICES
Appendix D

Table D.1
Fremantle Harbour Trust and Fremantle Port Authority Commissioners since 1903

Name	Period Served	Background
LAURIE, Robert [Captain]	1903	Stevedore and Member of the Legislative Council; Chairman of FHT, 1903-1907
HUDSON, Charles	1903-1905; 1908-1911	Manager (and later partner) William Sandover, hardware merchants, 1884-1901; Manager, Fremantle Branch of Commercial Union Assurance Company; and local director of the AMP Society
COOMBE, Thomas Melrose	1903-1905	Director of timber merchant Coombe Wood & Co.
SANDOVER, Alfred (MBE)	1903-1905	Chairman, West Australian Shipping Association; and Chairman of Directors of Harris, Scarfe and Sandover Ltd.
LEEDS, Arthur George	1903-1911	Fremantle Manager for Dalgety & Co.; Chairman of FHT, 1908-1911.
VILES, Frank	1906-1908	Representative of Chamber of Mines
EYRES, Thomas	1906-1911	Hardware merchant in Perth; and founding member of the Perth Chamber of Commerce
ALLNUTT, Ernest (JP)	1906-1913	Managing Director of D & J Fowler Ltd.
BARKER, Henry Gell	1909-1911	H.G. Barker & Co., Ship and Insurance Brokers

Name	Period Served	Background
TAYLOR, John Henry George	1912-1930	Member of the Legislative Assembly for Mount Margaret; Colonial Secretary in 1904; Member of Australian Workers' Union
IRVINE, Charles James (Captain)	1912-1916	Chief Harbour Master for the state of Western Australia
THOMPSON, James	1912-1916	Engineer-in-Chief, WA; Chairman of FHT, 1912-1917.
OLIPHANT, Arthur Morris	1912-1918	Manager, Western Australian Producers' Co-operative Union; Nominated by Perth Chamber of Commerce
EVANS, William Herbert	1913-1917	Manager of James Bell & Company (which was involved in shipping and grain finance); Insurance Broker and Chairman of Marine Underwriters Association; and Fremantle Chamber of Commerce
NICHOLAS, Frank	1917	Representative of Fremantle Chamber of Commerce
CARTER, Tom (JP)	1917-1944	Sub-Manager, Fremantle Branch of Dalgety and Co. Ltd.; Chairman, FHT, 1917-1944; Nominated by Perth Chamber of Commerce
MURRAY, Basil L.	1918-1925	Died, April 1925; Represented Farmers and Settlers Party Political Association

Name	Period Served	Background
PAYNE, George Gwythyr Frederick	1918-1926	Co-head, Elder, Shenton & Co. Ltd., merchants, shipping agents, stock and station agents; Shipping manager, Elder Smith & Company; Nominated by Perth Chamber of Commerce
BATEMAN, Lewis Lindsay	1919-1956	Director, J & W Bateman Pty. Ltd.; Chairman, FHT, 1945-1956
McMAHON, Patrick Gregory	1925-1944	Died, December 1944; No other details available
TANNER, Henry William Afrie	1927-1934	Farmer; Primary Industry representative
SIMPSON, George William	1930-1931	Career public servant; Public Service Commissioner from 1931 to 1945, when he retired
WILSON, Kenneth David	1931-1950	Accountant of Treasury
ANGWIN, Hon. William Charles (CMG and JP)	1934-1935	Member of the Legislative Assembly for North East Fremantle, 1904-1927; Minister in various Labor governments; Agent-General for Western Australia in London ,1927-1933
MANN, Frederick (JP)	1936-1956	Former General Secretary of the Farmers' Union; Secretary of Fremantle Trades Hall
WAUHOP, William (MBE and JP)	1945-1946	Mayor of East Fremantle; Chairman Fremantle Hospital Board; Chairman of Western Australian Licensing Court, 1949-1958.

Name	Period Served	Background
HOOPER, H.J.R.	1945-1953	Employed by Elder Smith & Company Ltd.; Deputy Director of Shipping, WA
ULRICH, Victor	1946-1947	Secretary of Clerks Union; Member of East Fremantle Council, 1932-1964; Mayor of East Fremantle, 1964-1974
NOAKES, Walter (JP)	1948-1950	Founder and first General President Farmers' Union of WA
PRATER, Hurtle John Barrrett (OBE)	1951-1956	General Secretary Farmers' Union of WA
BYFIELD, Herbert William	1951-1959	Under-Treasurer and Commissioner of Stamps, WA; Chairman FHT, 1957-1959
BROWNE, Eric Hablot	1953-1956	Director and joint manager for Victoria of P&O Lines of Australia Pty. Ltd.
GRACE, Maxwell Norman Burton	1956-1974	Employed by Elder Smith & Co. Ltd., 1927-1972; Honorary Consul for the Netherlands
McKENZIE, Norm A.	1957-1959	Secretary, Western Australian Branch of the Waterside Workers' Federation; Councillor, Town of East Fremantle
HALLETT, John Mead	1957-1963	Farmer and MHR for Canning (Country Party), 1963-1975; Former Treasurer, Farmers' Union of Western Australia
HUGHES, William John	1957-1971	Businessman and past President, South Fremantle Football Club; Member of Fremantle City Council

Name	Period Served	Background
McCONNELL, James (JP)	1960-1974	Government representative; Former Under Secretary for Works; Chairman, FHT/FPA ,1960-1974
MANFORD, John Glaholm (DFC and CStJ)	1960-1983	Retired company director of Frank Manford Pty. Ltd., customs agents and transport contractors
CARMICHAEL, Thomas	1964-1968	Retired farmer
FORRESTER, Lorimer Richard	1969-1972	Farmer and President Farmers' Union
COOPER, Joseph Henry (JP)	1972-1974	Former President, Western Australian Branch of the Waterside Workers' Federation.; Mayor of Cockburn Council
CARTER, Charles	1972-1977	Farmer
WATSON, John Richard	1975	General Manager, Maritime Agencies of WA Pty. Ltd.; Chairman, Australian Chamber of Shipping (Western Australian Branch)
IRELAND, Phillip William	1975-1983	President of the Western Australian Branch of the Waterside Workers' Federation
LEWIS, Thomas James (ISO)	1975-1987	Under-Secretary, Public Works Department; Chairman, FPA, 1975-1987
SAMSON, James Samuel. (OBE)	1978-1987	Farmer and President, Pastoralists and Graziers Association of Western Australia; Member of Esperance Port Authority, 1969-1977

Name	Period Served	Background
CLARKE, James T.	1984-1991	Former President Western Australian Branch of the Waterside Workers' Federation; Retired from waterfront in December 1987
TEMPLE, James McLaughlin	1984-1988	Director of Temples Transport Ltd.
SUMICH, "Jack" Zlatko	1988-1992	Chief Executive Sumich Group
POUSTIE, Archibald Trevor	1988-1989	Assistant General Manager, Co-Operative Bulk Handling; Appointed General, Manager FPA, 1985; Chairman FPA Board, 1988-1989
McCULLOUGH, William Ian	1990-1993	Civil Engineer at Westrail, rising to Commissioner of Westrail; Chairman, FPA Board ,1990-1993
TAPLIN, John Harold Eaton	1990	Director General of Transport WA; Chairman, FPA Board, 1990
CARTER, Anthony Robert	1991-1995	Former Chairman and Managing Director of Jebsens International Australia Pty. Ltd.; Former Chairman of the WA Committee of the Australian Chamber of Shipping

Name	Period Served	Background
SANDERSON, Kerry Gaye	1992-1995	Former Deputy Director General of Transport and Director, Economic and Financial Policy Division, State Treasury; Appointed Acting General Manager of the FPA in 1991 and appointed permanently in 1992; Member of FPA Board ,1992-1995; Currently Chief Executive Officer of the FPA
PRITCHARD, Walter John	1992-1995	West Australian State Secretary of the Seamans' Union of Australia; When the Seamans' Union merged with the Waterside Workers' Federation to form the Maritime Union of Australia, he became the Joint State Secretary
STRAHAN, Ernest Eric	1993-	Retired businessman with wide experience in a variety of businesses, including tourism, farm machinery and furniture
HORWOOD, James Kentish (AM)	1993-1996	Farmer and former Chairman of Chamberlain-John Deere; Past President of the Royal Agricultural Society and the Confederation of WA Industry; Chairman of FPA Board, 1993-1995

Name	Period Served	Background
McKAY, Joe C.	1995-	Founding partner and Director of Healy, McKay and Wright Investment Services; Past employee of the Armstrong Property Group and the Australian Taxation Office
AITKENHEAD, Ron	1996-	Grain and sheep farmer; Inaugural and current Chairman of the Central Wheatbelt Enterprise Centre; Past Branch President and Secretary of the WA Farmers' Federation; Past President of the Central Wheatbelt Zone of the WA Council of State Schools Association; Chairman, of FPA Board, 1997-
ALLEN, Russell D.	1996-	Heads the Employee Relations Practice of the legal firm Freehill, Hollingdale and Page; National Chairman of the firm's Employee Relations Practice Group
O'CALLAGHAN, Michael J.	1997-	Past President of the WA Shippers' Council and has a background in mining and transport

Sources: FHT and FPA, *Annual Reports*; FPA, 35/31, Minutes, 20 November 1931; FPA, 3467/31/1-3, Commissioners - Appointments, etc.; J.S. Battye, *The Cyclopedia of Western Australia* (Perth, 1912); J.A. Alexander (ed.), *Who's Who in Australia 1938* (Melbourne, 1938); *Leading Personalities of Western Australia* (Perth, 1950); R. Erickson (ed.), *Dictionary of Western Australians*. V: 1889-1914 (Nedlands, WA, 1986); H.J. Gibbney and A.G. Smith, *A Biographical Register 1788-1939* (2 vols., Canberra, 1987); and unpublished information supplied by Lorraine Stevens of the Fremantle City Library.

Table D.2

General Managers of the FHT and FPA

F.W.B. Stevens (as Secretary)	1903-1929
G.V. McCartney (as Manager 1929-1946)	1929-1950
F.W.E. Tydeman	1950-1965
H.C. Rudderham	1965-1972
Captain B.L. Noble	1972-1984
A.T. Poustie	1985-1992
K.G. Sanderson	1992-

Sources: See table D.1.

Bibliography

Manuscript Materials

Department of External Affairs, Correspondence Files, Alphabetical Series, 1925-1942 (Australian Archives, Canberra, Deposit CRS A981).

Department of Trade and Customs, Papers of the Secretary Commonwealth Board of Trade, 1917-1925 (Australian Archives, Canberra, Deposit CP 703/5).

Fremantle Port Authority, Records, 1989 onwards (Fremantle Port Authority Basement).

Fremantle Harbour Trust and Fremantle Port Authority, Records, 1903-1988 (J.S. Battye Library of West Australian History, Perth, Accessions 87, 88, 3468, 3469, 3470, 3471, 3728, 4008, 4804, 5341).

Harbour and Lights Department Records, 1903-1939 (J.S. Battye Library of West Australian History, Perth, Accessions 1056 and 1066).

Public Works Department Records, 1905-1939 (J.S. Battye Library of West Australian History, Perth, Accessions 689 and 748).

Waterside Workers' Federation, Federal Records, 1902-1939, and Fremantle Branch Records, 1891-1939 (Australian National University, Noel Butlin Archives' Deposits T62 and N28).

Official Australian

Australian Stevedoring Industry Authority. *Annual Reports*, various years.

Australian Stevedoring Industry Board. *Annual Reports*, various years.

Australian Yearbooks. Canberra, various years.

Basten, H. *Report on the Turn-round of Ships in Australian Ports*. Canberra, 1952.

Buchanan, G. *Report on Transport in Australia with Special Reference to Port and Harbour Facilities*. 2 vols. Canberra, 1927.

Bureau of Transport and Communication Economics. *Review of the Waterfront Industry Reform Program*, Report 91. Canberra, 1995.

Bureau of Transport Economics. *A Study of Western Australian Ports*. Canberra, 1981.

Bureau of Transport Economics. *A Study of Liner Shipping Services into and out of Australia*. 2 vols. Canberra, 1986.

Commission of Inquiry Into the Maritime Industry. *Report on Adequacy of Australia's Ports*. Canberra, 1976.

Commonwealth Report of the Royal Commission on the Navigation Bill. Canberra, 1906.

Department of National Development, *Atlas of Australian Resources: Ports and Shipping*. 2nd ed. Canberra, 1971.

Department of Resources and Energy, *A History of British Atomic Tests in Australia*. Canberra, 1985.

Industry Commission. *Port Authority Services and Activities*. Canberra, 1993.

Inquiry into Ship Safety. Report from the House of Representatives Standing Committee on Transport, Communications and Infrastructure. Canberra, 1992.

Inter-State Commission. *Waterfront Investigation: Preliminary Findings and Discussion Papers*. 3 vols. Canberra, 1988.

Report from the Royal Commission on Ocean Shipping Services. Canberra, 1906.

Report from the Senate Select Committee. *The Container Method of Handling Cargoes*. Part 1. Canberra, 1968.

Report of Committee of Inquiry Into the Stevedoring Industry. Canberra, 1957.

Report of Commonwealth Committee on the Co-ordination of Transport in Australia. Canberra, 1929.

Report of Royal Commission into Pillaging of Ship's Cargoes. Canberra, 1921.

Report of the Committee of Economic Inquiry. 2 vols. Canberra, 1965.

Report of the Royal Commission on the Navigation Act. Canberra, 1924.

Royal Commission into Alleged Payments to Maritime Unions. Canberra, 1976.

Royal Commission on Mineral Oils and Petrol and Other Products of Mineral Oils. Canberra, 1935.

Royal Commission on the Wheat, Flour and Bread Industries. 2nd Report. Canberra, 1935.

Tariff Board. *Report and Recommendations on Bunker Coal - Imposition of Duty or Payment of Bounty*. Canberra, 1932.

Official South Australia

First Progress Report of the Parliamentary Standing Committee on Public Works. Adelaide, 1934.
South Australian Committee on Public Works. *Minutes of Evidence*. Adelaide, 1934.

Official Western Australia

Bulk Handling of Wheat: Reports of Investigations Conducted by Direction of Hon. J. Lindsay Minister for Works and Labour. Perth, 1932.
Fremantle Harbour Trust and Fremantle Port Authority. *Annual Reports*, 1903-04 to 1995-96.
Leslie, W. "Report as to the best method of providing Appliances and Accommodation for dealing with Cargo and Vessels at Fremantle." WA, *Votes and Proceedings*. Vol. 2, 5-13.
Report of the Royal Commission on Ocean Freights. Perth, 1905.
Report of the Royal Commission on the Bulk Handling of Wheat. Perth, 1935.
Report of the Royal Commission on the Collie Coal Industry. Perth, 1916.
Report on Fremantle Harbour and Cross-River Communications. Perth, 1917.
Stephenson, G. and Hepburn, J.A. *Plan for the Metropolitan Development of Perth and Fremantle*. Perth, 1955.
Tydeman, F.W. *Report on Port of Fremantle*. 3 vols. Perth, 1949.
Tydeman, F.W. *Report on Albany Harbour*. Perth, 1948.
Western Australia. *Yearbooks*, various years.

Official British

Report of Royal Commission on Shipping Rings. 1909 (Cd. 4668).
Royal Commission on the Dominions. *Final Report*. 1917 (Cd. 8462).
Royal Commission on the Dominions. *Second Interim Report*. 1914 (Cd. 7210).

BOOKS

Adams, J. *A Pinch of Salt*. Perth, 1996.
Alexander, J.A. (ed.). *Who's Who in Australia 1938*. Melbourne, 1938.

Alexandersson, G. and Norstrom, G. *World Shipping*. New York, 1963.

Allbrook, A.M and H. Cattalini, H. *The General Langfitt Story*. Canberra, 1995.

Appleyard, R.T. and Manford, T. *The Beginning: European Discovery and Early Settlement of Swan River, Western Australia*. Nedlands, WA, 1979.

Bach, J. *A Maritime History of Australia*. Melbourne, 1976.

Barker, A.J and Jackson, L. *Fleeting Attraction. A Social History of American Servicemen in Western Australia during the Second World War*. Nedlands, WA, 1996.

Battye, J.S. *The Cyclopedia of Western Australia*. Perth, 1912.

Beasley, M. *Wharfies. A History of the Waterside Workers' Federation of Australia*. Rushcutters Bay, NSW, 1996.

Beaumont, J. *Australia's War 1939-45*. St. Leonards, NSW, 1996.

Berson, M. *Cockburn the Making of a Community*. Cockburn, WA, 1978.

Bestic, A.A. *Kicking Canvas*. London, 1957.

Bird, J. *Seaport Gateways of Australia*. Oxford, 1968.

Bird, J. *Seaports and Seaport Terminals*. London, 1971.

Blainey, G. *The Tyranny of Distance*. Melbourne, 1966.

Board of Trade, *Overseas Economic Surveys: Australia*. London, 1954.

Boehm, E.A. *20th Century Economic Development in Australia*. 3rd ed. Melbourne, 1993.

Booth, K.E. and Chantrill, C.G. Materials *Handling with Industrial Trucks*. London, 1962.

Branch, A.E. *Elements of Shipping*. London, 1981.

Brazil, P., Kolsen, H. and Evans, J. *Liner Shipping Cargoes and Conferences. Review of Part X of the Trade Practices Act*. Canberra, 1993.

Brennan, F. *The Australian Commonwealth Shipping Line*. Canberra, 1978.

Broeze, F.J.A. and G. Henderson. *Western Australians & the Sea. Our Maritime Heritage*. Perth, 1986.

Broeze, F.J.A. (ed.). *Brides of the Sea. Port Cities of Asia from the 16th-20th Centuries*. Kensington, NSW, 1989.

Broeze, F.J.A. (ed.). *Maritime History at the Crossroads: A Critical Review of Recent Historiography*. St. John's, NF, 1995.

Broomham, R. *Steady Revolutions. The Australian Institute of Marine and Power Engineers*. Kensington, NSW, 1991.

Brown, P. *The Merchant Princes of Fremantle. The Rise and Decline of a Colonial Elite 1870-1900*. Nedlands, WA, 1996.

Buckley, K. and Klugman, K. *The History of Burns Philp*. Sydney, 1981.
Burley, K. *British Shipping and Australia 1920-1939*. Cambridge, 1968.
Butlin, M.W. *A Preliminary Annual Database 1900/01 to 1973/74*. Canberra, 1977.
Butlin, N.G. *Australian Domestic Product, Investment and Foreign Borrowing 1861-1938/39*. Cambridge, 1962.
Butlin, N.G.; Barnard, A., and Pincus, J. *Government and Capitalism*. Sydney, 1982.
Cairns, L. *Fremantle's Secret Fleets*. Fremantle, 1995.
Chida, T. and Davies, P.N. *The Japanese Shipping and Shipbuilding Industries. A History of Their Modern Growth*. London, 1990.
Commission Internationale d'Histoire Maritime. *Les grandes voies maritimes dans le monde XVe-XIXe siècles*. Paris, 1965.
Corlett, E. *The Ship. The Revolution in Merchant Shipping 1950-1980*. London, 1981.
Crowley, A.F. (ed.). A *New History of Australia*. Melbourne, 1974.
Crowley, F.K. *Australia's Western Third*. Melbourne, 1970.
Crowley, F.K. *Westralian Suburb: The History of South Perth, Western Australia*. Perth, 1962.
Crowley, F.K. and de Garis, B.K. *A Short History of Western Australia*. Melbourne, 1970.
Day, D. *Contraband and Controversy. The Customs History of Australia from 1901*. Canberra, 1996.
Deakin, B.M. and Seward, T. *Shipping Conferences*. Cambridge, 1973.
Dharmasena, K. *The Port of Colombo 1860-1939*. Colombo, 1980
Dyos, H.J. and Aldcroft, D.H. *British Transport. An Economic Survey from the Seventeenth to the Twentieth Centuries*. Leicester, 1971.
Dyster, B. and Meridith, D. *Australia in the International Economy*. Cambridge, 1990.
Economic Research Associates Pty. Ltd. *Economic Impact Study. Port of Fremantle*. Nedlands, WA, 1993.
Erickson, R. (ed.). *Dictionary of Western Australians*. Vol. 5: 1889-1914. Nedlands, WA, 1986.
Evans, A.A. *Technical and Social Changes in the World's Ports*. Geneva, 1969.
Ewers, J.K. *The Western Gateway*. Perth, 1971.
Fair, M.L. *Port Administration in the United States*. Cambridge, MA, 1954.
Falkus, M. *The Blue Funnel Legend. A History of the Ocean Steam Ship Company, 1865-1973*. Basingstoke, 1990.

Fall, V.G. *The Sea and the Forest: A History of the Port of Rockingham, Western Australia*. Nedlands, WA, 1972.

Farnie, D.A. *East and West of Suez*. London, 1969.

Firkins, P. (ed.). *A History of Commerce and Industry in Western Australia*. Nedlands, WA, 1979.

Fischer, L.R. (ed.). *From Wheel House to Counting House: Essays in Maritime Business History in Honour of Professor Peter Neville Davies*. St. John's, 1992.

Fitchett, T.K. *The Vanished Fleet. Australian Coastal Passenger Ships 1910-1960*. Sydney, 1976.

Ford, C.R. (ed.). *Ports into the Next Century*. London, 1991.

Forster, C. *Industrial Development in Australia 1920-1930*. Canberra, 1964.

Forster, C. (ed.). *Australian Economic Development in the Twentieth Century*. London, 1970.

Forsyth, P. *Microeconomic Reform in Australia*. St. Leonards, NSW, 1993.

Frankel, E.G. *The World Shipping Industry*. London, 1987.

Fyfe, C. *The Bale Fillers. Western Australian Wool 1826-1916*. Nedlands, WA, 1983.

Gallagher, F.D. *Options for Western Australia- Europe Container Traffic*. Perth, 1977.

Gibb, A. and Partners. *Report on the Fremantle Harbour*. Perth, 1929.

Gibbney, H.J and Smith, A.G. *A Biographical Register 1788-1939*. 2 vols. Canberra, 1987.

Glyn, S. *Government Policy and Agricultural Development*. Nedlands, WA, 1975.

Goss, R.O. *Studies in Maritime Economics*. Cambridge, 1970.

Goss, R.O. (ed.). *Advances in Maritime Economics*. Cambridge, 1977.

Griffiths, B. *Wharfies. A Celebration of 100 years on the Fremantle Waterfront 1889-1989*. Perth, 1989.

Hardy, A.C. *Bulk Cargoes*. London, 1926.

Harlaftis, G. *Greek Shipowners and Greece 1945-1975*. London, 1993.

Harlaftis, G. *A History of Greek-Owned Shipping. The Making of an International Tramp Fleet, 1830 to the Present Day*. London, 1996.

Hartman, P.T. *Collective Bargaining and Productivity*. Berkeley, 1969.

Hitchcock, J.K. *The History of Fremantle. The Front Gate of Australia*. Fremantle, 1929.

Holm, P., and Edwards, J. (eds.). *North Sea Ports and Harbours - Adaptations to Change*. Esbjerg, 1991.

Hunt, L. (ed.) *Westralian Portraits*. Nedlands, WA, 1979.

Hutton, J. *Manufacturing Industry and Western Australian Development*. Nedlands, WA, 1966.

Hyde, F.E. *Far Eastern Trade 1860-1914*. London, 1973.

Indecs. *State of Play 8*. St Leonards, NSW, 1995.

International Labour Organization. *Social and labour Problems Caused by Structural Adjustments in the Port Industry*. Geneva, 1996.

Jackson, G. *The History and Archaeology of Ports*. Tadworth, 1983.

Jackson, R.V. *Australian Economic Development in the Nineteenth Century*. Canberra, 1977.

Jerome, H. *Mechanisation in Industry*. New York, 1934.

Johnson, K.M. and Garnett, H.C. *The Economics of Containerisation*. London, 1971.

Kelly, M. (ed.) *Nineteenth-Century Sydney*. Sydney, 1978.

Kerr, A. *Australia's North-West*. 2nd ed. Nedlands, WA, 1975.

Kimberly, W.B. *History of West Australia. A Narrative of Her Leading Men*. Melbourne, 1897.

Kitz, J.F. *Shattered City. The Halifax Explosion and the Road to Recovery*. Halifax, 1989.

Kornhauser, A.; Dubin, R.; and Ross, A. (eds). *Industrial Conflict*. New York, 1954.

Levinson, H.M. (ed.), *Collective Bargaining and Technological Change in American Transportation*. Illinois, 1971.

Lowenstein, W. and Hills, T. *Under the Hook: Melbourne Waterside Workers Remember Working Lives and Class War: 1900-1980*. Prahran, VIC, 1982.

Maber, J.M. *North Star to Southern Cross*. Prescot, 1967.

MacElwee, R.S. *Port Development*. New York, 1925.

MacIntyre, S. *Militant. The Life and Times of Paddy Troy*. Sydney, 1984.

Maddock, R. and McLean, I. (eds). *The Australian Economy in the Long Run*. New York, 1986.

Mallett, A.S. and Bell, A.M.B. *The Pirrie-Kylsant Motorships 1915-1932*. Coltishall, 1984.

Mansfield, E. *The Economics of Technological Change*. London, 1969.

Markus, T. and Ricklefs, M.C. *Surrender Australia? Essays in the Study and Uses of History*. Sydney, 1985.

Marriner, S. (ed.) *Business and Businessmen. Studies in Business, Economic and Accounting History*. Liverpool, 1978.

Marx, D. *International Shipping Cartels: A Study of Industrial Self-Regulation by Shipping Conferences*. Princeton, 1953.
Mathews, R. *Public Investment in Australia*. Melbourne, 1967.
Mathewson, S.B. *Restriction of Output Among Unorganised Workers*. New York, 1931.
McDonnell, R. *Build a Fleet Lose a Fleet*. Melbourne, 1976.
McKellar, N.L. *From Derby Round to Burketown*. St. Lucia, 1977.
McPherson, K. *The Indian Ocean. A History of People and the Sea*. Oxford, 1993.
Moore, K.A. *The Early History of Freight Conferences. Background and Main Developments Until Around 1900*. London, 1981.
Morgan, F.W. *Ports and Harbours*. London, 1958.
Page, J.S.H. *Building a State*. Perth, 1986.
Pemberton, B. *Australian Coastal Shipping*. Melbourne, 1979.
Perkins, A.J. *Macro-Economic Policy in Australia*. Melbourne, 1971.
Perlman, M. *Judges in Industry*. Carlton, VIC, 1954.
Petersen, K. *The Saga of Norwegian Shipping*. Oslo, 1955.
Pinkstone, A.B. *Global Connections. A History of Exports and The Australian Economy*. Canberra, 1992.
Powell, J.M. and Williams, M. (eds.). *Australian Space, Australian Time*. Melbourne, 1975.
Proudfoot, P. *Seaport Sydney. The Making of the City Landscape*. Sydney, 1996.
Reece, R. and Pascoe, R. *A Place of Consequence. A Pictorial History of Fremantle*. Fremantle, 1983.
Rendel and Partners. *Port and Urban Systems*. Canberra, 1976.
Reserve Bank of Australia. *Australian Economic Statistics, 1949-50 to 1994-95*. Sydney, 1996.
Rice, M.R. and Lloyd, B.E. *Professional Engineers in Australia. Population Analysis*. Brighton East, VIC, 1990.
Royal Australian Navy. *Australia's Navy, 1993-94*. Canberra, 1994.
Rimmer, P.J. *Freight Forwarding in Australia*. Canberra, 1970.
Sandford, J. *Walter Harper and the Farmers*. Perth, 1955.
Sanklecha, S.N. *Tramping to Success.Story of the Great Eastern Shipping Company Limited*. Bombay, 1994.
Shore, H. *From the Quay*. Sydney, 1981.
Sinclair, W.A. *The Process of Economic Development in Australia*. Melbourne, 1976.
Snooks, G.D. *Depression and Recovery in Western Australia 1928/29-1938/39*. Nedlands, WA, 1974.

Stannage, C.T. *The People of Perth*. Perth, 1979.
Stannage, C.T. (ed.). *A New History of Western Australia*. Nedlands, WA, 1981.
Statham, P. (ed.). *The Origins of Australia's Capital Cities*. Cambridge, 1989.
Stearns, P.N. *Lives of Labour*. London, 1975.
Stephens, A.M. *The Stateships Story*. Perth, 1977.
Stevens, D. (ed.). *The Royal Australian Navy in World War II*. St. Leonards, NSW, 1996.
Sturmey, S.G. *British Shipping and World Competition*. London, 1962.
Tauman, M. *The Chief, C.Y. O'Connor*. Nedlands, WA, 1978.
Thomas, W.L. (ed.). *Man's Role in Changing the Face of the Earth*. Chicago, 1956.
Todd, J.A. *The Shipping World*. London, 1934.
Trace, K. *Towards Efficient Transport*. Perth, 1986.
Trade and Professions Directory of Western Australia. Perth, 1933-34.
Tucker, K.A. (ed.). *Business History. Selected Readings*. London, 1977.
Tweedie, A.S. *Trading Partners. Australia and Asia 1790-1993*. Sydney, 1994.
Uren, M. *Land Looking West*. London, 1948.
Walker, K.F. *Industrial Relations in Australia*. Cambridge, MA, 1956.
Wendemuth, L. and Bottcher, W. *The Port of Hamburg*. Hamburg, 1927.
White, C. *Mastering Risk. Environment, Markets and Politics in Australian Economic History*. Oxford, 1992.
Whitwell, G. *The Treasury Line*. Sydney, 1986.
Williams, J. *The First Furrow*. Willagee, Perth, 1976.
Williams, V. *The Years of Big Jim*. Perth, 1975.
Willinge, J. *Full Steam Ahead. Bunbury Port Authority 1909-199*. Bunbury, WA, 1996.
Williams, T.I. (ed.). *A History of Technology*. Vol.VII, Part II. Oxford, 1978.
Wilson, A.T. *The Suez Canal. Its Past, Present and Future*. London, 1933.
Woodruff, W. *The Suez Canal and the Australian Economy*. London, 1957.
Wotherspoon, W. (ed.). *Sydney's Transport. Studies in Urban History*. Sydney, 1983.
Xavier, H. *Disturbing Element*. Melbourne, 1963.

Articles, Pamphlets and Papers

Adams, W.E. "Australian Ports in Relation to Modern Ships and Shipping." *Report of British Association for the Advancement of Science* (1914), 508-510.

Association of Employers' of Waterside Labour, "The Stevedoring Industry in Australia: Submission to the Commonwealth Government in Connection with the Industrial Situation and Employment Arrangements." Typescript prepared by the Sydney Branch of the AEWL. Sydney, December 1964.

Bickford, C.R. "The Development of the Port of Sydney." *Journal of the Institution of Engineers* (Australia), XXIX (1957), 113-125.

Bickford, C.R. "The Handling of Bagged Wheat at Glebe Island, N.S.W." *Journal of the Institution of Engineers* (Australia), III (1931), 325-329.

Bonds, A.T. "Early History of the Port of Fremantle." *Port of Fremantle Quarterly*, III (1969), 22-23.

Broeze, F.J.A. "Western Australia Until 1869: The Maritime Perspective," *Early Days Journal and Proceedings of the Royal W.A. Historical Society*. VIII, Part 5 (1981), 38-52, and Part 6 (1982), 103-116.

Broeze, F.J.A.; Reeves, P.D.; and McPherson, K.I. "Port Cities in the Indian Ocean Region 1815-1939: Functional and Methodological Issues." Unpublished paper presented at the Second International Conference on Indian Ocean Studies Perth, WA, 1984.

Broeze, F.J.A. "Our Home is Girt by Sea. The Passenger Trade to Australia and New Zealand 1788-1914." Unpublished paper presented at the International Congress of Historical Sciences, Stuttgart, 1985.

Broeze, F.J.A.; McPherson, K.I.; and Reeves, P.D. "Imperial Ports and the Modern World Economy: The Case of the Indian Ocean." *Journal of Transport History*, VII (1986), 1-20.

Broeze, F.J.A. "'A Great Frankenstein:' The West Australian Shipping Association 1884-1906." *Studies in Western Australian History*, XIII (1992), 49-62.

Broeze, F.J.A. "Private Enterprise and Public Policy: Merchant Shipping in Australia and New Zealand, 1788-1992." *Australian Economic History Review*, XXXII (1992), 8-32.

Brown, P. "Western Australian Merchants And Political Agitation: The Struggle For Fremantle Harbour In The Late 19th Century." *The Great Circle*, XII (1990), 75.

Brown, P. "'Rich Men In Their Castles, Poor Men At Their Gates:' Status And Paternalism Of A Colonial Elite 1870-1900." *Studies in Western Australian History*, XIII (1992), 36-48.

Buchanan, R.A. "The British Contribution to Australian Engineering: The Australian Dictionary of Biography Entries." *Historical Studies*, XX (1983), 401-419.

Buchanan, R.A. "Institutional Proliferation in the British Engineering Profession 1847-1914." *Economic History Review*, XXXVIII (1985), 42-60.

City of Fremantle. *Victoria Quay and Its Architecture. Its History and Assessment of Cultural Significance*. Fremantle, 1991.

Co-Operative Bulk Handling Ltd. "A Co-operative Enterprise." Undated pamphlet, Fremantle Port Authority Library.

Davies, J. "The Role of Contestability Theory in the Economic Analysis of Liner Shipping." *Maritime Studies*, No. 22 (March/April 1985), 2-8.

Davies, P.N. "The Rise of Japan's Modern Shipping Industry." *The Great Circle*, VII (1985), 45-56.

De Garis, B.K. "An Incident at Fremantle." *Labour History* (May 1966), 31-37.

Deery, S. "Industrial Relations on the Australian Waterfront: A Policy of Laissez-Faire." *Journal of Industrial Relations*, XIX (1977), 93-97.

Deery, A.S. "The Impact of the National Stevedoring Industry Conference (1965-67) on Industrial Relations on the Australian Waterfront." *Journal of Industrial Relations* (June 1978), 202-222.

Ferrier, R.W. "The Oil Company as a Shipowner - The Case of British Petroleum." Unpublished paper presented at a conference on "The Shipowner in History," Greenwich, 1984.

Fischer, L.R. and Nordvik, H.W. "The Context of Maritime History: The New International Journal of Maritime History." *International Journal of Maritime History*, I (1989), vi-ix.

Fletcher, T. "Stevedoring Efficiency at Fremantle, 1829-1903.The Problems Experienced by a Waterfront Industry in a Developing Port." *The Great Circle*, XVII (1995), 22-38.

Fraser, J. "The 1950 Voyage of the *Anna Salen*." *Bureau of Immigration, Multicultural and Population Research Bulletin*, No. 16 (March 1996), 26-27.

Fremantle Port Authority. Future Port Options Auxiliary Study. *Final Report*. Fremantle, 1991.

Fremantle Port Authority. *Victoria Quay Study Report*. Fremantle, 1993.

Gifford, P. "The Effects of the British Seamen's Strike of 1925 on Fremantle." *The Great Circle*, XIV (1992), 73-87.

Gillman, S. "An Investigation into Some Effects of New Handling Technologies on the Structure of Maritime Transport Systems." *Maritime Studies and Management*, II (1975), 165-180.

Harcourt, F. "P&O and Orient: A Cool Partnership, 1886-1914." *The Great Circle*, XVII (1995), 73-94.

Henning, G.R. and Trace, K. "Britain and the Motorship: A Case of the Delayed Adoption of New Technology." *Journal of Economic History*, XXXV (1975), 353-385.

Jarvis, A. "The Port of Liverpool and the Shipowners in the Late Nineteenth Century." *The Great Circle*, XVI (1994), 1-22.

MacQueen, R. "Report on the Medical Examination of Sydney Waterside Workers with Disability Cards." Typescript in National Library, Canberra.

McCallum, Hon. A. *Fremantle Harbour: Proposals for Extension. Schemes Outlined and Compared*. Perth, 1928.

McLean, I.W. and Pincus, J. "Did Australian Living Standards Stagnate between 1890 and 1940?" *Journal of Economic History*, XLIII (1983), 193-202.

Mitchell, W. "Home Life at the Hungry Mile: Sydney Wharf Labourers and Their Families, 1900-1914." *Labour History*, No. 33 (1977), 86-97.

Morris, R. "Australian Stevedoring and Shipping Labour under the Transport Workers Act 1928-47." *The Great Circle*, XI (1989), 17-31.

Moynihan, J. "Linking Rottnest and Fremantle." *Telecom News* (June 1982), 12-13.

Moynihan, J. "Twelve Miles West of Fremantle."*Australian Post Office Journal* (June/July 1970), 2-4.

North, D.C. "Ocean Freight Rates and Economic Development 1750-1913." *Journal of Economic History*, XVIII (1958), 537-555.

Proudfoot, P.R. "Wharves and Warehousing in Central Sydney, 1790-1890." *The Great Circle*, V (1983), 73-86.

Proudfoot, P.R. "Maritime Land Uses in Central Sydney, 1890-1970," *The Great Circle*, VI (1984), 110-121.

Proudfoot, P.R. "A Model for Government Control in Urban Waterfront Renewal." *International Journal of Maritime History*, VIII (June 1996), 183-198.

Review of the Fremantle Port Authority for the Minister of Transport. Final Report. 2 vols. Fremantle, 1991.

Rimmer, P.J. "The Problem of Comparing and Classifying Seaports." *Professional Geographer*, XVIII (1966), 83-91

Robertson, J.R. "The Foundations of State Socialism in Western Australia 1911-1916." *Historical Studies: Australia and New Zealand*, vol. X (1962), 309-326.

Shaw, B.J. and Jackson, J.T. "A Comparative Study of Residential Development in Perth and Fremantle." *Australia 1888*, Bulletin No. 5 (September 1980), 151-159.

Sheridan, A.T. "Shipowners, Stevedores and Foremen: Divergent Management Attitudes to Waterfront Labour in the 1950s." *Journal of Industrial Relations*, XXXVIII (1996), 412-440.

Sheridan, T. "Australian Wharfies 1943-1967: Casual Attitudes, Militant Leadership and Workplace Change." *Journal of Industrial Relations*, XXXVI (1994), 258-284.

Sheridan, T. "Public Image of a Cartel: The Australia/UK-Continental Conference, 1950-1965." *Australian Economic History Review*, XXXIV (September 1994), 24-58.

Sheridan, T. "Baggage Taken Ashore: The Outlook of Senior Waterfront Management in the 1950s." *Journal of Industrial Relations*, XXXVII (1995), 562-586.

Slack, B. "Pawns in the Game: Ports in a Global Transportation System." *Growth and Change*, XXIV (Fall 1993), 579-588.

Smith, E. "Swan Dock Fremantle Harbour. Its Origin and Construction." *Maritime Heritage Association Journal*, VII (1996), 5-8.

Smith, G.R and Buxton, I.L. "The Development of the Bulk Carrier." Unpublished paper presented at a conference on Tanker and Bulk Carrier Terminals, Institution of Engineers, London, 1969.

Snooks, G. "The Arithmetic of Regional Growth: Western Australia 1912/13 to 1957/58." *Australian Economic History Review*, XIX (1979), 63-74.

Statham, P. "The Australian Sandalwood Industry." Unpublished paper presented at the Sandalwood Conference, East-West Centre, Honolulu, 1990.

Stodden, K.M. "The Post-War Migrant Ships." *Bureau of Immigration, Multicultural and Population Research Bulletin*, No. 16 (March 1996), 24-25.

Stonham, P.E. "User Costs in Port: An Australian Study." *Australian Economic Papers*, VIII (1969), 178-192.

Stonham, P.E. "Conferences and Competition in Australia's Overseas Liner Trades." *Economic Record*, XLVI (1970), 197-207.

Symonds Travers Morgan Pty. Ltd. and Meyrick & Associates Pty. Ltd. *Fremantle Port Authority Review of Alternative Structural Models. Final Report*. Perth, 1995..

Trace, K. "'Revitalisation of Australian Shipping:' A Critique of the Crawford Report." *The Great Circle*, IV (1982), 125-130.

Trace, K. "Contestable Market Theory Applied to Australian Overseas Liner Shipping Arrangements." *Maritime Studies*, No. 22 (January/February 1985), 1-11.

Tull, M.T. "The Development of Port Administration at Sydney 1901 to 1936." *The Great Circle*, IV (1982), 92-104.

Tull, M.T. "American Technology and the Mechanisation of Australian Ports 1942 to 1958." *Journal of Transport History*, VI (1985), 79-90.

Tull, M.T. "The Development of the Port of Fremantle, Australia's Western Gateway." *The Great Circle*, VII (1985), 116-138.

Tull, M.T. "Blood on the Cargo: Cargo-Handling and Working Conditions on the Waterfront at Fremantle, 1900-1930." *Labour History*, No. 52 (May 1987), 15-29.

Tull, M.T. "The Financial Performance of the Fremantle Harbour Trust, 1903 to 1939." *Australian Economic History Review*, XXVIII (1988), 21-42.

Tull, M.T. "The Development of Port Administration in Australia: The Case of Fremantle, 1903-1939." *The Journal of Transport History*, X (March 1989), 41-58.

Tull, M.T. "Profits and Lifestyle: Western Australia's Fishers." *Studies in Western Australian History*, XIII (1992), 92-111.

Tull, M.T. "The Development of the Australian Fishing Industry: A Preliminary Survey." *International Journal of Maritime History*, V (June 1993), 95-126.

Vanden Driesen, I.A. "Confrontation and Reconciliation on the Waterfront: The Fremantle Lumpers' Strike - 1899." *Labour History*, No. 40, (May 1981), 29-48.

Ward, J. "Australian Mineral Exports-Pattern in the 1960s and Possible Future Trends." *Australian Mineral Industry Quarterly Review*, XXIII (1971), 117-138.

Weigend, G.G. "Some Elements in the Study of Port Geography." *Geographical Review*, XLVIII (1958), 185-200.

Whitlam, A.G. "Australian Port Charges." *The Economic Record*, Supplement (1930), 202-224.

Williams, D.M. "The Progress of Maritime History." *Journal of Transport History*, XIV (September 1993), 126-141.

Williams, J.P. "The Problems Facing Australian Shipping in the Next Decade." Unpublished paper presented at a forum on transport by the Economics Society of Australia and New Zealand (Victorian Branch), Melbourne, 1960.

Wong, Lin Ken. "Singapore: Its Growth as an Entrepôt Port, 1819-1941." *Journal of Southeast Asian History*, IX (1978), 50-84.

Newspapers and Periodicals

The Australian
Australian Financial Review
Evening Mail
Port of Fremantle Quarterly
The Daily News
The Mail
The Sunday Times
The West Australian

Oral History Transcripts

Bass, George. Interview by Jack Darcey. FIRDC Oral History Project on the Western Australian Fishing Industry, 7 November 1989. J.S. Battye Library, Perth. OH 2266.

Bonds, Alan. Interview by M. Howroyd. FPA and Fremantle City Library Oral History Project, 24 November-1 December 1988.

Donnes, Michael. Interview by M. Howroyd. FPA and Fremantle City Library Oral History Project, 7 November 1988.

Peraldini, John. Interview by M.T. Tull. 25 March 1997.

Poustie, A.T. Interview by M.T. Tull. 26 March 1997.

Tydeman, F. Interview by M.T. Tull. 17 February 1983. The typescript is in the Battye Library.

Willis, William. Interview by M. Howroyd. FPA and Fremantle City Library Oral History Project, 9 March 1989.

Worthington, Captain. Interview by M. Howroyd. FPA and Fremantle City Library Oral History Project, 29 November 1988.

Wrightson, Len. Interview by M. Howroyd. FPA and Fremantle City Library Oral History Project, 19 January 1989.

Theses

Bonds, A.T. "The Economics of Outer Harbour Development in the Port of Fremantle." Unpublished MA thesis, University of Western Australia, 1969.

Harcourt, G. "Bulk Grain Handling Facilities at the Port of Fremantle and the Development of a Work Culture 1933-1977." Unpublised Honours thesis, Murdoch University, 1991.

Hartley, C. "Western Australia: The Decline of the Colonial Merchant Shipping Industry 1870-1890." Unpublished Honours thesis, Murdoch University, 1982.

Henderson, G. "From Sail to Steam: Shipping in Western Australia, 1870-1890." Unpublished MA thesis, University of Western Australia, 1977.

Hopper, P. "The 1919 Fremantle Lumpers' Strike." Unpublished Honours Thesis, University of Western Australia, 1975.

Hyams, B.K. "The Political Organisation of Farmers in Western Australia 1914-1944." Unpublished MA thesis, University of Western Australia, 1964.

Manford, T. "A History of Rail Transport Policy in Western Australia, 1870-1911." Unpublished PhD thesis, University of Western Australia, 1976.

McCarthy, M. "Charles Edward Broadhurst (1826-1905): A Remarkable Nineteenth Century Failure." Unpublished MPhil thesis, Murdoch University, 1989.

Rees, C. "Microeconomic Reform and the Waterfront. A Case Study of the Fremantle Port." Unpublished Honours thesis, Murdoch University, 1995.

Trace, K. "Australian Overseas Shipping 1900-60." Unpublished PhD thesis, University of Melbourne, 1965.

Tull, M.T. "The Development of the Port of Fremantle, Australia's Western Gateway, 1903-39." Unpublished PhD thesis, Murdoch University, 1985.

Vance, J. "Some Aspects of Industrial Relations and Economics of the Western Australian Waterfront Industry." Unpublished MA thesis, University of Western Australia, 1960.

Index

Printed and bound by CPI Group (UK) Ltd, Croydon, CR0 4YY

16/09/2026

14963458-0006